Edited by

Roger Desmond

University of Hartford

COMMUNICATION *in the Digital Age*

Kendall Hunt
publishing company

Kendall Hunt
publishing company

www.kendallhunt.com
Send all inquiries to:
4050 Westmark Drive
Dubuque, IA 52004-1840

ISBN 978-1-4652-7595-0

Printed in the United States of America

Dedication

To Tracey and Seth: The two great loves of my life

Contents

About the Author

Dr. Roger Desmond is Professor of Communication at the University of Hartford. He teaches a variety of courses in journalism as well as the basic course for all communication majors. He grew up in Los Gatos, California and received his Ph.D. from the University of Iowa. He has published research articles and book chapters on media and children for more than thirty years. He was awarded the Roy E. Larsen Award for excellence in teaching in the spring of 2015.

Foreword

This volume represents a broad sweep of the communication field for the student who is just meeting the discipline. By definition a book in the digital universe is somewhat outdated even before it is published. As in many academic fields, every day brings new thinking and research in communication that can't possibly be captured on paper bound into a volume. But what changes much more slowly are the sub-disciplines of a field, the ways that we divide an area of study into many pieces so that we can investigate them more easily.

The authors of the individual chapters are all experts, in many cases, nationally known research professionals who represent all of the major sub-disciplines in the field of communication. My chapter on journalism is a distilled version of my own thinking, research and practice that in my judgment introduces the student of communication to the major elements of journalism in the digital age.

My hope is that these readings will stimulate you and help you to decide if a major in the field is a good fit for you. Most universities offer entire courses centered on the major ideas of each chapter. Hopefully, this book will help you to decide where you might fit in the growing enterprise that is communication study.

Communication: A Broad Introduction

Part 1: Why Study Communication?

OBJECTIVES

After reading this chapter, you should understand the following concepts:

- Communication is a complex, multidisciplinary process in which participants create meaning by using symbols and behavior to send and receive messages with a social and cultural context.
- The freedoms of speech, of the press, of association, of assembly, and of petition constitute the freedom of expression represent—the right to communicate.
- The rapid growth of technology enhances our abilities to communicate, but also complicates the issues of communication.
- Several themes are woven into this text, each involving values that are represented in your rights and responsibilities to communicate.
- This book is designed to help the reader formulate strategies and learn the skills necessary to accomplish communication goals, with the understanding that expertise is not acquired over a semester but is honed with time and practice.

KEY TERMS

communication **freedom of expression** **culture**

INTRODUCTION

Have you ever experienced a communication gap? Try this. Which of the following statements can you interpret or translate?

> Hey, don't bogart the brewski. Everythingi copasetic. It's gnarly.[1]
>
> What It Is, What It Is? The Man came around today, can you dig it? Yeah, that's sick.[2]
>
> The dinks next door just barf me out. They are such hosers.[3]
>
> The straight edge is a buzz kill. Let's dip. Don't go there! Back in the day we were tight![4]

From *Communication: Principles of Tradition and Change* by Samuel P. Wallace, Kimberly N. Rosenfeld, David L. Bodary, and Beth M. Waggenspack.

© digitalskillet, 2008, Shutterstock.

Why would you have to study communication when you do it everyday?

When you first signed up for this course, you might have thought that communication is too simple. It's too "obvious" to study, and it's just silly to have a whole course about it! You probably told others that you communicate all the time, and you feel pretty proud of your abilities. Perhaps those phrases have given you second thoughts. But they're just words, right? Can't you just speak more clearly and resolve any confusion those phrases might have created? Do you really need a whole course just about word choice? Is that what this course is?

You might think that studying communication is a waste of time because it's nothing more than common sense. Because you have been communicating all your life and seem to be reasonably good at it, you figure there *can't* be much to it, right? You should be spending your academic time more profitably, considering topics that *should* be studied. We should be studying how to fly an airplane or how to practice medicine, because those things are complex and people don't just intuitively learn how to navigate through heavy clouds or how to successfully remove a spleen. However, there is no need to study communication—we do that every day!

Because communicating is so familiar to everyone, it is often taken for granted and, as a result, it is ignored. The only time we really ever pay attention to or notice the communication process is when something goes wrong or if some rule is violated. Instead of waiting around for a communication disaster to strike, the purpose of this course is to challenge you to call your participation in the communication process into question and raise it to the level of conscious awareness. At this level you can examine it, take it apart, put it back together, and use that new awareness to improve your own abilities as a communicator.

Think for a minute *how* and *how often* you communicate. Not only do you carry on conversations with others, work successfully in groups with them, participate in interviews, make presentations, and tell entertaining stories, but you also have to have a pretty good facility with various electronic communication tools that provide you with efficient means of reaching out to others. In their book *Connecting to the Net.Generation: What Higher Education Professionals Need to Know about Today's College Students,* Reynol Junco and Jeanna Mastrodicasa revealed the following information gathered in a survey of 7,705 college students in the United States:[5]

- 97 percent own a computer.
- 94 percent own a cell phone.
- 76 percent use instant messaging.
- 15 percent of IM users are logged on 24 hours a day/7 days a week.
- 34 percent use Web sites as their primary source of news.
- 28 percent own a blog, and 44 percent read blogs.
- 49 percent download music using peer-to-peer file sharing.
- 75 percent of students have a Facebook account.
- 60 percent own some type of expensive portable music and/or video device such as an iPod.

Do these figures surprise you? Do you think these media have an effect on how you communicate and what you expect from others? Add in the work groups, commuting partners, friends and family members that you talk with daily. All of these influence how you develop relationships with others, your awareness of things going on near and far, the ways that you view time, what you think is important, and a thousand other perceptions. Your beliefs, attitudes, and values are all affected by the amount, type, and success of your communication efforts. For example, if you use many of those media, you probably expect responses more quickly than someone from a previous generation. You might think that finding information is better done on a computer than by personal interviews or even reading a book or a print newspaper. Your means of telling others about yourself have expanded, leaving both privacy and personal safety at risk. You can create images of yourself that reflect what you'd like to be, rather than what you are. Your language evolves with blinding speed, with new words being coined daily and shared immediately. You live in a communication-saturated world, where symbols evolve, media change, and people adapt.

How does the media you use affect your communication with others?

Are you starting to believe that communication is much more complex than you first realized? Theorists and researchers have studied it for hundreds of years, attempting to discover what constitutes effective communication, involving different sources, messages, audiences, contexts, and purposes. Other studies have investigated the use of technology ranging from Sumerian writing and its impact on later Egyptian hieroglyphics, through the impact of print and photography, to electronic means ranging from the telegraph to the computer, PDAs, cell phones, and emerging new technologies. These studies have been undertaken by researchers in diverse fields such as art, anthropology, history, philosophy, computer science, linguistics, sociology, psychology, English, and a relatively new field called **communication.**

Today, the study of communication spans multidisciplinary interests and has developed interlocking and independent theoretical approaches. This text will introduce you to the basics of the theories and practice of some of those approaches to communication in different contexts. Ranging from the situational contexts of intrapersonal, interpersonal, and small group communication, to interviewing and finally public speaking, you'll traverse the discipline. Although you will find that these different contexts allow you to examine the communication process more clearly, the categorization is not perfect, because you'll find overlap among the strategies suggested in different contexts. For instance, you'll learn about being seen as credible, understanding an audience, and how to engage in verbal and nonverbal communication. There are some basic assumptions and ideas about each of these topics, but the contexts in which you use the strategies will differ. You'll see that when you prepare a speech, you'll want to engage in critical thinking, research, organization, and consider delivery strategies. You might also have to conduct an interview or participate in a small group discussion. In a small group, you still will have to think critically, analyze your audience, and organize and present your ideas.

Depending on the situation, different communication strategies are most effective.

But delivery concerns are different in public speaking than they are in interviewing. Participating in an interview requires a different mind-set (roles and norms) than does leading a small group. Good communication depends on developing a set of strategies designed to help you to understand one another and cooperate to create meaning with others. As a result of taking this class, you'll discover that you have a broad view of strategic choices to consider in a number of different communication contexts.

Maybe you're starting to be convinced that this text might teach you some necessary skills, but you'll be exposed to more than skill competency. Communication involves considering cultural values and issues, along with developing shared meaning with others.

WHAT IS THE IMPACT OF COMMUNICATION STUDY BEYOND SKILLS?

© Laurence Gough, 2008, Shutterstock.

Why is competent communication important to almost anything we do?

Communication is important and central to nearly all that we do. Think about it. We make our laws through a process of debate and voting in legislatures. Our legal system depends on people to make a good case; to present and interpret evidence in a compelling way to allow important decisions to be made. Our political system requires citizens to make decisions concerning candidates for office, laws to adopt, and where to spend tax money. Religion, culture, science, and education all involve a series of beliefs passed along to each new generation by the people who hold those beliefs. It's all done through communication. Fundamental to our American culture is the right to use our ability to communicate. Let's consider the freedoms and responsibilities inherent in that right in an attempt to discover the complexity of communication.

The freedoms of speech, of the press, of association, of assembly, and of petition: this set of guarantees, protected by the First Amendment, constitutes the concept of **freedom of expression.** They represent the right to communicate. Without this freedom, other fundamental rights, like the right to vote and to participate in our own governance, would lack force. Members of a democratic society have both the right and responsibility to participate in governance. At the very least, you should be an informed voter. But being an informed voter requires doing research and interpreting and critically analyzing information and values related to candidates and issues. This activity often means that you have to sift through and weigh heaps of campaign slogans, sound bytes, and promises to get to the "meat" of the matter.

The essence of being a citizen in a democratic society goes beyond the privilege of voting, however. From childhood, you may have been taught the core values of being an individual, of tolerating the differences and diversity of others, or of having the right to speak and think as you want. You learn to express your mind, to speak out against decisions you disagree with, to praise people who do a good job, to associate with whomever you want, and to criticize both individuals and government. This freedom of expression is the essence of a democracy. Let's consider a few examples that demonstrate the nation's commitment to freedom of expression and how it has been tested.

When the country music group the Dixie Chicks' lead singer Natalie Maines said at a London concert on March 10, 2003, that she was "ashamed the president of the United States is from Texas," the backlash started. Country music stations across the country pulled Dixie Chicks' songs from their playlists, others called for boycotts of their concerts, and some organizations sponsored bonfires in which the group's CDs were destroyed.[6] In response, on his Web site, Bruce Springsteen defended the group's right to say what they believe. He asserted that they are American artists who were using their right to free speech, and that anyone who thought it was right to punish them for speaking out is un-American.[7]

Is burning the American flag an issue of the freedom of expression? In 1989, the Supreme Court ruled in the case of *Texas v. Johnson* that the First Amendment rights of citizens to engage in free speech, even if that speech is "offensive," outweigh the government's interest in protecting the American flag as a symbol of American unity. The action of flag burning, as repugnant as it may be to many citizens, was defined by the Supreme Court and Texas Court of Criminal Appeals as an example of "symbolic speech."[8] For the majority opinion, Justice Brennan wrote: "If there is a bedrock principle underlying the First Amendment, it is that the Government may not prohibit the expression of an idea simply because society finds the idea itself offensive or disagreeable. Punishing desecration of the flag dilutes the very freedom that makes this emblem so revered, and worth revering."[9]

What about protest marches and sit-ins? What about protesting the actions of the courts? Are these activities representative of freedom of expression? In 1963, the Southern Christian Leadership Coalition mounted a campaign that focused on direct action, committed to ending segregation in Birmingham, Alabama. The campaign began with a series of mass meetings, including one featuring civil rights leader Martin Luther King Jr., who spoke about the philosophy of nonviolence and appealed to the volunteers to practice its methods. The actions included lunch counter sit-ins, marches on City Hall, a boycott of downtown merchants, sit-ins at the library, and a voter registration march. When the city government obtained a court injunction directing an end to all protests, King and the SCLC disobeyed the court order, and on April 12, King was arrested in Birmingham. He was kept in solitary confinement and was allowed only minimal contact. It was at this time that King penned his famous Letter from the Birmingham Jail.[10]

The rapid growth of technology enhances our abilities to communicate and adds additional cautions to what we say and how we say it. It has multiplied the channels by which we can create relationships, gather information, conduct business, and make decisions. The 2005 Pew Foundation's Major Moments Survey showed increases in the number of Americans who report that the Internet played a crucial or important role in various aspects of their lives.[11] Consider the growth of blogs, "web logs," which allow anyone with a computer to post thoughts, opinions, histories, anecdotes, and political ideas to a worldwide platform, unhindered by time and distance. Blogger and public relations writer Jeneane Sessum of Atlanta is the founder of Blog Sisters, a group blog with more than 100 female members from around the world. The group discusses everything from gender

© Kurhan, 2008, Shutterstock.

How has technology changed the way we communicate with others?

Martin Luther King Jr.'s Letter from Birmingham Jail

Sometimes a law is just on its face and unjust in its application. For instance, I have been arrested on a charge of parading without a permit. Now, there is nothing wrong in having an ordinance which requires a permit for a parade. But such an ordinance becomes unjust when it is used to maintain segregation and to deny citizens the First Amendment privilege of peaceful assembly and protest.

I hope you are able to embrace the distinction I am trying to point out. In no sense do I advocate evading or defying the law, as would the rabid segregationist. That would lead to anarchy. One who breaks an unjust law must do so openly, lovingly, and with a willingness to accept the penalty. I submit that an individual who breaks a law that conscience tells him is unjust and who willingly accepts the penalty of imprisonment in order to arouse the conscience of the community over its injustice, is in reality expressing the highest respect for law.[12]

and international politics to family life and career quandaries, without fear of being censored. Sessum says, "Blogs make it really easy to express yourself. It's an amazing tool to help you figure out who you are, what you care about and to connect with other human beings. Plus, it's a place for me to exercise my voice. I've been so busy writing for clients that I've never kept up with my personal writing. Blogging has really helped me refine my voice."[13]

Does the existence of blogs raise questions about freedom of expression? Some critics assert that bloggers have transformed the Internet into a virtual soapbox, resulting in an impact on the public dialogue with questions about social responsibility and the law. Bradley Smith, chairman of the Federal Elections Commission (FEC), has suggested that there is a need to regulate political speech in blogs, saying that bloggers could soon invite federal punishment if they improperly link to a campaign's Web site.[14]

Broadcast media have a responsibility to check sources when providing news coverage. On September 20, 2004, CBS news anchor Dan Rather apologized for a "mistake in judgment" in relying on apparently bogus documents for a *60 Minutes* report about President George W. Bush's time in the Texas Air National Guard. In his on-air statement, Rather said,

> Now, after extensive additional interviews, I no longer have the confidence in these documents that would allow us to continue vouching for them journalistically. I find we have been misled on the key question of how our source for the documents came into possession of these papers. That, combined with some of the questions that have been raised in public and in the press, leads me to a point where—if I knew then what I know now—I would not have gone ahead with the story as it was aired, and I certainly would not have used the documents in question. But we did use the documents. We made a mistake in judgment, and for that I am sorry.

Rather's admission of a mistake resulted in great damage to the CBS news division's credibility. Boston *Phoenix* media writer Dan Kennedy said, "They were way too late in acknowledging there may be problems with this. The short-term damage is just horrendous. You have a large percentage of the public believing—falsely, I would argue—that the media are suffused with liberal bias, and this just plays right into that."[15]

There are many examples of the impact of communication rights and responsibilities that span the entire history of the United States. Freedom of expression is codified in law, and it is part of who we are as Americans. The core values represented in the right to express your thoughts and to communicate freely with others are central to our society. These values are vital to the attainment and advancement of knowledge and the search for the truth. These are only a few examples of instances where the privilege and attendant responsibility of freedom of expression have impacted your life. In this text, we will "bring it home" by your participation in discussions about the freedom of expression in your daily life in personal and public arenas.

Now it's time to ask: How does this concept of communication responsibilities impact what you'll learn in this course?

SUMMARY

You're now ready to begin your study of unique features of the communication discipline, along with its attendant values and responsibilities. You will bring your established abilities into the mix, but you will also begin to take into account aspects of communicating that you never considered before. *Communication is serious, complex, and important!* By the end of this book, we want you to believe this is true. Perhaps more importantly, though, we want to challenge you to become a full and influential participant communicating in personal, business, and civic affairs.

Before you can accept this challenge and begin your exploration of the strategies communication requires, you need to consider the scope of communication via a definition. *Communication is a process in which participants create meaning by using symbols and behavior to send and receive messages within a social and cultural context.* This book is devoted to helping you understand and apply this definition so you will be able to formulate strategies and learn the skills necessary for accomplishing all of your communication goals. You are not likely to become an expert communicator by the time you complete this course, but you should have a good start. You'll be exposed to a series of questions in every chapter that will lead to some beliefs, attitudes, and values, along with skills. Like any expertise that you learn, your competence improves with time, practice, and use. The goal of this text is to assist you in developing strategies and practicing skills in a variety of communication contexts.

NOTES

1. Samples of 1960s slang, defined at 1960s slang, http://www.cougartown.com/slang.html (accessed Sept. 23, 2007).
2. 1970s slang, http://www.inthe70s.com/generated/terms.shtml (accessed Sept. 23, 2007).
3. 1980s slang, http://www.i80s.com/80s_slang/slang1.htm (accessed Sept. 23, 2007).
4. http://www.inthe90s.com/generated/terms.shtml (accessed Sept. 23, 2007).
5. Junco, Reynol and Jeanna Mastrodicasa, *Connecting to the Net.Generation: What Higher Education Professionals Need to Know About Today's College Students.* (Washington, DC: National Association of Student Personnel Administrators, 2007).
6. CNN.Com/Entertainment. Dixie Chicks pulled from air after bashing Bush. March 14, 2003 (accessed June 14, 2007).

7. BBC News (bbc.co.uk) Springsteen backs under-fire Dixies. April 28, 2003 (accessed June 14, 2007).
8. *Texas vs. Johnson,* 491 U.S. 397. (June 21, 1989).
9. PBS.Org PBS Online. United States v. Eichman. Issue: Burning the American Flag. (Undated) (accessed June 18, 2007).
10. Stanford University. King Encyclopedia. "Birmingham Campaign." (accessed June 18, 2007).
11. Horrigan, John and Lee Rainie. "The Internet's Growing Role in Life's Major Moments." (April 19, 2006.) Pew Internet & American Life Project, http://www.pewinternet.org/PPF/r/181/report_display.asp (accessed June 20, 2007).
12. MLK Online. "Letter from Birmingham Jail, April 16, 1963." (accessed March 30, 2008).
13. Trimbath, Karen. "Women Go Blogging and Find Freedom of Speech." Women's eNews. August 2, 2004 http://www.womensenews.org/article.cfm/dyn/aid/1934 (accessed June 22, 2007).
14. "Are Blogs Protected under the First Amendment?" http://www.legalzoom.com/articles/article_content/article14006.html (accessed June 22, 2007).
15. Kurtz, Howard. "Rather Admits 'Mistake in Judgment.'" (September 21, 2004) http://washingtonpost.com/wp-dyn/articles/A35531-2004Sep20_2.html (accessed June 22, 2007).

Part 2: What Is Communication?

OBJECTIVES

After reading this chapter, you should understand the following concepts:

- The goal of communication is to build theory used to guide communicators in the formulation of strategies to achieve communication goals.
- There are many definitions of communication, but they share common characteristics: Communication is a process, messages are sent and received, participants interact in social contexts, and meaning is created and shared through symbols and behavior.
- The action model was the necessary first step in the evolution of communication models, but it has a weakness in that it lacks interaction.
- The interaction model includes the important aspect of feedback.
- The transactional model recognizes that communication is a process, it is irreversible, it means shared responsibility, and it occurs in context and culture.

KEY TERMS

theory
empirical
Aristotle
Claude Shannon
Warren Weaver
source
message
code
encoded
transmitted
channel
receiver
decodes
destination
noise
action model
interaction model
Wilbur Schramm
David Berlo
feedback
transactional model
process
participant
carrier
environmental noise
psychological noise
physical context
social context
culture

INTRODUCTION

"Oh, that's just a theory. It doesn't mean anything!"

Have you heard this before? There is a common misconception that a **theory** is the same thing as a "guess." A theory is a "shot from the hip," or it's a "Monday morning quarterback's" explanation of why his team won or lost on Sunday. Sometimes you hear people express doubt about "relativity" or "evolution" because they are "only theories," and not fact. Not true! A theory is not idle speculation unsupported by evidence that is spontaneously created or made up.

Theories are not guesses! Littlejohn states, "Any attempt to explain or represent an experience is a theory; an idea of how something happens."[1] Kerlinger says that a theory is "a set of interrelated constructs (concepts), definitions, and propositions that present a systematic view of phenomena by specifying relations among variables, with the purpose of explaining and predicting the phenomena."[2]

WHAT IS THE NATURE OF COMMUNICATION THEORY?

Our definition is that a theory is *an attempt to describe, predict, and / or explain an experience or phenomenon.* The purpose of generating a theory is the attempt to *understand* something:

- Theory is a collection of statements or conceptual assumptions.
- It specifies the relationships among concepts or variables and provides a basis for predicting behavior of a phenomenon.
- It explains a phenomenon.

Here's an illustration from the distant past:

Og the cave dweller comes out of his cave in the morning and sees the sun shining in the east. When Og visits the village well later in the day, he and his friends are able to *describe* what happened: "When I came out of my cave, I saw the bright light in the sky!" They can all try to agree on the description, and they will all know what happened.

Og the cave dweller systematically observes the environment.

Over the next several months, Og and his pals emerge from their caves every morning, and every morning they see the sun in the eastern sky. They also notice that the sun has moved to the western sky when they return to their caves in the evening. After several conversations at the village well, they discover or recognize that a *pattern* seems to exist in the behavior of the sun. In the morning, the bright light is over there. But in the evening, the bright light is on the other side. They set up an observational plan to see if their pattern holds up. In the mornings, when Og comes from his cave (which faces south), he looks to his left and he *expects* to see the sun. There it is! Eureka! The observations support the hypothesis (or informed assumption) that the sun will rise in the east! Og and his associates can now *predict* the behavior of the sun!

Og is attempting to build a theory. He is able to describe and predict, but he still comes up short because he does not understand *why* the sun behaves as it does. Og still has much uncertainty about the sun's behavior, and that makes him and all the rest of us humans uncomfortable. So we continue to study it. Now, please "fast forward" from this point several thousand years when, after gathering lots and lots of information, we were finally able to *explain* why the sun appears to rise in the east and set in the west.

Observation → Pattern Recognition → Theory → Hypotheses → Observation

Og and his buddies made some observations of phenomena and were able to describe it, then they noticed patterns in the phenomena and were able to predict its behavior. They might have even tried to explain the activity they observed, but they did not have enough knowledge to make a good explanation. The explanation came much later and is beyond the scope of this book. But you can go look it up!

What they *did* do was create a partial theory, and that theory was based on empirical observation. Not bad for cave dwellers! **Empirical** means that knowledge claims are based on observations of reality (i.e., the real world) and are not merely subjective speculation based on the observer's perspective. The conclusions are based on *observed* evidence, which helps the observer remain more objective.[3] The cycle of study is repeated over and over: Observation is made, which leads to recognizing a pattern; attempts to predict and explain are made, which become basic theories; the theories help the observer create new hypotheses (predictions) about the behavior of the phenomenon; observation is made and the information analyzed in search of patterns; and those recognized patterns add to the basic theory.[4] As this cycle repeats itself, the body of theory becomes larger and more sophisticated, and the field of study matures.

The goal of any field of study, including communication, is to *build theory*. The body of communication theory is subsequently used to guide communicators in the formulation of strategies for achieving communication goals and to help communicators understand what skills are necessary for carrying out the strategies.

The purpose of this chapter is to help you understand the basic theory supporting human communication behavior. The skills and strategies necessary to accomplish your communication goals are derived from this theory. This chapter includes the following:

- A definition of communication
- An evolution of conceptions of communication
- A transactional model of communication
- A discussion of essential terms

HOW IS COMMUNICATION DEFINED?

Defining communication is not quite as easy as it sounds because almost all people, even scholars, think they know what it is. We all communicate every day, so we all have an opinion. The problem is that nearly nobody agrees! Clevenger says that the term *communication* is one of the most "overworked terms in the English language."[5]

To try to make sense of the literally hundreds of different definitions, we will examine some significant attempts to define communication, and then we will draw out the commonalities in the attempt to build our own point of view. Here are some influential examples:

- An individual transmits stimuli to modify the behavior of other individuals.[6]
- Social interaction occurs through symbols and message systems.[7]

Take a Closer Look

What do these definitions have in common?

- ❒ Communication is a process.
- ❒ Messages are sent and received.
- ❒ Participants interact in social contexts.
- ❒ Meaning is created and shared through the use of symbols and behavior.

- A source transmits a message to receiver(s) with conscious intent to affect the latter's behavior.[8]
- "Senders and receivers of messages interact in given social contexts."[9]
- "Shared meaning through symbolic processes" is created.[10]
- There is mutual creation of shared meaning through the simultaneous interpretation and response to verbal and nonverbal behaviors in a specific context."[11]
- "Communication occurs when one person sends and receives messages that are distorted by noise, occur within a context, have some effect, and provide some opportunity for feedback."[12]

The perspective of this book is that *communication is a process in which participants create meaning by using symbols and behavior to send and receive messages within a social and cultural context.* This perspective will be expanded and explained in the remainder of this chapter.

HOW HAVE THE CONCEPTIONS OF COMMUNICATION EVOLVED?

Now that we have a working definition of communication, let's examine where it came from. This section looks at classic models of communication spanning about 2,500 years. The goal of this section is to illustrate the evolution of the communication perspective taken by this book; to show you how we arrived at the point of view that influences every strategy and skill that we teach. We believe that if you understand why we teach it, you will be more motivated to learn and to use this point of view to plan and execute your own communication strategies!

WHAT ARE THE MODELS OF COMMUNICATION?

You have seen and used a map many times. If you are looking for a particular street in your town, you pick up a map to find where the street is and to learn how to get there from where you are. A map is not your town, however, but a *representation* of your town. It's a picture or drawing that helps you understand the way your town is arranged. A *model* is the very same thing. But instead of representing a physical space, like a town, the model represents a process, or the way something happens.

The models discussed here represent three views of communication that have enjoyed popularity over the years. Those three views are action (or linear), interaction, and transaction. These models help illustrate and explain the current view of communication, the transactional perspective. Each will be discussed in the following pages.

As a map represents a place, a model represents a process.

The Action Model

Although many perspectives of communication contributed to what we are calling the action model, Aristotle and the Shannon and Weaver models had the most impact.

We'll start with **Aristotle,** a philosopher, scientist, and teacher who lived in ancient Greece. Educated by Plato and the son of a physician, he was trained as a biologist.[13] He was skilled at observing and describing, and at categorizing his observations.[14] Aristotle found himself interested in nearly all things that occupied the attention of the citizens of Athens, including the study of speaking.

Ancient Athens was a democracy, and all citizens had the right and opportunity to influence public affairs and public policy. The more articulate citizens were able to affect events by persuading or influencing other citizens and law makers in public meetings. Because individual citizens had a voice, teachers of public speaking and persuasion were always in demand.

Aristotle's *Rhetoric* is a published collection of his teachings,[15] and it has been suggested that it is the "most important single work on persuasion ever written."[16] The focus of the *Rhetoric* is primarily on the speaker and the message. Some, but little, attention is paid to the audience. The philosophy is that a well-crafted message delivered by a credible speaker will have the desired effect with the audience. If Aristotle had a model of persuasion, the simple version would probably look something like this:

Aristotle used his observation skills to study communication in ancient Greece.

WELL-CRAFTED MESSAGE + CREDIBLE SOURCE = DESIRED EFFECT

Aristotle's contribution to communication would not have been this model. His contributions came in the form of instructions for how to use logic and emotions (*logos* and *pathos*) to craft a message, and how to establish and build credibility as a speaker or source of a message *(ethos)*.

For the second time in this chapter, please fast forward in time, but this time only about two thousand years. Stop when you get to the 1940s, and we'll take a look at **Claude Shannon** and **Warren Weaver.** Claude Shannon was a mathematician who worked at Bell Labs, and he was interested in ways to make more efficient use of telephone lines for the transmission of voices. He was not concerned about human communication, but he was very focused on electronic communication. Shannon teamed with Warren Weaver, a scientist and mathematician, to publish the *Mathematical Theory of Communication.* Shannon's focus was on the engineering aspects of the theory, while Weaver was more interested in the human and other implications. Communication scholars found this model to be very useful in helping them to explain *human* communication.[17]

The Shannon–Weaver model is consistent with Aristotle's point of view, and it extends it to include a transmitter, a channel, and a receiver. It also introduces the concept of *noise* to the explanation. The process is illustrated in Figure 1.1. The **source** (a person) initiates a **message** that is turned into a **code** (language), and the **encoded** message is sent **(transmitted)** through a **channel** (sound waves created by the voice, or some mediated signal). The **receiver decodes** the signal (turning it again into a message), which is sent to the **destination** (the other person). **Noise** is anything that can interfere with the signal. See Figure 1.1.

This model helps to understand human communication, but it has a significant shortcoming: it doesn't adequately capture the reality or the complexity of the process. It assumes that the participants in the process take on discrete speaker or listener roles, and that while one person speaks, the other person quietly listens with no response, until the speaker is finished. Then the roles are reversed. Then the roles are reversed again, and again and again, until

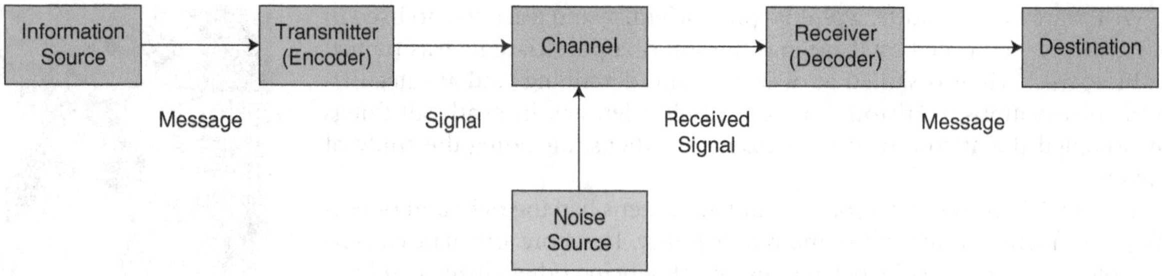

Figure 1.1
The Shannon–Weaver Mathematical Model

A message in a bottle lacks the interaction we have in everyday conversations.

the conversation is complete. *Human communication is arguably not that linear!* It is equivalent to placing a message in a bottle, throwing it into the sea, and waiting for it to reach the proper destination. The person (receiver) removes the message from the bottle, reads the message, writes a new message, places it back in the bottle, and throws it back into the sea. The model works, but it doesn't represent the way that we communicate in everyday conversations. It lacks *interaction!*

As you consider the two models just discussed, you can see that they are primarily concerned with the source of the message and the content of the message itself. The focus is on the source and how he or she constructs and delivers the message. So a source that creates well-designed messages has done everything possible to ensure effective communication. Say the right thing and you will be successful! If something goes wrong, or if the source is not clearly understood by the potential receiver, the **action model** states that the fault is with the source. However, when everything goes well and the message is clearly understood, it is because the source crafted and sent a good-quality message. See Figure 1.2 for a depiction of the action model. The action model was the necessary first step in the evolution of the contemporary communication model.

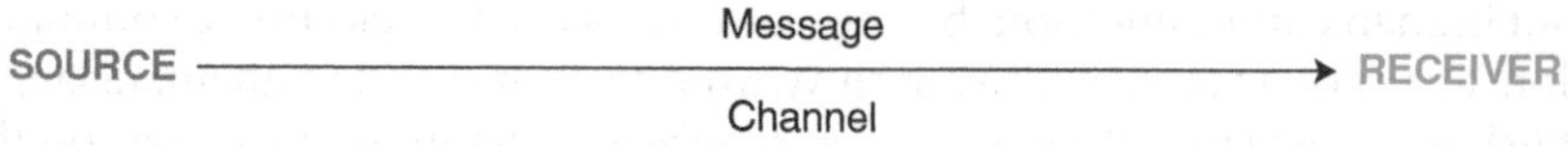

Figure 1.2
Action Model

The Interaction Model

The **interaction model** remains linear, like the action model, but it begins to view the source and receiver as a team in the communication process.

Wilbur Schramm introduced a model of communication that includes a notion of *interaction.*[18] The Schramm model does not consider the context or environment in which the communication takes place, and it does not explicitly treat codes (language) or noise. Although it is still very linear, it describes the dual roles played by the participants instead of viewing one as a source (speaker) and the other as a receiver (listener), and it makes a strong case for *interaction* among the participants. The flow of information can be seen as more ongoing or continuous, rather than a linear, back-and-forth type of flow. The conception of communication is emerging as a *process.* See Figure 1.3.

David Berlo, in *The Process of Communication,* began to discuss process and the complexity of communication.[19] This model fully includes the receiver,

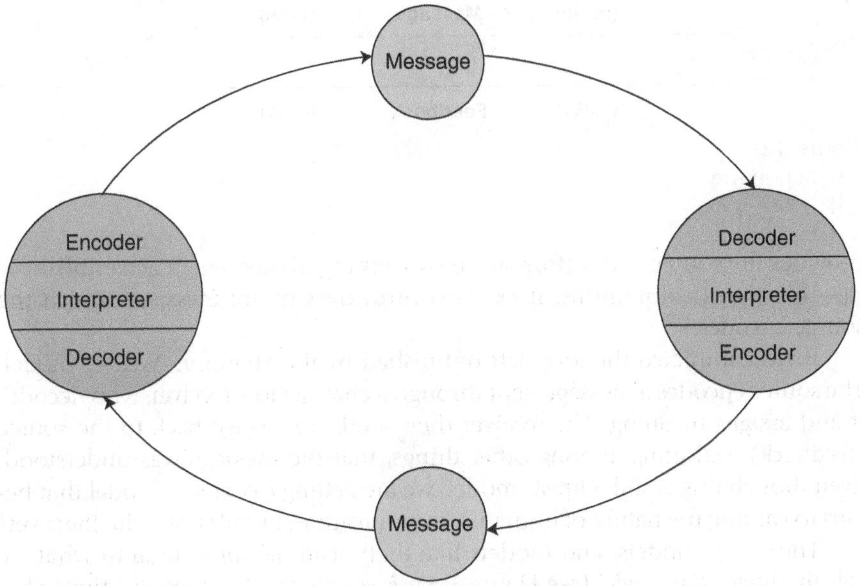

Figure 1.3
Schramm's Model of Communication

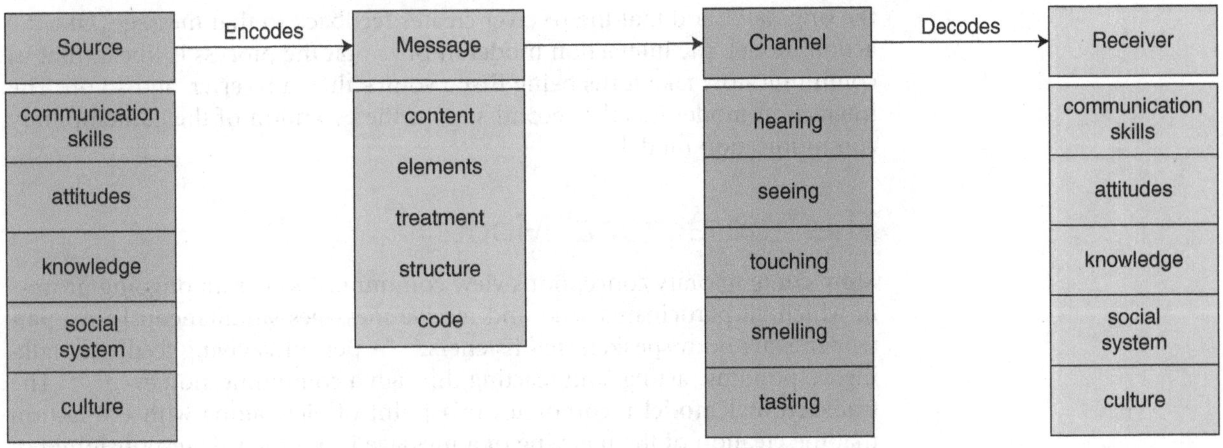

A Source encodes a message for a channel to a receiver who decodes the message: S–M–C–R Model.

Figure 1.4
Berlo's Model of Communication

and it places importance on the *relationship* between the source and receiver. It also illustrates that the source and receiver are not just reacting to the environment or each other, but that each possesses individual differences based on knowledge and attitudes, and that each operates within a cultural and social system that influences meaning. Because we all have different knowledge and attitudes, we interpret or give meaning to messages in different ways. This makes human communication very complex!

Although it was not explicitly mentioned in the model (see Figure 1.4), Berlo discussed the notion of **feedback** in his book. Feedback is information that is routed to the source, or fed back, from the receiver. Berlo said, "Feedback

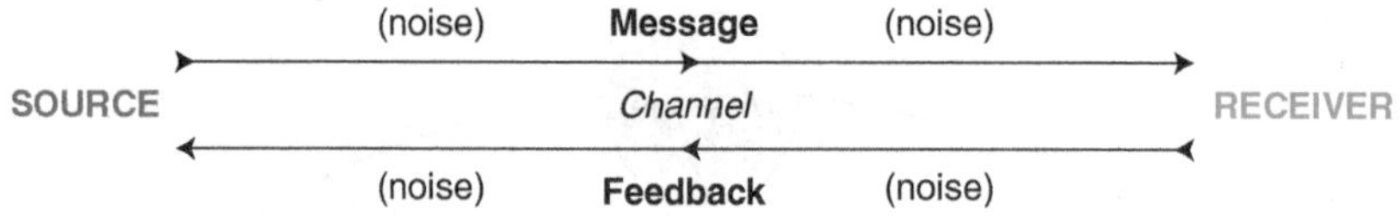

Figure 1.5
Interaction Model

provides the source with information concerning his success in accomplishing his objective. In doing this, it exerts control over future messages which the source encodes."[20]

Berlo completed the loop left unfinished by the Shannon–Weaver model. The source encodes a message, sent through a channel to a receiver, who decodes it and assigns meaning. The receiver then sends a message back to the source (feedback) indicating, among other things, that the message was understood. Even though this is still a linear model, we are getting closer to a model that begins to capture the nature of human communication. But it's not quite there yet!

These two models, and models like them, can be *summarized* in what we call the *interaction model* (see Figure 1.5). A source sends a message through a noise-filled channel to a receiver. The receiver responds to the source through feedback, which is a message sent by the receiver to the source through a noise-filled channel. The core of the interaction model is that the source is the originator and that the receiver creates feedback to that message. Like the action model, the interaction model implies that the process is linear; that is, communicators take turns being first a source then a receiver, and so on. The interaction model was the second step in the evolution of the contemporary communication model.

The Transactional Model

More contemporary conceptions view communication as an ongoing process in which all participants send and receive messages simultaneously. All participants are both speakers *and* listeners.[21] "A person is giving feedback, talking, responding, acting, and reacting through a communication event."[22] The **transactional model** incorporates this point of view along with the notion that the creation of the meaning of a message is not the sole responsibility of the source or the receiver, but a responsibility that is shared among all participants in a communication situation or event.

Properties of Transactional Communication. To get a clear view of the transactional model of communication, it is necessary to understand the important properties of communication. Properties include process, irreversibility, shared responsibility, context, and culture. These five properties are discussed in this section.

Communication Is a Process. Many conceptualizations of communication describe it as a **process.** The notion of process is not unique to communication; it comes to us from the literature of *theoretical physics.* A little closer to home, the notion of process and its relationship to human behavior can be found in *general systems theory.*[23] Although we use this term all the time, it's important to understand what the term *process* implies.

Process implies that communication is *continuous* and ongoing. It is *dynamic:* It never stops. Barnlund[24] says that a process has no beginning and no end. It constantly changes and evolves, new information and experience is added, and it becomes even more complex.[25] There is ongoing and constant mutual influence of the participants.[26] Participants are *constantly* sending and receiving verbal and nonverbal messages. You can try to take a "snapshot" of a single episode, and you can observe the date and time of its beginning and ending, but you can't say that this is where the communication began and ended. Heisenberg stated that to observe a process requires bringing it to a halt.[27] This gives us a fuzzy look at what is really happening, because stopping a process alters the process. So we have to do the best we can to observe, understand, and participate in communication events.

Consider, for example, a father asking his son to practice his saxophone. The father says, "Pete, please go to your room and practice your saxophone for 20 minutes." Pete (clearly annoyed) responds, "Come on, Dad! I'm right in the middle of this video game. Can't I do it later?" The father immediately gets angry and sends Pete to his room "to think about what he has done," followed by 20 minutes of saxophone practice.

The episode seems to be over, but we wonder why the young man was so annoyed at being asked to practice and why the father got angry so quickly. Could it be that this was only *one* installment in a series of episodes in which the father tries to get Pete to practice? Or could it be that Pete was having some difficulty with the saxophone that made him not want to practice? Or is there something else going on that we can't see in only this one episode? Will this episode affect future episodes?

The answer to the last question is yes! Communication is influenced by events that come before it, and it influences events that follow it.

Communication Is Irreversible. Messages are sent and received, and all participants give meaning to those messages as they happen. Once the behavior has occurred, it becomes part of history and can't be reversed. Have you ever said something that you wish you could take back? It doesn't matter if you meant it or not; once it's out there, you have to deal with it.

> *"You are the master of the* unspoken *word. Once the word is spoken, you are its slave."*
>
> —Anonymous

As mentioned in a previous section, the prior experience or history of the participants influences the meaning created in the current interaction. Even if you try to take something back or pretend it didn't happen, it still has influence in the current and future interactions. Occasionally, in a court case, an attorney or a witness will say something that the judge decides is inappropriate to the case, and he or she will instruct the jury to "disregard" the statement. Do you think the members of the jury are able to remove the statement from their memories? Have you ever heard that as a member of a jury? What did you do?

A friend of ours was asked the question that no married person wants to hear. While clothes shopping, the spouse asked, "Do these pants make me look fat?" Instead of pretending not to hear the question or saying an emphatic no, our friend said, "The pants are very nice, honey. It's your backside that makes you look fat!" For almost a whole minute, it seemed pretty funny. Multiple attempts to take back the comment failed. That communication episode affected the meaning of nearly every conversation they had for several months. *Communication is irreversible.* And you thought this book would have no practical advice!

Communication Means Shared Responsibility. Poor communication is not the fault of *one* participant in a conversation. If communication breaks down, you can't blame it on the "other guy." It is the fault of *all* the participants. The transactional perspective implies that it is the responsibility of all participants to cooperate to create a shared meaning. Even if a few of the participants are deficient in some communication skills, it is the responsibility of each person to adapt to the situation and ensure that everyone understands. Even the less capable have responsibilities: If they do not understand, they have the responsibility to ask the other participants to help them understand. *All participants cooperate to create meaning.*

How does your culture affect communication?

Communication Occurs in a Context. The participants in the communication event affect or influence each other, and they are also affected and influenced by the context or environment in which the communication event occurs.

Communication Occurs within Cultures. Much like context, the participants are affected or influenced by the culture of which they are members and by the culture in which the communication event takes place.

Specifics of the Transaction Model. The evolution of communication theory through the action and interaction models has brought us to the current perspective, the transaction model. This book is based on the transaction model, and all of the communication strategies we suggest are based on the model and its properties.

Wallace and others view the transactional perspective as *the joint creation of shared meaning through the simultaneous perception of verbal and nonverbal behaviors within a specific context.*[28] Although you are speaking or sending messages, you constantly receive and give meaning to information from the environment and from other participants. Similarly, while you are listening to another participant, you are sending nonverbal messages through eye contact, facial expressions, posture, and body movements. So we don't really take turns being the source and receiver as illustrated by the action and interaction models. Instead, we are constantly sending *and* receiving messages!

How do you prepare for a meeting with a new business associate?

For example, a husband asks a wife if she minds if he plays golf on a Saturday afternoon. All the time he is asking the question, he is constantly scanning for every nonverbal clue to find out how she really feels. It might be her posture, or the way she looks at (or away from) him, or a particular facial expression, or some combination of everything that provides her response long before she speaks. Lots of information is being exchanged in this situation, which helps this couple create and share meaning.

Think about the first time you met your girlfriend's or boyfriend's parents. Think about your first date with somebody you were really interested in. Or consider meeting a potential client for a business deal. Doing business is important to both participants, so you both are very careful to gather all the available information to reduce uncertainty, become more

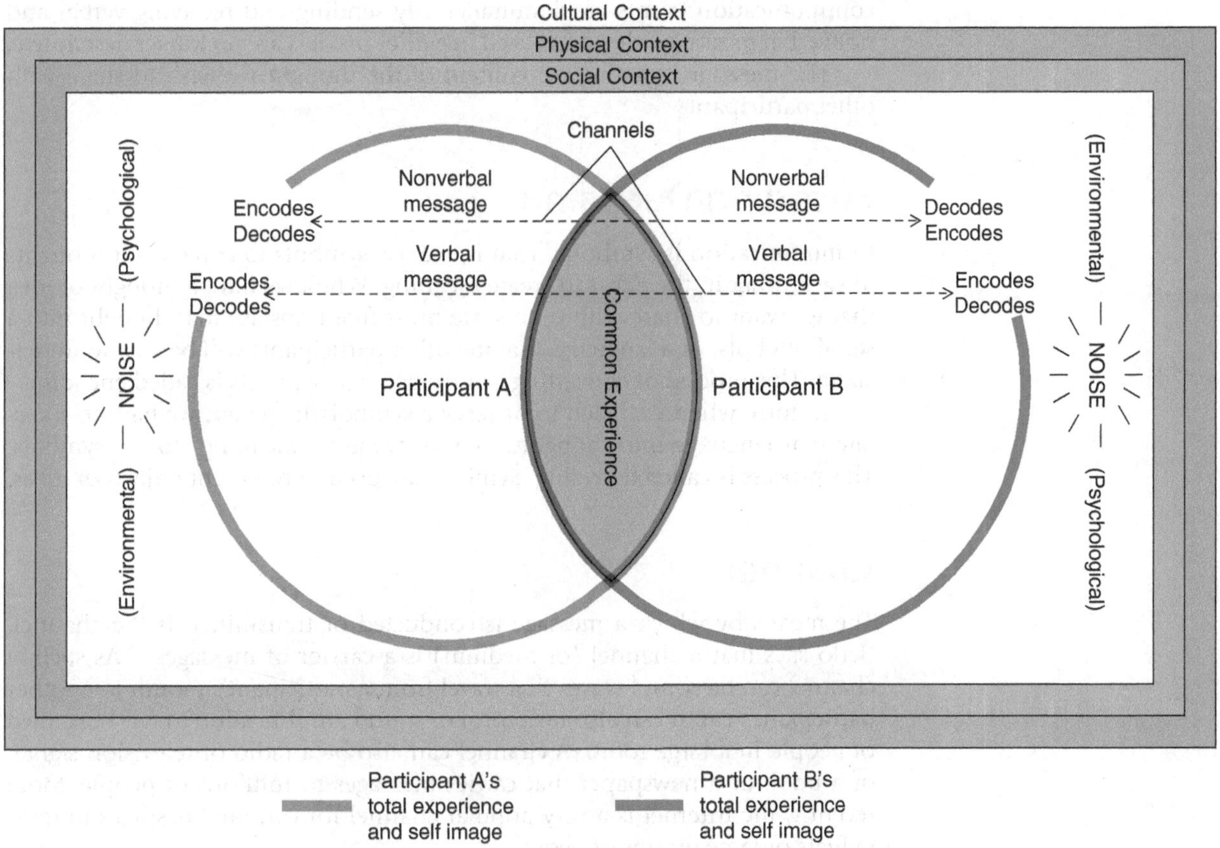

Figure 1.6
Transactional Model

comfortable, and formulate and confirm strategies for accomplishing communication goals. You use the information to create and share meaning!

In the transaction model, *participants create shared meaning* by simultaneously sending and receiving verbal and nonverbal messages within a specific context. Please see Figure 1.6 for a depiction of the model. The transaction model is reflected and applied in every chapter of this book.

WHAT DO THE TERMS MEAN?

We know that you're tired of all the theory talk, but we have to define some terms so that we are all on the same page. All of these terms have been used in this chapter, but some have been used in different ways in the various models. This section will establish the way each term will be used throughout the book.

Communicators/Participants

Although the action and interaction models use the terms *source* and *receiver* or *speaker* and *listener,* we will simply use the term **participant.** Because there is no exchange of speaker and listener roles, and because all persons in communication events are simultaneously sending and receiving verbal and nonverbal messages, the terms used in earlier models are no longer descriptive.

The message contains the content of the thought we wish to share with other participants.

Encoding/Decoding

Communication is symbolic. That is, we use symbols to convey our thoughts to each other in the effort to create meaning. When we have a thought or idea that we want to share with others, we must first translate that thought into a set of symbols, or a language, that the other participants will be able to understand. This process of converting our thoughts to symbols is called encoding.

In turn, when we listen to or receive symbols/language, we have to translate that language into thoughts. That is, we give "meaning" to the symbols. This process is called decoding. Symbols are used to represent objects or ideas.

Channel

The means by which a message is conducted or transmitted is the channel. Berlo says that a channel (or medium) is a **carrier** of messages.[29] As such, a channel can be sound waves that travel from a participant's mouth to another participant's ear. It can also be a form of sound amplification to reach a crowd of people in a large room. A channel can also be a radio or television signal, or a book or a newspaper that carries messages to millions of people. More recently, the Internet is a very popular channel for carrying messages to individuals or large groups of people.

Noise

Noise is anything that interferes with or distorts the transmission of the signal. **Environmental noise** is interference with the signal as it moves from the source to the destination. This could take the form of sounds in the room that prevent the receiver from hearing the message; it could be static on a telephone line, or even a dropped call on a cellular phone. **Psychological noise** takes place inside the sender or receiver, such as misunderstanding or failing to remember what was heard.

How does an event's context affect communication?

Context

Context can be viewed as physical or social. The **physical context** is made up of the space surrounding the communication event, or the place in which the communication event occurs. The context could be a classroom, a meeting room at work, a church, a physician's office, your house, your favorite "night spot," or about any other place you can imagine. The place in which the event takes place influences communication behaviors and the meanings attributed to them. How would your behavior change if you moved from your favorite night spot to a classroom? Would you behave the same way?

The **social context** considers the nature of the event taking place in a physical context. The social expectations tied to particular events influence meaning attributed to communication. Even though you were still in a classroom, you would behave differently during an exam than during a group work session. You would behave differently in church during a funeral than celebrating a festive holiday, and you would certainly behave differently while playing bingo in the church basement!

Culture

The **culture** in which the communication occurs and the native cultures of the participants can influence meaning. People belong to a variety of nations, traditions, groups, and organizations, each of which has its own point of view, values, and norms.[30] A culture is made up of the collective beliefs or principles on which a community or part of a community of people is based. These beliefs are often passed from generation to generation and provide a perspective through which the community makes sense of its experiences. The culture, then, provides a very powerful context or backdrop for communication events and has a profound influence on the meaning that participants create and share.

SUMMARY

That's enough of the theory, at least for the moment. Let's get to the application! Keep in mind, however, that a solid understanding of the basics of the transactional model will provide a lot of help to you as you attempt to plan strategies and practice your skills to help you achieve your communication goals.

NOTES

1. S. Littlejohn, *Theories of Human Communication* (Belmont, CA: Wadsworth, 1999), 2.
2. F. Kerlinger, *Foundations of Behavioral Research* (New York: Holt, Rinehart, and Winston, 1973), 9.
3. M. Polanyi, *Personal Knowledge* (Chicago: University of Chicago Press, 1958).
4. W. Wallace, *The Logic of Science in Sociology* (Chicago: Aldine, 1971).
5. T. Clevenger, "Can One Not Communicate? A Conflict of Models," *Communication Studies* 42 (1991), 351.
6. C. Hovland, I. Janis, and H. Kelley, *Communication and Persuasion* (New Haven, CT: Yale University Press, 1953).
7. G. Gerbner, "On Defining Communication: Still Another View," *Journal of Communication* 16 (1966), 99–103.
8. G. Miller, "On Defining Communication: Another Stab," *Journal of Communication* 16 (1966), 92.
9. K. Sereno and C.D. Mortensen, *Foundations of Communication Theory* (New York: Harper & Row, 1970), 5.
10. J. Makay, *Public Speaking: Theory into Practice* (Dubuque, IA: Kendall/Hunt, 2000), 9.
11. L. Hugenberg, S. Wallace, and D. Yoder, *Creating Competent Communication* (Dubuque, IA: Kendall/Hunt, 2003), 4.
12. J. DeVito, *Human Communication: The Basic Course* (Boston, Allyn & Bacon, 2006), 2.
13. J. Golden, G. Berquist, W. Coleman, and J. Sproule, *The Rhetoric of Western Thought, 8th ed.* (Dubuque, IA: Kendall/Hunt, 2003).
14. D. Stanton, and G. Berquist, "Aristotle's Rhetoric: Empiricism or Conjecture?" *Southern Speech Communication Journal* 41 (1975), 69–81.
15. L. Cooper, *The Rhetoric of Aristotle* (New York: Appleton-Century-Crofts, 1932).
16. Golden etal., 65.

17. C. Shannon, and W. Weaver, *The Mathematical Theory of Communication* (Urbana: University of Illinois Press, 1949). Also W. Weaver, "The Mathematics of Communication," in C.D. Mortensen (ed.), *Basic Readings in Communication Theory* (New York: Harper & Row, 1979).
18. W. Schramm, "How Communication Works," in W. Schramm, (ed.), *The Process and Effects of Communication* (Urbana: University of Illinois Press, 1954).
19. D. Berlo, *The Process of Communication* (New York: Holt, Rinehart, and Winston, 1960).
20. Ibid pp.111–112.
21. Barnlund, D. (1970). "A Transactional Model of Communication," in *Foundations of Communication Theory*, Sereno, K. and Mortensen, C. D. (eds.). New York: Harper & Row, 1970. Also P. Watzlawick, *How Real Is Real? Confusion, Disinformation, Communication: An Anecdotal Introduction to Communications Theory* (New York: Vintage, 1977).
22. M. Burgoon and M. Ruffner, *Human Communication.* (New York: Holt, Rinehart, & Winston, 1978), 9.
23. E. Lazlo, *The Systems View of the World: A Holistic Vision for Our Time* (New York: Hampton Press, 1996). Also L. von Bertalanffy, *General System Theory: Foundations, Development, Applications* (New York: Braziller, 1976).
24. Barnlund.
25. F. Dance, "Toward a Theory of Human Communication," In F. Dance (ed.), *Human Communication Theory: Original Essays* (New York: Holt, 1967).
26. K. Miller, *Communication Theories: Perspectives, Processes, and Contexts* (New York: McGraw-Hill, 2005).
27. W. Heisenberg, *The Physical Principles of Quantum Theory* (Chicago: University of Chicago Press, 1930).
28. S. Wallace, D. Yoder, L. Hugenberg, and C. Horvath, *Creating Competent Communication,* 5th ed. (Dubuque, IA: Kendall/Hunt, 2006).
29. Berlo.
30. Yoder, Hugenberg, and Wallace. *Creating Competent Communication.* (Dubuque, IA: Kendall/Hunt, 1993).

REFERENCES

T. Newcomb, "An Approach to the Study of Communicative Acts," *Psychological review* 60 (1953), 393–404.
P. Watzlawick, J. Beavin, and D. Jackson, *Pragmatics of Human Communication* (New York: Norton, 1967).

chapter 2

Creating Your Message

OBJECTIVES

After reading this chapter, you should understand the following concepts:

- If your ideas and message are disorganized, your communications will be as well.
- Selection is a decision strategy of determining your topic and purpose, meeting the audience's needs, and choosing the proper supporting evidence.
- Once the topic is selected, the general purpose of a speech will guide all other decisions. The specific purpose will narrow the focus to what you want to accomplish from the speech.
- Evidence should be relevant, accurate, and appropriate for the audience, and it should be presented truthfully.
- Sequencing strategies help you organize the message into a logical order of introduction, body, and conclusion.
- The body of the message contains the main points and is developed first.
- The introduction motivates the audience to listen and prepares them for the subject.
- The conclusion should close the speech with an effective, appealing summary.
- Connectives create a dynamic flow between the sections of the speech.

KEY TERMS

selection
topic
audience interest
speech purpose
informative speech
persuasive speech
ceremonial speech
general purpose
specific purpose
evidence
main points
chronological order
spatial order
categorical (topical) order
cause-effect order
comparison and contrast
problem-solution order
Monroe's motivated sequence
attention step
need
satisfaction
visualization
action
primacy
recency
specificity
introduction
thesis statement
initial summary
speech preview
final summary
conclusion
connectives
transitions
signposts
previews
internal summary

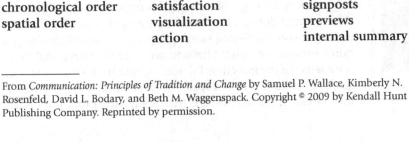

INTRODUCTION

I enjoy making baked goods for my family. I know where every ingredient, recipe, and utensil is in my kitchen, and I can bake pretty efficiently (even if not always successfully). I have several books that tell me how to bake elaborate to simple things, and I even have a folder on my computer that is filled with baked goods yet to be tackled. There are pictures of completed pies, delicious-looking cakes, and yummy cookies to inspire me. When planning to spend an afternoon baking, I make sure I have all the needed ingredients, prepare and measure them, and line them up in the order in which they'll be needed. I set aside time to do this all. Even the most complicated baking project seems uncomplicated once I have everything laid out, and my planning and organization give me some sense of control over the eventual outcome.

How can you expect to accomplish anything when your surroundings are in complete disarray?

However, in the chaos of my home office, a different scenario exists. Although I write all the time, the process is often made more painful because of the disarray I attempt to work in. Usually, I know the task I have to complete: Write a report, develop a lecture, create some slides, construct a test. I know the general materials that need to go into those, and most of the time, I'm pretty sure I have a sense of what the end result product should look like. Although I sort of know where most things are, I usually end up wasting time looking for long-lost papers buried in stacks. To begin my project, I sit at the computer and stare, stuck from the start without a coherent plan. I have good intentions to file papers where they need to go (witness all of my folders), but somehow, everything seems to end up in heaps. My computer desktop has icons galore, and while I can eventually find the folder I've put work into, guessing what I've named something has to come first. When faced with complicated projects, I have wasted hours looking for a book or document that I know is here somewhere, in some electronic or hard-copy form. Books surround me, leaning in haphazard piles. At my feet are various blank CDs and DVDs, along with a printer, a jumble of cords, pencils and markers, and some old computer disks. Eventually, because I can't find anything or something falls over on me, I'll have to stop working and straighten things up before I can continue in my stumbling way.

Do you notice a difference between my baking structure and my office organization? The similarity is that doing something and thinking about something probably require the same discipline. Both require strategic planning and goal setting. You have to be motivated to engage in both, and it would be nice if you enjoyed the activity. The difference is that although I like both baking and writing, my structural deficiencies in my office make writing much more painful than it has to be.

A neat office atmosphere makes it more inviting to get down to work.

Now, let's imagine that we all believe that strategic planning is desirable; I seem to do it when baking, don't I? I know that it will help in understanding, finding, developing, and relating information. Strategic planning gives organization and form to thinking and doing. How could I employ that structure on my writing missions? Before starting a project, I could jot down a quick summary of what I have to accomplish. That should give me a sense of the materials I'll need to gather. Setting some time goals never hurts; I'm not really good at all-nighters, and sometimes I can stress over details that really aren't that important.

I could decide to reorganize my office: Papers could be filed in neatly labeled drawers or boxes; books could be shelved alphabetically or by topic. I could decide that only the left wall will be used for bookshelves. I could rearrange my computer desktop into well-designed folders, with clear headings that follow a specific pattern. I could move off anything that wasn't currently in use and store it off my computer. All the clutter on the floor could find a new home in the closet, on specific shelves designed for office use. I could buy a desk organizer that holds pencils and pens, clips and markers, so that they weren't all over the desk and floor. Come to think of it, any one of those strategies would probably help me to have a more structured office and successful writing program!

The same organizational strategies are true for communicating. Thinking and doing are both harder when you, your ideas, and your materials are disorganized. You learned about the audience in Chapter 12. Considering their demographics and psychographics will help you to design a message that will fit their needs. The context can impact the ideas that you develop, because if you're expected to inform but instead decide to entertain, for instance, your poor context analysis will leave the audience feeling cheated. Once you have a sense of audience and context, you'll move to the next steps of topic selection and goal setting, gathering evidence, and structuring the message. Determining your goal for the audience is essential, because that will guide you in making some decisions about the direction your message should take and the evidence you must gather. Once you have considered those necessary elements, you can structure your message.

When you have ideas or issues that you want to share with others, there's a choice among several decision strategies that can help you and your audience. You just have to learn which ones to choose and how to use them, and which contexts call for certain approaches. *Constructing any message can be accomplished through the two primary decision strategies of selection and sequence of ideas.* As you impose coherence on the jumble of data that you'll be gathering, you'll apply these strategies and will become a more effective communicator.

WHAT TWO DECISION STRATEGIES AID IN CONSTRUCTING MY MESSAGE?

Two decisions strategies work together to help you construct a message. The first is selecting your topic, its purpose, and its supporting evidence. The second strategy is organizing your message in an efficient sequence. Let's look at how to use these strategies effectively.

Decision Strategy 1: Selecting Your Topic, Purpose, and Evidence

The concept of selection suggests that you have choices to be made from a range of options. In communication, **selection** involves determining your topic and purpose, meeting the audience's needs and expectations, and recognizing the kinds of supporting materials that you will use to build the message.

You can't process too many pieces of information at one time.

When you read about critical thinking earlier in the text, you discovered that the selection of stimuli is necessary and typical of our perceptual process. As you take in all the data that bombard you, you can't make it all relevant; there's just too much there to process, and it's difficult to structure it in a meaningful way. You choose to focus on the stimuli that you define as important to the task at hand.

Stop and pay attention to the variety of stimuli around you right now. Is there is noise from other people, the TV or music source, or even environmental noise such as a fan blowing or a siren in the distance? Did you notice them until you stopped to listen for them? Are you paying attention to only the ideas that are highlighted in this text in some way, or are you just reading the examples? Did you look at the objectives listed for this chapter? Have you ever considered how you approach a text? Are you marking in the text, taking notes, or rereading paragraphs over and over again because you aren't really focusing? Have you developed an effective way to make the words significant and able to be retained?

What stimuli are impacting you, and which ones are you ignoring? The same need to make certain stimuli relevant, immediate, or intense exists for your audience. As the speaker, you have to help that audience to focus on the important stimuli—those you have chosen to highlight for them. That means you have to select topic, purpose, and supporting materials.

Speakers are most often asked to talk about their specific areas of expertise.

Selecting a Topic. The starting point in selection is to determine your **topic.** On the face of it, this seems pretty challenging: You might be asking, what do I know that would be interesting to anyone? You can answer this question in several ways. Many times, of course, you are asked or told to speak on a specific topic. You're asked for a progress report, you're told to explain how to do some process, someone inquires about an experience you've had. When that happens, topic selection has been taken out of your hands. After college, you will mostly be invited to speak on topics related to your work or your passions. Speakers are nearly always asked to speak in areas of their expertise, be it gardening, geography, radiation, or radio frequency identification. Even on those occasions, you'll find it necessary to narrow the subject so you can meet the needs of the audience and the context. Sometimes, the occasion or issue determines the topic, like when you're giving a nomination speech, a wedding toast, or the introduction of a speaker. But on those occasions where you have complete freedom in selecting the subject, there are some simple guidelines you can use that should help to erase the majority of your worry.

Topic selection should begin with you. What do you care about? What interests you? What do you know something about? If you don't feel the topic is important, it's likely that you won't be able to make the audience feel any differently. You might think that telling college students about the importance of creating a burial plan is a "good idea," but if you really don't believe that it's true, then find something else to talk about. How about creating a speech about the difference among different types of life insurance policies? Can you competently lay out the pros and cons? If not, choose again. If you are taking a history class at the same time you are taking your speech class, why not speak about the significance of some historic event you are already studying? If you enjoy reading a particular blog, consider the emerging role of blogging as a topic for your speech. Remember, however, that not only do you have to be interested and have some degree of expertise, but you also have to make sure that you make the audience the target of that message. You shouldn't be speaking just to hear yourself do it! Filter that topic through a fast audience analysis (you'll flesh this out more once you've settled on your subject).

Is your speech one that others will think worthy of their time and attention?

That notion of **audience interest** is also an initial challenge. Keep in mind that others are interested if what they're hearing gives them new, useful information; if it provides a solution to something that concerns them; if it relates to their own experiences; or if it shows a connection to what they know and something new. As a speaker, each of us has an ethical obligation to bring the audience something of value, to challenge listeners by sharing something they do not already know, or to ask listeners to rethink something they are familiar with. Unlike our grade school "what I did on my summer vacation" speeches, a speech to an adult audience must offer something of value to the listener. An interesting phenomenon is that sometimes, audience interest can actually be a detriment. If you're presenting the company's plan for budget cuts, it's pretty likely that the employees will have a vested interest. However, the threat that they feel when they hear "budget cuts" can actually weaken their ability and desire to listen to the ideas you intend to present. Their unique bias may create a block to effective listening. In another scenario, interest might be determined by the audience's sense that what they're hearing is or is not worth their time. How many meetings do you go to grudgingly, feeling that you have better things to do? What if you had to listen to a speech about how make a peanut butter and jelly sandwich? Think about what it would be like to sit and listen to such a speech. Would you consider it worth your attention and time? Even if you have never made a sandwich before, you probably do not need a six-minute speech to describe the process, unless some really unique spin is put on the description. A speaker in this situation fails to honor the audience by ignoring the value of their time and ignoring if they would be better off after hearing the speech.

Finally, you should not only avoid topics that waste audience members' time and attention, you must also be sure that your topic doesn't harm or intentionally misinform. Carefully weigh the impact of examples and ideas that could reinforce negative stereotypes or slander others. Knowingly including false or misleading information in a speech is unethical and should be avoided. Just as harmful is selecting a topic because it seems funny without considering how audience members might be affected. Although it might seem humorous to give a speech on how to get drunk fast, for example, it would be ethically irresponsible and it could be highly offensive to a classmate who lost a friend or family member to binge drinking. Use language that respects others: Avoid demeaning, sexist, or racist words. As a speaker, you must exercise your opportunity to speak responsibly.

Now that you have an idea of the guidelines for determining a good topic, how do you select one? Sources of topics exist within public issues you care about (immigration reform, global warming, big box stores' impact on local retailers); they can come from personal experiences you can open up to the audience (the time you got a flat tire can become "how to change a flat," or your camping fiasco could relate tips for safe camping); or they might be stimulated by media exposure (ideas present in news magazines, interviews that generate awareness). In all honesty, if you spend a bit of time brainstorming about the ideas that catch your attention, you'll probably be faced with the task of narrowing the field to the best one for this audience and situation.

The Role of Speech Purpose. I attended church last week, as I normally do. The sermon surprised me, though. Rather than hearing a homily that enlightened or stimulated me, I listened to a report on the church's finances. I felt uncomfortable as the service progressed, although I couldn't really figure out why, since the rest of the rituals included all the usual elements of songs, prayers, and readings. So what caused my discomfort? It was that the purpose of the sermon was compromised: I expected one thing and was given something else.

Speech purpose is a statement of a goal and the desired audience response. It usually is determined by the audience and the occasion: Why were you asked to speak? Think of purposes as having two dimensions: general and specific. The general purpose is the broad, overall speech goal. Traditionally, we perform one of three general purposes in speaking: to inform, to persuade, or to entertain. An **informative speech** is one whose goal is to produce shared understanding, to increase knowledge, to cultivate appreciation, or to develop skills or abilities. A **persuasive speech** involves the process of social influence in order to influence beliefs, values, attitudes, or actions of others. **Ceremonial speeches** reaffirm common values and strengthen ties among a community. The first two purposes are covered in Chapters 15 and 16; the third can be found on the companion Web site.

© Tomasz Trojanowski, 2008, Shutterstock.

How do you attempt to persuade someone to act in a specific manner?

Your **general purpose** will guide all the choices to come: what evidence or supporting materials you'll gather and use, how you'll structure your ideas, and even the delivery techniques you'll employ.

The second dimension of speech goal setting lies in determining the specific purpose. Your **specific purpose** states precisely what you hope to accomplish in your speech: What response do you expect from your audience? What is it that you want the audience to know, believe, do, or feel by the end

Take a Closer Look

Let's consider a few simple examples to show how the general purpose dictates what the specific purpose will be.

If your general purpose is to *inform*, then your specific purpose would be:

1. To create awareness in my audience about the services provided by the American Red Cross in our community
2. To demonstrate to the audience how to choose among cell phone plans
3. To describe how recycling saves the environment

If your general purpose is to *persuade*, then your specific purpose would be:

1. To convince my audience to donate their time to the upcoming Red Cross blood and bone marrow drive
2. To recommend to the audience that they select Verizon's cell phone plan
3. To urge my audience to participate in campus recycling

of your message? The specific purpose is a limitation placed on the audience's focus that develops your general purpose.

When formulating your purpose statement, here are a few strategic guidelines. A well-planned specific purpose contains one distinct idea worded in terms of the desired audience response. For example, if you said, "To persuade my audience to volunteer their time with the Red Cross and to learn more about marrow donation," you'd have different general and specific purposes working here. Either you can persuade your audience to volunteer, or you can inform them about marrow donation. It is impossible to reach both purposes in one speech. Second, your specific purpose should match your general purpose. If your general speech purpose is to persuade, your specific purpose can't be "to tell my audience about the negative effects of cigarette smoking." Third, you should word your specific purpose as a statement, not a question. A question doesn't tell the audience about the response you're seeking from them: "Do we need capital punishment?" isn't as directive as, "The state should revoke its statue permitting capital punishment." Finally, your specific purpose statement guides your speech focus in terms of time: Can you really achieve your goal in the time allotted? Could you "explain about golf" in a five- to seven-minute speech? How would you need to refine the focus of this specific purpose?

Think of the selection of general and specific purposes as the step that provides you a target: Where do you want to be by the end of the speech? That answer will guide the formation of your speech purpose statement. If you have a clear idea of your direction, then the next element of selection can be achieved. You're ready to start gathering evidence.

Collecting Evidence. In Chapter 3 on critical thinking, you learned about the various categories of evidence or supporting material (examples, statistics, testimony, narratives, and analogies) that a speaker can consider. During the selection stage, you'll employ *knowledge gathering,* identifying the evidence you will need to reach your communication purpose of information giving, persuading, or expressing value. Rather than repeating the categories, let's think about how your own cognitions work. Why do you believe the things you do? Do you know how to search Internet databases? Why do you have the attitudes you hold? Do you feel that the draft should be reinstated, or that people should buy only American goods? How about the things you value; where did those judgments come from? Why do you believe that your football team is the best, or that the worst role models for young girls are found in Hollywood? All of these views come from someone or something in your life that gave you evidence from which you built your perspectives. Most of these pieces of evidence came to you from an external source: a friend who shared a personal experience, a teacher who explained a concept, a Web site or television show that exposed you to something new, a poll that revealed national trends, or even the comparisons that your parents made between your life and theirs. All of these contributed to the convictions that you hold. In the same way, when you select **evidence,** or supporting materials, you will make decisions about what kinds of cognitions (beliefs, attitudes, and values) you hope to create in your audience.

We learn by sharing our experiences with friends.

Some of the cognitions you want to support in a message are pretty fundamental; you can use your own experience or a friend's narrative to explain what you mean, and the audience will see the similarities with their own way of thinking. However, other ideas will require more compelling supports from credible external sources; your personal statement just isn't enough. Why should we believe your claim that the school mascot should be changed because it is a racist symbol? Why should we agree that the town should sell a plot of land to a developer in order to improve the tax base? You have to support these claims or assertions with evidence that helps to solidify (or prove) them in your audience's frame of reference. Evidence is necessary because it helps to prove your point, and it helps to make your ideas more valid.

© Damir Karan, 2008, Shutterstock.

Where do you go to research for evidence about your topic?

You can gain acceptance from a wider group of people when you support your ideas with evidence beyond your own word. When you support your statements with external proof, you can show that it's not just your opinion that is being given. You can show that you are not alone in your line of thinking. Take a simple example: You want to inform your audience of the dangers of young adult depression. You might be brave enough to share your own personal experience (a narrative) with your listeners, but they could just as easily dismiss you as being an exception. But when you bring in statistics from the American Psychological Association demonstrating the increased suicide rate among young adults, and then you follow it up with testimony about undiagnosed depression from the surgeon general and the campus psychologist, and cap it off with a list of depression symptoms for your audience to compare with their own feelings, your speech will be made believable and acceptable to a wide-ranging audience.

You know that the evidence created by examples, statistics, testimony, narratives, and analogies can amplify, clarify, personalize, capture attention, visualize, aid in retention, and link ideas in any message. Here are a few reminders about the selection of supporting materials:

- *Represent the evidence truthfully.* Do not present a hypothetical illustration as a real one, for example, or present only part of a piece of testimony. You might remember that in October 2005, Oprah Winfrey named as her book club selection *A Million Little Pieces,* author James Frey's nonfiction memoir of his vomit-caked years as an alcoholic, drug addict, and criminal. In January 2006, following the discovery of Frey's "embellishment" of the facts of the narrative he had depicted as all true, Oprah castigated him on her hour-long show for the lies he had told.[1]
- *Make sure that your evidence is clearly relevant to the point you're making.* If you were giving that speech about young adult depression and only gave statistics for mental illness in postwar veterans, the statistics would fail.
- *Present accurate evidence; check your examples, testimony, and statistics to make sure you have not misspoken or left anything out.* Cite the sources for your evidence. Make sure that those sources are credible and will have meaning for your audience. Former Secretary of State Colin Powell was reminded of this guideline when he admitted in September 2005 that information he gave to the United Nations in a February 2003 speech was flawed. He told Barbara Walters that he had relied on information he received at Central Intelligence Agency briefings. "There were some people in the intelligence community who knew at the time that some of those sources were not good, and shouldn't be relied upon, and they didn't speak up," Powell said. He called his prewar speech to the United Nations accusing Iraq of

harboring weapons of mass destruction a "blot" on his record and admitted, "I'm the one who presented it to the world, and (it) will always be a part of my record. It was painful. It is painful now."[2]

- *Make sure the evidence is appropriate to the audience.* Does the analogy fit their knowledge level? Can they understand the quotation?

Early in the process of message creation, you have to gather supporting evidence. How do you know when enough is enough? There really is not a quantifiable statement to be made here, so let's just say this: Gather more than you think you will need. You'll have the opportunity to limit the range of evidence after you structure your speech. Remember, *selection* means that you determine your topic and purpose and begin to amass your supporting materials to help your audience to achieve your goal. It's in the next process step of sequence that you'll start to structure the ideas that you've selected.

Decision Strategy 2: Using Sequencing Strategies

© iofoto, 2008, Shutterstock.
Organization is essential form any tasks, including a successful shopping trip.

Imagine you are planning to do some shopping for a new cell phone, a new pair of shoes, and some food for the family dinner. Your time is important to you, so you want to be efficient. You've done some Internet searches to find out current national prices on the phone and shoes, but you really want to buy local. However, your funds are limited, so you want to conserve gas and do all the shopping at once. This will require several stops, because you want to compare prices locally, too. How will you organize your trip? You could plan your trip based on what you are most excited to buy, or you could focus on the most important items first. You might plan your trip based on a particular route that is efficient. You could plan your trip based on the order of "greater need," so you pick up food for dinner first and the new cell phone last. While you plan your mission, you would think about how to accomplish all of your objectives in the time available and with the limited resources you have. The sequence choices you make give progression and order to your day.

Organizing a message is much like organizing a shopping trip. It will involve reviewing your goals, considering your audience, and several strategic choices. When you organize, you can pull your evidence, analysis, and ideas together from the fragmented pieces you've gathered. Creating order from these elements then allows you to figure out their best sequence. What's the best progression of ideas for your purpose, audience, and occasion? You can determine the relationships between the "big" ideas and the ones that are subordinate to them. In addition, effective organization should help you and your listeners to achieve shared meaning; ideas will be clearer, easier to follow, and less complicated to remember. Finally, clear organization will reflect favorably on you; your audience will perceive that you have prepared and given thought to what you want to say, and your credibility should be enhanced.

Remember what you learned about perception in an earlier chapter? We all try to structure perceptions in order to make sense of them. If you've never been to a flea market, the stimuli of antiques, collectables, clothing, farm goods, people, and food will assail you. You have to decide which stimuli to keep or to abandon, which are more important than others, and even where to turn your attention first. That organizational sorting and arranging is based on your personal reasons for going to the flea market in the first place. Was your purpose to see what was out there? Were you on a mission for that perfect lamp? Did you hope to find some organic vegetables? Did you just want to see what a flea market was? Those purposes guide how you structure your walk through the flea market and will help you to make sense of the stimuli that you're receiving. Now think about presenting a message to others. You're going to give them stimuli in the form of ideas and evidence. You want them to perceive those stimuli in a specific way so shared meaning will be established. That means you need to arrange the stimuli for the audience so that they have a better chance of perceiving through your lens.

How you structure ideas should be based on the needs of the situation and audience. Those analyses will have given you a sense of their knowledge level and interest. Now you must strategically decide how to put your evidence and ideas into a progression that will meet those findings. The most basic step in developing your organization is to think of the three basic parts of sequence: introduction, body, and conclusion. But we're going to take a twist here and consider them out of order!

HOW DO I CONSTRUCT THE BODY OF THE MESSAGE?

The body of your message is the "meat" of the content. It's where the audience will learn the most, will be given the most evidence, or will be given arguments to influence them. As a result, it's the most important part of your message, and it should also be the longest. If you structure the main part of the speech first, developing the introduction and conclusion can be made much easier.

Importance of the Main Points

The **main points** are the ideas generated by your specific purpose; they divide your message into manageable units for you to present and your audience to consider. They need to be selected carefully and arranged strategically to meet your purpose. How do you decide what main ideas to consider for inclusion? Your specific purpose provides a simple starting point: it tells the audience what you expect of them. Let's take the earlier example of this informative specific purpose: to create awareness in my audience about the services provided by the American Red Cross. What kinds of questions could you ask yourself to determine how best to develop that awareness? Consider these for a start:

- What is the Red Cross's purpose?
- What is the history of the Red Cross?
- What does the audience already know about the Red Cross?
- Who are the people in my community involved in Red Cross activities?
- Who receives benefits from the Red Cross?
- Is there a difference between the national Red Cross services and local ones?
- Does the Red Cross have divisions?
- How does the Red Cross raise money?

Now, you can see that there is no way you could answer all of these in one speech, considering the time it would take to adequately answer each question. Learning the history of an organization is a speech unto itself. The question about what the audience already knows is answered by your audience analysis;

it's possible that you'll find out they've never heard of the Red Cross, so you need to start pretty basic in your speech. You probably also realize that some of these questions don't really relate to your specific purpose, since it's a focus on services provided by the Red Cross. Would it be important to know the difference between the national Red Cross services and local ones? That lets you eliminate several questions, and end up with maybe two or three:

- What is the Red Cross's purpose?
- Who receives benefits from the Red Cross?
- Does the Red Cross have division?

If you inspect these questions, you'll see that even they can be further divided. "Who receives benefits from the Red Cross?" could be split into something like, "How does the Red Cross help meet emergency needs from natural disasters?" and, "How does the Red Cross help meet emergency needs from accidents?" You can carry out this exercise until you feel comfortable with the main points you think are important in order to meet your purpose. Then you can add depth to those main points by including the supporting materials you have gathered.

Generally, the guidelines suggest dividing your specific purpose into between two and four main points; this is enough to be specific and focused and still meet a gamut of time limits. Remember: Your main points must be directly relevant to your specific purpose; if they're not, you either reconsider and refine those points or rethink your specific purpose. In addition, you would like to have a balance among the main points. You don't want to load up most of the information under one point and have the other two be entirely subordinate. If, for instance, you wanted to change your specific purpose to a more in-depth look at the Red Cross overall, you might want to talk about what services it offers, what values it represents, and how it is funded. If you find yourself spending the majority of your time detailing the services the Red Cross offers, then you can go back and restrict your specific purpose. Maybe your specific purpose is better stated as "to learn about the Red Cross organizations' outstanding (or unheralded) services." In that case, your main points could be disaster services, blood services, and health and safety services. If you can create parallel wording in the structure, that can help the progression and retention of ideas. The example about natural disasters and accidents is created in parallel structure. Compare that with two points that say, "The Red Cross gives help in natural disasters" and, "If there's a local emergency the Red Cross is there." Similarly, the three services are easy to create in parallel wording. Once you've settled on some possible main points (they still can be refined), you're ready to decide on their order.

Your speech topic may answer how a volunteer group helps those who've suffered a natural disaster.

Sequencing Choices

As with the shopping trip scenario, there may be many "right" ways to organize your ideas, deciding what to do first, second, and last. A list of organizational patterns could go on forever, because we arrange our perceptions through our own experiences and needs. However, there are some simple, standard patterns that you can use as you help your audience to take meaning from your message:

- **Chronological order** *structures ideas according to time orientation.* It is used most often when explaining how to do something or how something occurs, since order of activities is critical. An example of chronological order would be an informative speech about the history of the World Wide Web would discuss its evolution from the 1980s to today. You can structure time order from the past to the present or vice versa. A speech on weight clubs in your community could start with the current state of affairs, then move backwards to the origins.

- **Spatial order** *arranges your main points in terms of their place or position.* Think about how sometimes we explain ideas in terms of how they're related to each other by location. Describing how Hurricane Katrina devastated the Gulf Coast could easily move from the impacts in Louisiana to Mississippi to Alabama. Another example would be a speech that identifies the various component pieces connected to create the Web, starting with your home computer. If you wanted to focus on global impacts of some issue and move closer to the audience's immediate context, that would also be spatial order: Uncontrolled pet population growth affects our nation, our state, and our community.
- **Categorical** or **topical order** *is the "natural" or "relevant" organization pattern.* As you think about your main points, they seem to fit best in this way. There is no required order other than what you impose. If you wanted to talk about the three impacts that social networking sites have had on interpersonal communication in the twenty-first century, what topical order would you use in discussing the ideas of privacy, job search, and politics?
- **Cause-effect order** *is used to show a relationship between a source and its outcomes.* You could also reverse the order and show how some effects can be traced back to their origins. Explaining how an animal became endangered could be shown by the causes of habitat depletion, pesticides, and invasive competing species, for example. The key is that you must be able to demonstrate that such a causal relationship exists.
- **Comparison and contrast** *structures ideas by showing that there is a similarity and/or difference of your topic with something the audience already knows.* You could explain how the changes the Internet has created are similar to the changes brought about by television's introduction, for example. Since your audience has always known television, its early impact may surprise the audience. You may have to decide whether to focus on only the differences or the similarities, or both. This is shown in a topic such as immigration issues of the early twenty-first century are both similar and dissimilar to those of the early twentieth century.
- **Problem-solution order** *structures ideas by pointing out a dilemma and offering (or supporting) its potential remedies.* If you use this structure, you must first demonstrate that a dilemma exists, that it's serious, and that it affects your audience. Then you are able to move into the potential solutions, perhaps even focusing on one resolution. Perhaps you feel that the allocation of special event tickets to currently enrolled students should be changed. The first main point you'd make is the extent of the problem: how ticket allocation is inefficient and how ticket allocation is unfair. You would then suggest a means for resolving this problem: Ticket allocation should be tied to class standing. The problem-solution order is quite common in advertisements. You are exposed to a problem you hadn't been aware of (you are alone and lonely, you have no opportunity to meet potential mates, you have no sense of how to talk to members of the opposite sex). Then, as if by magic, Dating Site X can resolve those issues by helping you to meet hundreds of compatible potential mates in your area, and they'll even coach you in how to fix your communication style.

If you assert that an animal became endangered because of habitat depletion, you need to demonstrate the cause-effect order.

Finally, there is **Monroe's motivated sequence,** developed by Professor Alan H. Monroe in the 1930s. This organizational pattern, used mostly in persuasion, combines logic and psychology, because it models the human thinking process and motivates the audience to action. When you read it, you may see it as an extension of the problem-solution order, but it does much more. The motivated sequence consists of five major steps: attention, need, satisfaction, visualization, and action. In the **attention step,** you want to cause the listeners to focus tightly on you and your ideas. This step comes in the introduction of the speech. The next three steps constitute the body. **Need** demonstrates to the audience that a serious problem exists that demands change. Potentially, four elements are covered:

1. *Statement:* a clear, concise statement or description of the problem(s)
2. *Illustration:* one or more detailed supports that picture the need for change
3. *Ramification:* any additional data to show the problem's extent
4. *Pointing:* convincing demonstration of how the need directly affects this group

Remember, in the need step of the body, you try to create in your audience an uncomfortable state that they will want to alter.

Satisfaction proposes a plan of action that will solve the need. Three elements should be covered:

1. *Statement:* Briefly state your plan.
2. *Explanation:* Clarify the details of the plan (who, what, when, where, how much).
3. *Practical experience:* If possible, give an actual example of how this plan has worked effectively elsewhere, or how this belief has been proven correct by others.

The third part of the body (or fourth step of the motivated sequence) is **visualization,** where you picture for the audience what the world will be like if your plan is adopted. This step projects the audience into the future to intensify their desire for change. You may visualize in one of three ways:

1. *Positive method:* Describe conditions as they will be if your advocated action is accepted. Each motive appeal and problem from the *need* step should be answered.

Take a Closer Look

If you have utilized the motivated sequence correctly, the audience will respond in a fashion somewhat like the following:

ATTENTION: Audience response will be, "I want to listen."

NEED: Response will be, "Something ought to be done. I can't live with things the way they are now." Or even, "I didn't know it was so bad. What can I do?"

PLAN: Audience will say, "This plan sounds like it will solve the problem."

VISUALIZATION: Reaction will be "I can see how I'll benefit" or, "Gee, without this solution, things will get worse."

ACTION: "I will do this."

Example: Five Ways to Organize a Speech about HIV/AIDS

Imagine that you plan to present a speech about HIV/AIDS. The speech design will influence the aspect of HIV/AIDS that you will discuss.

Match each of the following five speech designs with their associated purpose statement.

1. Chronological
2. Topical
3. Spatial
4. Logical
5. Compare/contrast

A. To inform the audience about the latest HIV/AIDS treatments

B. To demonstrate for the audience the process of how HIV becomes AIDS

C. To inform the audience about the causes of HIV/AIDS and its effect on the world's population

D. To compare and contrast the magnitude of the HIV/AIDS epidemic in South Africa and India

E. To inform the audience how HIV/AIDS spread, beginning in Africa and moving east

Answers: (A. 2, B. 1, C. 4, D. 5, E. 3.)

2. *Negative method:* Describe adverse conditions that will prevail in the future if advocated belief/action is not accepted. Describe unpleasant conditions that will result.
3. *Contrast method:* Combine the negative and positive approaches.

It's important to remember that the visualization step must stand the test of reality. The conditions you picture must seem probable. The visualization step should be a logical counterpart to all of the ideas brought up in the need step. Finally, the last step is **action,** where you urge the audience to do a specific, definite act. You want to give them specific information on how to accomplish this action, so that they will know how to commit themselves. One caution: Asking your audience to "think about this" isn't an action! What behavior do you want them to do?

Integrating My Evidence with My Main Points

As you make the selection of your order, you'll begin to arrange your supporting materials. Main points are nothing without the evidence that clarifies them. But how exactly do you organize your evidence within your main points? What if you have a great set of statistics, a quote or two, and an example, all of which support the first main point? What goes first? Sometimes, the answer is based on the same structural choices as the body: you might move chronologically through your evidence, for instance. In some cases, you can use the principles of primacy and recency to guide you. **Primacy** arranges ideas in terms of how convincing they are, moving from most important to least important. The belief is that by putting the most important first, you will compel the audience to believe what comes after. **Recency** is the opposite; it moves from the least convincing to the strongest. You might use this technique when you have some simple examples that lead naturally to a major example, for instance. With recency, the last thing heard is the one that is best remembered. Finally, you might choose to arrange by **specificity**; you could start with a general illustration and move to a specific one, or vice versa. You could present national statistics, regional ones, and end on local ones.

Because you probably have gathered more supporting materials than you really need, here is when you start to edit. You'll want to use your audience as your guide: What examples, statistics, testimony, narratives, and analogies will help them to achieve meaning? Which ones fit into the time limits you're facing? Are there some that are easier to explain than others? Do some require additional explanation through presentational aids? There is no magic number of supporting materials that any one point should have; that's totally dependent on your purpose, your audience, and your context.

You need to determine which supporting materials you ultimately use for your speech.

WHAT GOES INTO A COMPELLING INTRODUCTION?

You now know about the structural choices to be selected from as you create the body of your message. You are able to start adding in evidence that augments and clarifies those main points. But sequencing isn't just about creating a pattern for the body. You have to develop the entire package of the message, which also includes a welcoming, compelling introduction and a reinforcing conclusion that establishes psychological closure.

The opening remarks made that provide the audience with initial message orientation is the **introduction**. This starting part of your message serves two important purposes: It motivates the audience to listen, and it prepares them to focus on the subject. You can meet these purposes by setting the stage through some strategically considered statements. Remember, you probably won't develop your introduction until you've already put the body of the speech together. Once the latter is done, you can then set up the introduction to reflect what will follow. How do you launch a speech? You do it by gaining attention, revealing the topic, suggesting to the audience a reason to listen, establishing credibility, and previewing the body through an initial summary.

Gaining Attention

You have probably heard the famous maxim, "You never get a second chance to make a first impression." That's certainly true about presenting a message. The first thing you say should capture the audience's attention; if you fail to establish that focus from the start, there's really no need to continue. Think about what captures your interest. Is it something creative? Something unique? Something surprising or unexpected? Popular television shows often begin with a powerful dramatic moment, perhaps the portrayal of a crime or a unforeseen circumstance. This "hook" is used to capture viewers' interest so that they do not switch the channel. This isn't a new idea. In 1947, Elmer Wheeler was one of the best-known salesmen of his time. Among the gems that he shared about initiating a sale were statements like, "Your first 10 words are more important than your next 10,000," and you must "Excite 'em, annoy 'em, or startle 'em, all in the first ten seconds."[3] His advice is good: Use your opening lines to capture your listener so he wants to hear what you have to say. Some popular approaches to capture an audience's attention are as follows:

- *Relate a narrative or anecdote.* Everyone likes to hear a riveting story. This may be accomplished in one of two ways. You could share a narrative, which is a story about someone else. You might share an anecdote, which is a story about yourself. If the story is told with conviction, it can capture the audience's imagination.
- *Create a hypothetical situation.* If you ask the audience to imagine something, they can be transported into a specific place, with accompanying emotions and images. We all like to imagine, but be sure to ask the audience to conceive of something they can realistically picture. Asking an audience composed of eighteen- to twenty-two-year-olds to imagine they are through with college, married with two kids, and contemplating a career change is a bit of a stretch. The audience may struggle to imagine finishing college, let alone anything beyond that. It would be better to ask this audience to image something within the realm of their current life, another reason to analyze your audience. Also, when you let the audience think of themselves in another place, be sure to bring them back to the present and your message. If your speech was about the advantages of taking a cruise and you asked us to see ourselves relaxing on deck, umbrella drink in hand with no cares in the world, we might just decide to stay in that daydream, rather than come back to the present.
- *Ask a series of rhetorical questions.* Rhetorical questions do not require the audience to answer aloud or by a show of hands. The answers are implied or are meant for audience members to think about. This mental participation can be very effective in creating immediate involvement. A speech talking about genocide in Darfur, for instance, could easily begin with the query: Do you know where Darfur is? Are you aware of the mass killings that are being perpetrated there? Do you know when you first heard about the crisis? The pitfall to avoid with this type of attention-getter is asking a question that is not thought-provoking or that should really have been asked as part of the audience analysis. An example of a question that should have been asked as part of a class survey would be, "How many of you are registered to vote?" It is not a rhetorical question and it certainly is not thought-provoking. A more effective rhetorical question to ask would be: "How many of you have thought about your voting rights being revoked? Would this threat motivate you to exercise those rights?"
- *Startle with some surprising information or statistics.* The Internet has enabled us to gather interesting statistics at the click of a button. Opening a speech with a startling statistic or shocking information can startle the audience into wanting to learn more. For example, you could begin a speech about the dangers of distorted body image with some shocking facts such as these. The average U.S. woman is 5′4″ and weighs 140 pounds, whereas the average U.S. model is 5′11″ and weighs 117 pounds. Young girls are more afraid of becoming fat than they are of nuclear war, cancer, or losing their parents. The "ideal" woman—portrayed by models, Miss America, Barbie dolls, and screen actresses—is 5′5″, weighs 100 pounds, and wears a size 5.[4]
- *Use a thought-provoking quote.* It's not unusual to find an authoritative or memorable statement by someone else that fits into your speech. This can

even add to your initial credibility, because that quotation will resonate with what you're about to say. The guiding principle to using such quotes is to be sure they are indeed interesting, related to your topic, and linked to the purpose of your speech. A quote such as, "Experience is a hard teacher because she gives the test first, the lesson afterward. And in the end, it's not the years in your life that count. It's the life in your years," by Abraham Lincoln can be a great way to interest an audience about speeches, ranging from financial planning to pursing a dream career.

- *Use humor.* A funny story, relevant joke, or witty comment can help to relax your audience, and ease any sense of anxiety, especially on subjects where they disagree with your position. But there are some pitfalls to consider with this attention getter. A joke can be offensive in its language or in the way it pokes fun at other groups (e.g., age, gender, ethnicity). If this is the type of joke you would like to share, it is not appropriate and is unethical to use. Also, some witty comments or jokes are grounded in cultural knowledge and a clear understanding of the language in which they were developed. If you are faced with an audience whose members are from diverse cultural backgrounds, you may run the risk of them not "getting" the punch line. Finally, to employ the delivery required to tell a joke well, the speaker must be at ease at the beginning of the speech. For novice speakers, this can be challenging.
- *Share some information counter to the audience's beliefs.* This could be in the form of stating a truth that was typically accepted but recently shown to be false. For example, many people believe senior citizens to be helpless, yet a recent *Los Angeles Times* article revealed that senior citizens are not as vulnerable as we might think. The article titled "U.S. Tourists Kill Mugger, Costa Rica Says," recounts an unfortunate incident in which a man who pulled a .38 caliber revolver on a group of senior citizen tourists was killed when the group jumped on him in self-defense.[5]
- *Refer to the occasion.* Sometimes, you'll be asked to speak at some special event or occasion, such as a holiday, a professional conference, or even graduation. It's appropriate to say something like, "I'm honored to be part of this celebration with you," and then continue with a reference to the event.
- *Play a short video or audio segment.* People respond well to visual messages. To do this well, however, remember that this will cut into your speaking time. The last thing you should do is play three minutes of video for a six-minute speech. Your message content is the important thing, not your introductory audio or video. Thus, for a six- or seven-minute speech, the use of a video segment should be fifteen to thirty seconds, tops. It is important to explain to the audience what they will be watching and what they should look for. Imagine for a moment that you are an audience member and the speaker begins his speech by walking over to the DVD player and playing a clip from *The Terminator.* You have no idea why you are watching the film but you sit back and enjoy the action. After the clip, the speaker says, "I am here to talk to you today about violence in the media." In this example, the speaker failed to set up the visual so that it motivated the audience to listen. The speaker should have begun by stating, "I am going to show you a clip from the film *The Terminator.* Count how many violent acts you see."

How would you toast the bride and groom?

You would know why you were watching the clip and would engage in the set task. After playing the clip, the speaker follows up by stating, "There were a total of fifteen violent acts performed in fifteen seconds. Watching such violence desensitizes us to real life violence in our communities." By explaining the clip and linking it to the speech, the speaker has created a compelling attention getter.

Whatever attention-getting technique you choose to use, your attention getter should establish interest, should be relevant to the message, and should prepare the audience for the thesis statement about to come.

Revealing the Topic

After capturing your audience's attention, you want to clarify for your audience exactly what you will talk about. This is achieved by providing a clear and simple **thesis statement** (or topic sentence, or central idea), which announces in one sentence what your speech is about. It's not the same as your specific purpose statement, but it certainly echoes that focus. If your specific purpose was "to create awareness in my audience about the services provided by the American Red Cross in our community," then your thesis statement could be: "A simple rule of thumb is that you should be able to say it in one breath, and it answers this question: 'If I were to ask to give one focused sentence that introduces the subject of my speech, what would that be?'" Few things frustrate listeners more than sitting through a speech attempting to figure out what you are talking about.

Moving the Audience to Listening

Consider how your information could possibly impact the listeners. Could it save them money or time? Do they lack of information or perspective? Why not give your listeners a reason to listen? By listening to your speech, they could be improving their understanding for another course or important life issue. Your audience analysis will help to reveal what reasons might motivate your particular audience to listen. You know about how and why we fail at listening, and you have some strategies for helping your audience to overcome those barriers. Keep all those elements at the center of your message preparation.

To be audience-centered means to find a way to add value to your audience's lives through your speech. It means giving your audience more for their money. It means connecting your speech topic with the needs of the listener. Remember Maslow's hierarchy of needs that you read about in Chapter 12? There is the basis of your reflection: What needs can I connect to early on in my speech? The audience should not have to work to see the link between their needs and the topic you have chosen. The link should be obvious in the introduction. This is analogous to sales training. Salespeople are taught to answer for customers the question, "What's in it for me?" (W.I.F.M.). In other words, the audience is silently wondering, "Why should I buy your product?" If the salesperson tells us what we gain from the purchase, then she motivates us to listen further to her sales pitch. You can create this reason to listen by showing the audience that what they're about to hear impacts them directly. You don't have to spend a great deal of time on this idea, but you do have to give the audience direction on why the topic is worth listening to. This could be something as simple as a statement saying, "You might not own this, but you probably know someone who does," or, "You might not think that what happens here is part of your life, but your tax dollars are going to support this effort." Part of creating a compelling introduction is telling the audience what they have to gain by listening. When you do that, you show them that you've thought about their perspective, and you have their best interest at heart.

Establishing Credibility in the Introduction

You've already read about the concept of ethos or credibility. You know that it's the audience's perception of you, seen through the lenses of character, intelligence, goodwill, and charisma. By helping the audience consider why they should listen, you have established a sense of goodwill. Another way to increase people's motivation to listen to your message is by offering a statement of your expertise. People are certainly interested in what Steve Jobs or Bill Gates has to say about technology, but why should they believe you? By offering a bit of information about how you are knowledgeable on the subject you have chosen, you boost your credibility, increasing the chance that your audience will listen to your ideas. Your competence might be built on personal experience and firsthand knowledge, or it might come from classes, reading, or even the experiences that others have shared with you.

For example, if you have trained show dogs as a hobby for ten years, tell your audience about your experience in a speech about caring for pets. If your have recently learned about the risks related to nano-technology through a chemistry class, share that in a speech about nano-technology. If you have volunteered during an emergency or given blood at a Red Cross center, then tell your audience your experience as you discuss American Red Cross services. A credibility statement in the introduction may be as simple as telling the audience about the amount of research done to prepare the speech: "Over the past couple of months, I have read numerous articles, books, and interviews about the Red Cross's history and services." When you help your audience to perceive you as believable, you are also giving them the opportunity to identify with you. If they think that they're like you and the topic is important to you, then by extension, it's also important to them.

Previewing the Body through an Initial Summary

The **initial summary** or **speech preview** forecasts what main points are about to come in the body. You want to let the audience know what the main points include so that they have a perspective on what to focus on. You're telling the audience what you're about to tell them, providing an initial listening guideline. But an initial summary can do more than that. Not only does it preview what's to come, but it can serve as a reminder to you, too. By telling your listeners that you plan to cover the ingredients, process, and cautions of making mortar, you review for yourself one last time where you're about to go. In a similar fashion, that initial summary serves as a bridge to the first main point in the body; it signals that the main content (body) of the speech is about to come. The initial summary is typically presented at the end of your introduction and should flow naturally from your thesis statement. In the speech about the American Red Cross, it might sound something like this: "Today I will explain three major services offered by the Red Cross in our community: disaster relief, health services, and military support services." This preview should be short, specific, and easy to understand. Avoid the temptation to state your preview as a question; an initial summary should state clearly what the speech will cover and the order in which it will be covered.

The tone and direction of your message are established when you create an effective introduction. This is done by gaining attention, revealing the topic, suggesting a reason to listen, establishing credibility, and previewing the body through an initial summary.

HOW DO I CONCLUDE THE SPEECH?

If you did a good job in the introduction, you set the stage for your audience to listen. The end of the speech should wrap up your ideas through a final summary and create closure for you and the audience. Have you ever read a book or gone to a movie that left you unsatisfied at the end? Do you recall one of those times when you weren't sure that it was over? This **final summary** helps the audience recall the main points, improving overall recollection and comprehension. You could signal the coming end with a simple review of your main points. In the Red Cross example, it might appear like this: "You've learned today about the services provided by our American Red Cross, which include disaster relief, health and safety, and military family services." An effective **conclusion** gives the audience one last time to hear your main points. By this time, you've now repeated your main points three times: first in the initial summary, then in the body, and now in the final summary. The final objective of the conclusion is to *close the speech* as powerfully as you began. Two important pitfalls to avoid: Don't assume that you'll "know" how to end the speech when you're done (the "lightning will strike me" approach") and make sure that it's really the end. One mistake speakers make is that they assume some inspirational ending will come to them as they're speaking. It doesn't happen. You need to know what your final statements will be, and you need to practice them so you wrap up with direct eye contact and strong delivery. Equally irresponsible is saying, "In conclusion," and then not concluding. We've all suffered through speakers who use that signal one or more times but then continue to drone on.

So how do you create closure? How do you end a speech? In the introduction, you try to capture the listeners' attention with a *hook*. Any of those techniques could be employed again in the conclusion. If you began by hooking the audience with a story, your closing might offer the moral of the story. If you started with thought-provoking questions, you might wish to return to those questions and offer answers, or you might ask the audience to reflect again on their answers. You could use the conclusion for a final appeal or challenge to the audience, telling them what response you expect from them. The key is to create a sense of closure in the same way that a well-written novel or movie leaves the audience feeling complete or satisfied.

HOW DO I USE CONNECTIVES TO BRIDGE MAIN IDEAS?

Now you have explored the most obvious structural aspects of sequence: creating an introduction, body, and conclusion. There is one more sequencing strategy to consider as you craft your speech: How do you connect those three structural elements into a seamless yet dynamic message? Unlike an interpersonal dialogue, where you can jump from topic to topic and still share meaning, in a speech you have to link the main ideas through connectives.

Connectives create the dynamic flow of a speech and help listeners to remember and to recognize where they have been and what to expect next in a speech. They are a subtle aspect of speechmaking that can turn a good speech into a great speech. The most common kinds of connectives are transitions, signposts, internal previews, and internal summaries.

Transitions consist of phrases or key words that we use to link ideas; they're typically used to bridge "big" ideas in a speech, such as a link between introduction and body, between main points, or between body and conclusion. A transition usually signals that one idea is done and the speech is moving to something new. Examples of transitions are phrases such as, "As I move to the next point . . ." or, "The final idea I want to make is . . ." Even "in summary" is a transition.

Signposts alert the audience to something important about to come; think of them as pointing a spotlight on an idea. "What you should remember is . . ." and, "The only thing that you should know is . . ." are signposts. So are numbers ("*the first cause* of obesity is . . ." They warn the audience of the importance of the next remarks.

Previews do just that: They give the audience a prompt or advanced warning that movement is about to occur, but they do it in a bit more detail than signposts or transitions. They can serve the same function as your initial summary did in the introduction, except on a much smaller scale. An example would be, "In order to understand the problems of the dangers of parasailing, we need to know first about equipment and then about the process."

Finally, an **internal summary** reviews what has just happened; it is the opposite of your internal preview. It reminds the audience of what they just heard in a preceding point, and it allows the audience to understand how new information connects to previous information. By saying, "Now that I've covered the equipment used in parasailing . . ." you have reminded the audience what they should have heard.

These connectives are very subtle, and what's important is the movement that they'll supply to your message. They're the last part of sequencing that should be considered as you work on your speech. When you use connectives well, you can bridge gaps between and among ideas, adding to the unity of your message.

The decision strategy of sequencing allows you to arrange your ideas and evidence for the audience so that they have a better chance of grasping and sharing your meaning. How you structure ideas should be based on the needs of the situation and audience. The most basic step in developing sequencing is to think of the three basic elements of organization: introduction, body, and conclusion. Each of these elements has specific functions, but each allows you to use your own creativity in adapting your structure to your audience and purpose. You strategically choose among organizational patterns so you can achieve your intended result. Then you add in your supporting materials to flesh out those ideas. Connectives are considered last, because they function to join ideas; they tie the main points into one cohesive whole.

SUMMARY

You've learned throughout life how important organization is in all sorts of ways. You may have been taught how to arrange your books and toys when you were young, or you quickly found that they were lost. Your middle or high

Established Rules for Outlining

Speeches are typically written as outlines, not essays. An outline not only helps to organize ideas, it also makes moving information easier. The outlining process begins with the planning outline, then progresses to a formal outline (the outline you turn in to your instructor), and ends with the development of a key word outline (a.k.a. a speaking outline).

With a well-developed planning outline, a speaker can easily visualize, in order, the ideas to be discussed. This makes it easier for the speaker to ensure the ideas are adequately clear and supported.

Here are some basic principles of outlining:

- *Follow consistent patterns of symbolization for main and supporting points.* For example, main points could be numbered with Roman numerals, while supporting points are capital letters.
- *Indent supporting points to indicate that they are related to the main point.* In our example, points A and B are subpoints of point I.
- *Use full sentences to articulate the information you plan to present.* The goal is to create a clear, succinct planning outline that does not leave the wording of important points to chance.
- *Make sure the organization of the points is logical.* Choose an appropriate pattern of order, based on the purpose and audience.
- *Construct a speaking outline that is a condensed version of the formal outline.* This will keep you from reading the outline when making the speech.

Figures 2.1 and 2.2 show how a formal outline and speaking outline should look.

Formal Outline:

I. The American Red Cross provides disaster relief services.
   A. The Red Cross supports families displaced by fires.
   B. The Red Cross supports communities hit by natural disasters.
II. The American Red Cross offers health services.
   A. The Red Cross provides baby sitter training.
   B. The Red Cross provides CPR and first aid training.
III. The American Red Cross offers military services.
   A. Red Cross offers veterans financial and support counseling.
   B. The Red Cross helps families connect with military personnel abroad.

Figure 2.1
Formal Outline

Key Word Outline:

I. The ARC provides disaster relief
   A. families displaced by fires
   B. communities hit by natural disasters

(Delivery Directions: Pause Here)

II. The ARC offers health services
   A. Baby sitter training
   B. CPR and first aid training

(Delivery Directions: Pause and Show Visual Aid #1 here)

III. The ARC offers military services
   A. financial and support counseling for veterans
   B. helps families connect with military personnel abroad

(Delivery Directions: Don't rush through the conclusion!)

Figure 2.2
Key Word Outline

school locker could easily become a black hole if you didn't impose some structure on what folders went where. How often do you lose your keys or cellphone? When you finally find them, don't you promise yourself that you'll put them in a place you can always find them? Why do you take notes? Can't you just listen to what your teacher tells you, without having to write ideas down? Are you that person who just can't go grocery shopping or pack for a trip without a list? All of these questions reveal the nature of organization: It compels you to configure stimuli into a meaningful structure that will help you to understand and to remember.

Effective message organization begins with careful consideration of your audience, situation, topic, and purpose. Whether your purpose is to inform or to persuade, you can utilize the same decision-making strategies of selection and sequence to construct your speech. The introduction, body, and conclusion each serve important purposes. The introduction attracts attention, develops audience focus on the topic and the speaker, and provides a preview of main points to come. The body presents the main ideas that meet your specific purpose, supported by a variety of evidence that interests the audience and increases shared meaning. The conclusion reminds the audience of the main points and challenges them to act on what they've heard.

A well-planned speech, like a structured office or a well-thought-out trip, allows you to complete your goals, avoid backtracking, and remain audience-centered in presenting your message.

NOTES

1. http://www2.oprah.com/tows/pastshows/200601/tows_after_20060126.jhtml (Oprah after the show). (accessed April 1, 2008).
2. "Powell calls pre-Iraq U.N. speech a 'blot' on his record," http://www.usatoday.com/news/washington/2005-09-08-powell-iraq_x.htm (accessed November 23, 2007).
3. Wheeler, E. *Tested public speaking,* 2nd ed. (New York: Prentice Hall, 1949), p.35.
4. "Shocking Statistics: Beauty of a Woman," http://www.colorado.edu/studentgroups/wellness/NewSite/BdyImgShockingStats.html (accessed November 23, 2007).
5. "U.S. tourists kill mugger, Costa Rica says," *Los Angeles Times* (February 23, 2007), A10.

chapter 3

Delivering Your Message

OBJECTIVES

After reading this chapter, you should understand the following concepts:

- Effective delivery involves both verbal and nonverbal message management, tailored for the intended audience and content.
- Speeches can be scripted, memorized, impromptu, or extemporaneous, depending on their purpose.
- Effective verbal delivery involves using volume, rate, pitch, pause, articulation, pronunciation, and dialects to engage the audience.
- Effective physical delivery involves proper use of eye contact, facial expression, gestures, movement, and attire.
- Presentational aids add dimension to your delivery and help communicate your message.

KEY TERMS

effective delivery
impromptu
SPREE method
PPF method
apples/oranges method
simple 6 method
extemporaneous (extemp) speech
volume
rate
pitch
pauses
articulation
pronunciation
dialects
eye contact
facial expression
gestures
movement
presentational aids
three-dimensional presentation aids
two-dimensional presentation aids
multimedia presentations
three T method

INTRODUCTION

What comes to mind when you read the following passages? After you've read them, try listening to them online. Does what you get from the message change?

> Nineteen years ago, almost to the day, we lost three astronauts in a terrible accident on the ground. But we've never lost an astronaut in flight. We've never had a tragedy like this. And perhaps we've forgotten the courage it took for the crew of the shuttle. But they, the *Challenger*

> Seven, were aware of the dangers, but overcame them and did their jobs brilliantly.
>
> —Ronald Reagan: The Space Shuttle "Challenger" Tragedy Address
> *http://americanrhetoric.com/speeches/ronaldreaganchallenger.htm*
>
> What we need in the United States is not division; what we need in the United States is not hatred; what we need in the United States is not violence and lawlessness, but is love, and wisdom, and compassion toward one another, and a feeling of justice toward those who still suffer within our country, whether they be white or whether they be black.
>
> —Robert F. Kennedy: Remarks on the Assassination of Martin Luther King, Jr.
> *http://americanrhetoric.com/speeches/rfkonmlkdeath.html*
>
> I—I feel it an honor to be here to come and say a final goodbye. I grew up in the South, and Rosa Parks was a hero to me long before I recognized and understood the power and impact that her life embodied. I remember my father telling me about this colored woman who had refused to give up her seat. And in my child's mind, I thought, "She must be really big." I thought she must be at least a hundred feet tall. I imagined her being stalwart and strong and carrying a shield to hold back the white folks. And then I grew up and had the esteemed honor of meeting her. And wasn't that a surprise. Here was this petite, almost delicate lady who was the personification of grace and goodness. And I thanked her then. I said, "Thank you," for myself and for every colored girl, every colored boy, who didn't have heroes who were celebrated. I thanked her then.
>
> —Oprah Winfrey: Eulogy for Rosa Parks
> *http://americanrhetoric.com/speeches/oprahwinfreyonrosaparks.htm*

These words offer you a glimpse into important moments in American history. What would happen if you were to read those words aloud, standing in front of your friends or class? Would you get the same response, be able to do it in the same way? Of course not! You don't have the same delivery style as any of these speakers; their tone, their pauses, their voice, and even their movements are unique to them. In the same way, you can develop your own delivery style that can effectively add dimension and depth to the message you develop.

Develop your own style to effectively add dimension and depth to your message.

Effective delivery usually is the result of a conversational style that blends energy, naturalness, and straightforwardness. Some occasions call for a more formal, manuscript-delivered presentation, but most of us will deliver messages that are more informal. That doesn't mean that you don't have to do a run through or two; in fact, good delivery is the result of preparation, training, and practice. **Effective delivery** *involves both verbal and nonverbal message management, tailored for the intended audience and context.* In this chapter, you'll be exposed to strategies for effective verbal and nonverbal delivery and the use of presentational aids to reinforce your message. You'll also learn a bit about the natural effects of communication apprehension on delivery. Just keep in mind that if you're successful, your delivery won't call attention to itself; the message will still be the most important thing the audience takes away.

WHAT METHOD OF DELIVERY IS MOST APPROPRIATE?

You have four different choices to make for your overall delivery plan: all involve a decision about the extent to which the written word will play in your speech.

Scripted

Some speakers like to deliver prepared remarks from a manuscript. This is especially true when exact language is crucial, such as in diplomacy issues or for a commencement address before a large audience. It is common for heads of state to speak from a manuscript in order to ensure accuracy in their messages. In these cases, word-for-word delivery is essential. Time limits may also play a role in the use of a manuscript; a candidate who purchases a one-minute spot needs to nail down that time. However, most of us do not find ourselves in these unique situations.

Using a manuscript might seem like an easy way to present your speech, but it can also have drawbacks. Crafting a manuscript takes an inordinate amount of time; you find yourself concentrating on word choice and sentence development in a way that you wouldn't do in other forms of delivery. Written and spoken language are essentially different; the way you write in long sentences with complex structures doesn't work well in the spoken form, where brief phrases and even incomplete sentences are more natural. Speaking from a script limits the speaker to only those comments prepared in advance. You don't have the chance to stray from the prepared remarks, and if an audience member seems confused, you can't elaborate. It is common for new speakers to make the mistake of just reading from a manuscript, leading to a drop in eye contact and vocal variety. If you do look up from the manuscript, it's easy to lose your place. A manuscript requires you to make the words "come alive" through vibrant vocal delivery, and that requires skill. It's very easy to find yourself reading *at* the audience through a manuscript, rather than talking *with* them.

What should you expect if you feel a scripted speech is appropriate for your occasion? Be sure to practice out loud so that you don't falter over words. Pacing must be timed perfectly; you don't want to pause in the wrong place, and you don't want to rush through the speech. Consider vocal tone: how can you emphasize words so that they sound conversational rather than scripted? Create a manuscript that is easy to read in larger print so that you can still develop and maintain eye contact; you want to be able to move off the script to look at the audience, even though you are tied to the words. Roger Ailes, a political media consultant, suggests that if a manuscript is called for, you should type your words in short, easy-to-scan phrases on the top two thirds of the notes so you don't have to look too far down.[1] A manuscript doesn't have to mean boring the audience with a monotonous tone, lack of eye contact, and stilted pacing; it does mean, though, that you'll have to work hard to overcome those pitfalls.

Memorized

At some point, we have all probably been expected to memorize a speech or poem. Perhaps it was the preamble to the Constitution or the Declaration of

Independence; maybe it was a poem or a prayer. You may have wondered why you needed this skill; after all, there is little call for long, memorized, complex speeches, and the effort you put into memorizing was painful. It's safe to say that while you might admire someone who can spout off long speeches from memory, it's probably not something you'd want to do yourself. However, the ability to memorize short passages still has its place in presentations. Memorization is a useful strategy to use for short speeches such as toasts, introductory remarks, or award acceptances. Even small portions of a speech where specific wording or language is important can utilize memorization. You just need to practice over and over, making sure to work on vocal variety as you do the words from rote memory.

© 2008, JupiterImages.

Memorization is effective for short speeches, such as accepting an award.

The negatives of a memorized speech are apparent. First, in order to memorize, you must create a full manuscript document. That means that the pitfalls of a scripted speech play a role here. Second, memorizing anything takes time and practice, more than you probably need to spend on a presentation. More obvious, though, as a danger of memorization is that the stress of a speaking situation can lead to memory lapses and occasionally even a complete loss of what was memorized. If you forget where you were, it's nearly impossible to pick up smoothly. Not only will you panic, but the audience will likely become very uncomfortable. All-in-all, memorizing an entire presentation is more trouble than help.

Impromptu

What would you do if a television reporter cornered you to get a response about an incident that just happened, an issue that's in the public eye, or a comment about the weather? If you're able to give a competent immediate response, you could be on the evening news! Even if that scenario doesn't hold much appeal, your ability to think and speak on your feet is essential in life. Meetings, interviews, unexpected reports, instructing or supervising others, and participating in general conversation all require the ability to organize thoughts quickly and delivery them effectively.

Speaking **impromptu** means talking about a topic with little or no preparation. Mark Twain said, "It usually takes me more than three weeks to prepare a good impromptu speech,"[2] and he was probably correct. Most of the time when we speak "off the cuff" or say a "few words," we do so in situations where we've given thought to the issue we're about to speak on. So, you might find yourself doing an impromptu speech at a community meeting when your opinion is sought, when your boss asks you to report on some incident, or when you're at a social function and a toast is called for.

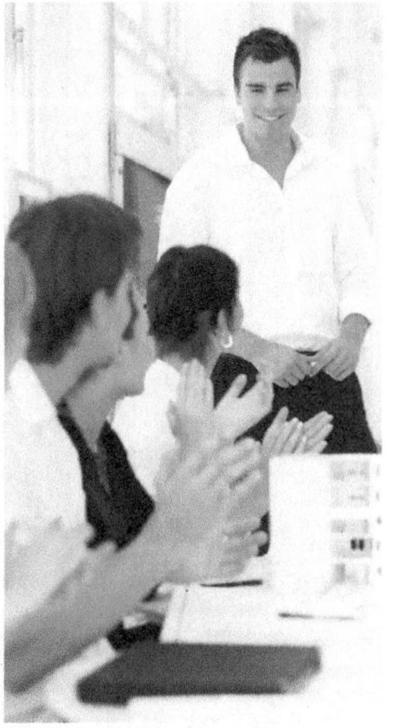
© Yuri Arcurs, 2008, Shutterstock.

An audience understands that an impromptu speech has not been carefully prepared.

A spur-of-the-moment or impromptu speech doesn't carry the same expectations of perfection as might a scripted or memorized speech. An audience usually is more forgiving in an impromptu speech because they understand you haven't had hours or days to prepare. However, that doesn't mean that you need to go into an impromptu situation stone cold. If you're in a meeting or listening to a presentation, take notes of the major points; this activity will likely cause you to consider your own opinion. If time allows you to do so, jot a few notes or outline of the points you want to make in case you're asked to respond.

Let's imagine that you've been asked for impromptu remarks of a minute or two. You need to be spontaneous and demonstrate your quick wit. What quick strategies can you call on?

If you do nothing else, make a note of how you want to open and conclude your remarks; remember, the first thing and the last thing the audience hears may be that which sticks with them. Make sure you understand what you've been asked to remark on, and make sure you answer it. Then structure the body of the message with two or four points, using some simple strategies:

- The **SPREE method** offers four points: State your Position, provide your Reason(s), Explain by experience or example, End with summary.
- The **PPF method** utilizes Past, Present, and Future as the main points. You can say something like this: We used to do this . . . but now we find ourselves doing this . . . and in the future we'll need to do this . . .
- The **apples/oranges method** begins by acknowledging that "there are two sides to this argument . . ." and then state the positions: One position says this, the other says that. End by giving your position on the issue.
- The **simple 6 method** uses the common questions of who, what, when, why, where, and how as the main points. Don't try for all of them, but use them to structure ideas and to jog your memory.

When delivering an impromptu speech, there are a few pitfalls to avoid. Don't apologize for a lack of preparation. If it's truly an impromptu occasion, give the best effort you can on short notice. When you offer an excuse, you damage your credibility. Focus your delivery on strong eye contact and vocal variety; you can't do much more. Don't ramble; stick to those main points, give some support, and make it short and sweet. You don't want to be accused of talking without saying anything.

To really speak effectively, you'd like to be able to prepare in advance. Even if you don't have that opportunity, you can still provide your audience with a clearly organized, brief message that makes a point. After all, you do impromptus all the time—you have ample chances to experiment with developing an effective strategy for their presentation.

Extemporaneous

You might hear people confuse impromptu and extemporaneous methods; often, people think they're one and the same. However, an **extemporaneous** (or **extemp**) **speech** is one that is carefully planned and practiced, that works from an outline or series of notes yet leaves room for message adjustment, and that maintains a conversational style.

The key to extemp is that outline of ideas. From it, you can adapt the words to the audience as they listen. The advantages of an extemp speech arise from the best of the other three methods. You can write out key ideas, as in a scripted speech. You can commit some lines (key data, phrases, quotations) to memory so word choice is exact. You can remain spontaneous and adapt to the audience and the occasion as you speak, just like in an impromptu. In addition, the extemp speech encourages you to use a conversational style, one that sounds spontaneous even though it's been well thought out and practiced.

How do you prepare an extemporaneous speech? Create an outline of main ideas and say it out loud. As you do, consider the amount and kind of supporting points you're developing, along with the purpose and time of your speech. Then think, am I saying too much or too little? Do my ideas coherently flow? Do I know the supports well enough to be able to present them in an interesting yet clear fashion? How are my introduction and conclusion? Next, revise that outline into a speaking outline, keeping the amount of written material minimal. Practice the speech all the way through, using only the outline. You may forget a few supports the first couple of times, but that's OK—keep going! Your goal is to keep yourself focused on the ideas of the speech, not the perfection of the words or the delivery. If you plan to use presentational aids, bring them into practice. After several run-throughs, you'll find that you are able to get through the ideas and their supports pretty well by thinking, not by checking your notes, and then it's time to work on delivery. Watch for eye contact by recruiting an audience of family or friends, or even watch yourself in a mirror. Record the speech if possible; listening to yourself (or watching on video) can point out distracting mannerisms. The key is that you must practice more than once; a single practice is a recipe for catastrophe. By giving yourself time to think the speech through, you'll find your confidence growing.

A combination of styles may work best to present your message.

Although each of these speaking styles is described separately, in reality, a combination of styles might be used in any given public speech or other communication situation such as an interview or meeting. You might consider memorizing a portion of the opening so that you can engage your audience without notes or other distractions. This lets you make strong eye contact with audience members and truly hook them into the speech. The body of a speech might involve the use of brief notes in an extemporaneous style. A question and answer session after a presentation resembles impromptu speaking, requiring a person to respond "in the moment." In meetings, you're called upon to offer your opinion on a plan: that's the place for an impromptu. Interviews are extemporaneous in the sense that you can plan and rehearse answers to questions, but you don't exactly know the directions those questions will take.

Remember: No one is born a great speaker. Effective public speaking takes practice, regular practice. The great thing about presenting a message is that, like riding a bike, when you can do it well, you can always do it well if you follow the same pattern of preparation, practice, and presentation.

WHAT STRATEGIES MAKE UP EFFECTIVE DELIVERY?

Do you want a surefire way to bore your audience to tears? To ensure audience members lose interest and drift away, stand in one place, never look up from your notes, use gestures minimally, and speak rapidly in a low-pitched, monotonous voice. Assuming that boring people isn't your goal, if you want to help the audience attend to, hear, and understand your message, you need to consider how to incorporate nonverbal delivery strategies.

Effective nonverbal delivery is critical in the success of any communication effort. This is true for any communication situation, whether it's interpersonal or small group, public or mediated. Effective delivery is a combination of verbal and nonverbal tactics, so factors such as eye contact, posture, vocal quality, and facial expression will play a major role in the audience's ability to listen and to follow your ideas. Even the presentational aids that supplement your words and nonverbal presence are aspects of effective delivery. Earlier in this chapter, you were told that a conversational style of delivery is the most desired, but you're probably thinking about more specifics, such as, "What do I do if I can't breathe?" or "What happens if my hands are shaking?" or "Is it OK to move around a little?" In order to impact the audience in a positive way and to answer those questions, let's consider some of the elements of effective vocal and physical delivery.

HOW DO I SPEAK TO CREATE UNDERSTANDING?

Have you ever met someone in person that you've spoken to on the phone many times? Was the image that you initially had skewed from his actual looks? Did you think he was older or younger than in reality? Was he taller or shorter? Did he dress as you thought he did? Were you shocked to learn that he was a she? Based on vocal cues, we do predict people's age, occupation, status, ethnicity, appearance, and a host of other things. Effective vocal delivery involves volume, rate, pitch, pauses, and the trio of articulation, pronunciation, and dialects, each of which can play a very important part in creating images and impressions. It's important that you present your ideas by using vocal delivery that enhances understanding and interest.

© 2008, JupiterImages.

How can you use the volume of your voice for effect in your speech?

Volume

Volume means projecting your voice loudly enough so that it can be clearly heard by those in your audience. Just how loudly you must speak depends on the room size, the audience size, and the amount and type of background noise. It's likely that your voice sounds louder to you than to your audience, but by watching your audience and adjusting to their feedback (leaning forward, looking puzzled, wincing), you can adjust the volume of your voice so that everyone in the audience can hear. If you have a soft voice, you don't want to cause your audience to strain to listen. They might decide it's not worth their effort. A quiet voice might require the use of electronic amplification, but realize that if you use a microphone awkwardly, the audience could interpret this as ineptness on your part. Your volume can also be manipulated for effect. Sometimes raising or lowering the volume can communicate importance or draw in the audience and emphasize a point. The key is to be aware of your volume and to adapt it according to your audience and setting.

Rate

Rate is the speed at which you speak. The normal rate of adult speech has been estimated to be between 120 and 150 words per minute. What matters is not how many words a speaker can get out, but how many (well-chosen) words are understood by the listener. People talk so fast because others around them do this, because they think erroneously that others will not take the time to listen to them, and because they do not realize the listeners are struggling. Speaking quickly doesn't mean you're unintelligible, however, and you can consider how using rate as a delivery strategy can enhance understanding.

Changing the speed of delivery to coordinate with different elements of your speech is one way to maintain audience interest. Varying your rate can improve the audience's ability to attend to your speech. You might start with a fast-paced, attention-getting story and then slow down as you reveal the topic and preview your main points. However, a study in 2000 found that speaking too quickly causes the audience to perceive you as tentative about your control of the situation.[3] A monotone rate, one that does *not* change, will lead your audience members to lose interest and make it more difficult for them to listen and learn from your message.

Pitch

Singing involves the alteration of the voice to produce the melody. That modulation of your voice is something you can also employ in effective delivery through awareness of pitch.

Pitch is your voice's intonation; how high or low in range your voice sounds to another. Your typical pitch is the range that you use when you're conversing normally, and in natural conversation, vocal pitch rises and falls and often helps listeners to understand a message. Your pitch may give others a perception of your mood and can show your enthusiasm for the topic or audience. Normally, women's voices are pitched higher than men's because women's vocal cords are shorter. However, individuals of each sex may display wide variations due to difference in physical structure. But keep in mind that no matter what nature supplies you for pitch, you still can manipulate it for strong effect.

In some cultures, inflection plays a major role in changing the meaning of words. Many of the languages of Southeast Asia and Africa are tone languages, meaning that they use pitch to signal a difference in meaning between words. In some of these languages, word meanings or grammar elements like tense depend on pitch level. Words can take on totally different meanings depending on their tones. In Mandarin Chinese, for example, the word *ma* means "mother" when spoken in the first tone, "hemp" when spoken in the second tone, "horse" in the third and a reproach in the fourth.[4]

Typically, our pitch in the United States goes higher when we ask a question and drops when we make a declaration of fact. Try the following activity. Say the following sentences, adding emphasis by raising your pitch on the italicized word each time.

This is a great class.

This *is* a great class.

This is a *great* class.

Now try it with a question mark at the end:

This is a great *class?*

Notice how the meaning shifts, depending on the emphasis of the words.

You can use this stress or inflection when you want to highlight a point, but don't overdo it. You might want to record a conversation with friends or family members and listen to changes in pitch to see what meanings you're suggesting. However, while it can assist you by underlining enthusiasm or importance, pitch change isn't a strategy you want to overdo.

© 2008, JupiterImages.

Vocalized pauses will detract from your meaning, not enhance it.

Pauses

Pauses add emphasis and impact to your speech by stopping your message briefly. Where and how you pause in your speech can have a dramatic effect on meaning. Pauses can be used to stress a point, to gain attention, to create a transitional effect, and to allow you time to think and catch up. They often are necessary for your listener just to think about what you've just said. Read the following line: "Woman without her man is nothing." Now think about possible ways to interpret those words. Through strategic pausing, the message meaning could be very different. Read it two more times, pausing at the commas:

> Woman without her man, is nothing.
> Woman, without her, man is nothing.

How you decide to deliver that line, including pauses, is critical to the message you communicate. Listeners do not "see" the commas in your speech; they must "hear" them through your strategic use of pauses in delivery

Vocalized pauses such as "um," "like," "you know," "stuff like that," or "Uhhhhh" detract from your speech. These involuntary fillers or bridge sounds are understandable in their way, because they are unintentionally included by speakers in order to maintain control. You are uncomfortable with silence, so you fill it up with sounds. These do not function in the same way that intentional pauses do. In fact, they detract from meaning, rather than enhancing it. To avoid vocalized pauses, try this easy test: Call yourself and leave at least a one-minute message about an upcoming assignment. Then listen to your voice mail and count the number of vocalized paused in your message. Give it a try. How many vocal pauses do you count? How do they impact your message? Are you surprised by the frequency of your vocalized pauses? The bottom line is, most of us find vocalized pauses to be annoying; you can eliminate them by paying attention.

Articulation, Pronunciation, and Dialects

Articulation is the physical production of a sound clearly and distinctly. **Pronunciation** is saying a word in an accepted standard of correctness and sound. While the two are interdependent, they are not the same. You can articulate a word clearly but still mispronounce it; for instance, if you say the "s" in the word *Illinois,* you're articulating the sounds but pronouncing it wrong! An example of misarticulation comes from Ohio, where students sometimes say *fur* when they mean "for" and *doin'* instead of "doing." Because some words sound similar, they require the speaker's careful articulation to avoid audience confusion. Consider, for example, the difference between *persecution* and *prosecution,* or the difference between *asking* someone and *axing* someone. It's not uncommon to mispronounce words, because you may not know how to say it correctly. Alphadictionary.com offers a list of the 100 most mispronounced words in English, which includes *athlete* (some people say "ath-a-lete"), *card shark* (the correct words are "card sharp"), *escape* ("excape"), and *herb* ("'erb").[5]

Articulation and pronunciation are further confounded by **dialects,** which are regional or ethnic speech patterns that have variations in grammar, accent, or even vocabulary. The United States has four major regional dialects: eastern,

Take a Closer Look

What strategies can you use to impact dialect, articulation, and pronunciation?

- Watch your audience's expressions to see if they seem to understand or if they look confused.
- Define your terms.
- Make sure you pronounce names or technical terms correctly.
- Slow down so you can articulate more clearly.
- Avoid regional words that may not mean the same thing elsewhere, or use both terms (yours and the local one) to show that they're synonyms.

All of these can aid you in avoiding confusing your audience with the way you say ideas!

New England, southern, and general American. There are also many ethnic dialects, including African-American English, Hispanic English, Cajun English, and Haitian English.[6] Your dialect has been shaped by your background, and it has meaning for those who share it. However, if you're speaking to an audience who doesn't share your dialect, you would want to avoid regionalisms that point out your differences. We're all familiar with those: Do you drink pop or soda? What goes on ice cream: jimmies or sprinkles? When grocery shopping, do you use a buggy or a cart? When washing your car, do you attach your outside hose to the spigot or the faucet? What you should keep in mind is that a distracting dialect may cause listeners to make negative judgments about your personality or competence.[7] This can be an important consideration if you're a nonnative English speaker, because your dialect, along with articulation and pronunciation, may be an additional barrier.

Your vocal delivery is unique; no one sounds exactly like you (which is why the FBI uses voiceprints in its investigative work). You have the ability to impact the audience by strategically using aspects of vocal delivery that you can control.

HOW DOES MY PHYSICAL DELIVERY AFFECT UNDERSTANDING?

In Chapter 4 you learned about nonverbal communication, the messages you deliver with appearance, movement, posture, eye contact, facial expression, and use of space and objects. Your nonverbal messages can assist audience members in interpreting the verbal message, or they can distract from that understanding. You know the phrase, "Actions speak louder than words." When you consider physical delivery, keep that in mind: An audience expects that good communicators will present their ideas clearly and in an interesting fashion. Your delivery can create (or destroy) emotional connections with your audience. If your nonverbal delivery contradicts what you're saying, the audience will more likely believe the nonverbal rather than the verbal. Think about shaking your head no side-to-side while saying in a flat voice, "I really had a good time tonight." What message will really be believed—the words or the nonverbal one?

© 2008, JupiterImages.

Your delivery can create emotional connections with your audience.

How you present yourself nonverbally is vital to your success as speakers. Effective physical delivery allows a speaker to develop immediacy with an audience and involves eye contact, facial expression, gestures, movement, and attire.

Eye Contact

Eye contact is the direct visual contact made with another person. Ralph Waldo Emerson said, "One of the most wonderful things in nature is a glance of the eye; it transcends speech; it is the bodily symbol of identity."[8] The significance of eye contact tells us about meaning in various cultures. Some cultures feel that strong eye contact demonstrates interest and respect in the other person. Conversely, other cultures hold that (especially when you are young) you should not look at others in the eye when speaking, or you'll show disrespect. Some Latin American and Asian cultures show respect by avoiding the glance of authority figures. In the United States, we value meeting another's eyes, because it is seen as demonstrating honesty. People in Brazil engage in intensive eye contact; here, we'd consider it staring.[9]

But since you're in an American classroom, let's consider why eye contact is seen in the United States as important for at least two reasons.[10] First, it creates a strong connection between listener and speaker. Audience members who feel more connected likely will listen more closely. Second, the speaker is able to gather feedback from audience members if eye contact is frequent and effective. Generally speaking, the longer the eye contact between two people, the greater the intimacy is developed.[11]

What strategies can you employ to meet your audience's gaze comfortably? Try looking briefly from one person to the next (you can even think about a "pattern" of gaze, from one corner to another, one row to an adjacent one). This scanning can let you acknowledge individuals without ignoring others. If you are sitting around a table, make sure you share eye contact with everyone in the group. Look for friendly people; conversely, if you're in the audience, smile at the speaker, for encouraging that person can create a pleasant interaction. If you see audience members looking at you with interest, leaning forward and seeming eager for more, you can assume that you are connecting with your audience. If, on the other hand, you see people nodding off or staring at your overhead with confused expressions, these are good indications that a problem should be corrected. By watching the feedback offered by your audience through eye contact, you can make corrections and improve your speech in the moment. Consider the type and amount of notes you use. Generally, the guideline would be to speak from an outline or a key word page, but if you feel you must use more, then make sure your notes are clear, large, and numbered in case you drop them. Effective eye contact tells the audience that you have confidence in yourself and care about their ability to understand your message.

Speakers must be alert to the cultural norms of the audience.

Facial Expression

Another way that you can display concern for the audience and passion for the subject is through your face. Research tells us that your face plays an essential role in expressing your thoughts, emotions, and attitudes.[12] Through your face, you have the initial opportunity to set the speech tone, even before you open your mouth. Think about it: when you don't like some kind of food, you probably make a face. That expression tells others how you feel about that morsel! The movements of your eyes, eyebrows, mouth, and facial muscles can build a connection with your audience.

Just like eye contact, your culture may dictate the kind and amount of **facial expression** you will display. For example, Koreans, Japanese, and Chinese do not usually show outward emotion through their faces, and in fact, may have learned to mask their emotions. Some Native American groups use far less facial animation than do other North Americans. Research also suggests that men and women use different facial displays.[13] In other cultures, people expect great animation when they speak, and they expect others to be similarly expressive. As a speaker, you need to be alert to the cultural norms of your audience.

Unfortunately, under the pressure of delivering a group presentation, many people solidify their expression into a grim, stone face, grimacing instead of smiling. Try to soften your face right from the start: when you greet the audience, smile! This is how you'd start a conversation with another, because you'd want to begin by establishing a warm, positive relationship. The same intent probably holds true for a speech. A relaxed smile to start your speech will help create a connection with the audience, perhaps even develop a closeness with them. You probably won't want to smile throughout the entire presentation, because your face should mirror your message. While figuring out how to "hold your face" isn't the most important delivery strategy you can employ, you need to make sure that your facial expressions are consistent with your words. Try taping yourself to discover your expressions just to make sure they're not contradicting your words.

Gestures

Gestures include movement of your head, arms, and hands that you use to emphasize, to reinforce, or to illustrate ideas. You probably don't even notice your gestures when you're in a relaxed conversation, but when you are giving a speech or presenting an important message in a group, you may become very self-conscious. Not everyone is naturally expressive with their gestures; they may not use their hands, cock their head to the side, or even shrug their shoulders to express some feeling. Some speakers try to get rid of their hands by putting them in pockets; others fidget or play with things.[14] As with other delivery techniques, cultural influences impact gestures. For example, Arab and Italian cultures expect a great deal of animation; German and Japanese expect a reserved style.[15] You can see this in how we greet others: Do we shake hands? Do we bow? Do we place our hands crossed on our chest?

Those accustomed to a reserved style of greeting would expect the same of a speaker's gestures.

Gestures can be used to reinforce your message, such as holding up fingers to reinforce the spoken words *first, second,* and *third.* Gestures can also be used to add emphasis to words; pounding one's fist on the podium demonstrates conviction or emotion.

If you're not sure what to do with your hands, then think about where you will place them during the speech: Are you going to be playing with notes? Giving a podium a death grip? Playing with keys in your pocket? When you stand, do you naturally do it with your arms crossed in front of you? What message

© 2008, JupiterImages.

Purposeful movement creates a connection and can signal changes in the speech.

does that send? Honestly, gestures will probably take on the form of your normal conversational style, and it really doesn't matter so much if you use many gestures or not. What does matter is *how* you use those gestures. They should support your message, not detract from it.

Movement

Movement involves the positioning of your entire body as you speak. By moving closer to the audience, a speaker removes the physical and psychological barriers that distance him or her from the audience. What does a podium, lectern, or table do to that space? Does it impact the trust that the audience might be feeling? The more willing you are to move toward the audience, the more attentive the audience becomes and the more similarity they feel with you.

You have probably experienced this with a professor who greets you as you enter, calls students by name, makes frequent eye contact with students, and moves among them throughout the class session. Contrast this to the classroom with a teacher who remains tied to notes behind the podium, paces nervously at the front of the room, and flashes up slide after slide with little or no attempt to the audience. Which would you prefer? What message are you taking from each of these instructors?

Posture also is an aspect of movement; slouching probably signals a lack of enthusiasm on your part. Sitting down while giving a formal presentation probably doesn't work, either, because it's too informal; this is unlike giving a short impromptu to a small group seated around a table, where standing would seem presumptuous. Purposeful movement not only creates a connection, but it can signal changes in the speech. You can change position or location by moving a step or two; that not only shows confidence, but it demonstrates that something "new" has happened in your message.

Consider how you will approach and leave the front of the audience; how will you establish yourself, how will you end? By approaching in a confident fashion, your audience will perceive you as someone to listen to. If you start "packing up" and shuffling notes before your message is finished, your message may be lost and your credibility damaged. Developing speakers should "fake it until they make it," meaning that even if you do not feel confident, you should try to appear confident. By standing tall, looking at your audience, and moving with purpose, you are able to convey a sense of confidence that positively impacts how your audience views.

Distracting movement is aimless. If you move around the room constantly, you may be creating a burden on your audience: they have to follow you and try to maintain eye contact. You'll likely end up with people tuning out; no one enjoys watching someone else pace. Shifting back and forth on your feet suggests nervousness. If you move so that you're blocking the screen you're using, or if you find yourself placing your back to the audience so you can look at something behind you, you're signaling a disinterest in the audience. How can you perceive their feedback, how can they hear you, and what happens to your eye contact?

How can you develop purposeful movement? Again, taping yourself doing a speech is a good way to see how others perceive you. But you can also watch others (professors, peers, public figures) to see how they move; these models might provide you some positive ideas on what to do, as well as pointing out negatives to avoid.

Attire

Your personal appearance makes that first impression. An unkempt, untidy speaker suggests that the message that is about to come will also be lacking in polish or disorderly. If you fiddle with your hair or glasses, wear a hat that shades your eyes, play with jewelry, or wear something distracting (clothes, hair, makeup), your audience will be sidetracked by that rather than being focused on the message. Students often ask if they have to get dressed up when they give their speech. The answer is, of course, that it depends on what impression you wish to make on your audience. Think about what nonverbal messages your attire or appearance makes as you speak. Does your appearance reinforce or contradict your message? If you're trying to enhance your credibility on a topic, is it appropriate to wear something that indicates your identification with that issue (uniform, school tie, name badge, etc.) Typically in most situations, you'd dress a bit more formally than your audience, but you should be comfortable in what you wear. Your appearance should help you to feel confident, and it should boost your credibility with the audience.

Your appearance should help you feel confident and comfortable.

Vocal and physical delivery surrounds your message; they help the audience to form initial impressions about the kind of person you are. The way you sound and the way you look can suggest confidence and concern or incompetence and unreliability. Your speech's impact is strongly impacted by how you deliver it. Having something important to say should take precedence, but saying it poorly will impact the audience's acceptance of your ideas. Good delivery presents your message in an interesting, clear way. One other group of strategies that can supplement your vocal and physical delivery involves the use of presentational aids. Let's examine how they can complement your message delivery.

HOW CAN PRESENTATIONAL AIDS AFFECT DELIVERY?

TV Guide selected NBC's Tim Russert's use of the dry erase whiteboard (November 7, 2000) on which Russert predicted "Florida, Florida, Florida" would be the pivotal state in the 2000 presidential election results, as number 68 of the "100 Most Memorable TV Moments" in history.[16] When Russert turned to a Tablet PC for election 2004, bloggers took note.[17] Why is the aid that the commentator used notable? Because Russert's use of presentational media demonstrated the advantages of this supplemental delivery strategy.

Presentational aids are any items developed for reinforcing a message. These include objects, models, charts, drawings, graphs, videos, and photographs. The importance of visual representations is reflected in common sayings across many cultures. A Saudi Arabian proverb says, "Believe what you see and lay aside what you hear." The Chinese are familiar with, "I hear and I forget, I see and I remember." In Nigeria, they say, "Seeing is better than hearing." Traditional American sayings are, "Seeing is Believing" and, "A picture is worth a thousand words." So what exactly are the advantages of presentational aids?

Advantages to the Speaker and Audience

Presentational aids add a dimension to your delivery. First, they help us to communicate clearly. If you are discussing an object, you can show it or a representation. If you're citing statistical trends, you can picture them. If you're explaining a technique, you can demonstrate it. All of these examples show that you can make your information more vivid to the audience by adding a visual element to your message. Hands-on instruction, math manipulatives, graphing, and recording data make learning easier for the visual and tactile learners, according to education researchers.[18] You may have been the recipient of such instruction, because you learned math more easily when you could see the number in a different way. The audience can see a sequence of events or process, so an actual demonstration or a series of visuals will reinforce how those procedures work.

Second, presentational aids can create and maintain interest and attention. Think of the difference between a newspaper, a textbook, and a web page. Which one springs to mind as having the most visual appeal? Where words might lack interest, a well-placed presentational aid can grab the audience's attention.

Third, presentational aids can help your audience to remember. Research tells us that in addition to aiding your audience's understanding, a well designed aid will reinforce ideas. Researchers estimate that you remember 10 percent of what you read, 20 percent of what you hear, 30 percent of what you see, and 50 percent of what you hear and see simultaneously.[19] Your memory might also be engaged by your presentational aids as they remind you of important aspects of your message.

Fourth (but not the most important reason to use them), some speakers feel that by using a presentational aid, the audience will focus on it rather than on them. You have to recall that an aid is only a supplement to you and your message; it won't speak for you, but it can be there to complement your ideas and your delivery.

> **A Closer Look**
>
> Review your presentational aids. Do they
>
> - ❒ Help clarify understanding?
> - ❒ Create interest?
> - ❒ Enhance memory and retention?

Bob enjoyed these benefits of presentational aids when he chose to give a speech to his college classmates on how to hit a baseball. He included a baseball bat that allowed him to effectively demonstrate how to grip the bat, to hold it back off the shoulder, and to swing it properly. The bat also was comforting to him, as hitting a baseball was something he knew well. Although he was not menacing with the bat, it did give him a feeling of being in control and in power. For him, the presentational aid choice helped him communicate his message and feel more confident doing it.

Types of Presentational Aids

You have a wealth of aids to choose from; that selection depends on your purpose, your ability to create the aid, the context you'll be speaking in, and your ability to use the aid successfully. Let's put the types into three categories: three dimensional, two dimensional, and multimedia.

Three-dimensional Presentational Aid. **Three-dimensional presentational aids** include people and other animate creatures, objects, and models. Ask yourself from the very start if there is another way that you could illustrate your point rather than employing something living, simply because there are pitfalls to their use that could be avoided fairly easily. Using *actual animate creatures* (people, pets, etc.) can be tricky. However, if you wanted to show how to style hair, demonstrate how certain tae-kwon-do moves work, or illustrate dance steps, then having a real person there might be fruitful.

Simple thought can make this easier on you and your model: Don't ask for spur-of-the-moment volunteers, don't bring that person up until needed, and make sure the person understands that she is simply a presentational aid, not your partner in delivering the message.

Animals require even more planning: You can't control their behavior most of the time in front of an audience, and it's easy for that creature to become the center of attention, even when it's not playing a role in the message at that moment. In addition, many creatures are difficult to see from all audience vantage points. Out of respect for you and your audience, think long and hard about using an animal as a presentational aid. You might think that it would be unique or more realistic to show the creature, but what if you have audience members who have fears or allergies, or what if the pet gets stressed out by the experience? Stories of "bad animal speeches" are legend in speech classes: the student who brought a live piranha in a zip-lock bag, which started to leak as the fish tried to attack the speaker's hand through the bag; the "how to bury your pet" speech, where the person brought in an actual dead rabbit he killed that morning; the speech about fear of snakes, accompanied by a burlap bag with two rather large boas in it, which, when shown, promptly sent the front row diving from their seats. Generally, it's better to consider other ways to illustrate or demonstrate your points, rather than using animate creatures, simply because the negatives likely outweigh any advantage you would get from them.

Objects can be either the actual item or a representation of it. Objects create interest because they're something the audience can see, hear, touch, and maybe even taste. We can respond to the real thing when we see it, because that tangible presence brings the idea to reality. The example of the baseball bat earlier in this section shows the use of an object. There are simple keys to using objects: Make sure that it's large enough to be seen, but not so large that you can't manipulate it (move, carry, etc.). Showing how to do a card trick may not work if you're not using a regular deck of cards: How do you perform that task with a normal deck? Make sure that there is no danger involved in the object's use (the swinging of a baseball bat could have tragic consequences in a classroom!). Practice how you will use the object, and keep it out of sight when you're not using it so that it doesn't become a focal distraction.

Models are useful when you can't bring the actual thing in but you want to help the audience visualize the object in a three-dimensional way. You can't show how to cut a real person's hair (think about those shaking hands holding scissors in front of an audience), but you can do the process on a wig. You can't bring a helicopter to class to explain why it flies, but you can bring in a model. Again, the use of models is pretty simple: Make sure it's large enough to be seen and practice its use.

Two-dimensional presentational aids are commonly used in speeches.

Two-dimensional Presentational Aids. **Two-dimensional presentational aids** make up the most commonly used category in speeches. These include images such as drawings, photographs, maps, graphs, charts, and overhead transparencies, to name a few. Because of an increased availability of electronic projection equipment in classrooms, conference rooms, and meeting places, images are nearly expected by contemporary audiences as the part of any presentation. Most of these can be developed through presentation software such as PowerPoint, which will be discussed after a brief review of the types of two-dimensional images you can utilize.

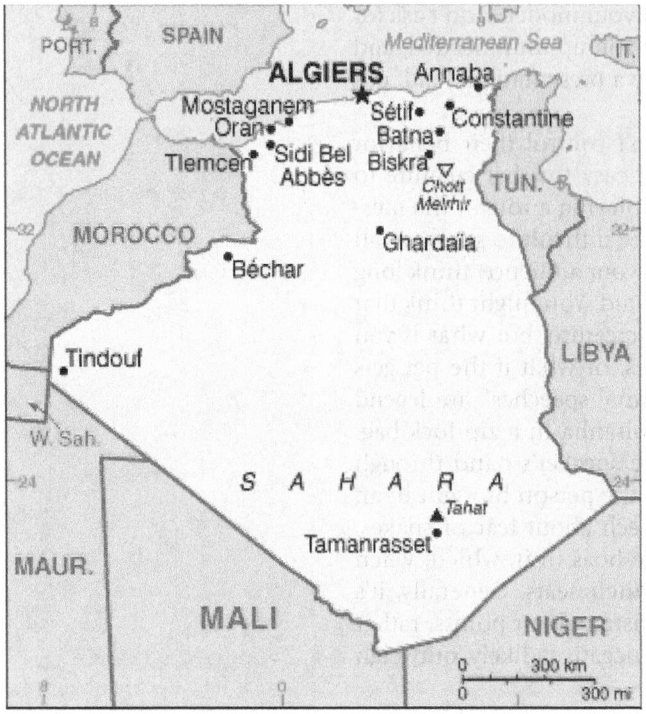

SOURCE: http://www.cia.gov/cia/publications/factbook/geos/ag.html (Accessed April 2, 2006)

Two important cautions should be considered from the start. You must keep in mind the relevance of the image to your message. This is true for all types of presentational aids, but because images are so readily available, many speakers tend to go overboard in their creation. Second, you must ensure that proper permissions have been sought if the images used are protected by copyright or a trademark. Just because it's available on a Web site or in a book doesn't mean you can automatically use it for your own purposes. Nearly every article, picture, photo, and cartoon is protected by copyright. Educational use of an image might be allowed in a single use, small audience situation. Repeated use of an image, even for educational purposes, might be a copyright violation.[20]

Drawings are inexpensive, can be designed for your exact needs, and are easily constructed with presentation software, so you don't have to be a master artist to create them. Simple drawings with large, dark lines are more effective for audience presentations than are detailed images. *Photographs* provide greater reality than drawings, but small detail is likely to be difficult to see, even when projected. Enlarging photographs to poster size is possible but relatively expensive (remember, ask yourself how necessary the photo is to your audience's understanding your message). Additionally, you don't want your speech to become a travelogue of "and then there's this," so you need to keep photos to a minimum, and make their impact strong. *Maps* share the size issue with photos; the detail on them is often difficult to see from an audience perspective.[21] Ali gave a speech to familiarize his classmates with his home country of Algeria. He was aware that helping them to picture Algeria's world location would be an essential part of the message. Ali found an image of Algeria in the *World Fact Book,* a resource available through www.cia.gov, which he incorporated into a PowerPoint presentation. In his speech he described where Algeria is located on the African continent and how Algeria was nearly three and a half times larger than the state of Texas. Using the visual aid shown here, along with his comparison to Texas, he was able to make his audience quickly understand both the country's size and location.

© 2008, JupiterImages.

Graphs serve to make information visually clear to the audience.

Graphs are representations of statistical data; while many in your audience might not understand numbers, they can grasp their meaning when shown visually. Bar graphs, pie graphs, line graphs, and picture graphs are able to show trends and relationships. Because most computer software programs have the ability to translate data into graphs, this is an easy way to include data in your message. The use of graphs can make information visually clear, something spoken numbers might not do. However, remember that the graph does not speak for itself. You must explain in words what the audience should be seeing.

Charts, like graphs, summarize information. They are easy to use in different formats: Flipcharts (large pads of paper on an easel) and whiteboards are inexpensive and low tech. However, because you often have to be writing while talking, their appearance is often unprofessional (not straight, hard to read), and speakers are prone to misspellings. Can you really think, talk, and write simultaneously in front of others? Won't you lose eye contact when you turn to write? The best charts are simple; their words use parallel structure or balanced points; their letters are large and bold. Don't overuse color (many colors might make the audience feel like you're enthralled with that new box of crayons). The audience needs to see a simple, plain image. Because presentation software is readily available, it's better in most cases to create a chart before you speak. However, if you're in a situation where an ongoing discussion requires writing while the message is being given, consider having someone else do the scribing for you.

Overhead transparencies are the precursor to contemporary electronic projection, using a plastic sheet called a *transparency.* Special markers are required for their creation, or you can usually print on them from a copy machine or home printer. This type of aid is simple to create, doesn't require you to dim the lights, lets you continue to face the audience while the transparency is projected, and can be developed prior to the speech but still allow you to add detail while speaking.

There are universal rules for the creation and use of all two-dimensional presentational aids. You should always practice their use, especially if you're going to be writing on them as you speak. If possible, go to the place where you'll be presenting and make sure that you can put the image's projector and image within easy view of the entire audience. Keep your images simple; bullet points and words or phrases are more effective than long sentences and paragraphs that will cause the audience to want to read. Watch your font size; what looks big to you when you're creating on your kitchen table or laptop may be tiny when projected. A simple rule of thumb is to use 32–36 point type for titles, 24 point type for subtitles, and 18 point type for the rest of the text. You want to use a simple font rather than a fancy, decorative, or specialized font. For example:

Times New Roman 24 point looks like this.

Brush Script 24 point looks like this.

Kuenstler Script Medium 24 point looks like this.

Imagine seeing this projected; which would satisfy your need for clarity and ease of recognition? Last, don't show your presentational aid until it's necessary, and when it's not, cover it up or insert a blank image. Again, you want to control the audience's focus on the message, not the image.

Many of these two-dimensional aids can be developed through graphics presentational software. Such software offers you a means to present information clearly and with visual interest, and they don't require great amounts of time or expertise on your part. Software allow you to create a uniform and distinctive look; save work as you prepare it; establish progression and timing

Guidelines for Using PowerPoint

- Limit the number of slides.
  - Rarely are more than five visual aids necessary in a speech. Remember that the visual aid is used primarily to clarify only when words are not enough.
- Simplicity is important.
  - PowerPoint can do many gimmicky things. It was created by people who wanted to show how much the program could do with no regard if it was good for speaking.
  - Avoid sounds and use the same transitions and animations throughout the speech.
- Use only photographs, charts and drawings in the presentation.
  - Do not list your main points. Do not type that which can be said.
- Include a blank black slide at the front and back of all content slides.
  - The blank black slides serves two purposes.
    - It allows the speaker to hide the content slides when not being used in order to keep the audience focused on the speaker.
    - It allows the speaker to remain in front of the screen without being blinded by the projection light and without the light shining on the speaker's face, causing a distraction.
- As with other audiovisual aids, the speaker should be familiar with the content.
  - The speaker should not talk to the screen while the slide is being projected.
- Speakers may look, briefly, at the slide to gain their bearings, but they should maintain eye contact with the audience as much as possible. Pointing to the slide's content may be necessary to ensure that the audience's attention is focused on the correct area of the visual aid.
- The speech is about you—not the software.

(Reprinted by permission of Professor Corey A. Hickerson.)

of ideas; and offer the audience a printout or electronic copy for later use. Presentation software such as Microsoft's PowerPoint, Apple's Keynote, Corel Presentation, Astound Presentation, and Lotus Freelance Graphics all allow their users to include two-dimensional images, words, sound, and animation in a presentation. Remember, though, that the software shouldn't dictate what you talk about; it's just a tool for supplementing delivery. Nor should you let special effects such as transitions, music, animation, and video clips attached to slides overwhelm the audience with needless images. PowerPoint is probably the most familiar presentational software and is the industry leader[22] so let's consider guidelines for its use.[23] Dr. Corey Hickerson developed a simple list of "how to's" that you can employ.[24]

One last caution about relying on any electronic creation: Equipment might not work the way you want. Have a backup plan, such as overhead transparencies or a handout ready, just in case. Remember, if something can go wrong, it likely will!

Multimedia Presentational Aids. **Multimedia presentations** involve the combination of sound and sight to create interest and excitement, along with information that is best presented in an audiovisual format. When played via CDs, DVDs, flashdrives, or laptops, audio and visual materials are easily combined into a professional-looking package. For example, if you are giving a speech about the music of the recording artist Prince, incorporating some sound clips might help your audience appreciate and understand the artist more fully. The danger of clips, music, and Web sites is that the audience may be conditioned to use these products in a passive fashion. If you're inserting multimedia in a speech, you want to get the audience to use these media in an active way, as a means to enhance clarity. The same cautions you've read for other presentation aids apply here. Make sure that what you're showing is really necessary; a movie clip might be interesting, but is it meant to be shown as a snippet for a supporting detail? A projected Web site might have too much detail on it to serve as a complement to your speech. CDs, DVDs, and flashdrives can give you a quick way to retrieve audio or visual information, but the temptation may be to put too much on them because of their storage capacity.

When using any multimedia source, make sure you introduce and explain it first, so the audience knows what to be looking or listening for. From a practical perspective, avoid playing an audio track while you are speaking. It might seem like a cool idea to play music as a background to your spoken message, but in the end, the audience will struggle to hear you because they can't listen to both the audio track and you at the same time.

If you don't know how to use the software, then multimedia will take a great deal of time to learn to use effectively. Make sure you're familiar with how to move forward in the presentation; how will you continue the information? Just like any technology, there's always the chance for breakdown or system incompatibility; have a backup plan in place. What will you do if everything falls apart? Remember, use multimedia presentation aids in a sparse fashion so you're not overwhelming the message. Many speeches have been dampened by unsuccessful attempts to use multimedia that did not work at all, did not include audio, or was not visible due to lighting limits or projection problems.

Using Presentational Aids Strategically

The three categories of presentational aids (three dimensional, two dimensional, and multimedia) offer you a range of ways to supplement your ideas. All cultures seem to recognize the value of visual expression accompanying verbal ideas, and they've become an anticipated part of business and academic life. But just because presentational aids are possible doesn't mean they have to be incorporated into a speech. Ask yourself if you learn better when you read something, when you see something, or when you do it? Different learning tasks require different techniques, don't they? The same holds true for presentational aids; some are more effective in representing specific ideas than are others. At the same time, there are many messages we present verbally that don't have "obvious" visuals, so we need to encourage the audience's understanding with additional presentational aids. The skillful use of any aid has become an expectation in our world, and you should consider their inclusion in your message preparation.

While each category has its own strategies and pitfalls, there are some general guidelines for you to consider to avoid the ineffective and enhance the effective.

Prepare in Advance. *Prepare your presentational aids in advance, and practice with them in the same way.* You need to have the resources and time necessary to create clear, memorable, and effective presentational aids. If you prepare in advance, you have a greater chance to make sure your information is accurate (no words are misspelled, ideas aren't missing or organized in a confusing fashion). You also need to be able to practice with them in "real time," as you would when giving the presentation to your audience. Practice helps you focus on the spoken message and augment it with your visual message, as opposed to the other way around. Second, practice is essential to successfully using aids when speaking. Taking time to practice with your presentational aids, whether they are three dimensional, two dimensional, or multimedia, will increase your confidence and readiness for the actual speaking situation.

Keep It Simple. *Keep your presentational aids simple.* Remember, it's the speech, not the dazzling graphics or multiple images, that matters. Too often speakers add transition features, animations, and sounds to a presentation that add little to their message effectiveness. In the same vein, avoid incorporating too many backgrounds or transition sequences just because they are trendy or exciting. You want attractive features that will ensure audience members will see your visual aid, but you want them to focus on your ideas, not the other way around.

The rule of thumb to employ is that you should include in your presentational aid only those things needed to make your point. Obey the 3 × 5 rule, which means that no more than three words and five lines or five words and three lines should be on any one slide or transparency. Essentially, this means you should not write out whole sentences or paragraphs for the audience to read. Instead, short phrases should be used to provide a visual reinforcement of the spoken message. Clutter is out; clarity is in. Intricate, detailed, and complicated ideas don't belong on a presentational aid; that's counter to the purpose.

You also need to consider color and font, as discussed earlier. Color can add energy and focus to a presentation, but it can also serve as a interruption to thought. Selecting foreground and background colors that are high in contrast will help text and images to be easy to see.[25] Television producers select cool background colors, such as blues and greens, because they create less strain on viewers' eyes. Similarly, careful attention to font selection can also impact clarity and visibility. Too much font variety can be distracting; you might use two (one for the title, the other for the rest), but in any case, you want to use a block-type font that is easier to read. The number and use of images is also important, as crowding a slide with pictures, especially animated ones, can quickly turn an effective presentation into a distracting one.

Make It Visible. *Make sure your presentational aids can be seen.* Your well-thought-out and well-designed presentational aid is worthless if the audience can't see it. That seems obvious, doesn't it? In most instances, modern corporate boardrooms and classrooms are designed to ensure audiences will be able to clearly see the visuals when projected. But not all speaking venues are designed for that purpose, so a little bit of planning can help. One strategy to use is the "floor" test. If using a nonprojected presentational aid (three-dimensional, some two-dimensional), create your visual aid and then place it on the floor in front of you. From a standing position you should be able to read the words and see all images in adequate detail. If you can, they probably will be appropriately visible when projected. If not, then corrections are necessary. Practice with the projected images, and make sure you're not standing in front of the screen. You don't want to be blinded by the light, and you don't want to cast a shadow.

Display It Selectively. *Display the presentational aid only when it's complementing your verbal message.* If a presentational aid is visible, it will be looked at by someone in the audience. That may mean that person isn't listening to you because she is admiring the artwork, wondering what you're going to be doing with it, or thinking that she could do something better. Cover three-dimensional objects or keep them out of sight. If using a flipchart, keep the blank page up until you need to point out the visual aspects. Slides can be blacked out, or you can insert a plain one into the presentation. You don't want to distract your audience by an unnecessary or ill-placed display.

The same goes for the use of sound. Avoid incorporating sound with your visual aids unless that feature improves understanding of your message. Sure, many presentational software programs can add neat sounds like cars screeching to a halt or the sound of a camera shutter clicking, but why would you do that? Before incorporating multimedia features into your presentation, ask yourself, "Will this feature help my audience understand my message?" and, "Can I use it without creating distraction?" If not, then don't incorporate the feature.

Control It. *Control your presentational aids; do not be controlled by them.* When using presentational aids, it is easy to be a slave to the tool. Instead of using the aid to help communicate an idea, the aid becomes the message. Audiences sometimes pay more attention to the background style or transitions used in presentational software slides than the intended messages. Sometimes speakers speed up their presentations to avoid allowing the screen saver to activate. A common mistake made with the best of intentions was made by a speaker who thought he would use the "timing" feature in PowerPoint. Unfortunately, his timing in the live presentation was different from his practiced timing (as it should be if a speaker is responding to the feedback of an audience). The result was a slide presentation that appeared possessed by a demon, bent on destroying his presentation.

This strategy is a reminder that you should talk to your audience, not to your aid. It's pretty easy to lose eye contact when utilizing an actual object or a projection, and your audience probably is looking at that aid, too. The message is the important item here, not the means by which it is being presented. A simple way to avoid this downside of using presentational aids is the **three T method.** First, Touch (or point to) the place you want the audience to focus their attention. Second, Turn your face to the audience. Third, begin Talking.

Three T Method

1. Touch (or point to) the focal point
2. Turn your face to the audience
3. begin Talking

With thought, preparation, and effort, presentational aids will enhance your delivery in an added dimension. Although they're not always required, they provide an appeal to multiple senses. Presentational aids can increase message clarity, interest, and retention. They can enhance your credibility when used effectively. Conceived of poorly, designed inaccurately, or used ineffectively, they'll frustrate or bore your audience. You have a tightrope to walk here: you want to enjoy the advantages of successful presentational aids and avoid the consequences of poor design and use. You should always base your strategic choice on this basic question: Will the effective use of presentational aids enhance my speech purpose?

SUMMARY

This chapter has focused on how your message is impacted by elements other than the content of spoken words. Effective delivery involves management of both verbal and nonverbal messages. Delivery should be tailored for the intended audience and situation. Effective verbal delivery considers volume, rate, pitch, pauses, and the trio of articulation, pronunciation, and dialects. Good nonverbal delivery involves appropriate eye contact, facial expression, gestures, movement, and attire. Presentational aids should reinforce and clarify the verbal message. Effective verbal and nonverbal delivery constitutes another strategic element in effective communication.

Roger Ailes summed up the importance of what he called the "composite you" as he explained the importance of communication elements beyond the message:

> "You are the message." What does that mean, exactly? It means that when you communicate with someone, it's not just the words you choose to send to the other person that make up the message. You're also sending signals about what kind of person you are—by your eyes, your facial expression, your body movement, your vocal pitch, tone, volume, and intensity, your commitment to your message, your sense of humor, and many other factors.
>
> The receiving person is bombarded with symbols and signals from you. Everything you do in relation to other people causes them to make judgments about what you stand for and what your message is. "You are the message" comes down to the fact that unless you identify yourself as a walking, talking message, you miss that critical point.
>
> The words themselves are meaningless unless the rest of you is in synchronization. The total you affects how others think of and respond to you.[26]

NOTES

1. Roger Ailes and Jon Kraushar, *You Are the Message: Getting What You Want by Being Who You Are* (New York: Doubleday, 1995), p.37.
2. *http://www.brainyquote.com/quotes/quotes/m/marktwain100433.html* (accessed August 27, 2007).
3. K.J. Tusing and J.P. Dillard, "The Sounds of Dominance: Vocal Precursors of Perceived Dominance during Interpersonal Influence," *Human Communication Research* 26 (2000), 148–171.
4. D. Deutsch, T. Henthorn, E. Marvin, H. Xu, "Perfect Pitch in Tone Language Speakers Carries over to Music," (Nov. 9, 2004), *http://www.aip.org/148th/deutsch.html* (accessed Sept. 1, 2007).
5. "The 100 Most Often Mispronounced Words in English," alphaDictionary.com, *http://www.alphadictionary.com/articles/mispronouced_words.html* (accessed Sept. 3, 2007).
6. For information on American dialects, see, for instance, the American Dialect Homepage, *http://www.evolpub.com/Americandialects/AmDialhome.html* (accessed Sept. 3, 2007), and "Varieties of English, Language Samples Project," *http://www.ic.arizona.edu/%7Elsp/index.html* (accessed Sept. 3, 2007).
7. Mary M. Gill, "Accents and Stereotypes: Their Effect on Perceptions of Teachers and Lecture Comprehension," *Journal of Applied Communication Research* 22 (1994), 348–361.
8. World of Quotes, Ralph Waldo Emerson, *http://www.worldofquotes.com/topic/Eye/1/index.html* (accessed Sept. 4, 2007).
9. See, for example, R. Axtell, *Dos and Taboos around the World,* 2nd ed. (New York: Wiley, 1990); and L. Samovar and R. Porter, *Communication between Cultures,* 4th ed. (Belmont, CA: Wadsworth, 2001).
10. Steven A. Beebe, "Eye Contact a Nonverbal Determinant of Speaker Credibility," *Speech Teacher* 23 (1) (Jan. 1974): 21.

11. For more information about the importance of eye contact, see, for instance, J.B. Bavelas, L. Coates, and T. Johnson, "Listener Responses as a Collaborative Process: The Role of Gaze," *Journal of Communication* (September 2002): 566–580.
12. Paul Ekman, Wallace V. Friesen, and S. Tomkins, "Facial Affect Scoring Technique: A First Validity Study," *Semiotica* 3 (1971).
13. L. Samovar, *Oral Communication: Speaking Across Cultures* (Los Angeles, CA: Roxbury, 2000), 102.
14. For more information about gestures, see, for instance, G. Beattie and H. Shovelton, "Mapping the Range of Information Contained in the Iconic Hand Gestures that Accompany Spontaneous Speech," *Journal of Language and Social Psychology* 18 (4) (1999): 438–462. Also J. Cassell, D. McNeill, and K.-E. McCullough, "Speech-Gesture Mismatches: Evidence for One Underlying Representation of Linguistic and Nonlinguistic Information," *Pragmatics & Cognition* 7 (1) (1999): 1–33; M. Gullberg and K. Holmquist, "Keeping an Eye on Gestures: Visual Perception of Gestures in Face-to-face Communication," *Pragmatics & Cognition* 7 (1) (1999): 35–63; A. Kendon, "Do Gestures Communicate?: A Review," *Research on Language and Social Interaction* 27 (3) (1994): 175–200; A. Melinger and W.J.M. Levelt, "Gesture and the Communicative Intention of the Speaker," *Gesture* 4 (2) (2004): 119–141; J. Streeck, "Gesture as Communication I: Its Coordination with Gaze and Speech," *Communication Monographs* 60 (4) (1993): 275–299 and J. Streeck, "Gesture as Communication II: The Audience as Co-author," *Research on Language and Social Interaction* 27 (3) (1994): 239–267.
15. Samovar, 103.
16. 68. Tim Russert Tallies the Vote (11/7/00) Decision 2000, "TV Guide and TV Land present the 100 Most memorable TV moments," *http://www.tvland.com/originals/100moments/page2.jhtml* (accessed Sept. 4, 2007).
17. "Election 2004 geekery: Tablet PCs are the new whiteboards" Peter Rojas, Engadget, *http://www.engadget.com/2004/11/02/election-2004-geekery-tablet-pcs-are-the-new-whiteboards/* (accessed Sept. 4, 2007).
18. Susan C. Jones, "Memory Aids for Reading and Math," Final Report U.S. Department of Education's Christa McAuliffe Fellowship (1991).
19. M. Patterson, D. Dansereau, and D. Newbern, "Effects of Communication Aids and Strategies on Cooperative Teaching," *Journal of Educational Psychology* 84 (1992): 453–61.
20. Indiana University's Copyright Management Center, *http://www.copyright.iupui.edu/fairuse.htm* has a good discussion of what constitutes fair use and the limits of using materials. (accessed Sept. 5, 2007).
21. Most libraries have online databases of maps, images, and other media. Check with your research librarian for assistance. See, for example, Images, maps, news sources, and other media, Virginia Tech University Libraries, http://www.lib.vt.edu/find/othermedia.html.
22. For an opposing view, see Professor Edward Tufte's, "PowerPoint is Evil," in *Wired* on line at *http://www.wired.com/wired/archive/11.09/ppt2.html.* There is ample information about the construction of PowerPoint slides. See, for example, N. Amare, "Technology for Technology's Sake: the Proliferation of PowerPoint," *Professional Communication Conference,* 2004. IPCC 2004. Proceedings. International Publication Date: 29 Sept.–Oct. 2004.
23. *http://office.microsoft.com/en-us/powerpoint/default.aspx* is the main Web site for PowerPoint, including tips and training points (accessed Sept. 5, 2007).
24. Corey A. Hickerson, Ph. D., Assistant Professor of Communication Studies: James Madison University.
25. For a discussion of the use of color, Microsoft PowerPoint has a brief discussion on choosing the right colors at http://office.microsoft.com/enus/powerpoint/HA010120721033.aspx.
26. Ailes, p.25.

chapter 4

Communication and the Self

OBJECTIVES

- Define the term self and explain why it is viewed as a complex process
- Define the term self-complexity and explain the benefits of high self-complexity
- Explain the three components of the self-system and discuss how each component affects interpersonal communication
- Discuss the development of the self with special emphasis on the individuals and groups of individuals that play important roles in the development of the self
- Explain attachment theory, including the three attachment styles that affect the way individuals view the self and others
- State the importance of direct definitions and identity scripts
- Discuss the significance of the self-fulfilling prophecy and social comparison processes for identify formation
- State the difference between state and trait approaches in studying communication
- Define communication apprehension and discuss its effects
- Discuss the way communication apprehension is typically measured and identify treatment options for individuals scoring high in communication apprehension
- Define willingness to communicate and distinguish it from communication apprehension
- Define and give examples of the two forms of destructive aggression
- Explain why some individuals are verbally aggressive
- Define and give examples of two forms of constructive aggression
- Define humor orientation
- Define affective orientation

KEY TERMS

self
self-complexity
self-concept
public self
inner self
self-esteem
self-regulation
reflected appraisal/ looking glass self
attachment theory
secure
anxious-avoidant
anxious-ambivalent
direct definitions
identity scripts
attachment security hypothesis

---

social comparison theory
behavioral confirmation/self-fulfilling prophecy
similarity hypothesis
perpetual conflict
state approach
trait approach
personality
communication apprehension
willingness to communicate
systematic desensitization
cognitive modification
skills training
constructive and destructive forms of aggression
hostility
verbal aggressiveness
argumentativeness
independent-mindedness
assertiveness
humor orientation
affective orientation

OVERVIEW

In an excerpt from a song by the 1980s rock band, The Talking Heads, the burning question "How did I get here?" is raised. Most of us, at one time in our lives, have asked the same question. Another profound question, "Who am I?" fixates our culture. It is asked in song lyrics from rock groups and Broadway alike, from No Doubt, Alanis Morisette, Will Smith, Elvis Presley, Seal, and the Smashing Pumpkins to the musical *Les Miserables.* The Talking Heads added another concern "How did I get to be this way?" The theme song of television's most popular show is "Who Are You?" and *CSI* and similar programs involve the audience in the weekly unraveling of someone's identity, seeking answers from his interactions with others. The preoccupying search for self is this chapter's concern. In the first half of this chapter we address these questions by discussing the process of identity formation. Special emphasis will be placed on the role that interpersonal communication and relationships play in this process. A definition of the term self is provided, along with an overview of relevant terms used to describe and explain various aspects of the self. Next, a detailed description of the development of the self is presented, with special attention given to those individuals and processes considered essential to identity formation.

© amygala imagery, 2007, Shutterstock.

In the second part of this chapter, we examine the impact of individual differences on interpersonal communication. When communication researchers want to learn more about the impact of individual differences on social interaction, they often turn their attention to communication-based personality traits. According to communication researcher John Daly (2002), "the greatest proportion of articles in our journals have explored topics directly or indirectly related to personality" (133). To learn more about how people differ in their communication patterns, we define the term personality, distinguish between trait and state approaches to interpersonal communication research, and provide explanations of a number of different communication based personality traits. While there are many traits that influence our communication with others, we focus on several that have been researched extensively. These have been identified as predispositions that can either hinder or facilitate communication with others. "Everyone thinks of changing the world, but no one thinks of changing himself," wrote Leo Tolstoy. By looking within instead of outwardly, we can choose to improve our ability to communicate.

DEFINITION OF SELF

While individuals use the term self frequently and with relative ease, it is quite challenging for researchers to offer a single consistent definition for the term (Baumeister 1998). The **self** has been defined as a psychological entity consisting of "an organized set of beliefs, feelings, and behaviors" (Tesser, Wood, and Stapel 2002, 10). Another way of understanding the **self** is as a complex system made up of a variety of interdependent elements that attain self-organization (Vallacher and Nowak 2000). In attempting to explain the self, theorists often emphasize the origins of self, noting that it emerges through communication and established relationships with others and is constantly developing and evolving (Epstein 1973; Park and Waters 1988). Take a moment to consider how your self-perceptions have changed over the years. Are you the same person you were five, ten, or fifteen years ago? You have probably changed and matured a great deal over the years and see yourself as being quite different from when you were younger. Thus, one's perception of self is often described as a process because it evolves and is largely determined by ongoing communication with significant others. This idea is further validated by social psychologist Arthur Aron (2003) who says, "What we are and what we see ourselves as being seems to be constantly under construction and reconstruction, with the architects and remodeling contractors largely being those with whom we have close interactions" (Aron 2003, 443). In later sections of this chapter we explore the specific individuals and processes that exert the greatest influence in shaping our self-perceptions.

The self is also recognized as highly complex and multidimensional. Researchers agree that there are numerous dimensions, or aspects, of the self that make up one overall perception of the self. While we might think of ourselves as relatively uncomplicated individuals, most of us are highly complex and can assume a variety of roles. For example, on any given day, you may assume the roles of student, employee, daughter, sister, friend, teammate, roommate, or resident comedian. This example illustrates how individuals vary in their **self-complexity** or number of self-aspects, also known as sub-selves. Individuals possessing higher levels of self-complexity reap a number of personal benefits. What does it mean to possess higher levels of self-complexity? Referring back to the example of the student, if she views her multiple roles (sister, teammate, friend, etc.) as separate or unique, and at the same time has encountered a number of life experiences associated with those roles, then she probably has a greater number of non-overlapping self-aspects, or higher self-complexity. On the other hand, a woman who views herself only in two closely-related roles, e.g., teammate and student, and has limited life experiences associated with these roles, will probably have fewer self-aspects, or lower self-complexity.

How does one benefit from higher levels of self-complexity? Individuals with higher self-complexity may be less prone to having mood fluctuations (Linville 1985) and may cope better with stress (Koch and Shepperd 2004). When individuals report lower self-complexity they are more likely to experience negative affect in response to a negative life event than someone who reports higher self-complexity. Individuals with lower self-complexity may not be able to separate the limited roles they assume and may experience what researchers call "spill over." Thus, a student athlete who has a bad game may not be able to separate her experience on the soccer field ("me as soccer player") from her experience in the classroom ("me as a student") and the negative affect from the soccer game will expand, or spill over, to other self-aspects (Koch and Shepperd 2004). The student athlete has a bad game, does not study for her chemistry exam because she is still angry about her performance on the field and, as a result, fails her chemistry test the next day.

© Robert J. Beyers II, 2007, Shutterstock.
How could her performance on the soccer field affect other aspects of this girl's day?

Higher self-complexity may actually act as a buffer for people by allowing them to mentally separate themselves from painful life events (Linville 1987). Furthermore, the buffer effect has direct interpersonal, or relational, implications. The buffer effect was observed for those higher in self-complexity faced with relationship dissolution. Individuals higher in self-complexity thought about the relationship less and were less upset about their relationships ending than individuals lower in self-complexity (Linville 1987). Familiar fictional characters demonstrate instances of high and low self-complexity following relationship disengagement. For instance, *Gilmore Girls'* Rory Gilmore, whose roles of daughter, granddaughter, friend, and student are emphasized more heavily than that of girlfriend, dealt with the end of relationships with various boyfriends by spending more time with her mother and friends, and by increasing her involvement at school. These actions served as a buffer for Rory, which kept relationship concerns from dominating her thoughts or actions. In contrast, the popular show *The O.C.* exhibited the character Marissa Cooper, who fell into alcoholism and depression after her own break-up with central character Ryan Atwood. Marissa allowed the role of romantic relationship, which she found self-defining, to affect all other aspects of her self. While typically not as extreme as these two situations, instances of lower self-complexity, compared to high, are more likely to produce negative effects.

Importance of Studying the Process of Identity Formation

Why should interpersonal communication scholars study aspects of the self and the process of self development? Similar to other frequently studied concepts, research and perspectives on the self are vast and vary greatly (see, for example, Tesser, Felson, and Suls 2000; Tesser et al. 2002). There are a number of terms related to self in the literature and definitions for them are often inconsistent, making it difficult to integrate and interpret research on the self (Houck and Spegman 1999). But, before we can engage in a meaningful discussion of the self and related processes, we need to offer clear definitions of terms such as self-concept, self-esteem, and self-regulation. We also need to highlight distinctions between key terms and concepts. In addition, if we want to understand how and why individuals vary in attitudes, beliefs, values, mannerisms, security, psychological states, etc., we need to take a closer look at both how and why people perceive themselves in a particular way. Exploring the communicative and relational processes that affect the development of the self either positively or negatively is important because it helps us to understand who we are and why we are this way. Once we understand differences in how individuals develop a sense of self as well as the processes associated with the development of a more positive self-perception, we can train individuals to interact more competently with those around them. As Houck and Spegman (1999) argue, "Given its manifestation of social competence, the development of the self is of fundamental importance not only to the well-being of individuals, but also to the well-being of others with whom they associate" (2).

There are three constructs related to the self that typically emerge in discussions about the self and developmental processes. These three specific aspects of the self are: self-concept, or cognitions about the self; self-esteem, or affective information related to the self; and autonomy/self-initiative, or self-regulation, processes. In order to better understand the self-system and its related components, it is important to define and distinguish between these related constructs. In this chapter, we present a detailed definition of each of these three components, offer examples of related terms used to discuss each of these key areas, and provide a brief overview of the importance of these concepts to interpersonal communication and relationships.

The Self System

Terms such as self-concept, self-esteem, self-schema, and self-regulation are used in dialogues about the self and identity development. Some of these terms have been used interchangeably and yet, as we will see, they are very different constructs.

Self-Concept/Cognitions about the Self. One term that often emerges in discussions about the self is self-concept. Houck and Spegman describe the **self-concept** as a cognitive construct which is a "descriptive reference to the self, or a definition of the nature and beliefs about the self's qualities" (Houck and Spegman 1999, 2). While there are a variety of other terms used when describing the self (self-cognition, self-image, self-schema, and self-understanding), self-concept is used most frequently. In the most basic sense, self-concept refers to what someone knows about himself.

Social psychologists and sociologists argue that people possess multiple perceptions of the self-concept, or different personas (Bargh, McKenna, and Fitzsimons 2002). For example, Goffman (1959) and Jung (1953) draw distinctions between a **"public" self**, or the self that we project during social interaction, and an **"inner" self** that we keep private and that may reflect how we really feel about ourselves. The public self is described as our "actual" self-concept while the inner self is presented as our "true" self. Psychologists note that individuals often project an actual self in public that is quite different from their true self. Individuals may not present their true selves for a variety of reasons. One reason could be the fear of evaluation from others. Or, in some instances, an individual may not yet fully know or understand his or her true self.

One place where individuals may feel more comfortable expressing their true selves is on the Internet (Bargh et al. 2002). According to researchers, the anonymity of the Internet gives people the chance to assume different personas and genders and to express aspects of themselves "without fear of disapproval and sanctions by those in their real-life social circle" (Bargh et al. 2002). Two different experiments were performed that used a reaction time task to access college students' perceptions of their true and actual selves. Researchers found that the true self-concept was more readily recalled during Internet interactions while the actual self was more accessible during face-to-face interactions. In a third related experiment, college students were randomly assigned to interact, either via the Internet or face-to-face. Students assigned to the Internet had an easier time expressing their true selves to their partners than those assigned to the face-to-face condition. If individuals feel more comfortable expressing their true selves during Internet exchanges, they are then more likely to establish relationships with individuals they meet on the Internet (McKenna, Green, and Gleason 2002). This research may provide some explanation for the fact that more individuals are using the Internet to establish romantic and platonic relationships.

Why do you think some people find it easier to express their "true" selves over the Internet?

An individual's self-concept influences how one views or interprets social interaction, and at the same time it regulates one's involvement in the interaction. Suppose the student council president is asked to speak to the superintendent of schools to discuss student views on proposed schedule changes. Her self-confidence in her role as a student leader causes her to assert herself in the interaction and offer suggestions for an alternative plan. Research on the relationship between self-concept and interpersonal processes has explored the effects of self-concept on social perception, the relationship between self-concept and selection of interaction partners, strategies individuals use to mold and interpret communication with others, and how individuals respond to feedback that is not consistent with their self-concept. Three of these areas of research—the relationship between self-concept and social perception, self-concept and partner choice, and self-concept and interaction strategies—are particularly interesting and relevant to understanding how and why our self-concept affects our communication with others.

Much of the research on the relationship between self-concept and social perception concludes that people are likely to view others as relatively similar to themselves (Markus and Wurf 1987). When you interact with your friends, family members, and co-workers, you perceive them to be more similar than dissimilar to you in attitudes, beliefs, values, goals, and behaviors. From an interpersonal communication perspective, similarity is an important variable that affects our interactions with others and, when used strategically as an affinity-seeking behavior, can potentially increase liking between interactants (Bell and Daly 1984).

The way one sees or defines one's self also affects both the choice of relationship partners and subsequent behavior in those relationships (Markus and Wurf 1987). Research on the relationship between self-perception and relationship satisfaction indicates that individuals report greater relationship satisfaction when they choose partners that validate views of themselves (Schlenker 1984; Swann 1985). In other words, individuals attempt to find a relationship partner who expresses similar or consistent views with their ideal or desired self. Much of the research on the role of the self in social interaction has examined the process of impression management during interpersonal encounters (Markus and Wurf 1987). Not surprisingly, individuals work diligently to present a particular image of themselves to both external (Goffman 1959) and internal audiences (Greenwald and Breckler 1985). Using impression management techniques consciously and effectively is linked to heightened self-awareness (Schlenker 1985). While we may not always be aware of our impression management efforts, our day-to-day choice of dress, hairstyle, choice of words, and artifacts are selected strategically to project a specific desired image of ourselves to those around us. Think about the choices you make when deciding what to wear and how to style your hair in various social situations. It is highly likely that impression management played a role in your decisions.

Self-Esteem/Affect about the Self. Another term used frequently when discussing the self is **self-esteem,** defined as the subjective perception of one's self-worth, or the value one places on the self (Houck and Spegman 1999). There are a number of related evaluative terms associated with self-esteem that include: self-affect, self-worth, and self-evaluation. All of these terms illustrate the evaluative nature of this concept with individuals typically experiencing either positive or negative feelings about themselves or their behavior. Self-esteem can be measured objectively, unlike self-concept. Research indicates that individuals typically vary in their reported levels of self-esteem. Those reporting higher levels of self-esteem feel more favorable about themselves and their behaviors than individuals with lower self-esteem.

How can a teacher influence a child's self-esteem?

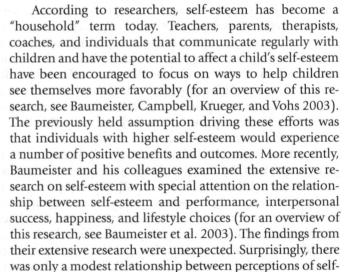

According to researchers, self-esteem has become a "household" term today. Teachers, parents, therapists, coaches, and individuals that communicate regularly with children and have the potential to affect a child's self-esteem have been encouraged to focus on ways to help children see themselves more favorably (for an overview of this research, see Baumeister, Campbell, Krueger, and Vohs 2003). The previously held assumption driving these efforts was that individuals with higher self-esteem would experience a number of positive benefits and outcomes. More recently, Baumeister and his colleagues examined the extensive research on self-esteem with special attention on the relationship between self-esteem and performance, interpersonal success, happiness, and lifestyle choices (for an overview of this research, see Baumeister et al. 2003). The findings from their extensive research were unexpected. Surprisingly, there was only a modest relationship between perceptions of self-esteem and school performance. Why? According to social psychologists, high self-esteem does not necessarily cause higher performance in school. Instead, researchers suspect that solid academic performance in school actually leads to higher self-esteem. When researchers investigated efforts to boost students' self-esteem, students did not improve in school and sometimes even performed at lower levels.

Similar to findings reported in the educational context, researchers concluded that occupational success may boost self-esteem rather than self-esteem leading to greater success in the workplace. The conclusions in this area are mixed, at best, with some research illustrating a positive relationship between self-esteem and occupational success and other research contradicting these findings (Baumeister et al. 2003). By this point, you might be asking yourself, "Are there any meaningful educational or occupational advantages associated with higher levels of self-esteem?" There *are* benefits to possessing higher self-esteem; they are just not as extensive as researchers initially estimated. For example, individuals with higher self-esteem seem to be more tenacious than those with low self-esteem. Social psychologists conclude that self-esteem may help individuals continue working on a task even after they failed initially (Baumeister et al. 2003).

What is the relationship between self-esteem and interpersonal communication and relationship success? Individuals self-reporting higher self-esteem typically indicate that they are well-liked and attractive, have better relationships, and make more positive impressions on others than those reporting lower levels of self-esteem. However, when researchers further investigated whether high self-esteem individuals were perceived this way by others using objective measures, the results were disconfirmed. The researchers further explain this finding by noting that while "narcissists are charming at first," they tend to eventually alienate those around them by communicating in ways that are perceived by others as inappropriate and ineffective (Baumeister et al. 2003, 1). The connection between self-esteem and the quality of romantic and platonic relationships is small to moderate, at best (Aron 2003). Some research indicates that there is a small consistent relationship between self-esteem and marital satisfaction and success over time (see, for example, Aube and Koestner 1992; Karney and Bradbury 1995). Based on research conducted thus far, couples' reported self-esteem does not appear to be a major predictor of marital satisfaction or persistence.

However, in addition to tenaciousness, there are some additional recognized benefits of having higher self-esteem. For example, higher self-esteem has been linked to feelings of happiness. Individuals reporting higher self-esteem are generally happier folks than individuals self-reporting lower self-esteem and are probably less likely to be depressed. Lower self-esteem has been repeatedly linked to greater incidence of depression under certain situations or circumstances. While it is disappointing to find that programs and initiatives created to boost individuals' self-esteem were generally ineffective in doing so, it is important to emphasize specific communication patterns that might be beneficial in helping others formulate positive self-impressions. Baumeister and his colleagues (2003) note that instead of giving children "indiscriminate praise" which may lead to excessive narcissism, parents and educators should focus on "using praise to boost self-esteem as a reward for socially desirable behavior and self-improvement" (1).

© Vartanov Anatoly, 2007, Shutterstock.

Rewarding children for good behavior gives them a boost in self-esteem.

As you can imagine, there is a great deal of information available on how to boost one's self-esteem in order to avoid depression, increase tenaciousness, and relate more effectively to others. Perceptions of one's self-esteem can change over time because of significant life experiences. There are numerous websites, books, workshops, and even computer games available for individuals who want to address problems with low self-esteem. See table 4.1 for an example of the type of information currently available to help individuals combat self-esteem problems.

Table 4.1 Ways to Boost Your Self-Esteem

1. *Think back to when you tackled a task for the very first time.*
   Trying something for the first time can be a daunting experience. The next time you feel under-confident, recall the first time you tried something new—and succeeded! This will help you to overcome your fears.
2. *Do something you have been putting aside.*
   Once you complete this task, it will help you feel as though you can follow through on something.
3. *Work on your ability to relax.*
   There are a number of different ways to reduce anxiety and stress in your life. Consider taking exercise classes, meditating, or involving yourself in something that helps you relax.
4. *Recall all of your accomplishments.*
   Take a minute to reflect on all of the times you have succeeded at doing something that you set out to do (e.g., passing your driver's test, passing exams, putting money away for vacation).

Adapted from an article that appears on the Uncommon Knowledge website *www.self-confidence.co.uk/self/esteem/tips.*

Research Brief: Playing Computer Games May Boost Self-Esteem

Mark Baldwin, a psychologist at McGill University in Montreal, argues that computer games offer another less conventional and interesting way to boost one's self-esteem. While these games are not recommended for individuals with serious self-esteem problems, Baldwin and his team of researchers found that the games helped people feel better about themselves and their relationships by focusing on the positive, not the negative (Dye 2004). Visit *http://abcnews.go.com/Technology/story?id=99532&page=1* to read the entire article.

Self-Regulation. The third and final component of the self-system, self-regulation, is occasionally referred to in literature as self-determination, independence, self-assertion, self-control, or internalization. Self-regulation is regarded by some as a highly significant component of human existence (Bargh and Chartrand 1999). Why is self-regulation so important? Because **self-regulation,** defined as "the capacity to exercise choice and initiation" (Houck and Spegman 1999, 3), allows us to pursue and engage in goal-directed activity. It is important to study the process of self-regulation in order to understand how and why individuals are motivated and make choices. Research in this area examines aspects of initiative, motivation, and decision-making in relation to morality and developing a conscience. It also sets out to discover why some individuals are motivated to achieve goals and others are not. The significant process of self-regulation can occur at either a conscious or a subconscious level (Bargh and Chartrand 1999). You probably exert self-regulation, whether you are aware of the process or not.

What is the relationship between self-regulation and interpersonal communication and relationships? Baumeister and Vohs (2003) offer several examples of how the process of self-regulation is related to interpersonal communication and relationships. Problems such as interpersonal violence between relationship partners and extradyadic sexual relations are obviously linked in some way to failures in self-regulation. Self-regulation is closely related to successful maintenance of close romantic relationships (Baumeister and Vohs 2003). Related research by Finkel and Campbell (2001) indicated that individuals reporting higher levels of self-regulation were more likely to exhibit accommodating behaviors in their romantic relationships. Not surprisingly, most individuals prefer being in relationships with partners that are accommodating, or willing to compromise, to meet each other's needs.

The extent to which one communicates effectively and appropriately with others is also linked to self-regulation or initiative. Recall from Chapter One our discussion of Spitzberg and Cupach's (1984) model of communication competence and its three components. This model advances the significance of motivation or initiative in communicating effectively with others. While individuals may posses the skills and knowledge necessary for communicating effectively, if they are not motivated to do so, they will not enact the appropriate behavior. Thus, the process of self-regulation directly affects our communication abilities and the quality of interpersonal relationships.

Now that we understand the three main components of the self-system and their relationship to interpersonal communication, we move on to the discussion of the development of self. Two important questions to consider are: Which individuals or groups of individuals are most influential in forming or shaping our self-perceptions? And why? Exploring these questions in much greater detail will help to answer the questions: Who am I? And how did I become this way?

Interpersonal Communication and the Development of Self

Most scholars agree that the self emerges and develops through communication with those to whom we are close (see, for example, Aron 2003). What exactly does this mean? This statement implies that, as infants, we do not possess a sense of self, but that one develops through our interactions with significant others (Cooley 1902; Mead 1934). Cooley (1902) was the first to advance "the **looking glass self**" metaphor which describes the impact of interpersonal communication on the development of self. Researchers (Felson 1989) extended the concept of looking glass self to include the term **reflected appraisal**, referring to the tendency to view ourselves based on the appraisals of others. Who are these significant others that affect our self-perceptions? Researchers have generally studied the influence of family and other significant individuals such as peers and relationship partners as they affect the development of self. We review the importance of interpersonal communication with family, peers, and significant others as it relates to the construction and reconstruction of the self over time.

A child who feels secure in the family environment will naturally expect positive peer relationships.

Family. Family plays a significant role in the development of one's identity. One theory that has received a great deal of attention from researchers studying the process of identity development is attachment theory. John Bowlby (1969, 1973) developed **attachment theory** in an attempt to explain the strong bond children form with the primary caregiver and the stress which results from separation from one another. Communication plays a pivotal role in creating the security associated with this attachment. Other theorists have expanded on the original theory advanced by Bowlby (1969) and typically recognize three different types of attachment relationships—secure, anxious-avoidant, and anxious-ambivalent (Ainsworth, Blehar, Waters, and Wall 1978).

When the primary caregiver behaves in a loving, supportive, and nurturing way towards her child, the child is likely to develop a **secure** attachment. A secure attachment is often "characterized by intense feelings of intimacy, emotional security, and physical safety when the infant is in the presence of the attachment figure" (Peluso, Peluso, White, and Kern 2004, 140). Because children raised in a secure environment typically have a history of responsive and supportive caretaking from their caregivers (Ainsworth et al. 1978), these experiences lead the children to believe that others will act in a supportive and caring way as well. Children who develop secure attachment styles are confident in their interpersonal relationships with their peers (Park and Waters 1988). Why is this the case? Bowlby (1973) and others (see, for example, Sroufe 1988) hold that children's first exposure to relationships is in the family context and that this experience helps them formulate expectations for subsequent relationships. Secure children, whose previous relationship experiences are generally positive, expect people in future encounters to act similarly, and therefore behave accordingly. Some research indicates that secure children recreate communication patterns and practices they experienced with their primary caregivers when interacting with peers, ultimately leading to more positive peer relationships (Sroufe 1988).

Conversely, individuals experiencing an insecure or **anxious-avoidant** attachment relationship with their primary caregiver often report trauma or neglect from their parents and exhibit significant developmental deficits (Peluso et al. 2004). Mothers of children who develop this attachment style act emotionally distant and rejecting, behaving with anger towards their children. Not surprisingly, this style of parenting can have long-term negative psychological and relational effects on individuals (Peluso et al. 2004). Unlike secure children, insecure children experience difficulty in forming relationships with others. Working from Bowlby's original theory (1973), insecure children, whose previous relationship experiences were negative, often develop a more negative "working model" of relationships and recreate negative communication patterns among peers. Some research supports this premise, with insecure children behaving more negatively and aggressively toward both known and unknown peers than secure children (Lieberman 1977; Sroufe 1988).

The third attachment style, labeled **anxious-ambivalent,** develops as a result of inconsistent and irregular treatment from parents (Ainsworth et al. 1978). Compared to secure children, those with anxious-ambivalent attachment styles experience more developmental delays, exhibit an unusual amount of conflict and confusion associated with their relationship with the primary caregiver, and are more accident prone (Ainsworth et al. 1978; Lieberman and Pawl 1988; Sroufe 1988). Both the anxious-avoidant and anxious-ambivalent attachment styles are problematic because children typically internalize perceptions of the self that are negative, which affect subsequent relationships with peers and romantic partners (Park and Waters 1988).

Communication with family members also affects how we define ourselves. Many of you have probably heard your parents describe your talents, personality traits, or other attributes in detail to other family members, friends, or even total strangers. **Direct definitions** are descriptions, or labels, families assign to its members that affect the way we see and define ourselves (Wood 2001). A child whose nickname is "slugger" may perceive herself to be an outstanding softball player. Consider the impact that the nickname "trouble" would have on a child's perception. Most of us can recall the way our family members referred to us and it is likely that many of these references were internalized. Researchers point out the significance of direct definitions by recognizing that positive labels can enhance our self-esteem while negative ones can have potentially deleterious effects on our self-perceptions (Wood 2001).

When you reflect back on your childhood, can you recall sayings or phrases that were repeated in your family? How about, "money does not grow on trees," "people who live in glass houses should not throw stones," "remember the golden rule," or "a family that prays together stays together?" Do any of these sayings sound familiar to you? Can you generate a list of phrases that were repeated in your family? These sayings are all examples of **identity scripts,** or rules for living and relating to one another in family contexts. Identity scripts help individuals to define who they are and how to relate to others (Berne 1964; Harris 1969). These phrases, which most have probably heard more than once, influence the way we relate to others and also our self-perceptions.

Peer relationships. While family relationships are important and clearly affect the development of the self, other relationships, such as peers, also play a significant role in identity development (Park and Waters 1988). The **attachment security hypothesis,** based on Bowlby's (1973) work, states that individuals are attracted to and seek out peers and relationship partners that can provide them with a sense of security. Not surprisingly, peers, like parents, can also provide a sense of security and social support for one another. Some research indicates that attachment related functions are eventually transferred from parents to peers over time (Surra, Gray, Cottle, Boettcher 2004).

Research by Meeus and Dekovic (1995) supports the significance of peer relationships later in life and indicates that peers, to a certain extent, are even more influential than parents in the identity development of adolescents. According to researchers, as young children age and mature they also begin the process of separation and individuation from their parents. Children begin to socialize more frequently with their peers, and to protest when they are separated from them. They begin to discover that most of their peer interactions are characterized by qualities such as equality and symmetry. Peer relationships, which tend to be more egalitarian, soon become more important than parental relationships and tend to influence child-parent relationship expectations. As children grow and mature, they expect to form new relationships with their parents, also based on symmetry and equality. When these relationships do not progress as expected, adolescents become frustrated and perhaps even more bonded with their peers (Meeus and Dekovic 1995). While initially researchers suspected that peers were only influential in certain areas of identity formation, research by Meeus and Dekovic (1995) illustrates the impact of peers on the formation of relational, educational, and occupational identity. Not surprisingly, best friends exerted the greatest influence on one's development of relational identity while peers or colleagues exerted the greatest influence on occupational and educational identities.

© paulaphoto, 2007, Shutterstock.

Have you ever compared your talents to those of your friends?

Peer relationships are also important in defining the self because individuals often use peers as a means of personal assessment. It is not unusual for individuals to compare themselves to others to determine whether they are smart, attractive, athletic or successful. When individuals compare themselves to others in order to determine their abilities, strengths and weaknesses, they are engaging in the process of social comparison. Leon Festinger (1954) developed **social comparison theory.** This theory suggests that most individuals have a basic need, or drive, to evaluate and compare themselves to those around them. Festinger holds that one of the only ways of validating an evaluation of oneself is to find out if similar others agree with it (Tesser 2003). Thus, if a student wants to evaluate his ability in school, he will typically compare his abilities to those of his fellow similar classmates. How many of you immediately consult with your peers after receiving a test or paper grade?

Another way that relationships with others affect the development of self is through a phenomenon called **behavioral confirmation,** or self-fulfilling prophecy (Aron 2003). Aron (2003) defines **self-fulfilling prophecy** as a process in which people act to conform to the expectations of others (see, for example, Darley and Fazio 1980). One of the classic studies that illustrated self-fulfilling prophecy was conducted in the classroom with teachers who were randomly informed that their students were academic overachievers. Academic performances improved significantly for those average students whose teachers were told that they were high achievers. Why did the students improve academically? Because the teachers communicated with the students as if they were overachievers, the students internalized these perspectives and acted accordingly (Snyder, Tanke, and Berscheid 1977). Researchers also found that previous relationship experiences can influence our expectations of new relationship partners' behaviors (see, for example, Andersen and Berensen 2001). Thus, if an individual experienced problems in previous relationships, he or she may expect similar negative experiences in the future and may circuitously contribute to how the relationship progresses.

© Losevsky Pavel, 2007, Shutterstock.

Your intimate relationships have a major influence on how you view yourself.

Relationship Partners. Over time, the bond formed between partners in a romantic relationship is sure to affect the development of the self. One particularly interesting study provides further support for this statement. Researchers found that married couples come to look more alike over extended periods of time. Zajonc and his colleagues (1987) found students were more successful in matching pictures of couples married twenty-five years compared with pictures of the same couples, newly married.

Intimate relationships are also important to the development of the self because they influence how positively or negatively one views oneself (Aron 2003). Some recent research indicates that getting married and having children can actually increase an individual's feelings of self-worth (Shackelford 2001).

According to the **similarity hypothesis,** also related to Bowlby's research on attachment theory, we are most attracted to individuals that exhibit an attachment style similar to our own (Surra et al. 2004). Not surprisingly, researchers found that college students with secure attachment styles were more attracted to relationship partners that had also developed this attachment style. As the similarity hypothesis would predict, anxious-attachment individuals were also more likely to date anxious-attachment partners and to report being satisfied with these relationships (Surra et al. 2004). This research indicates that we often seek out individuals with similar attachment styles that also verify our perceptions of self-worth.

Relationships with family members, peers, and significant others affect the way we define ourselves and influence our evaluative perceptions of the self. Another way that we define ourselves, and simultaneously distinguish ourselves from others, is by describing our predominant personality traits.

In the second part of this chapter, we explore some of the ways people differ in how they communicate with others. While individual differences such as age, culture, ethnicity/race, sex/gender, and cognitive traits certainly affect the way we communicate. with others, interpersonal researchers have turned their attention to the powerful role that communication-based predispositions play in making sense of social phenomena (Daly 2002). In the next sections we discuss: (1) the impact of individual differences on social interaction, (2) differences between state and trait approaches to research, and (3) a number of personality traits that affect our communication with others. Because students are often interested in finding their scores on the communication-based personality instruments, we have included ways to measure many of the traits discussed in the chapter.

THE IMPACT OF INDIVIDUAL DIFFERENCES ON SOCIAL INTERACTION

Most of us have interacted with someone we might label "difficult" because of his or her communication behaviors. It is not unusual for students to share stories of the "difficult" or "less-than-popular" roommate who lives with them. This roommate is often described as difficult because he acts in a consistently problematic manner or manages regularly to offend others. Not surprisingly, this roommate's poor behavior not only impacts all of the housemates, but also affects relationship partners, friends, classmates and neighbors that must hear about and interact with the difficult roommate. A number of authors have written books about dealing with difficult people (see, for example, Keating 1984). Dealing with difficult personality types is an important and relevant topic for a number of reasons: (1) we all have to deal with difficult people, whether at home, school, or work, (2) we might be one of those "difficult people" because we have communication challenges linked to our personality, and (3) asking an individual to completely change his or her personality is unreasonable and can damage relationships. Social psychologist John Gottman (1999) describes **perpetual conflict** as disagreements between relationship partners that are often directly related to personality issues. This type of conflict is pervasive and not easily fixed because it often involves fighting over matters that cannot be easily resolved, like differences in couples' personality traits. It is very frustrating when someone tells you, matter-of-factly, to "completely change your personality" in order to become a better relationship partner. We know that this unproductive criticism is an unreasonable request.

When someone asks you repeatedly to change the same aspect of your personality, e.g., to talk more or to talk less, it is likely that this person is requesting a change in a personality trait. Much of the communication research conducted to date has adopted a trait approach to studying personality differences, which is quite different from a state approach.

A COMPARISON OF TRAIT AND STATE APPROACHES TO RESEARCH

When communication researchers investigate differences in communication behaviors, they clarify whether they are studying these behaviors from either a trait or a state approach. When they adopt a **state approach** to studying communication behaviors, they examine how individuals communicate in a particular situation or context. For example, an interpersonal communication researcher might examine how individuals feel right before they ask someone out on a date. Researchers might measure an individual's state anxiety to determine if this affects his or her ability to advance a request for a date. Thus, when researchers adopt a state approach to communication research they examine situationally specific responses (Daly and Bippus 1998).

When researchers adopt a **trait approach,** they attempt to identify enduring, or consistent, ways that people behave. If a researcher adopts a trait approach to studying communication behaviors, it means that he is interested in examining how individuals interact the majority of the time. Guilford (1959) defines a trait as "any distinguishable, relatively enduring way in which one individual differs from another" (6). Daly and Bippus (1998) identify several conclusions about traits: (1) they define ways in which people differ, (2) they can be broad or narrow in focus, (3) some address social characteristics while others emphasize cognitively-oriented variables, and (4) some can be measured using questionnaires while others are recognized by observing behaviors. Daly and Bippus comment on the distinction between state and trait approaches in research by stating, "The differences between trait and state are, in actuality, primarily differences in emphasis. Personality scholars tend to emphasize the trait over the state" (2).

Why are communication scholars so interested in studying personality traits? Communication scholars study traits because they are related to communication variables in a number of different ways. For example, in the following sections of this chapter we will learn about individuals who are highly apprehensive about communicating with others. These individuals are described as having trait-CA (Communication Apprehension) because they are consistently apprehensive about communication with others. Explained another way, high CA individuals tend to exhibit high levels of apprehension across a wide range of situations and with varied persons. Not surprisingly, research indicates that these individuals tend to exhibit a variety of behavioral disruptions when forced to interact with others (Allen and Bourhis 1996). This example illustrates the relationship between a trait (CA) and communication variables (behavioral disruptions, stuttering, pauses, etc.).

Because our **personality,** or predisposition to behave a certain way, is an important and relatively enduring part of how we see and define ourselves, interpersonal communication researchers are naturally interested in learning more about the impact of individual differences on social interaction. In

How is your communication affected by those around you?

addition, most researchers argue that communication behaviors linked to personality differences are explained, at least in part, by social learning; that is, we learn how to communicate by observing and imitating those around us. While a number of communication scholars have argued that one's genetic background best explains his or her personality predispositions (Beatty, McCroskey and Heisel 1998), it is still important to consider both explanations.

Finally, by learning more about how individuals with specific personality traits approach social interaction, we can advance some predictive generalizations about how they interact and plan our own behaviors accordingly. You might ask, why do communication researchers not just study self-concept? Unlike one's self-concept, which is subjective and could change from moment to moment, one's personality is relatively stable and consistent over time. For example, if you complete one of the communication-based personality measures in this chapter today and then complete the same one a year from now, it is very likely that your scores will be highly similar or even the same. Learning more about communication behaviors that are trait-based helps researchers understand the impact of individual differences across different contexts. In the remaining sections of this chapter, we review research that adopts a trait or personality approach to studying differences in communication behaviors.

COMMUNICATION APPREHENSION AND WILLINGNESS TO COMMUNICATE

In John Maxwell's (2002) book, *The Seventeen Essential Qualities of a Team Player,* he emphasizes communication as one of the most important skills needed for succeeding in teams. Other essential skills included in his list are adaptability, collaboration, enthusiasm, and the ability to establish relationships with team members. Not surprisingly, all of these qualities also require strong communication skills. Maxwell and countless other authors from a variety of academic and professional fields emphasize the relationship between communication skills and success at work. Throughout our own textbook we continually emphasize the link between communication and relationship stability and professional success. However, what if you are not comfortable communicating with others? If you or someone you know often avoids talking in most situations and with most people, it is likely that this individual would score high in communication apprehension and low in willingness to communicate. In the following sections, we examine these two related communication-based personality traits. For each communication-based personality trait we provide a general overview of the construct, describe ways to reliably measure the trait, and discuss research on the link between the personality trait and communication behaviors. Because high levels of communication apprehension can be extremely debilitating for individuals, treatment options are also discussed.

Approximately one in five individuals in the United States is considered high in communication apprehension (McCroskey 2006). For highly apprehensive individuals, even anticipated communication with others evokes a significant amount of stress and psychological discomfort (McCroskey, Daly, and Sorensen 1976). James McCroskey (1977) conducted the seminal

Highly apprehensive individuals are more stressed and lonely than those who are low in communication apprehension.

research in this area and defines **communication apprehension** as an "individual's level of fear or anxiety with either real or anticipated communication with another person or persons" (78). Communication apprehension (CA) can be measured in a variety of ways, but is frequently assessed using the Personal Report of Communication Apprehension (PRCA) developed by McCroskey (1978). The PRCA is a twenty-four-item five point Likert-type measure that assesses individuals' communication apprehension in general, as well as across four different areas: public, small group, meeting, and interpersonal/dyadic situations (see Applications at the end of this chapter). Individuals scoring high on the PRCA are generally quite anxious about communicating with others and will attempt to avoid interaction. Highly apprehensive individuals are less communicatively competent, less disclosive, and are more stressed and lonely than individuals low in communication apprehension (Miczo 2004; Zakahi and Duran 1985). Highly apprehensive college students are more likely to be considered "at risk" in college settings (Lippert, Titsworth, and Hunt 2005) and are less likely to emerge as leaders in work groups (Limon and La France 2005).

Willingness to communicate (WTC) is similar to communication apprehension because it also taps into an individual's propensity to avoid or approach communication with others. The willingness to communicate construct does not assess fear or anxiety, only one's tendency to approach or avoid communication in varied situations and with varied persons. McCroskey and Richmond (1987) coined the term willingness to communicate (WTC) and describe this construct as a person's tendency to initiate communication with others (McCroskey and Richmond 1998). WTC is further described as a "personality-based, trait-like predisposition which is relatively consistent across a variety of communication contexts and types of receivers" (McCroskey and Richmond 1987, 134). WTC can be measured via the WTC scale, which is a twenty-item measure that assesses an individual's willingness to interact with different individuals in different situations (see Applications section at the end of this chapter). Individuals completing the WTC scale indicate the percent of time they would choose to communicate in public, during a meeting, within a group, in a dyad, with a stranger, and in situations with acquaintances. For example, individuals are asked to indicate how often they would "talk with a service station attendant" or "talk with a physician." When individuals consistently indicate that they would not want to talk in most of the contexts listed, they are described as low in WTC. Conversely, individuals who indicate that they are willing to interact with others in a wide range of contexts are described as high in WTC.

Not surprisingly, highly apprehensive individuals are more likely to be low in WTC. Richmond and Roach (1992) summarize a significant body of research on the benefits and drawbacks for employees described as quiet, or low in WTC. First, they identify several positive factors associated with lower WTC. For example, individuals reporting lower WTC are typically less likely to initiate or perpetuate gossip and are also less likely to emerge as "squeaky wheels" within the organization. In addition, quiet individuals are less likely to take long breaks, unlike their more social high WTC counterparts. Finally, individuals with lower WTC are more likely to be discreet than more talkative individuals. Thus, organizations do not have to worry as much about quiet individuals sharing corporate secrets or new developments.

While there are some benefits of employing quiet individuals, Richmond and Roach (1992) note that, in general, quiet employees "are considered at risk in an organizational setting" for various reasons (Richmond and Roach 1992). More often than not, quiet individuals are perceived as less competent and intelligent because they do not contribute to discussions or share their accomplishments with others. Consequently, quiet employees are often mislabeled as incompetent and lacking business savvy. Research indicates that we tend to formulate negative impressions of employees who are quiet and, as a result, they are often less likely to get interviewed or considered for promotions. In research by Daly, Richmond, and Leth (1979), it was found that when individuals were described as quiet or shy in recommendation letters, they were less likely to be granted interviews than highly verbal individuals. Unfortunately, low WTC individuals may be more likely to experience the "last hired" and "first fired" syndrome than their high WTC counterparts (Richmond and Roach 1992).

What can be done to help individuals who are either high in CA or low in WTC? There is a significant amount of research that has identified treatment options for high CA individuals. Communication apprehension can be treated with methods similar to other types of phobias and neurotic anxieties (Berger, McCroskey, and Richmond 1984). According to McCroskey and his associates (1984), high levels of CA can be overcome or managed by applying three widely accepted treatment options. If these treatment options are not available, "there are other options available for individuals in the absence of these more formal treatments" (153). The three primary treatment options available for individuals high in communication apprehension are systematic desensitization, cognitive modification, and skills training.

One of the most effective means of treating high levels of CA is **systematic desensitization** (SD), a type of behavior modification derived from learning theory. Eighty to ninety percent of individuals who use systematic desensitization eliminate completely their high level or fear or anxiety. The basic premise behind systematic desensitization is that anxiety related to communication is learned and, as such, can be unlearned. **Cognitive modification,** also based on learning theory, is the second method of managing high levels of CA. "The underlying rationale for this treatment is that people have learned to think negatively about themselves, in this case, how they communicate, and can be taught to think positively" (Berger et al. 1984). The third and least successful way to treat high levels of CA is skills training. Skills training, when used as the sole method, is typically considered the least effective method for treating high levels of CA. Communication **skills training** might involve taking courses to help individuals learn to communicate more effectively. For example, individuals may take public speaking courses to improve their ability to design and deliver speeches. Experts recommend that persons with high levels of communication apprehension first employ systematic desensitization or cognitive modification as a means of reducing their anxiety and then participate in skills training courses to help manage deficient communication skills. Whether you or someone you know is highly apprehensive about communication, it is important to note that the tendency to fear communication can be treated successfully.

> *And I think that those who consider disabled people 'broken' fail to see that while some of us have disabilities that are physically obvious, in truth all people are disabled in one way or another—including disabilities of character and personality.*
>
> —Kyle Maynard

AGGRESSIVE BEHAVIOR

Infante (1987a) recognizes a behavior as aggressive when it "applies force . . . symbolically in order, minimally to dominate and perhaps damage, or maximally to defeat and perhaps destroy the locus of attack" (58). He further explains that there are two types of aggressive behavior; he labels them destructive and constructive. **Destructive** forms of aggression are those that can potentially damage individual's self-esteem or, to use Infante's words "destroy the locus of attack." Two widely recognized types of destructive aggression are hostility and verbal aggression.

Hostility

Hostility is defined as "using symbols (verbal or nonverbal) to express irritability, negativism, resentment, and suspicion" (Infante 1988, 7). When someone expresses hostility, he or she might say, "I am so angry I did not get chosen for the lacrosse team and I blame the selection committee!" Individuals presenting hostile personalities generally devalue the worth and motives of others, are highly suspicious of others, feel in opposition with those around them, and often feel a desire to inflict harm or see others harmed (Smith 1994). One way to measure hostility is to use Cook-Medley Hostility Scale (Cook and Medley 1954) which is one of the most commonly used means of assessing trait hostility and appears to have construct, predictive, and discriminant validity (Huebner, Nemeroff, and Davis 2005; Pope, Smith, and Rhodewalt 1990). Sample items on the hostility measure are "I think most people will lie to get ahead," and "It is safer to trust nobody." Individuals completing the hostility measure indicate the extent to which they either agree or disagree with the statements using a five-point Likert scale.

Needless to say, feeling consistently hostile toward others affects the way one views the world and impacts relationships with others. Hostile individuals tend to be quite unhappy individuals who are more likely to report depression and lower self-esteem (Kopper and Epperson 1996). From a communication perspective, researchers try to accurately identify people or communication situations that evoke feelings of hostility in order to better understand this construct. If we can identify the types of situations or people that cause others to feel hostile, perhaps we can make attempts to modify or improve these situations. Recent research by Chory-Assad and Paulsel (2004) examined the relationship between students' perceptions of justice in college classrooms and student aggression and hostility toward their instructors. As expected, when students felt instructors were not fair in regard to course policies, scheduling, testing, amount of work, etc., they were more likely to feel hostile toward their teachers. Now that we know that perceptions of injustice in college classrooms leads to greater hostility in students, we can make recommendations on how to alter these situations and to reduce hostile reactions.

Hostile individuals are more likely to experience problems in committed romantic relationships. Rogge (2006) and his colleagues examined communication, hostility, and neuroticism as predictors of marital stability and found that couples were less likely to stay together when spouses reported higher levels of hostility and neuroticism. The researchers noted that while communication skills distinguished those who were married-satisfied and those who were married-unsatisfied, they did not always predict marital dissolution. It is important to note that hostility and neuroticism "contribute to a rapid, early decline in marital functioning" (Rogge et al. 2006, 146). In addition, an inability to empathize with relationship partners and manage conflict in a productive way may negatively impact future chances at relationship success. From an interpersonal communication perspective, it is important to determine the kinds of behaviors that elicit feelings of hostility from others, to then reduce or eliminate those behaviors, and to attempt to repair the damaged relationship using relationship maintenance strategies.

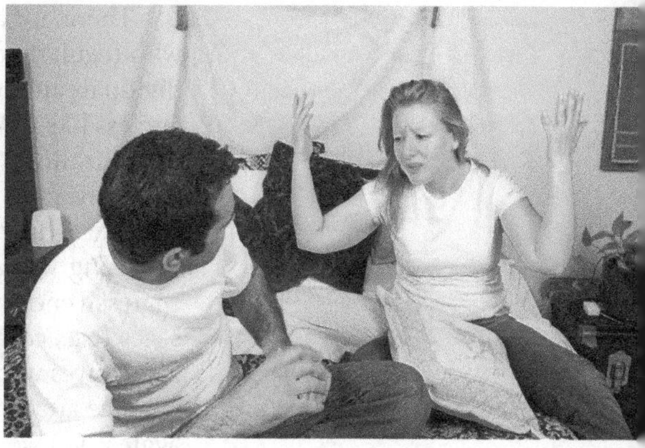

Verbally aggressive attacks can permanently damage relationships.

Verbal Aggression

Another personality trait labeled difficult, or problematic, during face-to-face encounters is verbal aggression. When individuals lack the ability to effectively argue, they often resort to verbally aggressive communication. Wigley (1998) describes **verbal aggressiveness** as the tendency to attack the self-concept of an individual instead of addressing the other person's arguments. Dominic Infante (1987; 1995) identified a wide range of messages that verbally aggressive communicators use. For example, verbally aggressive communicators may resort to character attacks, competence attacks, background attacks, physical appearance attacks, maledictions, teasing, swearing, ridiculing, threatening, and nonverbal emblems. On occasion, they might also use blame, personality attacks, commands, global rejection, negative comparison, and sexual harassment in their attempts to hurt others. As Wigley (1998) notes, "there seems to be no shortage of ways to cause other people to feel badly about themselves" (192).

Infante and Wigley (1986) developed the Verbal Aggressiveness Scale, which is a twenty item self-report personality test that asks people to indicate whether they are verbally aggressive in their interactions (found in Applications at the end of this chapter). Infante and Wigley were aware of the fact that people might not self-report their use of aggression. With this in mind, the researchers designed items on the measure to make it seem like they approved of aggressive messages. The researchers developed the Verbal Aggressiveness instrument to learn more about the behavior of people who were verbally aggressive.

For those of us who have ever interacted with someone who is highly verbally aggressive, one of the more common questions is why this person acts this way. There are a number of viable explanations for why some individuals possess trait verbal aggressiveness. Individuals may be verbally aggressive because they learned this behavior from others. Thus, social learning, or modeling effects explain why verbally aggressive parents have children that also become verbally aggressive. Another explanation for this trait is that verbally aggressive individuals lack the ability to argue effectively and, as a result, are more likely to become frustrated during arguments. The inability to defend one's position is frustrating and often causes the highly aggressive person to lash out at others. In this case, trait levels of verbal aggression are linked to argument skill deficiency (ASD). Researchers note that if verbal aggression is linked to ASD, then one way to combat this problem is to train individuals in effective argumentation (Wigley 1998).

There are a number of significant negative consequences for individuals who regularly communicate in verbally aggressive ways. Verbally aggressive individuals are more likely to use a variety of antisocial behaviors and, as a result, are less liked (Myers and Johnson 2003). Research by Infante, Riddle, Horvath, and Tumlin (1992) compared individuals who were high and low in verbal aggressiveness to determine how often they used different verbally aggressive messages, how hurtful they perceived these messages to be, and their reasons for using verbally aggressive messages. Individuals who were high in verbal aggressiveness were more likely to use a wide range of verbally aggressive messages (e.g., competence attacks, teasing, and nonverbal emblems). High verbal aggressives were less likely than low verbal aggressives to perceive threats, competence attacks, and physical appearance attacks as hurtful. When high verbal aggressives were asked to explain their behavior, they stated that they were angry, did not like the target, were taught to be aggressive, were in a bad mood, or were just being humorous. Wanzer and her colleagues (1995) found that verbally aggressive individuals are less socially attractive and more likely to target others in humor attempts than to target themselves. Their inappropriate use of humor may explain why acquaintances rate them as less socially attractive.

College students scoring high in verbal aggressiveness were more likely to be considered academically at risk in college settings than students scoring low in verbal aggressiveness (Lippert et al. 2005). Lippert and his colleagues (2005) call for more research to understand why verbally aggressive college students are more academically at risk. They suspect that verbally aggressive students' inappropriate classroom behavior may lead to negative evaluations from teachers and peers. Consistently negative experiences in the classroom may contribute to verbally aggressive students' at risk status.

What can be done to help high aggressives? From a communication perspective, it is important to recognize when we are being verbally aggressive with others and to attempt to eliminate these behaviors. Recognize that when you communicate in a verbally aggressive way, others may model your behavior. Have you ever had a younger sibling mimic your verbal or nonverbal messages? There is a substantial amount of research on this trait and the potentially negative effects of high amounts of verbal aggression on relationships in married (Infante, Chandler, and Rudd 1989), family (Bayer and Cegala 1992), and organizational contexts (Infante and Gorden 1991). If you are predisposed to using verbal aggression, enroll in courses that might help you improve your ability to argue. One of the most widely recognized ways to address or treat verbal aggression is to train individuals who are skill deficient in argumentation to defend their positions more effectively.

Next, we turn our attention to several communication-based personality traits that may help individuals communicate more effectively during social interaction. More specifically, we examine argumentativeness, assertiveness, humor orientation, and affective orientation.

CONSTRUCTIVE AGGRESSIVE BEHAVIOR

Argumentativeness and assertiveness are described by Infante as constructive forms of aggression. Both of these behaviors are considered **constructive** forms of aggression because they are more active than passive, help us achieve our communication goals, and do not involve personal attacks (Rancer 1998). For some individuals, arguing with friends, colleagues, or family members is considered enjoyable and challenging. For others, arguing leads to hurt feelings, confusion, or even anger.

Argumentativeness

According to Rancer, individuals vary extensively in their perceptions of argumentative behavior. Infante and Rancer (1982) define **argumentativeness** as "a generally stable trait which predisposes individuals in communication situations to advocate positions on controversial issues and to attack verbally the positions which other people hold on these issues" (72). When individuals are argumentative, they attack issues and positions. When individuals are verbally aggressive, they attack others by using competence or character attacks, or possibly even swearing. When someone exhibits high levels of argumentativeness, they are able to both advocate and defend positions on controversial issues. Infante and Rancer (1982) developed the Argumentativeness Scale, which is a twenty-item Likert-type scale that asks people to record how they feel about responding to controversial issues. Ten items on the scale assess motivation to approach argumentative situations and ten items assess motivation to avoid argumentative situations (see Applications section at the end of this chapter).

There are a number of benefits associated with argumentativeness. Highly argumentative individuals are more effective in their attempts to persuade others. They employ a wider range of persuasion and social influence tactics and tend to be more tenacious in their persuasion attempts (Boster and Levine 1988). Highly argumentative individuals are more resistant to compliance attempts from others and generate more counterarguments in response to persuasive encounters (Infante 1981; Kazoleas 1993). Argumentative individuals are viewed as more credible and competent communicators who are also more interested in communicating with others (Infante 1981; 1985). More recently, research by Limon and La France (2005) explored communicator traits associated with leadership emergence in work groups. As predicted by their hypotheses, college student participants low in CA and high in argumentativeness were more likely to emerge as leaders in work groups than students high in CA and low in argumentativeness. These findings illustrate the significance of this communication skill as it relates to one's potential to become a leader.

As mentioned previously, the inability to argue effectively is extremely problematic for individuals and for relationships. Research by Andonian and Droge (1992) linked males' reported verbal aggressiveness to date rape, which is an especially aggressive form of interpersonal behavior. They found that males' tendency to report acceptance of date rape myths, e.g., females might say no to sexual intercourse but really mean yes, was positively related to verbal aggressiveness and negatively related to argumentativeness. Again, this study, like others, emphasizes the constructive nature of argumentativeness and the destructive nature of verbal aggression. Similarly, in the organizational setting, the best conditions for organizational communication are when managers and employees are both high in argumentativeness and low in verbal aggression (Infante and Gorden 1987; 1989). Research on the benefits of argumentativeness in organizational contexts supports the notion of **independent-mindedness,** which refers to the extent to which employees can openly express their own opinions at work (Rancer 1998). The research on the benefits of argumentativeness in different contexts illustrates the significance of this skill.

Can we train individuals to argue more constructively? A number of programs have achieved successful results in training individuals to improve their ability to argue effectively. Anderson, Schultz, and Staley (1987) implemented cognitive training in argument and conflict management to encourage individuals to argue with one another. For individuals who are low in argumentativeness, this can be a daunting task. The researchers were pleased that they were able to see results from females who were low in argumentativeness. This study, as well as others, indicates that individuals can be trained to argue more effectively.

Assertiveness

© Yuri Arcurs, 2007, Shutterstock.

How can assertive behavior contribute to individual success?

Another form of constructive aggression is **assertiveness,** which is defined as the capability to defend your own rights and wishes while still respecting and acknowledging the rights of others. When individuals act in an assertive way, they stand up for themselves and are able to initiate, maintain, and terminate conversations to reach interpersonal goals (Richmond and Martin 1998). One way to measure assertiveness is by using the Socio-Communicative Orientation Scale developed by Richmond and McCroskey (1990). This measure includes ten assertiveness items and ten responsiveness items. Individuals are asked to report how accurately the items apply to them when they communicate with others. Some examples of assertive characteristics include: defends own beliefs, independent, and forceful. Individuals use Likert-type responses to indicate whether they strongly agree or strongly disagree that these characteristics apply to them (see the Applications section at the end of this chapter).

There are innumerable benefits associated with the assertiveness trait. By acting in an assertive manner, individuals are able to defend themselves, establish relationships, and take advantage of opportunities. Richmond and Martin (1998) note that assertive communication is more beneficial than aggressive communication and can lead to "long-term effectiveness while maintaining good relationships with others" (136). Assertive individuals are perceived as more confident and self-assured and often rated as more effective teachers and managers than unassertive individuals. When it comes to practicing safe sex, sexually assertive males are more likely than unassertive males to use condoms to protect themselves (Noar, Morokoff, and Redding 2002). Researchers say that increasing sexual assertiveness in males may lead to long-term increases in safer sexual behaviors (Noar et al. 2002).

Humor Orientation

Booth-Butterfield and Booth-Butterfield (1991) developed the concept of **humor orientation** and define it as the extent to which people use humor as well as their self-perceived appropriateness of humor production. Humor orientation (HO) can be measured using the Humor Orientation Scale (found in the Applications section at the end of this chapter), which is a seventeen-item questionnaire that assesses how often people use humor in their day-to-day communication and how effective they are at enacting humorous messages. When developing the HO measure, M. Booth-Butterfield and S. Booth-Butterfield (1991) examined the different types of humorous communication behaviors people used when they were attempting to be funny. They found that individuals scoring higher on the HO measure (also called high HO's) accessed more categories of humorous communication behaviors such as nonverbal techniques, language, expressivity, and impersonation. Persons who enacted humor frequently and effectively perceived themselves as funny, and utilized a variety of humorous communication behaviors across diverse situations. Wanzer, Booth-Butterfield, and Booth-Butterfield (1995) later confirmed that high humor-oriented people were perceived by others as funnier than low HO's when telling jokes. Thus, being humorous is not simply in the eye of the high HO.

© Zsolt Nyulaszi, 2007, Shutterstock.

Humor can add more than just laughs to the work environment.

There appear to be a variety of intrapersonal and interpersonal benefits associated with the humor orientation trait. For example, high HO's are typically less lonely (Wanzer et al. 1996a), are more adaptable in their communication with others, have greater concern for eliciting positive impressions from others, and are more affectively oriented, i.e., are more likely to use their emotions to guide their communication decisions (Wanzer et. al. 1995). Honeycutt and Brown (1998) found that traditional marital types, which usually report the highest levels of marital satisfaction (Fitzpatrick 1988), were also higher in HO than other types. When managers are perceived as more humor-oriented by their employees, they are also viewed as more likable and effective (Rizzo, Wanzer, and Booth-Butterfield 1999). Not surprisingly, there are a number of benefits for teachers who use humor effectively in the classroom. For example, students report learning more from instructors perceived as humor-oriented (Wanzer and Frymier 1999) and also report engaging in more frequent communication outside of class with humor-oriented teachers (Aylor and Opplinger 2003).

More recently, researchers have examined whether high humor-oriented individuals are more likely than low humor-oriented individuals to use humor to cope with stress and whether they benefit from this "built in" coping mechanism (Booth-Butterfield, Booth-Butterfield, and Wanzer 2006; 2005). In two different, yet similar studies, employed participants reported their HO, whether they used humor to cope with stressful situations, coping efficacy, and job satisfaction. The researchers speculated that individuals employed in highly stressful jobs, such as nursing, would: (1) benefit from the ability to cope using humor, and (2) would vary in this ability based on HO scores (Wanzer et al. 2005). Nurses who reported higher HO were more likely than low HO nurses to use humor to cope with stressful work situations and to perceive their coping strategies as effective (higher coping efficacy). In addition, humor-oriented nurses reported greater coping efficacy, leading to higher job satisfaction. Researchers found the same relationships between HO, coping and job satisfaction in a similar study of employed college students (Booth-Butterfield, Booth-Butterfield, and Wanzer 2006). These studies illustrate how humor can help individuals cope with difficult or stressful situations.

Can we train people to use humor more appropriately and effectively? Perhaps. We know that people often participate in improv classes and classes on stand-up comedy to improve their ability to deliver humorous messages. It seems likely that if people understand why certain messages are universally perceived as funny, they could be trained to improve their ability to deliver humorous messages with greater success. For now, researchers who study humor and the effects of humor recommend that individuals avoid using any type of humor based on stereotypes, or humor viewed as racist, sexist, ageist, or homophobic. Individuals need to be aware of audience characteristics that influence the way humorous content is interpreted and make attempts to use humor that is innocuous. For example, individuals who want to incorporate more humor into their day-to-day communication may use more self-disparaging humor, making certain not to overuse this type of humor as it may damage one's credibility.

Affective Orientation

Affective orientation refers to the extent to which individuals are aware of their own emotional states and use them when making behavioral decisions (Booth-Butterfield and Booth-Butterfield 1990). Individuals described as affectively oriented tend to be quite aware of their affective states and consult them before acting. Conversely, individuals described as low in affective orientation tend to be relatively unaware of their emotions and tend to reject their emotions as useful (Booth-Butterfield and Booth-Butterfield 1998). Affective Orientation (AO) can be measured via the Affective Orientation (AO15) Scale which is a fifteen-item instrument used to assess the extent to which individuals are aware of and consult their affective states and can be found in the Applications section at the end of this chapter. The revised fifteen-item measure "offers a more definitionally focused and concise operationalization of AO, exhibits minimal gender differences in mean scores and it is psychometrically more sound than the original AO scale" (Booth-Butterfield and Booth-Butterfield 1998, 180).

What are some of the benefits and/or drawbacks of higher AO? Individuals that exhibit higher levels of AO tend to be more nonverbally sensitive and better at providing comfort to others (Booth-Butterfield and Andrighetti 1993; Dolin and Booth-Butterfield 1993). Interestingly, individuals with higher AO also tend to utilize humor more frequently than lower AO individuals (Wanzer et al. 1995). The researchers suspect that higher AO individuals might use humor as one method of treating or managing negative affective states. From a relationship perspective, higher AO individuals tend to be more romantic and idealistic in their beliefs about intimate relationships (Booth-Butterfield and Booth-Butterfield 1994). More recent research on AO has examined the relationship between this trait and health behaviors. Specifically, researchers have been examining the relationships between AO and specific health practices such as smoking. Higher AO individuals are more likely to smoke than low AO's (Booth-Butterfield and Booth-Butterfield 1998). These findings are important and can be used to formulate successful persuasive campaigns. For example, the researchers note that since smokers are more affectively oriented, persuasive prevention campaigns should generate negative affective states (e.g., fear) and then connect them in some way to smoking (Booth-Butterfield and Booth-Butterfield 1998).

© Serghei Starus, 2007, Shutterstock.

What kind of campaign might work to persuade this individual to quit smoking?

Individuals may reap a variety of personal and interpersonal benefits when they exhibit higher levels of argumentativeness, assertiveness, humor orientation, and affective orientation.

While these traits are not the only ones that have proven to be beneficial for sources (e.g., cognitive complexity), they are studied frequently, and can be assessed via self-report instruments, and are linked to other positive traits and characteristics.

SUMMARY

The goal of this chapter was to help you learn more about the complex, evolving, and multidimensional nature of the self. To learn more about who we are and why we act a certain way, we explored the role of interpersonal communication and relationships in identity formation. Communication with family members, peers, and relationship partners influences how we see ourselves and how we relate to others. Our personality differences also affect the way we relate to others. In this chapter we discussed differences between state and trait approaches to studying personality and the connection between personality traits and communication behaviors. Communication based personality traits such as CA, WTC, hostility, verbal aggression, argumentativeness, assertiveness, humor orientation, and affective orientation were discussed in this chapter. Some of the behaviors associated with these communication traits can be problematic for both sources and receivers. We hope that after reading this chapter you now have a better understanding of these traits and how some can either hinder or facilitate our communication with others.

APPLICATIONS

Discussion Questions

A. Write about or discuss in small groups the person/persons that were most influential in your life. What other individuals play a role in the process of identity formation that were not identified in this chapter?

B. Visit several websites that offer suggestions for improving one's self-esteem. Critique these websites based on the following criteria: (1) Quality and quantity of information presented, (2) Inclusion of a discussion of both the pros and cons of high and low self-esteem, (3) Credentials of the individuals posting these sites, and (4) Ease of navigation of these sites. Based on your analysis of these sites, would you use these sites or send friends to these sites for information?

C. Complete one or more of the personality measures included in this chapter and score them. Recruit a friend that knows you quite well to complete the measure based on how the friend perceives your communication behaviors. Next, draw comparisons between self and other reports of the communication-based personality assessments. After examining the self and other reports closely, write about the following: (1) Are there similarities in the self and other reports, (2) Are there differences in the self and other reports, (3) Are these scores valid—do they accurately explain your communication tendencies, (4) After completing these assessments, do you feel it is necessary to change any aspect of communication behaviors? Why or why not?

ACTIVITIES

Activity #1: Personal Report of Communication Apprehension

This instrument is composed of twenty-four statements concerning feelings about communicating with other people. Please indicate the degree to which each statement applies to you by marking whether you (1) strongly agree, (2) agree, (3) are undecided, (4) disagree, or (5) strongly disagree. Work quickly; record your first impression.

______ 1. I dislike participating in group discussions.

______ 2. Generally, I am comfortable while participating in group discussions.

______ 3. I am tense and nervous while participating in group discussions.

______ 4. I like to get involved in group discussions.

______ 5. Engaging in a group discussion with new people makes me tense and nervous.

______ 6. I am calm and relaxed when participating in group discussions.

______ 7. Generally, I am nervous when I have to participate in a meeting.

______ 8. Usually I am calm and relaxed while participating in meetings.

______ 9. I am very calm and relaxed when I am called upon to express an opinion at a meeting.

______ 10. I am afraid to "press" myself at meetings.

______ 11. Communicating at meetings usually makes me uncomfortable.

______ 12. I am very relaxed when answering questions at a meeting.

______ 13. While participating in a conversation with a new acquaintance, I feel very nervous.

______ 14. I have no fear of speaking up in conversations.

______ 15. Ordinarily I am very tense and nervous in conversations.

______ 16. Ordinarily I am very calm and relaxed in conversations.

______ 17. While conversing with a new acquaintance, I feel very relaxed.

______ 18. I'm afraid to speak up in conversations.

______ 19. I have no fear of giving a speech.

______ 20. Certain parts of my body feel very tense and rigid while I am giving a speech.

______ 21. I feel relaxed while giving a speech.

______ 22. My thoughts become confused and jumbled when I am giving a speech.

______ 23. I face the prospect of giving a speech with confidence.

______ 24. While giving a speech, I get so nervous I forget facts I really know.

SCORING: In order to compute the total score follow this formula: Total = 72 + (sum of the scores from items 2, 4, 6, 8, 9, 12, 14, 16, 17, 19, 21, 23) – (sum of the scores from items 1, 3, 5, 7, 10, 11, 13, 15, 18, 20, 22, 24)

The average score for college students is typically 65.6. Scores of 80 and higher indicate high levels of CA. Scores of 50 and lower indicate lower levels of CA.

Source: From Communication Apprehension, Avoidance And Effectiveness, 5E by Virginia P. Richmond & James C. McCroskey, Published by Allyn & Bacon, Boston, MA. Copyright © 1998 by Pearson Education. Reprinted by permission of James C. McCroskey.

REFERENCES

Ainsworth, M. D. S., M. C. Blehar, E. Waters, and S. Wall. 1978. *Patterns of attachment: A psychological study of the strange situation.* Hillsdale, NJ: Erlbaum.

Allen, M., and J. Bourhis. 1996. The relationship of communication apprehension to communication behavior: A meta-analysis. *Communication Quarterly, 44,* 214–226.

Andersen, S. M., and K. Berensen. 2001. Perceiving, feeling, and wanting: Motivation and affect deriving from significant other representations and transference. In J. P. Forgas, K. D. Williams, and L. Wheeler (Eds.), *The social mind: Cognitive and motivational aspects of interpersonal behavior* (231–256). New York: Cambridge University Press.

Anderson, J., B. Schultz, and C. Courtney Staley. 1987. Training in argumentativeness: New hope for nonassertive women. *Women's Studies in Communication, 10,* 58–66.

Andonian, K. K., and D. Droge. 1992. *Verbal aggressiveness and sexual violence in dating relationships: An exploratory study of antecedents of date rape.* Paper presented at the annual meeting of the Speech Communication Association, Chicago, IL.

Aron, A. 2003. Self and close relationships. In M. R. Leary and J. P. Tangney (Eds.), *Handbook of self and identity.* New York: The Guilford Press.

Aube, J., and R. Koestner. 1992. Gender characteristics and adjustment: A longitudinal study. *Journal of Personality and Social Psychology, 70,* 535–551.

Aylor, B., and P. Opplinger. 2003. Out-of-class communication and student perceptions of instructor humor orientation and socio-communicative style. *Communication Education, 52,* 122–134.

Bandura, A. 1986. *Social foundations of thought and action.* New York: Prentice Hall.

Bargh, J. A., and T. L. Chartrand. 1999. The unbearable automaticity of being. *American Psychologist, 54,* 462–479.

Bargh, J. A., K. McKenna, and G. M. Fitzsimons. 2002. Can you see the real me? Activation and expression of the "true self" on the Internet. *Journal of Social Issues, 58,* 33–48.

Baumeister, R. F. 1998. The self. In D. Gilbert, S. T. Fiske, and G. Lindzey (Eds.), *The Handbook of social psychology* (680–740). New York: Oxford Press.

Baumeister, R. F., and K. D. Vohs. 2003. Self-regulation and the executive function of the self. In M. R. Leary and J. P. Tangney (Eds.), *Handbook of self and identity.* New York: The Guilford Press.

Baumeister, R. F., J. D. Campbell, J. I. Krueger, and K. Vohs. 2003. Does high self-esteem cause better performance, interpersonal success, happiness or healthier lifestyles? *Psychological Science in the Public Interest, 4,* 1–44.

Bayer, C. L., and D. J. Cegala. 1992. Trait verbal aggressiveness and argumentativeness: Relations with parenting style. *Western Journal of Communication, 56,* 301–310.

Beatty, M. J., J. C. McCroskey, and A. D. Heisel. 1998. Communication apprehension as temperamental expression: A communibiological perspective. *Communication Monographs, 65,* 197–219.

Bell, R. A., and J. A. Daly. 1984. The affinity-seeking function of communication. *Communication Monographs, 49,* 91–115.

Berger, B. A., J. C. McCroskey, and V. A. Richmond. 1984. Communication apprehension and shyness. In W. N. Tinally and R. S. Beardsley (Eds.), *Communication in pharmacy practice: A practical guide for students and practitioners* (128–158). Philadelphia, PA: Lea & Febiger.

Berne, E. 1964. *Games people play.* New York: Grove.

Booth-Butterfield, M., and A. Andrighetti. 1993. *The role of affective orientation and nonverbal sensitivity in the interpretation of communication in acquaintance rape.* Paper presented at the annual convention of the Eastern Communication Association, New Haven, CT.

Booth-Butterfield, M., and S. Booth-Butterfield. 1990. Conceptualizing affect as information in communication production. *Human Communication Research, 16,* 451–476.

———. 1991. Individual differences in the communication of humorous messages. *Southern Communication Journal, 56,* 32–40.

———. 1994. The affective orientation to communication: Conceptual and empirical distinctions. *Communication Quarterly, 42,* 331–344.

———. 1996. Using your emotions: Improving the measurement of affective orientation. *Communication Research Reports, 13,* 157–163.

———. 1998. Emotionality and affective orientation (171–190). In McCroskey et al. (Eds.), *Communication and personality.* Cresskill, NJ: Hampton Press.

Booth-Butterfield, M., S. Booth-Butterfield, and M. B. Wanzer. 2006. Funny students cope better: Patterns of humor enactment and coping effectiveness. *Communication Quarterly.* (In Press)

Boster, F. J., and T. Levine. 1988. Individual differences and compliance-gaining message selection: The effects of verbal aggressiveness, argumentativeness, dogmatism, and negativism. *Communication Research Reports, 5,* 114–119.

Bowlby, J. 1969. *Attachment and loss: Vol. 1. Attachment.* New York: Basic Books.

———. 1973. *Attachment and loss: Vol. 3. Loss, sadness, and depression.* New York: Basic Books.

Chory-Assad, R. M., and M. Paulsel. 2004. Classroom justice: Student aggression and resistance as reactions to perceived unfairness. *Communication Education, 53,* 253–273.

Cook, W. W., and D. M. Medley. 1954. Proposed hostility and pharisaic-virtue scales for the MMPI. *Journal of Applied Psychology, 38,* 414–418.

Cooley, C. H. 1902. *Human nature and the social order.* New York: Scribner's.

Daly, J. A. 2002. Personality and interpersonal communication. In Knapp and Daly (Eds.), *Handbook of interpersonal communication* (133–180). Thousand Oaks, CA: Sage Publications.

Daly, J. A. and A. M. Bippus. 1998. Personality and interpersonal communication: Issues and directions. In McCroskey et al. (Eds.), *Communication and personality* (1–40). Cresskill, NJ: Hampton Press.

Daly, J. A., V. P. Richmond, and S. Leth. 1979. Social communicative anxiety and the personnel selection process: Testing the similarity effect in selection decisions. *Human Communication Research, 6,* 18–32.

Darley, J. M., and R. H. Fazio. 1980. Expectancy confirmation processes arising in the social interaction sequence. *American Psychologist, 35,* 867–881.

Dolin, D., and M. Booth-Butterfield. 1993. Reach out and touch someone: Analysis of nonverbal comforting responses. *Communication Quarterly, 41,* 383–393.

Dye, L. 2004. Researchers design games to boost self-esteem. Retrieved on 12/20/2006 from *abcnews.go.com/Technology/print?id.*

Epstein, S. 1973. The self-concept revisited: Or a theory of a theory. *American Psychologist, 28,* 404–416.

Felson, R. B. 1989. Parents and reflected appraisal process: A longitudinal analysis. *Journal of Personality and Social Psychology, 56,* 965–971.

Festinger, L. 1954. A theory of social comparison processes. *Human Relations, 7,* 117–140.

Finkel, E. J., and W. K. Campbell. 2001. Self-control and accommodation in close relationships: An interdependence analysis. *Journal of Personality and Social Psychology, 81,* 263–271.

Fitzpatrick, M. A. 1988. *Between husbands and wives: Communication in marriage.* Newbury Park, CA: Sage.

Goffman, E. 1959. *The presentation of self in everyday life.* Garden City, NY: Doubleday.

Gottman, J. M. 1999. *The marriage clinic: A scientific based marital therapy.* New York: Norton.

Greenwald, A. G., and S. J. Breckler. 1985. To whom is the self presented? In B. R. Schlenker (Ed.), *The self and social life* (126–145). New York: McGraw-Hill.

Guilford, J. P. 1959. *Personality.* New York: McGraw-Hill.

Harris, T. 1969. *I'm OK, you're OK.* New York: Harper & Row.

Honeycutt, J., and R. Brown. 1998. Did you hear the one about?: Typological and spousal differences in the planning of jokes and sense of humor in marriage. *Communication Quarterly, 46,* 342–352.

Houck, G. M., and A. M. Spegman. 1999. The development of self: Theoretical understandings and conceptual underpinnings. *Infants and Young Children, 12,* 1–16.

Huebner, D. M., C. J. Nemeroff, and M. C. Davis. 2005. Do hostility and neuroticism confound associations between perceived discrimination and depressive symptoms? *Journal of Social and Clinical Psychology, 24,* 723–740.

Infante, D. A. 1981. Trait argumentativeness as a predictor of communicative behavior in situations requiring argument. *Central States Speech Journal, 32,* 265–272.

———. 1985. Inducing women to be more argumentative: Source credibility effects. *Journal of Applied Communication Research, 13,* 33–44.

———. 1987. Aggressiveness. In J. C. McCroskey and J. A. Daly (Eds.), *Personality and interpersonal communication* (157–192). Newbury Park, CA: Sage.

———. 1988. *Arguing constructively.* Prospect Heights, Illinois: Waveland Press.
———. 1995. Teaching students to understand and control verbal aggression. *Communication Education, 44,* 51–63.
Infante, D. A., and W. I. Gorden. 1987. Superior and subordinate communication profiles: Implications for independent-mindedness and upward effectiveness. *Central States Speech Journal, 38,* 73–80.
———. 1989. Argumentativeness and affirming communicator style as predictors of satisfaction/dissatisfaction with subordinates. *Communication Quarterly, 37,* 81–90.
———. 1991. How employees see the boss: Test of an argumentative and affirming model of superiors' communicative behavior. *Western Journal of Speech Communication, 55,* 294–304.
Infante, D. A., and A. S. Rancer. 1982. A conceptualization and measure of argumentativeness. *Journal of Personality Assessment, 46,* 72–80.
Infante, D. A., B. L. Riddle, C. L. Horvath, and S. A. Tumlin. 1992. Verbal aggressiveness: Messages and reasons. *Communication Quarterly, 40,* 116–126.
Infante, D. A., and C. J. Wigley. 1986. Verbal aggressiveness: An interpersonal model and measure. *Communication Monographs, 53,* 61–69.
Infante, D. A., T. A. Chandler, and J. E. Rudd. 1989. Test of an argumentative skill deficiency model of interspousal violence. *Communication Monographs, 56,* 163–177.
Jung, C. G. 1953. *Psychological reflections.* New York: Harper and Row.
Karney, B. R., and T. N. Bradbury. 1995. The longitudinal course of marital quality and stability: A review of theory, methods, and research. *Psychological Bulletin, 118,* 3–34.
Kazoleas, D. 1993. The impact of argumentativeness on resistance to persuasion. *Human Communication Research, 20,* 118–137.
Keating, C. 1984. *Dealing with difficult people: How you can come out on top in personality conflicts.* New York: Paulist Press.
Koch, E. J., and J. A. Shepperd. 2004. Is self-complexity linked to better coping? A review of the literature. *Journal of Personality, 72,* 727–760.
Kopper, B. A., and D. L. Epperson. 1996. The experience and expression of anger: Relationships with gender, role socialization, depression and mental health functioning. *Journal of Counseling Psychology, 43,* 158–165.
Lieberman, A. F. 1977. Preschooler's competence with a peer: Relations with attachment and peer experience. *Child Development, 48,* 1277–1287.
Lieberman, A. F., and J. H. Pawl. 1988. Clinical applications of attachment theory. In J. Belsky and T. Nezworski (Eds.), *Clinical implications of attachment* (327–351). Hillsdale, NJ: Erlbaum.
Limon, S. M., and B. H. LaFrance. 2005. Communication traits and leadership emergence: Examining the impact of argumentativeness, communication apprehension and verbal aggressiveness in work groups. *Southern Communication Journal, 70,* 123–133.
Linville, P. W. 1985. Self-complexity and affective extremity: Don't put all your eggs in one cognitive basket. *Social Cognition, 3,* 94–120.
———. 1987. Self-complexity as a cognitive buffer against stress-related illness and depression. *Journal of Personality and Social Psychology, 52,* 663–676.
Lippert, L. R., B. S. Titsworth, and S. K. Hunt. 2005. The ecology of academic risk: Relationships between communication apprehension, verbal aggression, supportive communication, and students' academic risk. *Communication Studies, 56,* 1–21.
Markus, H., and E. Wurf. 1987. The dynamic self-concept: A social psychological perspective. *Annual Review of Psychology, 38,* 299–337.
Maxwell, J. C. 2002. *The seventeen essential qualities of a team player.* Nashville, TN: Thomas Nelson Publishers.
McCroskey, J. C. 1977. Oral communication apprehension: A summary of recent theory and research. *Human Communication Research, 4,* 78–96.
———. 1978. Validity of the PRCA as an index of oral communication apprehension. *Communication Monographs, 45,* 192–203.
McCroskey, J. C. 2006. Personal communication with the author.
McCroskey, J. C., and M. J. Beatty. 1984. Communication apprehension and accumulated communication state anxiety experiences: A research note. *Communication Monographs, 51,* 79–84.
McCroskey, J. C., J. A. Daly, and G. A. Sorensen. 1976. Personality correlates of communication apprehension. *Human Communication Research, 2,* 376–380.
———. 1995. Correlates of compulsive communication: Quantitative and qualitative characteristics. *Communication Quarterly, 43,* 39–52.
———. 1998. Willingness to communicate. In McCroskey et al. (Eds.), *Communication and personality* (119–132). Cresskill, NJ: Hampton Press.

McCroskey, J. C., and V. P. Richmond. 1987. Willingness to communicate. In J. C. McCroskey and J. A. Daly (Eds.), *Personality and interpersonal communication* (129–156). Newbury Park, CA: Sage.

McKenna, K. Y. A., A. S. Green, and M. E. J. Gleason. 2002. Relationship formation on the Internet: What's the big attraction? *Journal of Social Issues, 58,* 9–31.

Mead, G. H. 1934. *Mind, self, and society.* Chicago: University of Chicago Press.

Meeus, W., and M. Dekovic. 1995. Identity development, parental and peer support in adolescence: Results of a national Dutch survey. *Adolescence, 30,* 931–945.

Mizco, N. 2004. Humor ability, unwillingness to communicate, loneliness, and perceived stress: Testing a security theory. *Communication Studies, 55,* 209–226.

Myers, S. A., and A. D. Johnson. 2003. Verbal aggression and liking in interpersonal relationships. *Communication Research Reports, 20,* 90–96.

Noar, S. M., P. J. Morokoff, and C. A. Redding. 2002. Sexual assertiveness in heterosexually active men: A test of three samples. *AIDS Education and Prevention, 14,* 330–342.

Park, K. A., and E. Waters. 1988. Traits and relationships in developmental perspective. In S. Duck (Ed.) *Handbook of personal relationships: Theory, research, and interventions* (161–176). Chichester: John Wiley & Sons Ltd.

Peluso, P. R., J. P. Peluso, J. F. White, and R. M. Kern. 2004. A comparison of attachment theory and individual psychology: A review of the literature. *Journal of Counseling and Development, 82,* 139–145.

Pope, M. K., T. W. Smith, and F. Rhodewalt. 1990. Cognitive, behavioral and affective correlates of the Cook and Medley Hostility Scale. *Journal of Personality Assessment, 54,* 501–514.

Rancer, A. S. 1998. Argumentativeness. In McCroskey et al. (Eds.), *Communication and personality* (149–170). Cresskill, NJ: Hampton Press.

Richmond, V. P., and D. K. Roach. 1992. Willingness to communicate and employee success in U.S. organizations. *Journal of Applied Communication,* 95–115.

Richmond, V. P., and J. C. McCroskey. 1990. Reliability and separation of factors on the assertiveness-responsiveness measure. *Psychological Reports, 67,* 449–450.

Richmond, V. P., and M. M. Martin. 1998. Sociocommunicative style and sociocommunicative orientation. In McCroskey et al. (Eds.), *Communication and personality.* Hampton Press: Cresskill, NJ.

Rizzo, B., M. B. Wanzer, and M. Booth-Butterfield. 1999. Individual differences in managers' use of humor: Subordinate perceptions of managers' humor orientation, effectiveness, and humor behaviors. *Communication Research Reports, 16,* 370–376.

Rogge, R. D., T. N. Bradbury, K. Halweg, J. Engl, and F. Thurmaier. 2006. Predicting marital distress and dissolution: Refining the two-factor hypothesis. *Journal of Family Psychology, 20,* 156–159.

Schlenker, B. 1984. Identities, identifications and relationships. In V. Derlega (Ed.), *Communication, intimacy and close relationships.* New York: Academic Press.

———. 1985. Identity and self-identification. In B. R. Schlenker (Ed.), *The self and social life* (65–99). New York: McGraw-Hill.

Self-Improvement. (n.d.). Retrieved September 29, 2005, from *http://www.mygoals.com/content/self-improvement.html.*

Shackelford, T. K. 2001. Self-esteem in marriage. *Personality and Individual Differences, 30,* 371–391.

Smith, T. W. 1994. Concepts and methods in the study of anger, hostility, and health. In A. W. Siegman and T. W. Smith (Eds.), *Anger, hostility, and the heart* (23–42). Hillsdale, NJ: Erlbaum.

Snyder, M., E. D. Tanke, and E. Berscheid. 1977. Social perception and interpersonal behavior: The self-fulfilling nature of social stereotypes. *Journal of Personality and Social Psychology, 35,* 656–666.

Spitzberg, B. H. and W. R. Cupach. 1984. *Interpersonal communication competence.* Newbury Park, CA: Sage.

Sroufe, L. A. 1988. The role of infant-caregiver attachment in development. In J. Belsky and T. Nezworski (Eds.), *Clinical implications of attachment* (18–38). Hillsdale, NJ: Erlbaum.

Surra, C. A., C. R. Gray, N. Cottle, and T. M. Boettcher. 2004. Research on mate selection and premarital relationships: What do we really know? In A. L. Vangelisti (Ed.), *Handbook of family communication* (53–82). Mahwah, NJ: Lawrence Erlbaum.

Swann, W. R. 1985. The self as architect of social reality. In B. R. Schlenker (Ed.), *The self and social life* (100–126). New York: McGraw-Hill.

Tesser, A. 2003. Self-evaluation. In M. R. Leary and J. P. Tangney (Eds.), *Handbook of self and identity.* New York: The Guilford Press.

Tesser A., J. V. Wood, and D. A. Stapel. 2002. Introduction: An emphasis on motivation. In A. Tesser, D. A. Stapel, and J. V. Wood (Eds.), *Self and motivation: Emerging psychological perspectives* (3–11). Washington, DC: American Psychological Association.

Tesser, A., R. B. Felson, and J. M. Suls (Eds.). 2000. *Psychological perspectives on self and identity.* Washington, DC: American Psychological Association.

Vallacher, R. R., and A. Nowak. 2000. Landscapes of self-reflection: Mapping the peaks and valleys of personal assessment. In A. Tesser, R. B. Felson, and J. M. Suls (Eds.), *Psychological perspectives on self and identity* (35–65). Washington, DC: American Psychological Association.

Wanzer, M. B., and A. B. Frymier. 1999. The relationship between student perceptions of instructor humor and student's reports of learning. *Communication Education, 48,* 48–62.

Wanzer, M. B., M. Booth-Butterfield, and S. Booth-Butterfield. 1995. The funny people: A source orientation to the communication of humor. *Communication Quarterly, 43,* 142–154.

———. 1996. Are funny people popular? An examination of humor orientation, verbal aggressiveness, and social attraction. *Communication Quarterly, 44,* 42–52.

———. 2005. "If we didn't use humor, we'd cry:" Humorous coping communication in health care settings. *Journal of Health Communication, 10,* 105–125.

Wigley, C. J. 1998. Verbal aggressiveness. In McCroskey et al. (Eds.), *Communication and personality* (191–214). Cresskill, NJ: Hampton Press.

Wood, J. T. 2001. *Interpersonal communication: Everyday encounters. (3rd ed.)* Belmont, CA: Wadsworth Publishing Company.

Zajonc, R. B., R. K. Adelmann, S. B. Murphy, and R. N. Niedenthal. 1987. Convergence in the appearance of spouses. *Motivation and Emotion, 11,* 335–346.

Zakahi, W. R., and R. L. Duran. 1985. Loneliness, communication competence, and communication apprehension: Extension and replication. *Communication Quarterly, 33,* 50–60.

chapter

5 Perception of Yourself and Others

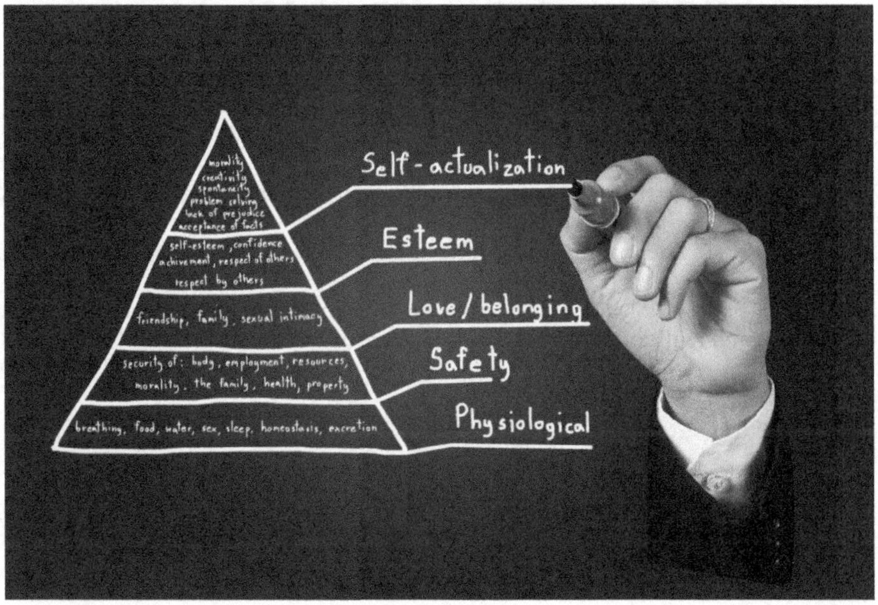

OBJECTIVES

- Explain how attributions are made.
- Explain how self-perception theory built on Kelley and Heider's work on attributions.
- Describe and explain the postulates of self-perception theory.
- Explain how self-perception theory is used to persuade.
- Describe two sequential request strategies and how they relate to self-perception theory.

KEY TERMS

Attributions
Consensus
Consistency
Counter-attitudinal advocacy
Dispositional attributions
Distinctiveness
Door-in-the-face (DITF)
External factors
Foot-in-the-door (FITD)
Internal factors
Locus of control

Non-normative behavior	**Pro-attitudinal advocacy**	**Situational attributions**

Fritz Heider's work with balance theory (1946, 1958) led to the development of a series of consistency theories culminating in the development of cognitive dissonance theory, a widely researched and valued theory. Ironically, Heider's (1958) work with interpersonal impression formation and attributions created a path of research culminating in a theory that challenged cognitive dissonance theory: self-perception theory. Just as cognitive dissonance theory built on prior work in the consistency realm, self-perception theory evolved from work in impression formation and the attribution processes. This chapter reviews the early basis for that work and explains self-perception theory.

HEIDER'S INTERPERSONAL IMPRESSION FORMATION AND ATTRIBUTION

In his examination of interpersonal relationships as well as persuasion, Heider (1958) focused on how people create their impressions of other people. How we relate to other people depends in part on what we think about them and why we believe they engaged in any given behavior. To make sense of the world around us, we create explanations for why things happen around us. The process of creating causal explanations for why things happen is referred to as **attributions**. Heider's work focused on how we make those attributions.

One of the central tenets of Heider's theory is that humans believe that behavior is *causal,* or that there is a reason for behavior. That cause can be **internal** or **external factors**. This is also referred to as **locus of control**—in other words, is the source of control for that behavior internal or external? As we observe the behavior of those around us, we can infer that some behavior is caused by factors internal to the individual. For example, if you observe a classmate arrive late to class just about every day, you might make an internal attribution. An *internal attribution* is when you infer the cause of the behavior as being within the person. You might suppose that the classmate doesn't care about being timely; thus, you would infer that the late arrival is a result of a personality characteristic of the individual.

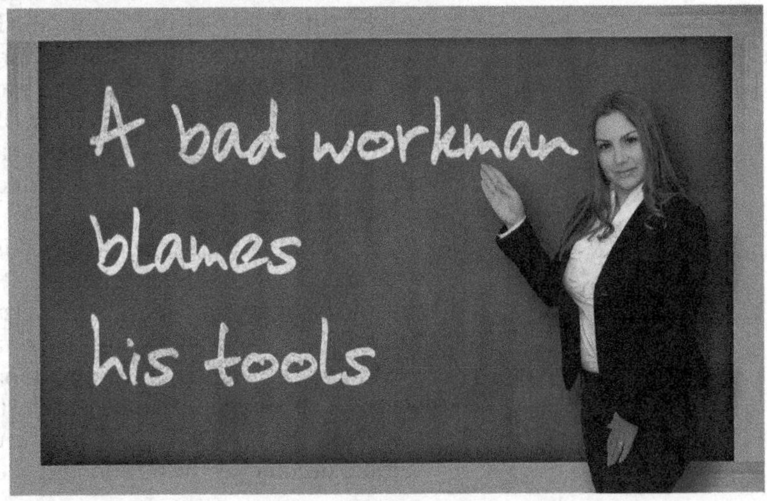

Alternatively, you could make an external attribution about your classmate's behavior. If that same classmate regularly arrived late but was out of breath and sweaty, you might guess that the classmate had a distant class right before this class that made it difficult to arrive on time. This guess would suggest that it wasn't an internal or personality characteristic that resulted in the behavior (late arrival) but instead external circumstances were the cause of the behavior—that is, an external attribution. An *external attribution* is when you infer the cause of the behavior as being outside the person. The attribution you make in this case would affect how you view the classmate. If you consider being late to be a negative behavior, then whether you made an internal attribution (blamed the lateness on some internal characteristic) or made an external attribution (blamed the lateness on some external factor) would affect your perception of your classmate.

The same attribution process occurs when you observe positive behavior, but the resulting impression of the individual is different. If you observed a roommate receiving an A on an exam in a persuasion class, you might make an internal attribution. In this case, you might assume that the good grade was the result of a bright and talented student working hard. However, you could also make an external attribution for this result. You might assume that the exam was easy or that your roommate was lucky in this case. Here, if you saw an A on an exam as positive behavior, you would think more of someone you made internal attributions about and less of someone you made external attributions about.

KELLEY'S ATTRIBUTION THEORY

Heider's work generated a great deal of attention. Another scholar, Harold Kelley (1967, 1971), elaborated on Heider's work on impression formation and developed attribution theory. Kelley was interested in how or why people made the choice of internal or external attributions. Kelley referred to internal attributions or personal characteristics as **dispositional attributions** and to external attributions based in influences around the individual as **situational attributions**. He argued that we operate as scientists in observing behavior and that some general guidelines lead us to make internal or external attributions for behavior.

The first factor involved in deciding whether the behavior is to be attributed to dispositional or situational factors is **consensus**. A behavior would have high consensus if most others behave the same way in that situation. In the example of your classmate who regularly arrives late to class, consensus could help you decide whether to make a dispositional or situational attribution. If most students in the class regularly arrived late, you are more likely to make a situational attribution for the lateness behavior and less likely to make a dispositional attribution about your classmate. If most students regularly arrive late, you might guess that the professor did not care about timeliness or that the class regularly started late. Those are factors of the situation rather than personal characteristics of your classmate. Thus, when a person's behavior reflects the consensus of behavior for others, we are more likely to make a situational or external attribution.

A second factor Kelley identified is **consistency**. This refers to whether the observed behavior occurs over time. If your classmate arrived late to class only once and was on time for all other class periods (low consistency), you would be less likely to make a dispositional or internal attribution. Instead, you might guess that something situational came up, such as a flat tire, a broken alarm clock, or a family emergency. However, if your classmate arrived late to class most days (high consistency), you would be more likely to make a dispositional or internal attribution and guess that the classmate did not care about being on time. The consistency of the late behavior would lead most of us to guess that it was a result of a lack of concern about timeliness on the part of the individual, a personality characteristic. Thus, consistency of behavior over time is more likely to lead to dispositional or internal attributions.

Distinctiveness is the third factor Kelley identified that affects the kind of attributions made about the behavior of others. This refers to how different the situation is among targets or situations. For example, if the classmate who arrived late to class was also late to student organization meetings, parties, and dates, you would probably make a dispositional or internal attribution because the lateness behavior was not distinctive for just that class. On the other hand, if the classmate arrived late to class regularly but was on time for meetings, parties, and dates, you would be more likely to make a situational or external attribution for the pattern of late arrival at class. You might guess that the student had another class before this one that ran late regularly or had a job that ended close to when class began. Thus, behavior that is distinctive to a situation is more likely to be attributed to situational or external factors.

In addition to Kelley's three factors, **non-normative behavior** is generally perceived as having an internal or dispositional cause. Non-normative behavior is behavior not standard or typical for a situation. When people behave in ways that are expected by social norms, we tend to assume that dispositional factors are not involved. When people violate social norms and expectations, however, then we tend to look for a cause for that behavior. For example, if your classmate regularly came to class on time, you probably would not assume that the person was particularly concerned about timeliness. Instead, you would expect that behavior is part of the social norms surrounding class attendance. It is when someone violates that norm and shows up late to class that internal or dispositional attributions are likely to be made.

Table 5.1 Attribution Summary Table

	CONSENSUS	CONSISTENCY	DISTINCTIVENESS
High	External	Internal	External
Low	Internal	External	Internal

Finally, we also tend to make internal attributions when *situational factors are lacking*. If a classmate arrived late to class regularly and you had no outside class experiences with that student, you would probably guess that the lateness resulted from a dispositional characteristic of a lack of concern for time. It may be that the student had a prior class at a distance across campus that made it difficult to come to this class on time, but in the absence of the student being out of breath and sweaty or announcing it, there would be no situational cues to tell you this. Research has shown that when there are less obvious situational cues in interpersonal situations, perceivers tend to make dispositional attributions.

Kelley's work, which built on Heider's research, is very useful in analyzing interpersonal relationships and impression formation, but it has also been used in persuasion settings. After all, the impressions we form about the source of a message can influence the acceptability of that message. Consider the example of a politician who visits a factory to talk with autoworkers before an election. Often, such politicians will don a hard hat and try performing some of the work done at the plant. In this case, the politician wants voters to make a dispositional attribution for the visit. The desire is for voters to believe that the politician made the visit because of genuine concern for the working class. However, some might make a situational attribution and guess that the politician made the visit because of the upcoming election. Many times, in persuasion, sources try to influence the kinds of attributions that receivers make about them.

We can also use Kelley's attribution factors to evaluate persuasive messages. If a message represented consensus in that it was reflective of the viewpoint of many people, represented consistency by being presented in different contexts to different people, and was distinctive by being tailored to the topic of the discussion, then the public should be more likely to accept the message. Eagly and Chaiken (1994, p. 353) provided a good example:

> Consider, for example, Professor Bargh's assertion that The Psychology of Attitudes is a great book. You will probably regard this statement as a valid description of the book's quality (entity attribution) and be persuaded by it to the extent that other faculty and students have also praised this book (high consensus), Professor Bargh has praised the book at various class meetings and cited it in his own writings (high consistency), and Professor Bargh has been critical of other recently published psychology books and articles (high distinctiveness).

In this case, the attributions were being made about a book rather than a person, but the attributions about the person's actions along the three attribution factors identified by Kelley were what led to the attribution about the book. Thus, acceptance of a message can be explained by attribution theory. However, like much research and theory development, attribution theory served as the basis for the development of another theory, self-perception theory.

SELF-PERCEPTION THEORY

Heider and Kelley's work generated considerable attention and as noted above, the theory was applied to persuasion. Daryl Bem's (1967, 1972) **self-perception theory** is based on the principles of Heider and Kelley's work on attribution theory. However, Bem's work was also in part a reaction to cognitive dissonance theory. Bem argued that self-perception theory could explain the same research findings that cognitive dissonance theory did and that self-perception theory could also explain findings that cognitive dissonance theory could not.

Self-perception theory relies on situational and dispositional attributions similar to attribution theory, but Bem argues that this is not just true in how we view others. Instead, we use the same attribution process to make sense of our own behavior. Within this theory, *we are observers of ourselves as we are observers of others,* and we use a similar process to make attributions about ourselves. According to self-perception theory, persuasion involves a person acting and then figuring out why he or she behaved in that way in order to understand his or her own attitudes.

Self-Perception Theory Postulates

Bem advanced two *postulates* for self-perception theory. The first is that "individuals come to 'know' their own attitudes, emotions, and other internal states partially by inferring them from observations of their own overt behavior and/or the circumstances in which this behavior occurs" (Bem, 1972, p. 2). In the previous examples of making interpersonal attributions about others, we inferred the cause of behavior by noting the behavior and any situational factors that might account for it. In persuasion, Bem suggests, receivers of messages look at themselves and make attributions in the same way.

The second postulate is that "to the extent internal cues are weak, ambiguous, or uninterpretable, the individual is functionally in the same position as an outside observer, an observer who must necessarily rely upon those same external cues to infer the individual's internal states" (Bem, 1972, p. 2). In this case, if you are the target of a persuasive message and are unaware of any situational influences on your behavior, then you are likely to make a dispositional attribution about your behavior. In persuasion terms, that generally means you perceive your attitudes as being in line with your behavior.

Recall the Festinger and Carlsmith (1959) study of cognitive dissonance theory described in Chapter 6 involving the boring task for which participants were paid $1 or $20 to lie to others. Take a moment to review this study and how cognitive dissonance theory explained the results. Self-perception theory can also explain the results of this study using the two postulates set out by Bem. In the study, participants engaged in the behavior of lying to other students about how interesting the task was and were paid either $1 or $20. Self-perception theory explains the results as follows. As the participants tried to decide how boring the task of putting spools on trays and turning pegs for an hour was, they were in the position of outside observers and looked to the situational cues to help them understand their internal states. Those who were paid $1 to lie to others saw a very weak situational cue for their behavior. Because the external cue was so weak, they needed to infer an internal reason for lying. In this case, it meant that participants saw their attitudes toward the task as more positive because there was no external explanation for their behavior.

Those who were paid $20 to lie to others, however, saw a situational cue that explained their behavior. They could infer that they were willing to lie for the researcher for the money (an external factor), and thus they had no reason to infer any internal reason for doing so. Those participants made a more negative evaluation of the task. If you were an outside observer, you would probably have made the same conclusions about another person's behavior. Thus, self-perception theory can explain the same research finding that was used to support cognitive dissonance theory.

Self-Perception Theory versus Interpersonal Impression Formation

Bem argued that the attribution process in persuasion via self-perception theory is similar to the attribution process in interpersonal impression formation, but he did note four differences when we examine our own behavior versus the behavior of others. First, when we examine our own behavior, we are an **insider** rather than an **outsider.** We have access to more information about ourselves than any outside person could. For example, we know internally if we are making an effort to work hard on a challenge, but that internal thought process would not be evident to outsiders. We would also be aware of situational factors such as a flat tire that caused us to be late to a class, whereas an external observer would lack this knowledge. In addition, we have more **intimate** knowledge than a **stranger** has about us. We have knowledge about our past behaviors that a stranger observing our behavior would lack. For example, we know if we are late to all kinds of events or to just the class in question. Third, we have more concerns for **ourselves** than we do for **others.** We often look at situations with an intent, conscious or not, of trying to protect our self-esteem. People tend to look for the best in themselves more consistently than they do with other people. This would motivate us to seek out more external reasons for negative behavior and more internal reasons for positively evaluated behavior. Finally, we focus on our **situation** rather than the **action** when looking at ourselves. We tend to focus on situational cues more than on our own behavior, but outside observers tend to focus on the behavior more. All four of these differences are subtle, but we generally do not tend to use the same processes to view ourselves as others use to view us.

A Self-Perception Model

Self-perception works in persuasion as a two-part model. First, *the individual must be induced to act.* That action can be any overt behavior, including things such as making a verbal statement, signing a petition, test driving a car, or sampling a food. In addition, *the environmental cues must be arranged so that a dispositional attribution results.* Too much pressure or forcing cooperation would lead to situational attributions. For persuasion to occur, the individual needs to make a dispositional attribution and think that his or her attitude led to the behavior. Consider the $1/$20 study discussed previously. For attitude change about how boring the task was to occur, there had to be little external justification ($1). A stronger pressure to lie ($20) led to situational attribution, so no attitude change about the boring nature of the task resulted.

Grocery stores frequently offer free samples to increase sales of particular products. Self-perception theory provides a rationale for the success of this sales strategy. In this case, a kind person offers the shopper a free sample. There is little external pressure to accept the sample, but most shoppers do so anyway. Once the sample is eaten, the shopper has to decide if the product was good and should be purchased. Self-perception theory would suggest that, given the lack of strong external cues, the shopper would look internally to find out why she or he ate the sample and conclude that it is probably because the food is good. If that is the case, the shopper is more likely to purchase the product. Of course, nothing works 100 percent of the time, but self-perception theory suggests that this would lead to a greater level of success and thus a greater level of sales.

As was the case with other theories, there are situations in persuasion where self-perception theory is most useful. Mary John Smith (1982) suggests that self-perception works in two kinds of persuasive situations. The first is "the formation of new attitudinal schemata in those cases where a person's attitudes are weak, ambivalent, or nonexistent" (p. 146). This is tied to Bem's second postulate. When we don't have preexisting attitudes, then our internal cues are weak, ambiguous, or uninterpretable, which is when, Bem argued, we operate as an outside observer relying on external cues to infer our own attitudes.

Self-perception theory can explain how people respond to marketing campaigns for new products. When Swiffer® dust cloths were introduced, it was a new kind of product unfamiliar to people. Not having any previous experience, people looked for external cues to discover how they felt about the new product. Marketers set up those external cues with demonstrations, free samples, coupons, and advertisements. People were encouraged to engage in behavior with the product, and then attributions needed to be made for those actions. Once having tried the product, individuals were more likely to develop positive attitudes about the product.

The second situation Smith (1982) identified as working best with self-perception theory is "the reinforcement and intensification of presently held attitudes" (p. 146). People who speak in favor of positions they currently support (or positions within their LOA in social judgment theory terms) are considered to be engaging in **pro-attitudinal advocacy**. Cognitive dissonance theory worked primarily with **counter-attitudinal advocacy**, in which individuals were induced to speak against their current attitudes. In the much-discussed \$1/\$20 study, subjects were asked to engage in counter-attitudinal advocacy and to tell others that the task was interesting when it was really boring.

Although self-perception can be used to explain these results, it is generally more useful in situations where individuals are being reinforced to maintain current attitudes or are being encouraged to take a positive stance to a stronger level. For example, students who already believe that they work hard and earn their grades would be engaging in pro-attitudinal advocacy in arguing against strict measures to control grade inflation. Proposals to limit the number of As in any given class or to require all class grade averages to be at a 2.0 level on a 4-point scale would be easy to reject. This would represent moving students farther along a continuum in the direction they were already inclined.

Eagly and Chaiken (1994) added an additional factor that limits the circumstances in which self-perception theory is useful. After a review of research, these scholars argued that *attitudes that are held strongly or are of particular importance to the receiver are less open to influence through self-perception*. In these cases, individuals do not need to seek external cues (or to observe their own behavior) to understand their internal states. They have invested a lot in those attitudes and beliefs and know exactly what they are. As explained with social judgment theory in Chapter 5 and the elaboration likelihood model in Chapter 9, involvement in a topic can modify responses to persuasion. People respond to persuasion differently when they are involved in the topic. Topics that individuals hold strong feelings about, such as on abortion, would be difficult to change with self-perception theory.

RESEARCH WITH SELF-PERCEPTION THEORY

An early study that supported the attribution and self-perception approaches to persuasion involved injecting participants with epinephrine, a stimulant (Schachter & Singer, 1962). Participants were told that the study involved investigation of the effects of a vitamin mixture called "suproxin" on vision. They were then placed into four groups. Three of the groups received the epinephrine injection; the fourth was a control group. The control group was given a placebo injection of saline solution, which had no effect. The first epinephrine group was *informed* about the side effects to expect from receiving the injection including an elevated heart rate, shaking hands, and warm or flushed faces. The second epinephrine group was *misinformed* about the effects of the injection; they were told that the expected side effects included numb feet, itching, and a slight headache. The final epinephrine group was left *ignorant* of the drug's effects and was told that it would cause no side effects at all.

The participants were asked to wait in the research room for about 20 minutes to let the supposed suproxin get into their system. Each participant was dealt with individually, and during the wait a confederate posing as another research participant was brought into the room. The confederate was instructed to act either *euphoric* or *angry* during the waiting period. In the euphoric condition, the confederate doodled on paper, made paper basketballs and shot them at wastebaskets, made paper airplanes, shot paper balls with a rubber band, and used a hula hoop that was lying in the room. The confederate talked about his activities and invited the participant to join him. In the anger condition, the two students were asked to fill out a long questionnaire while they waited. The confederate complained about the injection, complained about the questions, and got angry about personal and insulting questions. Finally, the confederate ripped up the questionnaire and stomped out of the room.

Participants' responses were measured in several ways. Secret observers of the participants' behavior rated the behavior according to the level of emotion displayed. In addition, each participant was asked to fill out a questionnaire after the waiting period. Participants were primarily questioned about their reactions to the suproxin but were also questioned about the emotions they experienced. Two five-point scales were used to evaluate how irritated, angry, and/or annoyed the participants felt, as well as how good or happy they felt. Finally, each participant's pulse was measured before the injection and after the waiting period.

According to self-perception theory, participants should base evaluation of their own attitudes on observations of their own behavior (in this case, the arousal from the drug) and the situational cues surrounding that behavior. Remember that we tend to make internal attributions for our behavior when situational cues are weak, ambiguous, or nonexistent. In the ignorant and misinformed conditions, the situational cues were weak or ambiguous about the true cause of the physiological arousal each participant experienced. However, the confederate's behavior served as a situational cue. In the informed condition, the participants had been given a situational explanation for the arousal (behavior) they experienced; thus, no further internal explanation was needed. Therefore, self-perception theory predicts that the participants in the informed condition are affected very little by the confederate's emotional state. Those in the ignorant and misinformed conditions attribute their physiological symptoms (behavior) to feelings expressed by the confederate. In those cases, the situational cues influence their attributions about their own feelings.

This is exactly what happened. Participants in the ignorant and misinformed condition were more likely to join in the behaviors of the confederate, and they were more likely to report either anger or euphoria based on the behaviors the confederate exhibited even though the physiological arousal was the same for both conditions. Thus, these participants were using situational cues that were more obvious (the behavior of the confederate) to explain their arousal because they had no good other explanation for what they experienced. Those in the informed condition were less likely to be influenced by the confederate's behavior because they had an explanation for the arousal (behavior) they observed in themselves.

The epinephrine results are not easily explained with cognitive dissonance theory because no cognitive dissonance should be generated. This is an example of forming new attitudes or schemata because there were no prior attitudes about the behavior experienced after the drug injection. There was no counter-attitudinal advocacy and no reason for the subjects to experience dissonance. As noted earlier, Bem has argued that self-perception can explain and predict most of the classic cognitive dissonance theory results (such as the $1/$20 study). However, when working with counter-attitudinal advocacy, self-perception predictions have not yielded as consistently supportive results as have cognitive dissonance predictions. On the other hand, when pro-attitudinal advocacy is involved, self-perception does a better job of explaining and predicting results.

Kiesler, Nisbett, and Zanna (1969) designed a study to investigate the impact of self-perception theory with pro-attitudinal advocacy. The researchers argued that pro-attitudinal advocacy should not arouse dissonance because the participants were arguing in favor of an issue they agreed with. Thus, if pro-attitudinal advocacy resulted in attitude change, it would support self-perception theory rather than cognitive dissonance. Air pollution was chosen as a topic for this study. A pretest had shown that the students at the university where the study was carried out were practically unanimous in agreeing that air pollution was a problem in their community. The researchers told the participants that they were recruiting students to serve as experimenters in a study about communication and persuasion. They asked the participants and a confederate (working with the experimenters) to agree to serve as experimenters by presenting some arguments to people on the streets of the university community. The researchers had prepared the arguments, and told the participants that they wanted different personalities to deliver the arguments to make sure that a particular personality was not responsible for the results. After the participants delivered the arguments, they were to ask each recipient of the message if he or she would be willing to sign a petition regarding air pollution. The participant was asked to speak about air pollution as a problem in the community; the confederate was asked to speak about automobile safety.

To ensure that the attitude change came from agreeing to engage in pro-attitudinal advocacy, the researchers had a control group that were told they were witnesses and part of another study. The witnesses heard the same instructions, but they were not asked to present a speech on any topic.

After assigning the topics, the researchers asked the participant and the confederate if they objected to the nature of the topic. The participants were always asked first and agreed verbally (e.g., "sure," "OK") or nonverbally (e.g., nodding). In the belief relevant condition, the confederate spoke up and said he agreed to participate because he did not mind convincing people about a topic he believed in. In the belief irrelevant condition, the confederate spoke up and said he agreed to participate because the study was important. The researchers expected the participant to model the behavior of the confederate about their own topic in their own minds about why they had agreed.

The researchers then asked the participants and the confederate for help with other studies in the future. The researchers explained that they were looking at future topics they wanted to work with students on, and they asked the participants to fill out a questionnaire about potential topics that included rat proliferation, air pollution, and auto safety. The participants were asked to rate each issue in terms of how important it was, how much needed to be done, the level of the threat to the local community, and how much effort should be put into solving the problem. Then, the participants were asked to fill out a departmental questionnaire about the study they were supposedly serving as experimenters for, because they would probably not have time when they returned from making the arguments to people on the streets. Participants were asked how much effort they expected to put into the task, how well they thought they would do, whether they would volunteer again, and how much they thought they would enjoy the task.

Those who had agreed to engage in the pro-attitudinal behavior had more positive or stronger attitudes about controlling air pollution than the witnesses did. In addition, those in the belief relevant condition (where the confederate said he agreed to make the arguments to others because of a belief in the topic) had stronger favorable attitudes than did those in the belief irrelevant condition (where the confederate agreed to make the arguments because of the importance of the study). Thus, a commitment to make a pro-attitudinal speech was enough to generate attitude change, and the attitude change generated was stronger when the participants thought they were doing it because they believed in the topic. Participants looked at external cues to determine their internal states or, in this case, their attitudes about the topic of air pollution. They used situational cues to make dispositional attributions about themselves. This supports the self-perception theory as operating in pro-attitudinal conditions.

ENCOURAGING OTHERS TO MAKE DISPOSITIONAL ATTRIBUTIONS

Because self-perception theory in operation requires the target public to make dispositional rather than situational attributions for their behavior, we need to understand what factors enhance this process in order to be more successful at persuasion. These factors are drawn from the interpersonal attribution research discussed previously, but the body of research surrounding self-perception theory also influenced them. As was explained in Chapter 4, any good theory should help explain, predict, and control persuasion. For self-perception theory to offer control, persuaders need to understand factors that influence the kind of attributions made in order to control the situation so that the preferred type is most likely.

First, individuals are more likely to make dispositional attributions when there is a *positive outcome*. When we engage in behaviors that accomplish our goal (e.g., results in a sale of our product) or benefit others (e.g., helps a needy child be fed), we tend to take personal credit through making dispositional attributions. These are tied to Bem's self versus other principles discussed earlier, which states we tend to consciously or unconsciously try to protect our self-esteem. Taking personal credit for positive outcomes helps us feel good about ourselves. Conversely, if the outcome is negative, we are more likely to look for situational factors as the cause. We might attribute the lost sale to the poor economy or the failure to give money to a homeless person to a lack of change.

A second factor that leads to a greater chance of dispositional attributions is having the *same behavior repeated in different circumstances*. This is similar to the consistency factor discussed by Kelley in attribution theory. When people engage in multiple behaviors that support the same position, they are more likely to make a dispositional attribution. If you signed a petition in favor of the local school levy, agreed to allow a pro-levy sign to be placed in your yard, and agreed to hand out literature favorable to the levy, you (and any external observers) are more likely to believe that you support the levy than if you only signed a petition. The result of multiple actions should be stronger support for the school levy.

A dispositional attribution is more likely to be made *when situational cues are weak, ambiguous, or nonexistent*. This statement is based on Bem's second postulate and was discussed when the postulate was introduced. If we do not observe a situational factor causing the behavior, we are more likely to look internally for the reason.

Fourth, *when situational cues suggest the behavior is consistent with your attitudes*, you are more likely to make a dispositional attribution. Imagine a student in a public speaking class giving a speech about abortion. If the feedback from classmates is positive and suggests that the speech was effective and/or the speaker sounded sincere, the student is more likely to make dispositional attributions about his or her stand on abortion rights. The external cues in this case tended to reinforce the speech (behavior) as being consistent with the student's attitudes about abortion. If the feedback was negative and/or there were indications that the speaker did not sound sincere about the topic, the speaker is less likely to make dispositional attributions. Instead, the student speaker could tell himself or herself that the speech was made simply to fulfill an assignment rather than to express personally held attitudes.

Finally, dispositional attributions are *more likely to occur when greater time passes between the behavior and the attribution made about that behavior*. We tend to forget the situational cues present over time and remember only the behavior. The reason a student attended a lecture on racism on campus may have been for extra credit in a class. However, over time the student may forget the extra credit as the reason for attendance and come to believe that the attendance at the lecture reflected internal beliefs about racism.

SHOULD WE START BIG OR LITTLE? SEQUENTIAL REQUEST STRATEGIES

Self-perception theory has been applied in multiple contexts, and its implications for successful persuasion outside a laboratory setting have been significant. One area of interest for self-perception application is sequential request strategies. A common question is whether it is better to start with a big demand and work down to a smaller request that you really want or whether it is better to ask for something small and work up to the bigger request you really want. Starting big and working down has been referred to as **door-in-the-face (DITF)**; starting small and working up is called **foot-in-the-door (FITD)**.

These kinds of strategies can be observed in multiple interpersonal and sales situations. Suppose a high school student wanted permission from his parents to drive a family car and stay out past curfew for prom night. A DITF approach would be to request use of the new car, $2000 for prom expenses, and permission to be out for 48 hours. Then when this request is refused, the teen would request the use of the old car to go to the prom—what he really wanted to begin with. Alternatively, the same high school student could try a FITD approach. In this case, he might first request permission to drive the old family car on errands—a small request that would probably be granted. Then, he would follow with a request to use that car for prom.

Both the DITF or FITD are effective strategies; however, they are each effective for different reasons. Self-perception theory is useful in explaining the FITD approach. Self-perception theory suggests that initial behavior creates or reinforces attitudes. People may have a hard time turning down a small simple request, leading to a high level of compliance to the small initial request. People who comply with the small initial request look at their behavior to understand what their attitudes are on the topic as long as they do not perceive the behavior as being forced (e.g., no strong external cues to explain the behavior). Because the behavior is in favor of the issue, they are more likely to assume that their attitudes are in favor of the issue. Then, when the larger request comes along, compliance with the larger request is likely.

Freedman and Fraser (1966) performed a classic research study in this area. The study examined how support for social issues and political issues were generated. Two fake organizations were created for the purpose of the study. One was called the Committee for Traffic Safety, and the other the Keep California Beautiful Committee. The resident participants were sorted into five groups. One group was a control group, and no initial request was made of these people. The second and third groups were asked to put a sticker in their windows for either the Committee for Traffic Safety or the Keep California Beautiful Committee. The final two groups were asked to sign a petition for one of the two committees. The four experimental groups were being asked for an initial small favor to support a good cause.

Two weeks later, a researcher representing himself or herself as a member of another fake group called Citizens for Safe Driving went to the home of each resident in the four experimental conditions (those asked for the initial small request) and those in the control group (those not asked for the initial small request). In this case, the residents were asked to place a large, poorly lettered sign in front of their homes. They were told it would block much of the front of their homes and needed to stay for over a week. In addition, the signs would leave a large hole in the yards when they were removed. This was a large request.

Self-perception theory and the FITD strategy predict that those who complied with the initial small request would be more likely to comply with the second larger request. Why? Because those who initially signed a petition or placed stickers in their windows would look at their own behavior to understand their attitudes about good causes. Because there was no pressure to comply, those engaging in the initial behavior would decide that they had favorable attitudes toward supporting good causes. That should lead to a greater willingness to help the good cause with a bigger request.

This is, in fact, what the study illustrated. Over 55 percent of the residents who had been asked to comply with the initial small favor agreed to put the signs in their yards despite the drawbacks of their appearance and the large hole left behind. However, less than 20 percent of the control group agreed to put the signs in their yards. No difference in compliance rates was found between those who had been initially approached by the Traffic Safety Committee and the Keep California Beautiful Committee. The kind of initial request (petition or window sticker) also did not make a difference in compliance rates. These results suggest that the type of initial request is not significant. Getting people to go along with an initial request for a good cause can be enough to activate self-perception theory. Thus, this research supported the FITD approach.

Substantial research on FITD has been conducted since Freedman and Fraser's work, with results indicating that the strategy works sometimes but not always. A study conducted in France (Gueguen, Marchand, Pascual, & Lourel, 2008) found that FITD worked better than a control group without FITD for initiating a date with a stranger. In this study, young women were approached by a young male they did not know (one of three confederates working for the researcher) and either asked for a light for a cigarette or directions to a location (initial request). Following the small initial request, the young man asked the women to join him for a drink. The control condition involved the young man asking the young woman to join him for a drink without an initial request. Only about 3 percent of the control group agreed to join the male for a drink, whereas 15 to 16 percent of those in the FITD conditions involving the initial request for a light or directions agreed to have a drink with the confederate. Thus, FITD led to a significantly higher success rate in this context, but the success rate was far from a sure thing.

Recent research has also found that the FITD strategy works in computer-mediated environments such as signing an electronic petition or providing online assistance to others (Gueguen, 2002; Gueguen & Jacob, 2001; Markey, Wells, & Markey, 2001). Burger (1999) reviewed more than 50 studies using meta-analysis to refine our understanding of the FITD strategy. Burger concluded that self-perception theory predicts when FITD is successful. First, consistent with self-perception theory, the more involved the receivers are with the initial request the more likely they are to comply with the second request. Second, if receivers perform the initial request as opposed to simply agreeing to perform it, they are more likely to comply with the second request. Both of these factors put greater pressure on receivers to examine their behavior and find an explanation for it.

Burger (1999) identified two additional factors that affect the effectiveness of the FITD strategy. The first is the *timing of the second request:* Does it immediately follow the first request, or is it delayed? Girandola (2002) specifically tested the timing of the request in a study on organ donation. Research participants were first asked to complete a five-question survey on organ donation (initial request) and then either immediately or 3 days later were asked if they were willing to become organ donors. Participants were significantly more willing to become organ donors when the request came 3 days after the initial request.

The second factor identified by Burger (1999) was whether the *person making the second request was the same or a different person making the first request.* Girandola (2002) also examined this factor in his study. In addition to some participants receiving the second request 3 days after the initial request, for some participants the second request came from the same person who made the first request, and for other participants the request was made by a different person. Girandola's results were quite clear: Participants were only influenced to be organ donors when the requester was the same for both initial and second requests when there was a 3-day delay between the requests. When the requester was different for the second request, it did not matter much if the second request was immediate or delayed. Why are these two factors important? Girandola explains that the *norm of reciprocity* dictates that requests and concessions are carried out in a reciprocal manner. In other words, if I ask a favor *of* you, I need to do a favor *for* you before I can ask a second favor. Therefore, when the same requester asks for the second favor immediately after the first, she or he is violating the norm of reciprocity. Girandola found that when the second request was delayed, it did not matter much if the requester was the same or not. This result most likely occurred because the norm of reciprocity was weakened by the delay; we don't keep that close track of whose turn it is to ask a favor.

Returning to our initial examples of the high school student wanting to borrow the car for prom, he would need to space out the first and later requests by several days or find a friend to make the second request. If time was of the essence, the DITF strategy would more likely be effective. The DITF strategy is discussed in greater detail in Chapter 11.

APPLYING SELF-PERCEPTION THEORY

Multiple paths can be employed in applying self-perception theory in the creation of persuasive messages. Imagine that you are in charge of a philanthropy project for your student organization and that it is your job to convince other students to participate in a dance marathon as a fundraiser for a local children's hospital. For self-perception theory to be an appropriate framework to employ, we would want to make this a case of pro-attitudinal advocacy. It is hard to imagine that anyone would be opposed to supporting a children's hospital, and students tend to be in favor of participating in philanthropic projects in general. Further, we might assume that most students like to dance, so a dance marathon to raise money for a children's hospital would be a case of pro-attitudinal advocacy. In a pro-attitudinal advocacy situation, our target audience has a favorable attitude, but we want them to engage in behaviors that support those attitudes.

Now that you have decided that self-perception theory is an appropriate approach to employ in our persuasive campaign, the next step is to induce an initial small behavior that will lead to the larger behavior of participating in the dance marathon. You have some options for that first step. You could ask students to sign a petition in support of greater funding for the children's hospital. Or, you could ask students to take some flyers about the event to post in their classrooms and/or residence areas. Alternatively, you could ask for small financial contributions or pledges from students for the event. All of these are small actions that would require your target public to engage in some kind of overt behavior that supports the ultimate goal of the philanthropic project. The challenge is to find a level of initial action that is large enough to cause students to make some kind of attribution but not so large as to be refused. For example, asking for a donation that would be perceived by students as large (perhaps for $20 or more) would probably result in refusal and be perceived as too much for an initial request.

In this first step, we want the targeted public to make an internal or dispositional attribution. As a result, we need to ensure that the situational factors are low key and involve little external pressure so that students decide it must be their favorable attitudes toward the children's hospital that caused them to sign the petition, distribute flyers, and/or make a small pledge. This means the project should not be set up as a requirement for membership in an organization or class project, nor should external incentives or rewards be offered for compliance with these initial small behaviors that might account for external reasons. If that was the case, the initial behaviors could be attributed to the external factors rather than to internal attitudes. In addition, those team members who made the requests need to be low key rather than high pressure in generating agreement to sign petitions, hand out flyers, or request modest financial support.

After these initial smaller behavioral steps are requested, you and your team are ready to move on to the larger task of getting individuals to commit to participating in the dance marathon itself. Soliciting participants for the dance marathon should be more successful among those who complied with the smaller requests initially. Even that process can involve smaller behavioral steps, as illustrated in the sample application form for participants in Figure 5.3. The form asks students for background information, but it also asks for addresses of friends and family so that the committee can send solicitation letters for pledges. Providing these names and addresses is an additional behavioral commitment step. These kinds of events have been quite successful at some locations. For example, Bradley University's dance marathon has generated more than $30,000 from one marathon on a campus with just 6,000 students. Indiana University, a larger school, raised more than $1.8 million in 2011 (see Figure 5.4). In part, the total money raised and the number of participants has increased each subsequent year for the events. Participants from one year tend to return in future years with even more pledges. This is also a part of self-perception theory in action. Their behavior of participating in one year of the dance marathon led to internal attributions about the value of supporting the children's hospital and being involved in the philanthropic event. That makes them more likely to return even stronger in the next year. Thus, self-perception theory can be applied very successfully to persuasive challenges.

STRENGTHS AND LIMITATIONS

A strength of self-perception theory is that it clearly *explains* some persuasion phenomenon quite well, such as pro-attitudinal advocacy and the FITD strategy. The explanation allows persuaders to accurately *predict* persuasive outcomes in research studies and in applied situations, and that prediction allows application of the theories in a manner that has been found to *control* the process. Clearly, at times, self-perception theory can be used to achieve persuasive goals. The social and political issues involved in research are good examples of the value of self-perception theory to those engaged in application of the process.

An additional strength of the theory is its contribution to our knowledge of the persuasion process. The theoretical foundation and the body of research it generated have supported the notion that there are indeed times when people operate as outside observers of their own behavior. The centrality of the attribution process and the importance of dispositional and situational attributions are clear in some circumstances.

Self-perception theory also emphasizes the importance of external cues in the success or failure of persuasion attempts. The persuader has more control over the persuasion process in some circumstances when he or she understands how the external environment influences the persuasion process. Although persuaders can rarely control what goes on inside someone's head, they can affect the setting and environment in which the persuasion occurs.

The self-perception theory also has weaknesses. Empirical research studies have supported both self-perception and cognitive dissonance theories, but empirical research studies have also challenged both theories. Although the theories seem to overlap and offer competing explanations for the same outcomes, the research on these two perspectives suggests limits for both. Fazio, Zanna, and Cooper (1977) argued that each theory has *boundary conditions* for when each applies.

There is considerable support for cognitive dissonance theory to offer better explanations, predictions, and control in situations where dissonance is aroused by counter-attitudinal advocacy and/or aversive conditions. There is evidence of physiological arousal that supports cognitive dissonance theory as a better model than self-perception theory in those conditions. However, there is considerable support for self-perception theory to offer better explanations, predictions, and control in situations of pro-attitudinal advocacy, when new attitudes are being formed, and/or when attitudes are about topics that are fairly uninvolving or weakly held by the target receivers. Fazio and his colleagues have argued that there are limits or boundaries under which each theory operates best. Thus, a weakness of self-perception theory is that it operates in limited situations. This means its explanatory, predictive, and control powers are limited.

Additionally, for explaining the FITD effect, self-perception theory is limited by the need to request initial behaviors that are large enough to generate attributions but not so large as to be refused. Nothing in the theory allows us to know what that level will be for any given topic. Instead, persuaders have to experiment to find the optimal level of initial request for each individual persuasive goal. This limits our ability to control persuasion.

Self-perception theory has also been criticized for viewing persuasion as a primarily passive process in which receivers are directed to action by external forces rather than thinking about decisions and actively deciding how to act (Smith, 1982). This is an after-the-fact justification for behavior rather than a proactive rationale before engaging in behavior. Some may support this view in some situations, but others are uncomfortable for the less active process implied by this theory.

Self-perception theory advanced our knowledge about the persuasion process, but it did not offer answers to all of our questions about persuasion. It offers a valuable perspective that gives us insight into some kinds of limited situations, but it does not answer broader questions about the patterns of persuasion overall. It offers another piece of the puzzle, but by itself it does not explain the larger framework. It built on prior theories and research and took us farther along the path of understanding how persuasion operates, but it is not the final and complete answer.

SUMMARY

- Fritz Heider's work in interpersonal impression formation and attributions laid the groundwork for self-perception theory.

- Heider looked at attributions as a way for people to make causal interpretations for observed behavior, and he saw those attributions as having an internal or external locus of control.
- Harold Kelley elaborated on Heider's work with attribution theory.
- Kelley referred to attributions as being either dispositional or situational.
- Factors involved in making dispositional or situational attributions include consensus, consistency, distinctiveness, non-normative behavior, and when situational factors are more subtle or less obvious.
- Daryl Bem's self-perception theory built on the basics of Heider and Kelley's work.
- Self-perception theory is based on two postulates: (a) individuals come to "know" their own attitudes, emotions, and other internal states partially by inferring them from observations of their own overt behavior and/or the circumstances in which this behavior occurs; and (b) to the extent internal cues are weak, ambiguous, or uninterpretable, the individual is functionally in the same position as an outside observer, an observer who must necessarily rely on those same external cues to infer the individual's internal states.
- Bem argued that there are four differences between attributions made for self-perception versus interpersonal attributions: insider versus outsider, self versus stranger, self versus other, and situation versus action.
- Self-perception offers a two-part model: (a) the individual must be induced to act, and (b) the environmental cues must be arranged so that a dispositional attribution results.
- Self-perception works best for the formation of new attitudes, the reinforcement and intensification of currently held attitudes, and when attitudes are less strongly held or are less important to the receiver.
- When using self-perception in persuasion, persuaders want the receivers to make dispositional attributions about themselves. The chance of dispositional attributions being made is greater when there is a positive outcome; when the same behavior is repeated in different circumstances; when situational cues are weak, ambiguous, or nonexistent; when situational cues suggest the behavior is consistent with the receiver's attitudes; and/or when greater time passes between the behavior and the attribution made about that behavior.
- Foot-in-the-door and door-in-the-face are two sequential request strategies. Self-perception theory helps explain the foot-in-the-door strategy.
- Foot-in-the-door works best when receivers perform the initial request, when the second request does not immediately follow the initial request, and when a different person makes the second request if there is less time between requests.
- Strengths of self-perception theory include clear explanation, prediction, and control for pro-attitudinal advocacy and the FITD phenomenon, adding to our knowledge about the persuasion process by building on the attribution process and focusing attention on the importance of external cues the persuader can control.
- Weaknesses of self-perception theory include very limited circumstances under which it operates effectively, a lack of clarity about the size of the initial request needed for the FITD effect, and the view of persuasion as a passive, after-the-fact kind of justification process.

Review Questions

1. What theories and theorists served as the prior basis for Bem's self-perception theory?
2. What are attributions? What role do they play in impression formation?
3. What factors are involved in deciding whether a behavior is attributed to dispositional or situational factors? How do they work?
4. What are the postulates of self-perception theory?
5. What are the differences between attributing causes for our own behavior and attributing causes for the behavior of others?
6. How does self-perception theory operate in persuasion?
7. What are sequential request strategies? Why are they important for self-perception theory?
8. Under what circumstances does the foot-in-the-door strategy operate best?
9. What are the strengths and weaknesses of self-perception theory?

Discussion Questions

1. Think of three things you observed others doing today. Which of these behaviors do you believe were due to external factors? Which were due to internal factors?
2. Think of a behavior you observed someone doing earlier today. Did you make an internal or external attribution about the behavior? Now consider why you made the attribution you did. Did you make the attribution because of observed consensus, consistency, or distinctiveness?
3. Is it ethical for persuaders to influence the attributions receivers make? What if the attempt is specifically to misdirect receivers from the true intent? In the example of the politician visiting a factory, wearing a hard hat, and performing some of the work, the politician may really just be out to get votes, but he or she may try to manipulate the attributions the workers and media make to convey more positive attributions. At what point is an ethical line crossed?
4. Compare self-perception theory with cognitive dissonance theory. What are the strengths of each theory? Which theory does a better job of explaining the research results of the various studies presented in Chapters 6 and 7?
5. Is it ethical for persuaders to arrange environmental cues in order to influence the kind of attribution to be made? Does that mislead the recipient of the message? Under what circumstances would you find this to be ethical? Under what circumstances would you find this to be unethical?
6. Think of times when someone has used either the foot-in-the-door or the door-in-the-face strategy on you. Was the person successful? Why do you think he or she was either successful or unsuccessful?

7. Is it ethical to make requests you aren't really interested in just to set up a foot-in-the-door or door-in-the-face strategy? Should we be more direct initially, or is it okay to use these strategies to "trick" receivers into acting the way we want them to?

REFERENCES

Bem, D. J. (1967). Self-perception: An alternative interpretation of cognitive dissonance phenomena. *Psychological Review, 74,* 183–200.

Bem, D. J. (1972). Self-perception theory. In L. Berkowitz (Ed.), *Advances in experimental social psychology* (Vol. 6, pp. 1–62). New York: Academic Press.

Burger, J. M. (1999). The foot-in-the-door compliance procedure: A multiple-process analysis and review. *Personality and Social Psychology Review, 3,* 303–325.

Eagly, A. H., & Chaiken, S. (1994). *The psychology of attitudes.* Fort Worth, TX: Harcourt Brace Jovanovich.

Fazio, R. H., Zanna, M. P., & Cooper, J. (1977). Dissonance and self-perception: An interactive view of each theory's proper domain of application. *Journal of Experimental Social Psychology, 13,* 464–479.

Festinger, L., & Carlsmith, J. M. (1959). Cognitive consequences of forced compliance. *Journal of Abnormal and Social Psychology, 58,* 203–210.

Freedman, J. L., & Fraser, S. C. (1966). Compliance without pressure: The foot-in-the-door technique. *Journal of Personality and Social Psychology, 4,* 195–202.

Girandola, F. (2002). Sequential requests and organ donation. *Journal of Social Psychology, 142,* 171–178.

Gueguen, N. (2002). Foot-in-the-door technique and computer mediated communication. *Computers in Human Behavior, 18,* 11–15.

Gueguen, N., & Jacob C. (2001). Fund-raising on the Web: The effect on electronic foot-in-the-door on donation. *CyberPsychology & Behavior, 4,* 705–709.

Gueguen, N., Marchand, M., Pascual, A., & Lourel, M. (2008). The effect of the foot-in-the-door technique on a courtship request: A field experiment. *Psychological Reports, 103,* 529–534.

Heider, F. (1946). Attitudes and cognitive organization. *Journal of Psychology, 21,* 107–112.

Heider, F. (1958). *The psychology of interpersonal relations.* New York: Wiley.

Kelley, H. H. (1967). Attribution theory in social psychology. In D. Levine (Ed.), *Nebraska Symposium on Motivation* (Vol. A5, pp. 192–238). Lincoln: University of Nebraska Press.

Kelley, H. H. (1971). *Attribution in social interaction.* Morristown, NJ: General Learning Press.

Kiesler, C. A., Nisbett, R. E., & Zanna, M. P. (1969). On inferring one's beliefs from one's behavior. *Journal of Personality and Social Psychology, 11,* 321–327.

Markey, P. M. Wells, S. M., & Markey, C. N. (2001). Personality and social psychology in the culture of cyberspace. In S. P. Shohov (Ed.), *Advances in psychology research* (Vol. 9, pp. 103–124). Huntington, NY: Nova Science.

Schachter, S., & Singer, J. E. (1962). Cognitive, social and physiological determinates of emotional state. *Psychological Review, 69,* 379–399.

Smith, M. J. (1982). *Persuasion and human action: A review and critique of social influence theories.* Belmont, CA: Wadsworth.

Weiner, B. (Ed.). (1974). *Achievement motivation and attribution theory.* Morristown, NJ: General Learning Press.

chapter

6

Verbal and Nonverbal Communication

Sidarta/Shutterstock.com.

OBJECTIVES

In this chapter, readers will explore the importance of verbal and nonverbal communication. By the end of this chapter, readers will be able to

- Define verbal communication and understand the history and functions of language
- Define nonverbal communication and discuss its functions
- Describe the various types of nonverbal communication that can be used in interpersonal interactions
- Explain how verbal and nonverbal communication have evolved in the digital age
- Use strategies to strengthen verbal and nonverbal communication competence

KEY TERMS

abstract symbol	**biased language**	**connotation**
affect blends	**confirming message**	**de facto language**

denotation
dialect
disconfirming message
emblems
eye gaze
formal language
gestural communication
haptics
inflection
informal language
intimate zone
jargon
kines
kinesics
nonverbal leakage
nonverbal vocalization
paralanguage
personal zone
phonology
pitch
proxemics
public zone
racist language
Sapir-Whorf hypothesis
sexist language
social zone
tempo
timbre
vernacular

INTRODUCTION

Janelle has been dealing with acne for years, but she is becoming increasingly frustrated and upset about being an adult who still struggles with pimples. It is her first visit with Dr. Abraham, a dermatologist, and she is nervous as she waits in the exam room. When Dr. Abraham enters about 10 minutes later, he reads Janelle's file. He does not make eye contact with her or shake her hand, though he does offer a perfunctory, "Hello, how are you? I'm Dr. Abraham." Janelle is immediately put off by Dr. Abraham's indifferent introduction, which frustrates her even further. He asks her a few brief questions, writes down her answers, and performs a quick examination of her skin. In a wavering voice, Janelle responds to Dr. Abraham's questions but keeps her eyes fixed on the floor. After about five minutes, Dr. Abraham suggests she use two prescriptions, which she can collect from the nurse at the front desk, and return in five weeks for a follow-up appointment. Almost as an afterthought, he asks Janelle if she has any questions. Janelle whispers, "No, thank you," and is barely able to hold back her tears of disappointment.

Have you ever had an awkward or frustrating encounter such as this? Perhaps you focused on your own and the doctor's verbal and nonverbal messages in an attempt to better understand the situation. As you learned earlier in this text, whenever people communicate, they attempt to share meaning by encoding messages in symbols and by decoding or interpreting the symbols used by others. These symbols may be verbal, consisting of words in oral or written forms such as Dr. Abraham's greeting and Janelle's answers to his questions. Symbols can also be nonverbal messages such as the tone or volume of your voice, your facial expressions, touching others, use of personal space or distance, and body movement and gestures. Janelle's soft and wavering voice, Dr. Abraham's lack of eye contact, and even the time Janelle spends waiting for the doctor are all examples of nonverbal communication.

When you communicate with others, your attention is not only focused on the words that are said but also on the characteristics of the other communicator's voice, his or her body language and physical distance from you, or even the environment in which the interaction is occurring. In the example above, Dr. Abraham uses appropriate verbal communication when he greets his patient, examines and diagnoses her condition, asks questions, and provides her with a treatment. But his nonverbal communication makes the visit unpleasant and upsetting for Janelle; his lack of "bedside manner" changes the overall meaning of the medical encounter.

You process others' nonverbal messages at the same time that you process their verbal messages, and you make judgments about others based on a combination of both. Others simultaneously make these same judgments of you. Nonverbal messages are usually more believable and more reliable than verbal messages. Verbal communication, or language, is crucial in forming and maintaining social relationships, and being competent in your verbal communication is essential to your personal and professional success. But an understanding of nonverbal communication is also essential given the sheer number of different nonverbal messages. In fact, findings from across a variety of research studies suggest that 60–65% of meaning in a social interaction is derived from nonverbal messages (Burgoon, 1994).

To account for the importance of both of these types of messages, Chapter 4 examines verbal symbols and nonverbal messages as they are used in interpersonal communication contexts. We combine information about verbal and nonverbal communication into a single chapter to understand how each are important individually, as well as to emphasize how much we rely on both types of messages in our interpersonal communication with others. We begin by exploring verbal communication with a brief history of language acquisition and the English language in the United States. Next we will consider the different ways that nonverbal communication functions in our interactions and discuss different types of nonverbal communication messages. We will also explore different verbal and nonverbal elements of communication, including how both operate in online settings, and we will identify ways in which we can improve both our verbal and nonverbal communication competence.

VERBAL COMMUNICATION

As we discussed in Chapter 1, *language* is defined as a system of human communication that uses a particular form of spoken or written words or other symbols. Language is the primary code humans use to communicate. It is crucial in forming and maintaining social relationships and is essential to your personal and professional success. You may consider speech natural and not always pay close attention to the words you use. However, you make language choices whenever you speak, although you may not always do so consciously. You become a more competent communicator when you become a more conscientious and responsible creator of messages. You can do this by making sure that your language is appropriate for the situation, the other person to whom you are speaking, and the purpose of the communication. Many languages, including English, have formal and informal language, and some types of informal language are considered derogatory or harmful to others.

Formal language is more careful and more mannered than everyday speech. It is used to express serious thought, which is generally clear, accurate, and not overly emotional. Formal language is the standard speech of the academic world and the appropriate language in most business and professional settings, with clients or customers, in professional writing, and in public speaking situations. Formal language avoids colloquialisms, slang, and biased language. In contrast, **informal language** describes a wide range of common and nonstandard English, including jargon, colloquialisms, idioms, and slang. Informal language is appropriate in casual conversation with peers or in special circumstances. However, it is usually not appropriate in written communication

WEB FIELD TRIP

English Language Timeline

The British Library (http://www.bl.uk/) provides a fascinating timeline of how the English language has evolved since 500 BCE. English has undergone a significant evolution through the ages: Though we would technically be speaking the same language as our English-speaking ancestors, it is likely we would have difficulty understanding one another. Conduct a search on the library's website for "Language Timeline," and then consider the following questions.

Critical Thinking Questions

1. At what point in this timeline do you think you could carry on a reasonable conversation with English speakers from the past?
2. Do you think we will be unable to understand individuals who are speaking English a few hundred years from now?

or in professional and academic settings. (Read the *Web Field Trip* feature for a quick look at the history of the English language and its evolution.)

The History of Language

Researchers agree that one characteristic sets humans apart from their animal cousins: communication. Language—in both spoken and written form—is unique to human beings and is considered by some to be the most exceptional behavior that humans can enact. It is also universal: All human societies throughout time are believed to have used language once they were able to do so (Pinker, 1994). Although there is no specific date that we can pinpoint as to when language was first "discovered," we can estimate that our ancestors have been verbally communicating for approximately a million years. In fact, physiologically, human beings are the only animals who are capable of producing spoken language. When humans started walking on two legs instead of four, the descent of the larynx—the organ that forms part of the air passage to the lungs and that contains our vocal chords—allowed the tongue to move in a way that could produce a variety of sounds, which were then used as a basis for verbal communication. The concurrency of these physiological developments means that the formation and growth of language likely occurred during the origin of modern human behavior.

Scholars do not uniformly agree on how to classify languages, and it is almost impossible to conduct a global census of all language speakers, so the number of estimated languages and number of speakers of each language around the world varies a bit from source to source.

Although no common global language exists, political, economic, and technological changes have dramatically increased the use of one particular language over the past few decades. That language is English (Campbell-Laird, 2004). Its use predominates in business, science and technology, and international maritime and aviation transactions. More than half of the world's books and three-quarters of international mail are written in English, and English sites dominate the Internet (Tonkin & Reagan, 2003). Today, English has the largest vocabulary of any language in the world, with perhaps as many as 2 million words (Monajemi, 2003). Like other languages, English is always growing and evolving. Old words continually gain new dictionary definitions, and new words are constantly being added to the **vernacular** through the creation of slang terms and newly coined words such as *staycation* and *googling*, which were recently added to many dictionaries.

The U.S. Constitution does not designate an official language; however, the widespread use of English has made it the recognized language, or **de facto language**, of the United States (Official English, 2010). American English derives from seventeenth-century British English. Mostly people from southern England, especially London, settled the original American colonies in Virginia and Massachusetts. The mid-Atlantic area, Pennsylvania in particular, was settled by people from northern and western England and by those of Scots-Irish descent. Southern speech, by comparison, was strongly influenced by the slave trade from Africa and from the Caribbean (Boeree, 2004).

Like many languages, American English has various **dialects**—geographic or social differences in the way groups of people use the same language. People who speak different dialects can usually understand one another because they have the same language. However, they have different vocabularies and unique **phonology**, the way the language sounds. For example, it is easy to recognize differences between British and American English. The two dialects have both vocabulary differences (such as *petrol* versus *gasoline* and *lift* versus *elevator*) and different phonology, or word pronunciations. The early settlement patterns of the eastern United States resulted in three primary dialects of American English: northern, midland, and southern. A western dialect began to develop in the late 1800s that was influenced primarily by northern midland speech. However, the original Spanish-speaking populations and immigrant Chinese also affected the western dialect. Figure 6.1 shows a regional map of American English dialects.

The influence of other immigrants (such as populations of Jews and immigrants from countries such as Ireland, Italy, and Poland) created regional variations and other dialects in the eastern region of the United States. Even today it is easy to see how different words came to be used for common objects in different regions of the United States. Table 6.1, for example, illustrates American English vocabulary differences for a well-known sandwich and beverage.

Functions of Language

We can use language for any number of reasons or to accomplish many different types of goals. Language can

1. Serve as an abstraction of reality
2. Sustain and transmit culture
3. Express imagination and creativity
4. Express confirming and disconfirming messages

These four functions of language are particularly important for understanding how and why we verbally communicate in interpersonal settings. Each of these functions is discussed next.

Language Serves as an Abstraction of Reality. Language is powerful because you can use it to construct your reality. You use the words of your

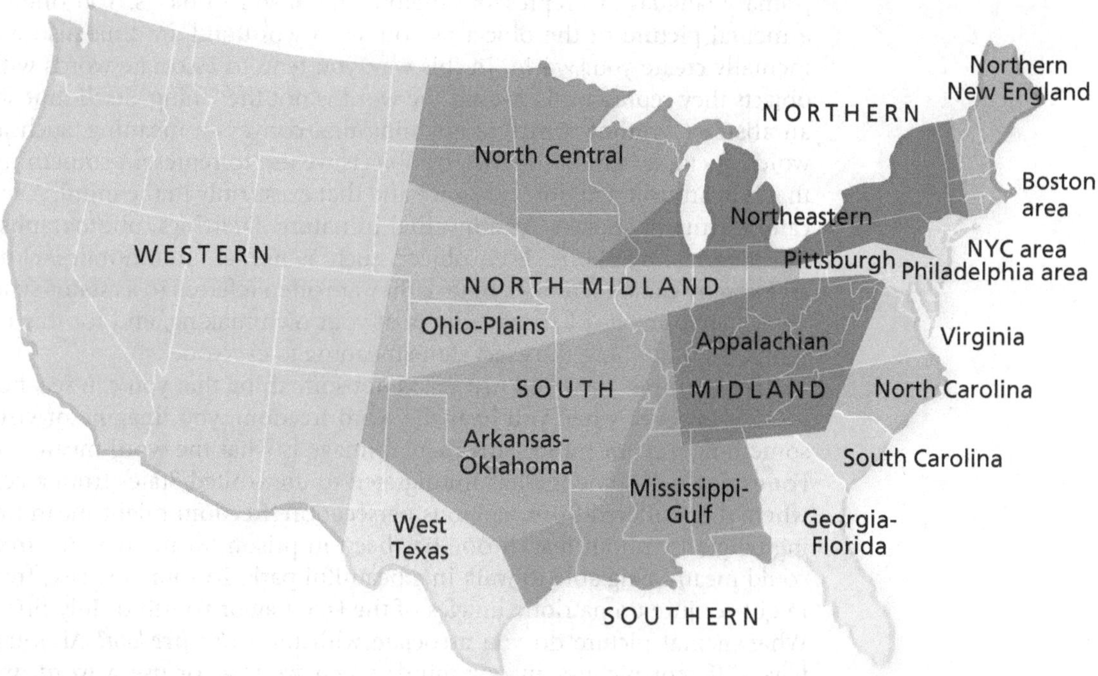

Figure 6.1
National map of regional dialects of American English
American English has many dialects, and, as the map indicates, many are associated with a geographic region of the country

Source: Copyright © 2004 by C. George Boeree. Reprinted by permission. Boeree, C. G. (2004). *Dialects of English*. Retrieved from Shippensburg University website at http://webspace.ship.edu/cgboer/dialectsofenglish. html. Used by permission.

Table 6.1 **Vocabulary differences in dialects of American English**

Food Type		Region of the United States
	hero	New York
	hoagie	Philadelphia
Sandwich	grinder	Boston
	poor-boy	southern
	submarine or sub	western
	tonic	Boston
	soda	northern and North Midland east of the Susquehanna River
Beverage	pop	northern and North Midland west of the Susquehanna River
	cold drink	South and South Midland
	coke (also cola, soft drink, soda pop, soda water, and phosphate)	Rhode Island

Source: Copyright © 2004 by C. George Boeree. Reprinted by permission.

primary language to represent tangible and abstract objects. You often form a mental picture of the object as you say a word and are thus also able to mentally create your world. In this way, you tend to associate words with the objects they represent. However, the word is not the "thing" itself, but simply an **abstract symbol**, which is anything that conveys a meaning, such as the words, pictures, sounds, marks, or objects we use to represent something else that is apart from tangible existence and that exists only in the mind. A symbol can be written, spoken, or nonverbal in nature. Drawings, photographs, and music can be symbolic. Even objects such as homes, automobiles, clothing, and jewelry can be symbols. In fact, they are often referred to as status symbols. Your mental image of the symbol is of your own making, and for this reason symbols do not have the exact same meaning to everyone.

For example, the word *freedom* is not something that you can see, hear, or touch. However, when you hear the word freedom, you imagine or visualize something in your mind. This mental image is what the word means to you. For example, if someone has immigrated to the United States from a country where they suffered from religious persecution, freedom might mean practicing religion without fear. If one has been in prison for many years, freedom could mean being able to walk in a beautiful park. To someone else, freedom might conjure up patriotic images of the U.S. flag or Fourth of July fireworks. What mental picture do you associate with the word *freedom*? Although we have different pictures in our minds when we hear or use a word, we can communicate with one another because words have common **denotations**. The denotation is the dictionary definition or description of what the word represents—a definition that most can agree upon. For example, if you look up the word *grandmother* in a dictionary, you will find it described in a manner similar to the following:

> Grandmother: The mother of one's father or mother.

The dictionary definition, or denotation, gives you the essential characteristics of what a grandmother is and helps you construct a basic mental picture of it. The denotations of concrete words such as *grandmother* are generally clear and descriptive. If you did not know what a grandmother is, it would be fairly easy for you to better understand one from this denotation.

Abstract words such as *freedom* also have denotations. However, the denotation of an abstract word is less specific and more subject to personal interpretation. For instance, a dictionary definition of the word *freedom* reads something like the following:

> Freedom: The power or right to act, speak, or think as one wants or to exercise choice and free will.

The definition, or denotation, of this abstract word is probably broad enough to encompass the various interpretations different people might give to the word. However, it does not specifically tell you what type of power or right that freedom provides or what obligations or duties you might have from which you need to be freed. What is meant by the word *power*, for example? Does it refer to physical strength, control or influence over others, or spiritual power? What is meant by "free will"? Answers to these questions are subjective; each person will answer them in his or her own way.

Beside denotations, words also have **connotations**. The connotation is created by the personal association you have with a certain word or the emotional meaning or impact of the word to you. Connotations are frequently shared among members of a particular society, but they also contain elements that are unique to each person. Connotative meanings exist along with denotative meanings, and they are generally either positive or negative. For example, when we first mentioned the word *grandmother,* you likely immediately imagined your own grandmother. But maybe what you picture is the general image of a grandmother in our society—an image of an older woman with white hair who wears glasses and is warm and welcoming. We can have connotations for any number of things that we use language to describe, including the things that we like and the food that we eat. See Figure 6.2 for a discussion of the connotations associated with the names of some common food products.

Language Sustains and Transmits Culture. Written and spoken verbal messages are a primary method that individuals use to sustain their culture, as well as to educate and transmit elements of their culture to others. We learn about our own and others' cultures by reading books, searching the Internet, and talking with others about their cultural experiences. Culture is passed down from generation to generation in multiple verbal forms: through spoken stories or oral histories, by writing down old family recipes, and via poetry, literature, and song. If we share a language with another culture that we are visiting, we rely on that form of communication in multiple ways: by asking natives for directions, by looking to street or public transportation signs in order to determine where we are and to find our way, and by reading written descriptions of places and things when visiting a culture's museums, parks, or memorials. (See *IPC Research Applied* for some insight into what your own name conveys about you.)

In addition, many communication theorists believe that the language that we use actually determines how we think and how we behave. In the early 1900s, anthropologist Edward Sapir posited a theory that there was a connection between culture and language. Sapir believed that the very structure of

In September 2010, the Corn Refiners Association applied to the federal government to change the name *high fructose corn syrup* on the labels of its food products that use this ingredient. The new name they want to use is *corn sugar.* Americans' consumption of products containing corn syrup fell to a 20-year low because studies show that consumers associate corn syrup with obesity, a perception for which there is little scientific evidence.

Corn refiners say the new name better describes the sweetener by more accurately reflecting the source of the food (corn) and identifying the basic nature of the food (a sugar). Renaming products has worked before. *Low erucic acid rapeseed oil* became much more popular when it was renamed *canola oil* in 1988, and *prunes* became *dried plums* in 2000. The group hopes the new name will help their product move away from negative associations (Fredrix, 2010).

Figure 6.2
What's in a name?
Connotations, usually shared among members of a society, can sometimes create negative associations between a phrase and the object it represents.

human language shapes our perceptions and how we view the world. Sapir's student, Benjamin Whorf (1940), developed what is known as the **Sapir-Whorf hypothesis**, which states that language is not just a way of voicing ideas, but it actually shapes and determines those ideas. The hypothesis states that we cannot think outside the confines of our language. In other words, we are so immersed in our language and our culture that we do not recognize how it influences our view of the world.

However, not all researchers accept the Sapir-Whorf hypothesis. Other theories suggest that our thoughts actually influence our language or that all languages have the same underlying structure. Psychologist Steven Pinker (1994) challenges the Sapir-Whorf hypothesis by asking, "If thoughts depended on words, how could a new word be coined? How could a child learn a word to begin with? How could translation from one language to another be possible?" (p. 47). What theorists do agree on, however, is that language, thought, and culture are inherently intertwined, and, together, they affect our view of the world.

IPC RESEARCH APPLIED

What Does Your Given Name Say about You?

Your first name—it is as much a part of you as the color of your eyes or your height. However, your name can also be considered a form of verbal communication, one that may be a clue about how individualistic your culture is. One interesting way to consider the interrelationship between culture and language is by tracing patterns of how U.S. parents name their children over time. In a research study that was conducted in 2007, social psychologists Jean Twenge, Emodish Abebe, and W. Keith Campbell analyzed naming data from the Social Security Administration from the years 1880 to 2007 to determine how many children were given common or popular names each year. This analysis included over 325 million names—a massive sample size for a study of language. Twenge and her colleagues (2007) argued that the number of children given common names would decrease over time, and that this decrease would reflect the growing individualistic nature of American culture.

The researchers found that the number of babies given common names by their parents has indeed decreased substantially: from 40% in 1890 to less than 10% in 2007 for boys, and from 25% to 8% for girls during this same time period. This decrease began to be steady in 1950 and then became particularly steep and continuous in 1983. The authors attributed this decrease to an increased interest in giving children names "that will help them stand out rather than fit in," which is a way to use language to increasingly emphasize being unique or individualistic in American culture (Twenge et al., 2007, p. 22).

Think about your own name. If you have a nickname that you prefer, why did you choose to use it instead of your full first name? For example, "Jennifer" was an extremely common name for baby girls in the United States in the 1970s and early 1980s, and having that name usually meant sharing it with at least one or two other females in school and at work. This common first name can be frustrating at times, because it means having to constantly distinguish yourself (e.g., by preferring to be called "Jen" or by using the first letter of your last name to set you apart). Keep this in mind as you consider the following questions.

Critical Thinking Questions

1. What does your own name say about you? Is it a common name or one that is a bit more unique?
2. How does the individuality of your name impact who you are and how you interact with others?
3. What effect might popular culture, in either a dominant or co-culture, have on baby name trends?

Language Expresses Imagination and Creativity. Because language is imaginative and creative, it allows you to construct entire worlds in your mind. Our capacity for language allows us to have a rich and vivid mental life in which we can suffer regret, reminisce about events that occurred decades ago, have complex wishes and yearnings, and reflect on what it is like to be ourselves. Language allows us to have not only real experiences, but experiences that we simply imagine. Through language, you can create and play with ideas that do not exist in the real world. You can recite stories, poems, rhymes, and riddles and engage in games of pretend by yourself or with others. Unlimited combinations of symbols are possible and, therefore, so are "mental creation[s] of possible worlds" (Chomsky, 2004, para. 12). Our use of symbols to represent physical objects, ideas, and emotions gives us the capacity to build cities, to make laws, and to create art and music.

In addition, if there is not a symbol for what you are envisioning in your mind, you can use language to create one. Human beings can agree to make anything stand for anything: S. I. Hayakawa (1964, p. 24) observed that, "we are, as human beings, uniquely free to manufacture and manipulate and assign values to our symbols as we please." Over time, we have agreed to make various sounds and written combinations of letters and marks stand for certain objects in the environment, for certain behaviors, or for experiences we pick up through our senses or that register in our nervous system and we call emotions (Hayakawa, 1964). Our ability to be creative and imaginative with language is evident in the fact that 15,000 to 20,000 words are added to the English language per year. For example, the word *unfriend*, which was coined to describe the act of removing an individual from one's list of approved Facebook friends, was the 2009 Oxford word of the year ("Oxford word of the year," 2009). This imaginative function of language thus allows you to use your creativity (Halliday & Webster, 2004).

Language Offers Confirming and Disconfirming Messages. As you have likely already figured out, language is a powerful tool for human understanding, and even just for basic survival. It can also be harmful or helpful in our interpersonal relationships. Through verbal communication, we can confirm or disconfirm those with whom we interact. A **confirming message** is one that provides a basic acknowledgment that the other person is present, as well as your acceptance of them, how they define or view themselves, and the relationship that you two share. Using confirming messages is associated with greater openness and essentially shows that you positively regard the other person (Dailey, 2006). Imagine your best friend is involved in a frustrating romantic relationship and often wants to discuss and dissect this relationship with you. After a while it begins to bother you, especially when your friend fails to take your advice, and it may be a struggle for you to continue to use confirming messages. However, you can still do so in a number of ways, such as by maintaining focus on the situation and being involved in the interaction. This does not mean that you always agree with your friend but that you recognize your friend's point of view. You can engage in a dialogue by being a simultaneous sender and receiver and express concern in a respectful way. And you can ask questions to reflect back what your friend says and show that you understand. Refer to Table 6.2 for more information about using confirming messages.

Table 6.2 Examples of confirming messages

Message	Explanation	Example Message
Communicator maintains focus on the situation.	Gives the other communicator exclusive attention.	"Ok, I'll put my laptop down so I won't be distracted."
Communicator is involved in the interaction.	Recognizes the other communicator's point of view, even if there is disagreement.	"I hear what you are saying, but I'm not sure if that is the way that I would go about it."
Communicator is engaged in a dialogue.	Simultaneously sends and receives messages and expresses concern in a respectful way.	"I'm listening to you, and I am worried about what I am hearing."
Communicator shows that he or she understands.	Asks questions to reflect back what the other communicator has said.	"It sounds to me as if you are really upset—am I right?"

Table 6.3 Examples of disconfirming messages

Message	Explanation	Example Message
Communicator ignores the other communicator.	Does not give the other communicator or the situation exclusive attention.	"I don't want to talk again so I'm going to let this call go straight to voicemail."
Communicator dictates the focus of the conversation.	Does not give the other communicator a chance to speak.	"Enough of this. You need to listen to what I have to say."
Communicator makes assumptions about the interaction.	Evaluates the other communicator's situation before hearing details.	"I don't need to hear your side; I already know what you *should* do."
Communicator dominates the interaction.	Discourages or interrupts the other communicator during the conversation.	"Do we really need to talk about this again, for the millionth time?"

In contrast, a **disconfirming message** does the opposite of a confirming message: You not only disregard the other person as an individual, you also ignore what the person says. The disconfirming message is thus one where you clearly indicate that that individual is not worth your time or effort, and that you have a negative regard for that person (Dailey, 2006). Consider again your best friend who is in a frustrating romantic relationship. When you feel frustrated by the discussions with your friend, you might start to use disconfirming messages in a number of ways: ignore your friend and her situation; do not give your friend a chance to speak; immediately evaluate your friend's situation; discourage or interrupt your friend during the conversation. See Table 6.3 for examples of disconfirming messages.

However, consistently disconfirming a person is not recommended, as it can reduce the person's self-esteem and damage your relationship. If you suspect that you are using messages such as those described in Table 6.3—ones that dominate, dictate, or ignore—try to be more aware of how the other person reacts when you use disconfirming messages. Do they seem upset or hurt, or become unusually quiet? Being more aware of the other communicator by trying to take that person's perspective can help you replace disconfirming messages with confirming ones.

Biased Language

You should be aware that some language is considered improper or unacceptable in almost all contexts. For example, **biased language** presents information in a way that shows preference for or against a certain point of view, shows prejudice, or is demeaning to others. Biased language usually refers to the use of words that intentionally or unintentionally offend people or express negative attitudes concerning a person's race, ethnicity, religion, sexual orientation, age, disability, or illness. This type of language has no place in professional or academic situations and should also be avoided in personal communication. Biased language is not objective; rather, it is offensive, negative, and reveals an individual's prejudices. Such language thus obstructs open-minded communication and cooperation between individuals and communities.

Racist language, for example, is the use of language to demean or insult people on the basis of their race or ethnicity. You know that intentionally using racial slurs constitutes racist language, but you can also insult people and express negative attitudes about race unintentionally when you use stereotypes regarding race or emphasize someone's race unnecessarily in your communication. For example, the public school district in Denver, Colorado, had to apologize for what it called a "well-intentioned but highly insensitive" attempt to celebrate Martin Luther King, Jr., Day by serving a school lunch consisting of fried chicken, collard greens, and sweet potatoes. Many criticized the district, saying that the meal was an offensive caricature and perpetuated stereotypes about black culture (Meyer, 2010). Pointing out someone's race when it is irrelevant can also be considered racist language, as when you state, for example, "I had an appointment with my Latino dentist yesterday."

Language responds to changes in society, and some language that is biased against specific groups of people and that might once have been used regularly is now considered improper and inappropriate. At one time, for instance, the word *man* was considered a generic word that referred to all humans. Today, such usage is considered **sexist language** because it excludes individuals on the basis of gender. It is considered inappropriate today to use the term *man* and the pronouns *he, him,* and *his* to refer to people of both genders. Instead of saying "Every employee must schedule his vacation" you might make the word *employee* plural and say, "All employees must schedule their vacations."

To communicate in an unbiased manner, you must be aware of and sensitive to the use of terms that others consider demeaning or offensive and refer to people using the terms that they prefer to describe them. (A type of language that can be unintentionally offensive is jargon, the topic addressed in *Everyday Communication Challenges*.) You must be particularly wary of language related to gender, sexual orientation, age, physical disability, or illness. For instance, including references to gender, when unnecessary, can be considered demeaning. Medical personnel, for example, can be male or female, so it is unnecessary and often insulting to state, "I had a male nurse when I was in the hospital recently," or "I met a lady doctor." Your language choices reflect your attitude toward a subject, so avoid derogatory phrases such as "little old lady" to refer to an older person or "handicapped" to describe a person with a disability. Instead emphasize the person first in the language, not the age, the disability, the race, or the illness. Use phrases like "people who are visually impaired" or "a man who is 55 years old" instead of "the blind" or "an old guy." If you are not sure which terms are best, ask the person you are referring to or ask others for guidance.

EVERYDAY COMMUNICATION CHALLENGES

Jargon in the Workplace

Have you ever overheard two people who work together talking about their job and had no idea what they meant? Did you understand only a handful of the words they used? They were probably able to express complex ideas to each other rather quickly and precisely with **jargon**, a set of words or phrases specific to a group or career field that may not make much sense to outsiders.

Jargon can help you to share meaning with coworkers easily because people in your industry or at your workplace know the ideas and concepts behind the words or abbreviations. For example, if you are in the medical profession, you could say that you "need a crash cart, stat" when you want a hospital employee to immediately bring a defibrillator machine to restart a patient's heart. People working in law enforcement may refer to an "UNSUB" or a "perp" when they want to discuss an unknown subject or perpetrator of a crime. Members of the U.S. Armed Forces, for example, often communicate through the liberal use of abbreviations and acronyms that they alone understand. Some examples include MOS (military occupational specialty, i.e., job) and PCS (permanent change of station). Most professions have their own jargon, and use of this type of language demonstrates your membership in the group. In this way, jargon usage can create and reinforce which groups we identify with.

When you are relatively new to a job, it takes a while to learn the jargon. Once you are fluent, it is important to be able to explain an abbreviation or to avoid jargon when talking to people who do not share your career or background. Jargon is acceptable, and often expected, in professional settings when all communicators understand the specialized language. In these circumstances, jargon can be a useful and efficient way for members of the group to communicate with one another quickly and easily.

However, jargon can make it difficult for someone outside the group to interpret your messages. It should not be used when outsiders are present because it can make others feel as if they are not members of your group. Jargon should also be avoided when you are trying to educate or inform others about what you do or what you have accomplished. In such instances jargon can make a communicator seem distant, evasive, and overly important (Obuchowski, 2006).

If you are unsure if your message contains too much jargon, seek out someone who is not familiar with your profession and explain your ideas and thoughts. Then, ask the person to explain what you said back to you to determine if your language needs to be simplified and broken down for a different audience. As a competent communicator, you should strive to adapt your language to your audience to promote shared understanding.

Critical Thinking Questions

1. When is it appropriate to use jargon? When is it inappropriate?
2. If you are in a group of individuals, some of whom understand jargon and some who do not, how should you communicate in a way that is competent?
3. How can you teach others jargon that they need without seeming distant and overly important?

NONVERBAL COMMUNICATION

Though we have thus far discussed verbal and nonverbal communication separately, they typically are encoded and decoded together in an interaction, and we rely on both to achieve shared meaning between communicators. Specifically, nonverbal communication may

- Reinforce, complement, or emphasize the words you speak
- Substitute for verbal communication entirely

- Interrupt or distract from verbal communication and be a form of noise
- Conflict with or contradict the verbal message entirely

In the following sections, we will examine nonverbal communication by identifying some of the important functions that this type of message serves in our interactions with others. We will also describe some of the different types of nonverbal communication, including voice, touch, body movements, and personal space and distance. As we discuss the different functions and types of nonverbal communication, it is important to remember that this type of message is bound by culture. This means that certain nonverbal messages are interpreted differently in different cultures, and that cultural mores determine what nonverbal behaviors are appropriate in particular situations. As you read the sections below, consider how members of cultures that you are a part of may communicate differently than the dominant U.S. cultural examples that we present here.

Functions of Nonverbal Communication

When you communicate nonverbally, you use every way other than language to send messages. Some of these messages are conscious and intentional, but many are innate aspects of your unique voice or body that you can do little to change. Still other nonverbal communication is unconscious and the result of habits that you have developed. These nonverbal messages serve four important functions in interpersonal communication, or "what the nonverbal message does and why it is sent" (Guerrero, Hecht, & DeVito, 2008, p. 10). The functions that are particularly important in terms of nonverbal communication include:

1. Managing your impressions and identities
2. Managing and interpreting your relationships
3. Regulating the flow of interactions
4. Engaging in and detecting messages of emotion, influence, and deception

We discuss these functions next, and then describe some of the different forms of nonverbal communication that are central in our interactions with others.

Manage Impressions and Identities. Even before another person opens his mouth to speak, you have likely already started to form an impression of him based on how he looks, what he is wearing, his posture, and whether he makes eye contact. At the same time, that other person is forming an impression of you using similar nonverbal cues. Physical appearance and body movements are particularly important in forming first impressions because these are examples of visual cues that are noticed first (Guerrero et al., 2008). Research identifies the importance of these initial impressions. For example, in one of the first studies on how individuals form impressions of others, researchers found that we tend to make accurate and enduring judgments about others we have just met (those we have zero acquaintance with) in only a short amount of time (less than 5 minutes) and with limited information—primarily the other person's physical appearance (Albright, Kenny, & Malloy, 1988).

As we form impressions of others via nonverbal messages, we also work to manage the impressions others have of us. Again, nonverbal communication is important in managing others' impressions, as evidenced when we dress up for a first date or buy a new suit and practice our handshake before an important job interview. The impressions we believe others have of us then contribute to our identities by serving as the looking-glass self that we learned about in Chapter 2. Thus, nonverbal communication is an important factor in how we perceive others and how others perceive us.

Manage and Interpret Relationships. In Chapter 1, we discussed the distinction between content and relationship messages and noted that we tend to gather more relationship information through nonverbal communication. This means that instead of verbally talking about your relationship, you tend to rely on nonverbal cues such as touch, personal space, facial expressions, and body movements to help you interpret the relationship. Nonverbal messages can in fact provide us with a great deal of relational information: what type of relationship it is; how intimate, close, or involved the individuals are; how comfortable they are with each other; even whether the relationship is more formal or informal in nature. The next time you are in a public place take a moment to observe, from a distance, two people communicating. Even if you cannot hear the discussion, you will be amazed by how much you can learn about the communicators simply by observing the nonverbal messages used during their interaction. For example, whether or not and how they touch each other can give you clues about the type of relationship that they share. The volume and pitch of their voices will indicate to you whether the topic they are discussing is something they are excited about or find uninteresting or boring. If they seem more interested in their mobile phones than in each other, then that is likely a sign that they don't have something to say to the other at that moment. Being more alert about nonverbal messages used by yourself and others can thus give you greater insight into your own relationships as well.

Regulate Interactions. Do you ever wonder how we are so seamlessly able to take turns in an interaction? How do we know when to speak and how do others know when it is their turn to talk? We rely on nonverbal communication in large part to regulate our conversations, or shorten and lengthen our nonverbal and verbal stream of messages. It is very rare for us to finish a point and then say, "It is your turn to speak now." Instead, a variety of subtle nonverbal cues serve this purpose, and there are four ways that we can use such cues to regulate an interaction. First, we exercise turn-requesting cues if we wish to speak. For example, we may raise our hand or lean in closer toward the other communicator. But if we do not want to talk, turn denying, we might look away or shake our head. Turn yielding occurs when a speaker is done and wants to invite others to contribute to the discussion. This individual could signal this shift by extending his arms and hands outward or by altering the pitch of his voice. However, if the speaker would like to continue talking, turn maintaining, he might put out his hand or raise the volume of his voice to stop a partner's turn request. Such nonverbal messages are thus integral tools we can use to manage the flow of conversation.

Engage in and Detect Emotional, Influence, and Deception Messages. The final function of nonverbal communication involves the pursuit of three specific communication goals. The first is to express emotion, and we depend on nonverbal communication a great deal when we want to share how we are feeling with others. For example, crying, frowning, hugging, and speaking in a higher pitch can indicate that sadness, whereas smiling, shouting, and jumping up and down are typically nonverbal cues of happiness. However, it is rare for someone to experience and express a single emotion. Instead, we tend to experience and express a mixture of emotions, which are called **affect blends**. For example, if your romantic partner proposes to you, you are likely to be both surprised and happy, and you will nonverbally express elements of both emotions. We also use nonverbal communication to determine what emotions others are experiencing. For example, a study by Sally Planalp (1998) found that vocal, facial, and body cues were frequently used to decode another person's emotions but that verbal cues (i.e., language) were considered less often.

BananaStock/Thinkstock.

We tend to experience and express a mixture of emotions. Vocal, facial, and body cues can reveal our emotions and help us decode others' emotions.

Nonverbal communication is also instrumental in influencing or persuading others. For example, advertisements in our culture use attractive, fit individuals to represent products. Descriptions of products and services also rely on vocal characteristics such as a soft voice that is not monotone or too high or shrill. In political campaigns, every element of a candidate's appearance, down to what she wears and how approachable she seems, is constantly monitored and scrutinized by the media and voters. We also employ nonverbal cues on an interpersonal level when we try to persuade others. One analysis (Segrin, 1993) found that we are more likely to convince someone to behave or act in a certain way if we engage in the following nonverbal behaviors: increase eye contact, lightly touch the person on the arm or shoulder, stand at a close but comfortable distance from the person, or wear formal, higher-status clothing. This study also found that these nonverbal tactics are as effective as verbal messages for gaining compliance in interpersonal interactions (Segrin, 1993).

Finally, nonverbal communication can be used to deceive others, as well as to detect the deceit of others. Unlike emotion and influence, however, the decision to focus on nonverbal communication in deception situations is not an effective strategy. Most of us believe that we can correctly detect deception, but our accuracy rate is approximately 55%, which means we are about as likely to detect deception as we are to correctly predict heads or tails in a coin toss. It is possible our accuracy rate is low because many communicators know that certain nonverbal cues—such as averting eye contact, fidgeting, or pausing before speaking—can decrease the credibility of a lie so they know to conceal such nonverbal cues. In a landmark study (Park, Levine, McCornack, Morrison, & Ferrara, 2002), college students were asked to recall actual situations where deception was detected (either they were themselves caught lying or they found out someone else was deceiving them). In only 2.1% of these instances were nonverbal behaviors (along with verbal messages) instrumental in detecting deception at the time the lie was told. Instead, the most common methods of discovery were information from others, a combination of methods, and physical evidence (Park et al., 2002). The take-away message here, then, is to actually depend *less* on nonverbal communication if you suspect someone is lying to you. Instead focus on the bigger picture, listen for verbal inconsistencies, and study the observations made by other communicators.

TYPES OF NONVERBAL COMMUNICATION

Because nonverbal communication involves every way other than language that we can communicate, there are many different nonverbal cues. How we look and dress, whether we touch someone or not, the sound of our voice, even how we smell can encode a message to others, among other nonverbal cues. Describing all of the different forms of nonverbal communication is beyond the scope of this text. Instead, we focus on the four types of nonverbal communication:

1. Body language, referred to as kinesics
2. Vocalics, referred to as paralanguage
3. Touch, referred to as haptics
4. Personal space, referred to as proxemics

We significantly rely on these four types of nonverbal communication during our interpersonal interactions, and each type is discussed in detail next. (Check out the *Web Field Trip* for a quick overview of nonverbal behaviors.)

Body Language/Kinesics

Body language, also called **kinesics**, is an important aspect of nonverbal communication because it is a broad category of nonverbal messages that includes any way that our body can move, including nodding your head in response to something someone says, leaning forward or backward, and crossing your legs. Facial expressions and eye behaviors, discussed in more detail below, are also

WEB FIELD TRIP

Dictionary of Nonverbals

The Center for Nonverbal Studies (http://center-for-nonverbal-studies.org/1501.html) is a private nonprofit center that aims to advance the study of nonverbal human communication. Visit the organization's website and explore the Nonverbal Dictionary. The entries and the discussion in this dictionary consider a range of nonverbal communications, which researchers in a variety of different academic fields study from the perspectives of their respective disciplines. Keep these examples in mind as you learn more about the different types of nonverbal communication, and consider two similar nonverbals, such as *smile* and *laugh*, when you evaluate the following questions.

Critical Thinking Questions

1. How do the separate usage and anatomy definitions differ between two similar nonverbals?
2. What is the significance of discussing media as it relates to the distinct nonverbals?

types of kinesics because they involve specific body movements. In fact, anthropologist Ray Birdwhistell (1952) identified 250,000 different **kines**, which are the smallest identifiable body movements, in the facial region alone.

Gestures. A wealth of unspoken information is communicated with your body, and **gestural communication**, which is communication related to how you use and move your body, plays a crucial role in interpersonal communication. These gestures usually reinforce or complement the verbal message. At times, however, you can use gestures without words. In these instances, gestures may carry the entire burden of the communication. Although the hands are the most common body parts used for gesturing, you can use other parts of your body, such as when you shrug your shoulders, nod your head, or wink. Table 6.4 describes some common gestures that are used in the United States. Consider how you would interpret each one in an everyday conversation.

Many gestures are **emblems**, which are gestures that are clear and unambiguous and have a verbal equivalent in a given culture (Poyatos, 2002a). When you use an emblem, you are doing so consciously and you might not need any verbal communication to get your point across. The hand signals that baseball and football coaches communicate to their players during games are emblems; they are used because verbal communication is difficult due to noisy stadiums, and they prevent the other team from understanding what is being communicated. Most emblems are culturally determined, and they can get you into difficulty if you use them in other countries. In the United States, some emblematic gestures are the thumb-up-and-out hitchhiking sign, the circled thumb and index finger OK sign, and the "V" for victory sign. However, be careful of using these gestures outside the United States. The thumb-up sign in Iran, for example, is an obscene gesture, and the OK sign has sexual connotations in Ethiopia and Mexico (Liebal, Muller, & Pika, 2007).

Facial Expressions. The face is a finely tuned visual channel for sharing information, with the ability to produce a range of expressions from the very subtle to the very dramatic. Faces also convey other types of important information. For example, arching an eyebrow can convey a look of disbelief or can convey a greeting or acknowledgement (Doherty-Sneddon, 2003). The face is the body part primarily used to express emotions. Researchers do

Table 6.4 Five common gestures used in the United States

Gesture	Description	Possible Meaning(s)
Shaking your finger at someone	Creating a fist with your index finger pointing outward and then moving the finger left and right three or four times	A reprimand for doing something incorrectly
Knocking on wood	Creating a fist with knuckle down and then moving it upward and downward in short movements	A superstitious behavior that is intended to ward off bad luck
Shrugging your shoulders	Moving your shoulders upward and downward several times	An act that indicates someone is unsure or does not know a piece of information; can also be a way to move rhythmically or in time to music
Rubbing your stomach	Making a circular movement with your hand on your stomach, palm inward	A gesture that shows that someone is hungry
Twiddling your thumbs	Interlocking the fingers of your hands and then moving your thumbs in circles around each other	An act of boredom or not knowing what to do in a particular situation

not agree on how many facial expressions can be formed, but psychologist Paul Ekman, who has studied facial expressions for more than 50 years, has catalogued more than 10,000 human expressions. His research suggests that some facial expressions are almost universal and others are culturally specific (Ekman, 1971). For example, people in all cultures seem to react to fear with similar facial expressions; however, people in different cultures are frightened by different things (Griffiths, 2008). Seven facial expressions—contempt, fear, surprise, anger, disgust, sadness, and happiness, appear in all or most cultures and are widely accepted by researchers as universal (Duenwald, 2005).

A few facial expressions appear to be innate, but others seem to be learned. Researchers, for example, report that just moments after birth, newborn babies make expressions of disgust in response to bitter tastes. As children mature, they learn to produce specific facial expressions, to understand the facial expressions of others, and to modify their own expressions to match those of others. Being able to understand and produce appropriate facial expressions is essential to a child's social development, and problems doing so are often signs of developmental disorders such as autism (Doherty-Sneddon, 2003).

Most adults are adept at controlling their facial movement and masking their feelings, if they work at it. However, this voluntary facial control is only one way that facial expressions are produced. Other facial expressions are spontaneous and involuntary, so they are much more difficult to disguise. These spontaneous expressions, called **nonverbal leakage** because our emotions involuntarily leak out, occur as a direct result of an emotional experience or feeling. So, when you feel sad or happy (two of the suggested universal emotional expressions mentioned earlier), your face will naturally reflect those feelings, unless you deliberately try to mask the expression. It appears that humans are born with the potential to produce the seven basic emotional expressions spontaneously and do not have to learn them. Children who were born blind have been found to produce these expressions, even though they have never seen them (Doherty-Sneddon, 2003).

Paying attention to and accurately interpreting the facial expressions of others is an extremely important skill you must acquire to be a competent communicator. Ekman (1999) also found that emotional expressions are crucial to the development and regulation of interpersonal relationships. Facial expressions are involved in forming attachments with people in infancy as well as in courtship and they are associated with the regulation, increase, and decrease of aggression. As with all forms of communication, nonverbal messages may be unclear or ambiguous, so providing feedback or questioning someone to make sure your interpretation of facial expressions is correct is an essential part of the communication process.

Eye Behavior. One of the most important aspects of nonverbal communication is eye behavior. Were you aware that every culture has unwritten rules about when it is permissible to look at someone, where you can look, and how long you can look? For example, in the United States total strangers usually think nothing of stopping someone on the street who is pushing a stroller to gaze at the baby, and caregivers usually think nothing about letting them do so. Americans tend to look at others above the neck or below the knees. Looking at other parts of a person's body is considered impolite, while looking at anyone for more than three to five seconds can be interpreted as staring. In Japan, however, direct eye contact makes many Japanese people uncomfortable and may be interpreted as an attempt to intimidate or an indication of hostility. Instead, it is advisable to gaze at a person's forehead or chin most of the time (Gesteland & Seyk, 2002).

Eye behavior communicates in many important ways. You can widen, narrow, close, or roll your eyes. You can raise and lower your gaze, and you can wink. You can hold your eyes steady, look over your shoulder, or turn your head and look behind. You can also raise or lower your eyebrows or scowl to draw your eyebrows close. Laughter is also reflected in the eyes, and they become bright when you laugh; however, your eyes can also glaze over when you are bored, and tears can fall from your eyes with sadness (Esposito, Bratanic, & Keller, 2007). Your eyes can send messages of love, hate, dominance, and empathy, and they are important indicators of your feelings.

The act of fixing your eyes on someone is called **eye gaze**. When you communicate with another person, gazing at him or her serves two primary purposes: (1) to help you monitor the conversation and know when it is your turn to speak; and (2) to obtain feedback (Esposito et al., 2007). Eye gaze typically does not involve steady fixation on one location on the face. Our gaze tends to move around the other person's face in brief fixations, primarily on the other person's eyes and mouth.

Creatas/Thinkstock.

You can use eye gaze to monitor the other communicator during a conversation and determine when it is your turn to speak.

Having someone gaze at you can be pleasant, especially if you look at someone you are attracted to and he or she returns your gaze. However, if you gaze at a person to the extent that it causes discomfort, the person may interpret the eye behavior as threatening or intimidating. As a result eye behavior is one area of nonverbal communication in which children are often given explicit instructions such as, "It's rude to stare at someone" (Doherty-Sneddon, 2003).

Vocalics/Paralanguage

Your voice reveals a great deal about you. Your vocal quality or tone, rate of speech, volume, pitch, and rhythm, along with your silences and the vocal fillers you use when you pause often communicate your feelings, intentions, and meanings in powerful ways. These vocal elements are called **paralanguage**. When people are angry, their voices usually get louder and shriller. When tired, their voices are often flat and dull. Trainers often instruct people in customer relations jobs to smile when they talk with customers on the telephone because the facial smile also tends to "put a smile in your voice."

You can recognize people by their voices. In fact, your individual voice is unique, and you can be identified by a voice print, a computer-generated analysis that can distinguish one person's voice from another. How often have you heard someone talking as they walked by and knew who they were before you looked up? When you communicate with others, what does your voice say about you? In addition to the primary vocal characteristics that give your voice its distinct character, you also use other aspects of paralanguage, such as sounds and silence, to send nonverbal messages about your attitude. Let's examine how aspects of your voice and elements of paralanguage contribute to your communication with others.

Timbre. The **timbre** (pronounced "TAM-ber") of your voice refers to its overall quality and tone and is often called the "color" of your voice. Timbre is often regarded as one of the primary characteristics of a person's voice. It is what makes your voice either pleasant or disturbing to listen to. Adjectives often used to describe the timbre of a person's voice include clear, brassy, mellow, breathy, resonant, piercing, harsh, nasal, warm, melodious, thin, and flat.

Pitch. One of the most important ways you convey messages with your voice is through **pitch**. Vocal pitch describes where your voice is on the musical scale and determines whether singing voices are soprano, alto, tenor, baritone, or bass. Your pitch goes up and down the musical scale as you express different thoughts and feelings. When you are excited, for example, you usually unconsciously tighten the muscles in your throat, which causes your voice to rise in pitch. Changes in pitch are called vocal **inflection** and can affect how interesting you judge a person to be. Someone who speaks at the same pitch all the time, with no changes in their voice to express emotions, is said to speak in a monotone, and you may find it boring and difficult to pay attention to that speaker. Vocal inflection is also an important element in creating meaning. For example, try this exercise: Say the sentence "I never said he stole money" six times, emphasizing a different word each time. The first time you say the sentence, emphasize the word *I*: "*I* never said he stole money." The second time, emphasize the word never: "I *never* said he stole money." Continue the exercise, emphasizing each of the last four words as you repeat the sentence. Did you get a different meaning from the sentence each time?

Tempo. **Tempo** refers to your rate of speech—how slowly or quickly you talk. Your speech tempo is influenced by whether you lengthen the syllables of a word (called a drawl) or shorten the syllables (called clipped speech). It is also influenced by how fast you deliver the sequence of words in a sentence, by how often you pause, and by how long you hold that pause between words or sentences. These vocal characteristics are all part of your individual vocal style, and they enable you to emphasize certain words when you speak. They can also indicate power, self-assurance, or dominance, as when you speak very deliberately and distinctly. On the other hand, if you speak very slowly or hesitate when you talk, the tempo of your speech can show a lack of self-confidence or suggest that you are uncertain about what you are saying (Poyatos, 2002b).

Nonverbal Vocalizations

Some of the vocal features that can convey meaning are specific sounds, noises, and behaviors called **nonverbal vocalizations**. These vocalizations include laughing, crying, shouting, sighing, gasping, panting, yawning, coughing or clearing the throat, spitting, belching, hiccupping, and sneezing. These behaviors, sounds, and noises—along with others we humans can produce such as "grrr" to indicate anger or frustration, "psst" to get someone's attention, or "ah" when we see a beautiful sunset—help us express our ideas and feelings without words (Poyatos, 2002b). Vocalizations can be voluntary or involuntary, but they modify our communication and send a nonverbal message.

Pauses and Silences. Sometimes when we communicate, we stop making sounds. The presence or absence of pauses or moments of silence, how often they occur, and how appropriate or inappropriate they are to the conversation can be important messages in our communication. "I do not want you to disturb me" is the message of the person sitting next to you in an airplane if he or she remains silent and does not initiate conversation or greet you when you arrive, and most of us get the message (Penna, Mocci, & Sechi, 2009).

Touch/Haptics

In recent years, researchers have begun focusing on the study of touch, called **haptics**, and how it contributes to interpersonal communication. Indeed, physically touching another, says Dacher Keltner, a psychology researcher at the University of California, Berkeley, is the first nonverbal cue that we learn, and it remains "our richest means of emotional expression" throughout our lives (Carey, 2010, para. 3).

The sense of touch is a particularly interesting type of nonverbal communication because it does not correspond to any single physical organ. We have receptors and nerve endings throughout our bodies that record pressure, temperature, pain, and movement when we touch something or someone. Touch can be receptive, such as when we receive a pat on the back. It can also be expressive and convey a wide range of emotions from a slap in anger to a gentle touch that communicates empathy to a high five that expresses jubilation. A touch can soothe and comfort or it can push someone away. It can also bring distant objects and people into proximity (Paterson, 2007). Touch can often convey a wider range of emotion than a gesture and sometimes more quickly and more easily than words. In a recent series of experiments, volunteers tried to communicate a list of emotions by touching a blindfolded stranger. The participants were able to communicate eight distinct emotions, from gratitude to disgust to love, some with about 70% accuracy (Carey, 2010).

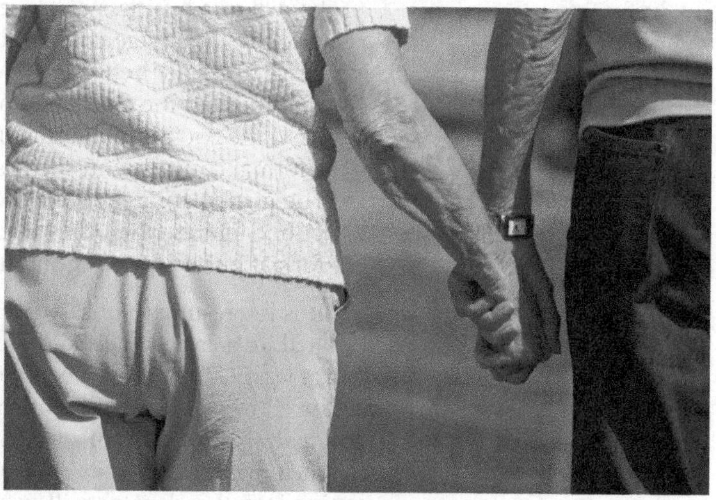
Huntstock/Thinkstock

Touch can be expressive and convey a wide variety of emotions, often more than can be expressed by a gesture.

Touch can convey so many different emotions, so use touch in interpersonal interactions only when you are relatively certain that its meaning cannot be misconstrued or in relationships where certain forms of touch are appropriate. Many people in many cultures object to being touched in any manner whatsoever, unless it is by someone with whom they are in a close relationship and to whom they have given tacit approval for the touch. In a business environment, a handshake is one exception. Among both men and women in professional business situations in the United States, a simple handshake upon meeting someone or leaving is an acceptable form of touch. A high five has also become popular as an informal touch among friends or peers—but not with people in positions of authority, unless they initiate the gesture. Kissing and extended periods of touch, in contrast, are typically reserved for romantic partners or our immediate family members. Therefore, consider your relationship when you touch another person; that is your best guide to what type of touch to use and how long it should last.

Personal Space/Proxemics

Another nonverbal cue that affects interpersonal communication is the use of physical space. The study of physical space is known as **proxemics**. This term was first suggested by anthropologist Edward T. Hall in his 1966 book *The Hidden Dimension*. Hall (1966) suggested that, in the United States, communicating with others happens from one of four primary personal space distances. Your personal space can be thought of as the invisible bubble you carry around your body at all times. These distances, which Hall referred to as spatial zones, are illustrated in Figure 6.3.

- The **intimate zone**, a distance of between 6 to 18 inches, is reserved for close, intimate relationships. A distance of 18 inches is about the length of your arm, so at an intimate distance, you can literally reach out and touch someone.
- The **personal zone**, from about 18 inches to about 4 feet, is the distance used for everyday encounters. This is the distance that feels most comfortable to Americans when they carry on a casual conversation with a friend or coworker. At this distance, people can move their arms around freely to gesture, without inadvertently touching someone, and this distance allows a normal tone of voice and volume.
- The **social zone**, a distance of approximately 4 to 12 feet, is sometimes known as a business distance. It is the distance generally used in business meetings at a large conference table and at other formal occasions. Most office desks are between 30 and 42 inches wide, so if one person sits at a chair behind the desk and another person sits on the opposite side of the desk, the two individuals will be positioned in this social zone to carry on a formal conversation such as a job interview.
- The **public zone**, between 12 and 25 feet, is the distance maintained by public figures when they speak to an audience, such as at a podium in a formal public speaking situation.

It is interesting to observe behavior when these personal spatial zones are violated. In a crowded elevator, for example, people are often unable to maintain at least 18 inches between themselves and other people. Instead, they may be forced to stand within someone else's intimate zone. Some people try to deal with this invasion of space in one of two ways. First, they will try to create as much distance between themselves and others as possible. The first person getting into the elevator will usually stand as far as possible to one side, the second person will stand at the opposite side, and a third person will stand in the middle, equidistant from the other two. Second, all three people will generally face forward and minimize their nonverbal signals. They will usually avoid eye contact with one another and reduce their facial expressions and body movements.

The distance between people can also send messages about the nature of their relationship. For example, Figure 6.4 illustrates a typical office arrangement

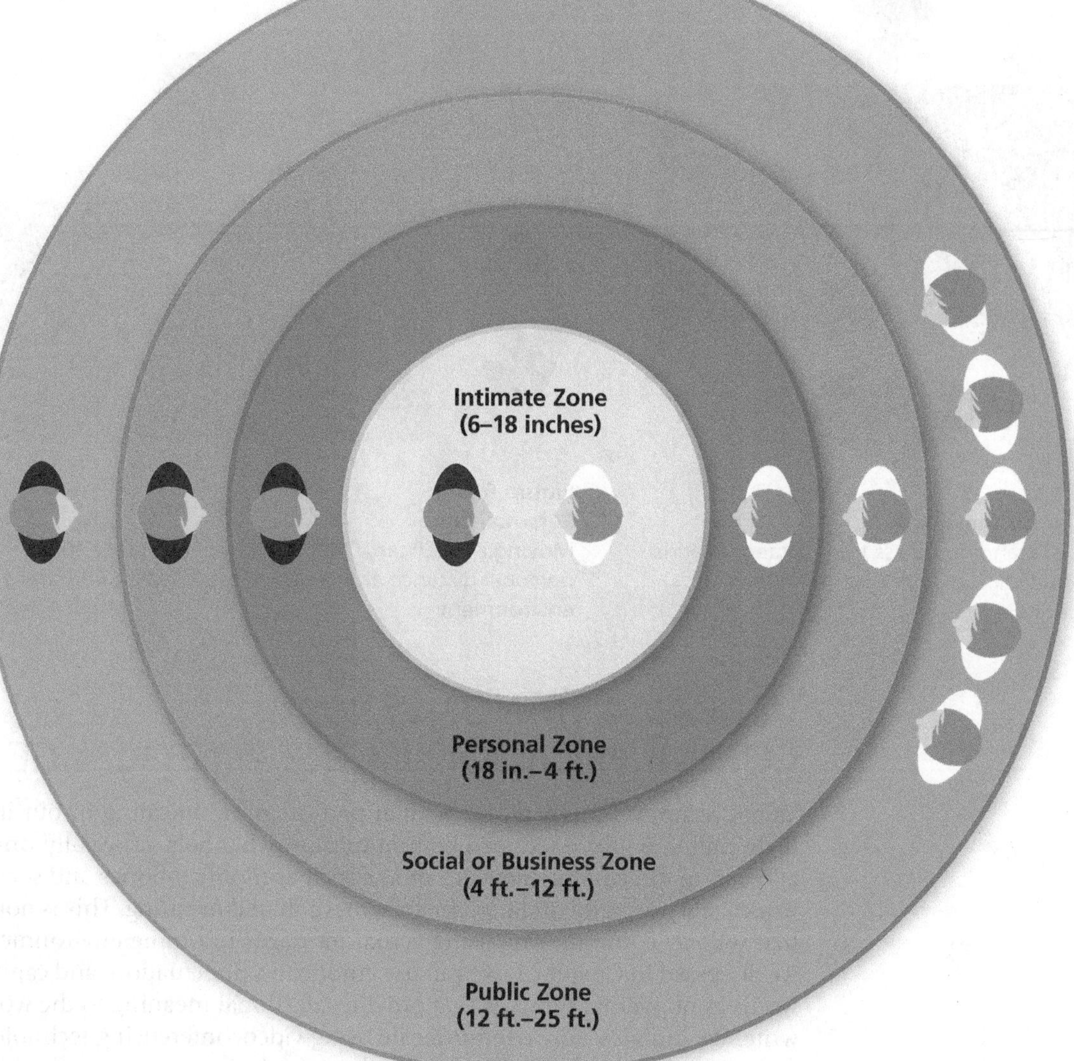

Figure 6.3
The four primary distances in U.S. culture
Hall (1966) proposed that communication can occur in four distinct personal distance zones: intimate, personal, social or business, and public.
Source: Adapted from Hall, E. T. (1966). *The hidden dimension*. New York, NY: Doubleday.

in which two people sit across a desk from each other. This positioning puts people at a social or business distance from each other where communication tends to be more formal. Studies also show that this positioning tends to promote competition or is the distance that people maintain when they do not like each other (Hill, Rivers, & Watson, 2008). Simply moving one chair to the side of the desk, as shown in Figure 6.5, reduces the distance between people and puts them at a personal distance from each other. Communication at this distance tends to be more relaxed and informal, and people tend to sit next to or adjacent to those with whom they have a cooperative relationship.

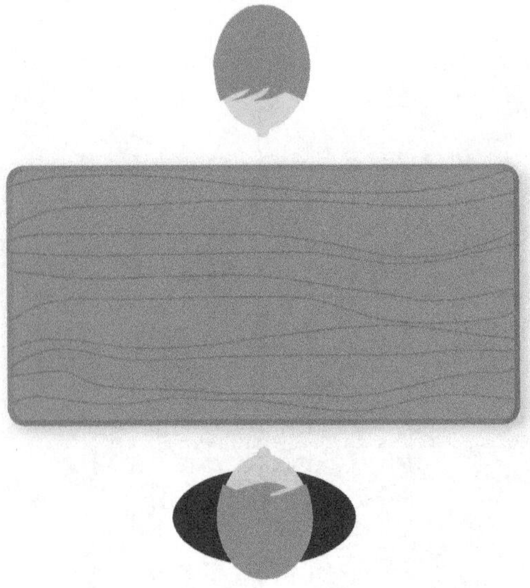

Figure 6.4
Social or business zone
Sitting or standing across from someone tends to be the typical distance for more formal interactions.

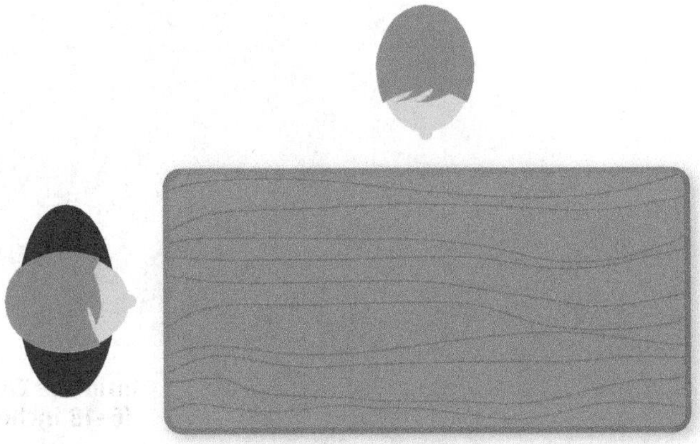

Figure 6.5
Personal zone
Moving a chair can change the social distance to a personal distance and create a less formal communication environment.

VERBAL AND NONVERBAL COMMUNICATION IN THE DIGITAL AGE

Verbal communication is an essential part of communicating in our increasingly online world. Mediated communication channels, especially ones that allow us to directly interact with others such as mobile phones and social networks, rely primarily on language to achieve shared meaning. This is not to say that we *only* communicate using verbal messages in online environments; as we discussed in Chapter 1, we can use emoticons, punctuation, and capitalized words as nonverbal symbols that provide additional meaning to the words we write. We can also now communicate using videoconferencing technology on our computers, tablets, and mobile phones—devices that allow both verbal and nonverbal messages to be encoded and decoded. As in our face-to-face interactions with others, both verbal and nonverbal messages are important when we communicate via mediated channels. Though we have not yet perfected a way to touch or smell one another over mediated channels, our current digital nonverbal communication is a vast improvement over earlier channels, such as electronic mail and listservs, which relied almost exclusively on written text. The following section describes the unique importance of both verbal and nonverbal communication in the digital age.

Verbal Communication in Mediated Contexts

As we noted above, we simply could not communicate online without language. When computer-mediated communication (CMC) began to grow and became a common way for us to communicate, communication researchers became more interested in understanding how communicating via CMC was different from interacting face-to-face. This early research on the differences between CMC and face-to-face interactions found that users rated CMC as less personal, more negative and task-oriented, and more focused on the self because online environments predominantly relied on verbal communication (e.g., Walther, 1992). Now, however, there is less of a division between CMC and face-to-face interactions because there are a greater variety of online and mediated methods of communication, and mediated audio and video technologies are increasingly available. In other words, though we once relied on e-mail text that we read on a computer screen, we now can use our mobile phones to instantly snap and share photographs online and to video chat with our friends via Skype or FaceTime. The addition of these sounds and visuals means that nonverbal communication is possible online, and it provides us with more information and context when communicating via CMC channels.

But unlike in face-to-face interactions, where we derive 60–65% of meaning from nonverbal communication (Burgoon, 1994), verbal communication—be it via text message, Facebook status updates, tweets, blog entries, or e-mail—is still the primary currency in our digital interactions with others. In fact, the sheer number of verbal messages that are exchanged via digital and new media is staggering, and this growth is primarily due to increased mobile phone use. Indeed, mediated verbal messages that once were only able to be sent and received via a computer are now also available on mobile phones, including e-mail, social networking, online game playing, video chatting, and text messaging. According to Online IT Degree (2011), 200 trillion (that's 200,000,000,000,000) text messages were received in America each day during 2011, which is more than the amount of regular ground mail items received in one year. In addition, sending and receiving text messages is the second most popular use for mobile phones, after checking the time (Online IT Degree, 2011). Further, 31% of Americans prefer being contacted by text message rather than the phone, and two-thirds of teens report being more likely to text than to call their friends (Lenhart et al., 2010; Smith, 2011).

Using mediated channels to communicate verbal messages, either via text messages or e-mails, can provide you with time to construct your message and a permanent record of what you said, and this can be helpful when you are engaging in formal interactions or with business and professional associates. The speed, convenience, and permanence of text messaging likely contribute to its frequent and preferred usage. However, compared to other ways that we can interpersonally communicate, texting does not offer very many message cues (Burgoon et al., 2002). For example, text messages are largely stripped of most nonverbal information, which can provide additional context, such as the emotions that an individual is feeling, or even contradict the verbal message entirely, such as when one's tone of voice indicates that the person is being sarcastic about what she is saying. However, in instances where only written text is available, removing nonverbal cues can actually focus users' attention on what is being verbally transmitted (Burgoon et al., 2002). In this way having limited information, such as we do when texting, could be beneficial for communication.

Nonverbal Communication in Mediated Contexts

Compared to verbal communication, researchers and communicators initially considered digital or mediated contexts less useful channels for nonverbal communication. Consider CMC in an online classroom: Online you do not have the benefit of the facial expressions, vocalics, and other nonverbal cues that you would have in a physical classroom, but you have more opportunities to contribute than you would have in a physical classroom where time constraints and group size may limit the number of people who can participate in a discussion. Limited nonverbal cues in e-mails or text messages, however, can create misunderstandings. To prevent these misunderstandings, many people use emoticons, or specific combinations of keyboard symbols, to replace physical facial expressions and help people interpret the meaning of a particular statement.

Gwyneth Doherty-Sneddon (2003) has examined how we change our communication style when we cannot see the other person, such as when we communicate by telephone. When there are no visual cues, turn taking in the conversation becomes more formal. We tend to speak in longer turns and avoid interrupting the other person. We also use phrases such as, "What do you think?" when we hand the conversation over to the other person, and we check about 50% more often to make sure the other person has heard and understood us by asking questions such as, "Do you know what I mean?" We also seek to confirm information more often by asking questions such as, "So, if I understand you correctly, you want me to . . . , right?" (Doherty-Sneddon, 2003). Providing feedback and paraphrasing the other person's statements are important listening behaviors in mediated communication, especially because technical noise in equipment, such as an intermittent cellular signal, can sometimes make listening more difficult. But as various forms of new media are introduced and grow in sophistication, the opportunities for nonverbal communication in mediated channels continue to expand.

rangizzz/Shutterstock.com.

In online environments, multimedia and other visually based elements make it easier for users to communicate and decode nonverbal signals.

Multimedia and other visual-based elements available in online environments make it easier for us to send and receive nonverbal communication through visual channels. For example, in 2012, 56% of Internet users viewed or posted photos or videos online (Rainie, Brenner, & Purcell, 2012). Some social media platforms such as Instagram and Pinterest primarily rely on communication through visual images. Instagram's objective illustrates the centrality of visual images shared via mediated contexts:

> Snap a photo with your mobile phone, then choose a filter to transform the image into a memory to keep around forever. We're building Instagram to allow you to experience moments in your friends' lives through pictures as they happen. We imagine a world more connected through photos. (Instagram Frequently Asked Questions, 2013, para. 2)

Such platforms are increasingly popular with Internet users. According to research, 12% of Internet users now use either Instagram or Pinterest (Rainie et al., 2012).

It is also possible to transmit auditory nonverbal signals in digital contexts. In addition to still images, computers, mobile phones, and tablets with built-in cameras allow users to send and receive videos. YouTube.com, a website where users share and view free video content, is the third most visited website in the world, with 450 million unique monthly visitors in July 2013 (Alexa.com, 2013). Videoconferencing applications such as Skype, Google Hangouts, and FaceTime also allow individuals to see, hear, and speak to one another in real time, over great distances, and with relative ease. We can now see and hear one another online better than ever before. We can even give someone a "thumbs up" when we like a friend's post on Facebook, and we can cycle through multiple profile photographs to carefully determine how to visually represent who we are to other Facebook users (e.g., Hum et al., 2011). Nonverbal communication's influence on mediated channels will continue to grow as technology offers more and more improvements in visual and auditory options.

As we saw, there are also benefits to using mediated channels to verbally communicate. Options for communicating via mediated channels are continuously emerging, and as they do we will respond by adapting our verbal and nonverbal messages to communicate competently and achieve shared

IPC IN THE DIGITAL AGE

Nonverbal Social Norms Online

There are unspoken rules regarding nonverbal communication in face-to-face interactions, but do we also follow these rules in online interactions? Nick Yee, a research scientist at the Palo Alto Research Center studying interactions in virtual environments, teamed up with colleagues to examine how those who play massively multiplayer online role-playing games (MMORPGs) such as Second Life observe nonverbal communication rules when interacting in these games. MMORPG players use three-dimensional avatars, or digital representations of themselves, in these games. The researchers predicted that players' avatars would follow similar social norms, as if these players were communicating face-to-face (Yee, Bailenson, Urbanek, Chang, & Merget, 2007).

By observing avatar interactions, Yee and his colleagues (2007) found that MMORPG players did indeed follow a number of nonverbal rules. For example, as in face-to-face interactions, the avatars stood closer to opposite-sex avatars compared to those of the same sex. In addition, when one avatar got too physically close, the other avatar compensated for this rule violation by looking away or moving back. Avatars who were talking to one another also stood close to and engaged in eye contact with one another. In other words, even though players in these games were not physically proximal to each other, they still feel the need to nonverbally communicate as they would in a face-to-face interaction. Yee and his colleagues (2007) concluded from their findings that the rules that govern our real, physical selves also direct our virtual, created selves when we interact online.

Critical Thinking Questions

1. Apply these findings to your own online interactions. If you play MMORPGs, do you notice that these nonverbal communication rules are followed?
2. When communication rules are broken, does it make you feel uncomfortable?
3. How do you think these rules change when we are videoconferencing with others and not communicating through avatars?

meaning in these digital and online contexts. Simply having these additional mediated channels to communicate provides us with more options for interacting with one another. Shifting seamlessly back and forth between face-to-face and mediated communication with a relational partner can increase how satisfied we are with that relationship (Caughlin & Shirabi, 2013) and can provide us with adaptability and flexibility in our interpersonal communication with others. (See *IPC in the Digital Age* to learn more about social norms in online communication.)

DEVELOPING VERBAL AND NONVERBAL COMMUNICATION COMPETENCE

You have already begun the work of becoming a more competent communicator by increasing your knowledge of language and how language works. Our ability to communicate both verbally and through mediated channels has a significant impact on our interpersonal communication. Nonverbal communication is also an important aspect of interpersonal communication. People vary in their ability to send and receive nonverbal messages, and difficulty understanding or interpreting nonverbal messages can be a serious challenge in interpersonal communication and can compromise our communication competence.

Success in your personal life, in school, and in the workplace thus depends on communication skills now more than ever. To be a competent communicator, it is important to analyze your own communications, observe how others communicate, and learn how to practice and adjust your skills in different contexts. Language skills include the ability to speak and write well and an understanding of grammar, punctuation, sentence structure, and language usage. However, research shows that another crucial skill is the ability to adjust language, make appropriate language choices, and accurately interpret messages (Halliday & Webster, 2004). Understanding and implementing these skills can improve your communication competence. Similarly, if you pay more attention to your own nonverbal behaviors and those of the people with whom you interact, you can make appropriate nonverbal communication choices too. Doing so will increase your knowledge, which then will help you to be a more motivated and skilled nonverbal communicator. The following strategies emphasize actions you can take to continue to improve both your verbal and nonverbal communication competency in a variety of contexts.

Analyze Your Own Communication

When you communicate, be conscious of the language you use and the nonverbal signals you send. Consider the purpose, receiver, and topic of the communication. Try this exercise:

> Make and evaluate a video of yourself talking with a friend or family member. Then review the video and critically analyze the language and types of nonverbal signals you use during the interaction. Is your word choice and vocabulary suitable for the situation, for the context, and for the topic of the interaction? Is your language biased or neutral? Then listen to your voice and consider the different vocalic elements. Also observe your body language and determine how you use

your eyes, your face, your body, touch, and personal space when you interact with the other communicator.

Using Figure 6.6, assess each of the issues concerning your vocal and visual behavior and ask the other communicator to perform the same assessment. The more you know about your communication choices the better able you are to evaluate the appropriateness of your choices and to adjust the communication as needed. This allows you to be more appropriate in your communication, contributing to your communication competence. Strive to use language that is most suitable to the situation, language that is not biased or unethical, and to be cognizant of how your body language, vocalics, touch, and treatment of personal space affect your interactions with others.

Boxed text provides a helpful guide for assessing personal vocal, visual, and touch behaviors used in a communication situation.

Observe How Others Communicate

Develop a habit of observing others in interpersonal communication settings, especially during your own interactions with others. Just as you monitor your own language choices and nonverbal signals, observe how others behave in different interactions. Pay attention to their language, vocal, spatial, and touch techniques. Consider how they use body language to build rapport. Sometimes it is a good idea to match the verbal and nonverbal communication styles of the other communicator. Consider again communication accommodation theory (CAT), which was introduced in Chapter 3. How does the communication either converge or diverge during an interaction? What happens if the communicator overaccommodates? Table 6.5 provides some examples of elements that you can monitor during an interaction.

Practice and Adjust Your Communication Skills

Develop strategies for improving your verbal and nonverbal communication skills, and be sure to practice. For example, reading as much as possible can be an excellent way to build your vocabulary. A similar strategy can also help

Table 6.5 Verbal and nonverbal elements to monitor during an interaction

Communication Types		What to Look For
Verbal	Spoken or written language	Is the language used formal or informal? Is the language used appropriate for the situation or context in which the interaction is taking place? Does the communicator use jargon or language that is not easily understood? Does the verbal message correspond with or contradict the nonverbal messages that are being used?
Nonverbal	Touch	What type of touch is occurring (e.g., kiss, handshake, hug)?
	Gestures	What emotions or moods are being expressed via body movement or the facial expressions?
	Space	How close or distant are the communicators from one another? Do both seem comfortable with the amount of space that is between them?

VOCAL

Timbre: What adjective could be used to describe your voice? For example, is it harsh, commanding, shrill, or melodious? Is it pleasant or unpleasant?

Pitch: Does your voice have sufficient vocal variety; do you vary the pitch of your voice to keep listeners interested in what you have to say?

Tempo: Do you talk at a rate of speech that allows people to follow you easily, or do you speak too quickly or too slowly at times?

General:

- Do any nonverbal vocalizations or dysfluencies interfere with your vocal effectiveness and appropriateness?
- In what areas of your vocal communication do you think that you excel? What areas could use some improvement?
- Do any of your vocal characteristics distract from or conflict with your verbal message?

VISUAL

Eye Behavior: Do you generally make eye contact with people during a conversation? Have you been told you make extended eye contact that could be construed as staring? Do you look at people appropriately or do you have any tendencies to violate norms about where you look?

Facial Expression: Do you make facial expressions such as frowning or scowling of which you are not conscious? Are your facial expressions natural? Do you smile appropriately or inappropriately? Do your facial expressions communicate that you are friendly or aloof?

Body Posture and Movement: Do you nod your head appropriately to provide feedback to others when they communicate? Do you lean forward when you interact with others to show interest in them? Is your body posture open and friendly, or do you tend to look uncomfortable in the presence of others?

Hand Gestures: Do you gesture naturally when you talk to reinforce your verbal messages? Do you gesture so much that you appear flighty or nervous? Do you hide your hands, keep them at your sides, or fold your arms, which can make you appear unapproachable?

Personal Space: Do you stand too close or too far away from others? Do you move closer and farther away from others along with the natural flow of conversation? Do you notice others moving away from you when you are speaking with them?

General:

- In what areas of your visual communication do you think that you excel?
- What areas could use some improvement?
- Do any of your visual characteristics distract from or conflict with your verbal message?

TOUCH

How much do you touch others? Does touching come naturally to you or do prefer not to touch or be touched?

Do you touch others in a way that is appropriate for your relationship of the situation?

How do others react when you touch them? How do you respond when you are touched? Do they (or you) stiffen up or seem comfortable?

General:

- In what areas of your haptic communication do you think that you excel?
- What areas could use some improvement?
- Do any of your touch messages distract from or conflict with your verbal message?

Figure 6.6
Assessment of vocal, visual, and touch behavior
The more you know about your communication choices, the better able you are to evaluate and adjust your behaviors as needed.

Table 6.6 Strategies for practicing and improving your communication skills

Strategies		Goals
Verbal communication	Read frequently and read a variety of sources, such as newspapers, books, and even social media posts.	To find and learn new terms and understand and use them in new contexts.
	Have a large and varied vocabulary to give you more word choices.	To help you encode and decode language accurately and appropriately.
	Offer feedback to other communicators about how you interpret their messages by rephrasing: "Let me make sure I understand:" or "Are you saying that…".	To help you and the other communicator negotiate and agree upon meaning in an interaction.
Nonverbal communication	Assess your nonverbal communication behaviors.	To learn how you uniquely nonverbally communicate and identify possible areas of improvement.
	Use feedback from others to adjust your nonverbal communication.	To better reflect the social norms of an interaction or the personal preferences of another communicator.

you identify elements of nonverbal communication that you can improve and practice. Consider again Figure 6.6 and your assessment of your nonverbal communication. See Table 6.6 to learn more about other strategies that can help you practice and improve such communication skills. But be aware that you may need to continually adjust your language and nonverbal communication for different interactions.

SUMMARY AND RESOURCES

Communication serves a wide range of needs in our lives, and language is the primary code we use to communicate with others. Language serves many functions in your life; it can be formal or informal, and is sometimes prejudiced or manipulated to suit political and social purposes. As children, you first learned the instrumental function of language as a means of expressing your needs, wants, and desires; soon, however, you learned that language has a regulatory function as well. As you became older and began to master your native language, your words began to help you form and maintain relationships.

We sometimes tend to take our use of language for granted, but good verbal skills are essential for personal and professional success, and they are critical to forming and maintaining relationships. Words are powerful tools; they create your reality, reflect your attitudes, and have multiple intentions and interpretations. Words do not have inherent meanings; rather, meanings are in people. Meanings are always personal and are the result of many factors, including your personality, your experiences, and the context in which the communication occurs. This interactional function of language helps you define yourself and your membership in groups and aids you in persuading others with your interpersonal communication. Language also allows you to participate with others in creating worlds that do not exist in the physical realm but only in your imagination, to participate with others in social customs, and to help establish your identity and distinguish yourself from those around you.

Language can be a primary communication vehicle during interactions, but nonverbal cues are also an important aspect of interpersonal communication. Nonverbal communication is the transmission of messages without the use of words, and this type of communication includes a wide range of vocal and visual signs and behaviors. Nonverbal messages have different characteristics, but they share common purposes: They primarily communicate your emotions and attitudes and contribute information to your conversations about how you are feeling and what you are thinking. They can also be a way to provide feedback to others, to show interest in them, and to help you regulate and maintain your conversations with other people. Some of the messages you send nonverbally are conscious and intentional, but many are innate aspects of your voice and body that you cannot easily change. Still other nonverbal communication is unconscious and the result of habits you have developed.

Nonverbal messages serve a variety of functions in interpersonal communication either in combination with or instead of verbal messages. You send messages to people by means of both nonverbal vocalizations and visible signs. Primary vocal characteristics, such as the quality and tone of a voice, are unique to each individual. But other vocal features, such as sounds, noises, behaviors, and pauses and silences, also contribute to your interpersonal communication. Similarly, some body language is personal and has meaning only to the communicators, but other visual signs convey a standard, shared meaning in a particular culture. When some visual signals, such as hand gestures, are used outside a specific culture they may have entirely different interpretations and thus be misinterpreted.

You can improve both your verbal and nonverbal communication skills by analyzing your communication, observing others as they communicate, and practicing and adjusting your communication. Improving your verbal communication skills is essential for educational and professional success. Some ways to improve your verbal communication competency are to improve your vocabulary, to increase your awareness of the language you use, to make appropriate language choices, and to adapt your language to communication situations. It is important to provide feedback and check for understanding to make sure that both the sender and the receiver of the communication share the meaning of words, and you must modify your language to ensure that your use of language is appropriate. The same is true for nonverbal communication. It is important to be more aware of what signals you send and how such signals are interpreted because you are then better able to adjust your behaviors for different interactions. Over time, this higher level of attention to both your verbal and nonverbal communication will help you increase your overall interpersonal communication competency.

Critical Thinking and Discussion Questions

1. Think again about the discussion from Chapter 3. What do you think is the relationship between language and culture? How do they interact with one another, specifically in your dominant culture?
2. In what ways are denotative or connotative meanings uniquely important in achieving shared understanding in an interaction?
3. Recall a conversation where someone used disconfirming or biased communication toward you. How did you respond and how did this response alter the tone of the interaction?

4. Think about a recent interaction you had. Did you derive more meaning from nonverbal or verbal communication in that encounter? Why was that type of message more important?
5. What form of nonverbal communication do you tend to focus on when communicating with others? Why do you think that you emphasize this particular type of nonverbal communication?
6. Consider the different forms and functions of verbal and nonverbal communication discussed in this chapter. Are there other functions of both verbal and nonverbal communication?

chapter 7

Communication and Culture

Photodisc/Thinkstock.

OBJECTIVES

In this chapter, readers will explore the essential associations between culture and interpersonal communication. By the end of this chapter, readers will be able to

- Define culture and co-culture
- Understand how culture and media are related
- Distinguish between primary and secondary identities, including explaining how cultural identity and communication are related
- Comprehend the role that cultural membership—including context, individualism, collectivism, and time orientation—plays in how we communicate with others
- Use strategies to strengthen interpersonal communication competence

KEY TERMS

acculturation
chronemics
co-cultures
collectivistic cultures
communication accommodation theory (CAT)
concurrency
convergence
culture
divergence
dominant culture

enculturation
ethnocentric
face
flexibility
high-context culture
identity
identity gaps
individualistic culture
intercultural communication
low-context culture
monochronic time system culture
normative
norms
open system
organizational temporal dimensions
ostracized
overaccommodation
polychronic time system culture
primary identity
secondary identity
separation
stereotypes

INTRODUCTION

In 2008, reporter Malcolm Gladwell published *Outliers: The Story of Success,* a compilation of human events that are extreme, unusual, and outside of one's normal experience. Chapter 7 of this book, entitled "The Ethnic Theory of Plane Crashes," recounts a particularly unusual pattern—one that even Gladwell himself admitted on his website was the most surprising to him ("What Is *Outliers* About?" 2013): the influence of commercial airline pilots' cultural background on how they communicate while in the air. Using examples from actual National Transportation Safety Board (NTSB) transcripts, Gladwell reveals that the causes of multiple plane crashes can be partially explained by the pilots' inability to competently communicate with one another or with Air Traffic Control (ATC), and that this communication difficulty is associated with culture.

When first officers, who are subordinate to captains in the hierarchy of the airline industry, tried to alert the captain of a problem, officers from cultures that prescribe deferential treatment to superiors used hints or softened speech to get their point across. In other words, even in potential life-or-death situations such as airline emergencies, cultural rules and norms were so ingrained in these first officers that they were simply unable to use direct and clear messages to notify their captains. Instead, the first officers chose to sugarcoat or downplay the significance of the situations. According to Gladwell (2008), NTSB transcripts present examples of the hints used by first officers in developing or actual airline emergencies, some of which include

- "Look how the ice is just hanging on his, ah, back, back there, see that?" (to captain, after noticing that there is a dangerous level of ice on the plane's wings, p. 196)
- "Climb and maintain three thousand, and ah, we're running out of fuel, sir." (to ATC, after being asked by the captain to tell ATC that they were in an emergency due to low fuel, p. 199)
- "Don't you think it rains more? In this area here?" (a subtle warning to the captain against doing a visual approach while landing in terrible, rainy weather, p. 213)

In each of the above instances, the plane crashed, and lives were ultimately lost. Gladwell summarizes this outlier when saying, "How good a pilot is, it turns out, has a lot to do with where that pilot is from—that is, the culture he or she was raised in" ("What Is *Outliers* About?" 2013, para. 6). Airlines with such issues during the 1990s, such as Korean Air, recognized these outlier patterns and took important steps to correct them, but miscommunications can still occur. However, the results of these efforts have been overwhelmingly successful, with a significant reduction in airline crashes in the last decade. This is a sobering example of just how much culture influences (and is influenced by) how we communicate, regardless of situation or context.

Chapter 3 examines the ways that culture and interpersonal communication shape and influence one another. In this chapter, we define *culture* and *co-cultures* and explore how certain cultural identity and characteristics are related to our interpersonal communication. The chapter also offers suggestions for improving your intercultural communication competence.

CULTURE AND COMMUNICATION

We are often unaware or not fully conscious of how culture influences our behavior and our communication, but it pervades almost every aspect of the lives of people in a society. Culture influences how we dress, how we act, what and when we eat, what and when we celebrate, how we raise and educate our children, and how we even view life and death. It affects our concepts of time, whether we prefer direct or indirect messages, if we view the world more as an individual or as a member of a group, and many other aspects of life that most people rarely think about. These characteristics of culture, in turn, affect the manner in which we communicate with other people. They influence our perception of the world, our verbal and nonverbal messages, and our relationships. If you desire to be a competent communicator, it is thus imperative that you understand the impact of culture on you, the people you encounter, and the interactions that you share.

What Is Culture?

When you travel to a new country, to a different region in the United States, or even to an event or environment that is unfamiliar to you, you will likely encounter people who speak different languages, wear different clothing, and have different customs from your own. Every society has a **culture**, or a number of different cultures—a relatively specialized set of traditions, beliefs, values, and **norms**, or standards of behavior that have been passed down from generation to generation by way of communication. Culture is often described as "the way we learn to do things." Everyday parts of our lives such as etiquette, values, customs, traditions, language, courtesy, and rituals such as shaking hands when you meet someone are at least partially formed, shaped, and changed by culture.

Culture provides structure in a society by defining the roles of group members and the hierarchy or status of various groups within the culture. In this sense, culture is **normative**, which means that it provides the rules, regulations, and norms that govern society and the manner in which people act with other members of that society. All societies have a system of social organization, and culture serves to provide an ordered and organized system for dealing with people within that society (Novinger, 2001). Culture is learned, but it seems natural because it is such an integral part of life. People are conditioned by culture to fit into a particular society, and the rules for interacting with other people are learned from birth. These rules become hidden, subtle influences on our behavior. You learn when to talk, when to keep quiet, and what tone of voice to use. You are taught which gestures are and are not acceptable. You learn what facial expressions are approved and which will earn a reprimand. You learn to sit up straight, cover your mouth to sneeze, and not to pick your nose (Novinger, 2001).

Tom Wang/Shutterstock.com.

Culture often seems instinctual because it is such an integral part of life, but its rules and norms are learned from birth.

Historically, most societies had a shared culture—a consistent set of cultural traits, norms, and customs among members of that society. Most modern societies, however, are a mix of different and often competing cultures because we have access to more foreign cultures today than ever before due to the increased rates of migration of people from one region of the world to another, military conquests, personal and professional travel, and global economics. But you do not have to travel abroad today to encounter cultural differences. **Intercultural communication**, which is a significant area of study in the communication discipline, is "the communication process in which individual participants of differing cultural and subcultural backgrounds come into direct contact with one another" (Kim, 2010, p. 454). The United States, for example, is an ethnically diverse nation of immigrants; in 2000 its foreign-born population was estimated at 30 million people, or 11% of the population (National Intelligence Council, 2001). Over America's 230-plus year history, it has become home to people from almost every other culture in the world, which likely explains why the United States is also currently one of the most racially tolerant nations in the world (Berggren & Nilsson, 2013). If you reside and work in the United States, you live in a multicultural environment, and you will regularly come into contact with people in your personal and your professional lives whose cultural backgrounds differ from yours.

We can view the United States as an **open system** culture: a culture that has continuous inputs and outputs from and to the surrounding environment. In other words, American culture is influenced by and can influence elements of other cultures. One example of this is our successful adaptation of British television shows such as *American Idol* and *The Office.* At the same time, who we are as a culture has also spread around the world in the form of movies and television shows. Celebrity international endorsements are also examples of the continued dispersal of American culture—for example, actor Ben Stiller's promotion of Chu-Hi, a Japanese canned alcoholic drink, or former wrestler and reality TV star Hulk Hogan's association with Hitachi air conditioner units.

Societies exert a great deal of pressure on people to conform to the way things are done in that specific culture, but this pressure is often subtle. You may be unaware of it until you do something unacceptable or encounter people from other cultures who do things differently. You may like to think of yourself as your own person, acting of your own free will. Although it is true that you can make choices about how to behave if your actions are not considered acceptable in your society, you usually suffer consequences or endure punishment for not behaving "properly." These consequences can vary. For example, you might be excluded from group parties, if your manners are poor. In a more extreme example, you might be **ostracized** or removed from a group or from society at large if you violate the formally stated laws of the land.

In summary, you could think of culture as a picture frame that surrounds and creates a border for your behavior and your communication. You are, in a sense, bound by your culture because the words in your language, your vocal characteristics, your nonverbal communication, and environmental influences can only be decoded correctly if someone is familiar with the cultural context. If you are not knowledgeable about a culture, you will often misread cues.

Dominant Cultures and Co-Cultures

Cultural diversity can enrich a society by infusing it with new ideas, new perspectives, and new ways of doing things. However, this diversity can also cause social unrest and conflict. As you learned in Chapter 1, belonging is a basic human need, and as we discussed in Chapter 2, self-image and self-esteem are equally strong needs. Immigrants to a new culture must often make difficult choices about whether to retain their cultural heritage, primarily adopt the behavior patterns of the dominant culture, or attempt to blend these different cultural characteristics in some way. The dominant culture, however, can also change when new populations are large and become significant subcultures, or co-cultures, within the society. The next sections will define and address these different aspects of culture.

Dominant Cultures. Although many societies are multicultural, they generally have a **dominant culture**—a term used by sociologists, anthropologists, and researchers in cultural studies to describe the established language, religion, behavior, values, rituals, and social customs of a particular society. The dominant culture may or may not represent the majority of the population; instead, it is considered to be dominant because it controls or has influence over social institutions such as the media, educational institutions, law, political processes, business, and artistic expression (Marshall, 1998). This power and control is not absolute, nor is it permanent: Other groups within the society may challenge the dominant culture. For example, because people from England, Ireland, and Scotland predominantly settled the original 13 colonies in the United States, many aspects of U.S. culture were based on British culture, which was itself a mix of English and other European traditions. As a result, the English language as well as the American legal and political system and many customs, religious views, attitudes toward work, recreational pastimes, and other characteristics of Anglo (English) culture became dominant in the United States (Mio, Trimble, & Arredondo, 1999).

When individuals are born into a particular society, they begin a process of **enculturation**, when they learn and adopt the norms, traditions, and beliefs of their dominant culture. Individuals are immersed in their dominant culture, and they acquire knowledge about that culture via direct experience. For example, they will eat food that is preferred by members of that culture, learn the primary language, and view and experience the major forms of media popular within that culture. Even immigrants usually undergo a period of **acculturation**, during which they learn and begin to adopt the norms of the dominant culture and the behaviors that are acceptable or preferred in the new society. Acculturation, for example, involves observing others who are members of the dominant culture to see how they behave, communicate, and what their preferences and dislikes are. From these observations, and by directly interacting with the newly adopted culture, the individual will begin to take on characteristics of that culture.

The acculturation process is not just one-way—as more and more new members join a culture, their values and beliefs will shape and influence the dominant culture as well. A society may celebrate its multicultural makeup, but its most widely shared customs, holidays, and traditions are usually those of the dominant culture, such as the U.S. holidays of Thanksgiving and Independence Day. The dominant culture of a society can change, but, unless a revolution or other major social upheaval occurs, this change usually happens slowly, over a lengthy period of time.

Table 7.1 illustrates some aspects of U.S. culture that can be troublesome for newcomers, but are likely to go unnoticed by most members of the dominant culture. These "Facts about American Lifestyle and Culture" were provided by the website www.path2usa.com to help visitors and immigrants understand and become familiar with various aspects of the dominant U.S. culture. Review the suggestions and consider whether the recommendations would be helpful for someone who is new to the United States. Do you think the recommendations

Table 7.1 Practical tips for visitors to the United States

Aspects of U.S. Culture Often Unfamiliar to Visitors or Newcomers
In America one has to keep to the right hand side of the road, and the driver's seat is on the left side of the car.
If a cop (police officer) asks you to stop while you are driving, just stop the car at the right side of the road and wait inside. Never get out of the car. The cop may consider it an offense.
You will find both "Hot" and "Cold" water in the tap at all places like your apartment, office, and public restrooms.
At restaurants, you won't get finger bowls. One can use paper napkins.
Electric switches are operated in the opposite direction, i.e., upside-ON and downside-OFF. Generally, there is no ON-OFF switch next to every plug point. They are always ON. Just connect the plug whenever necessary.
The TV channels can't be tuned according to your wish. For example, ESPN will come on channel 39; you can't change it. This is applied according to your area and the cable company.
At work or elsewhere while talking, if you want to say yes, just say "YES." Don't nod your head up and down. Moving your head side to side is very confusing, and it's mostly taken as NO.
Never, ever talk in your native language in the presence of Americans during a gathering.
When standing in a line, make sure there is enough space between you and the person standing in front of you. If you stand too close to strangers, they feel you are invading their personal space.
FREE is a buzzword here. You may get hundreds of ads with FREE in bigger fonts. Make sure that you read and understand all terms and conditions. Look for any hidden costs (Generally referred as the Catch) before accepting such offers. Note: Generally, the Catch is written in almost unreadable font size.
Don't be surprised if complete strangers greet you. Be polite and greet them back. Generally, Americans are very polite, friendly, and helpful, but have little patience with interference in their private lives.
Don't offer chewing gum or a breath freshener to others. It gives them a message that they have a bad breath. Your intention may not be that, but it is easily mistaken.

Source: "Facts about American Lifestyle and Culture." http://www.path2usa.com/facts-about-usa. Used with permission of www.Path2usa.com.

are all appropriate advice for those new to the United States? Would you alter any of these suggestions or include additional suggestions?

Co-Cultures. In addition to a dominant culture, most societies have several **co-cultures**—regional, economic, social, religious, or ethnic groups that are not the dominant culture but still do exert influence in the society. These co-cultures have characteristic customs and patterns of behavior that are unique to them and that distinguish them from the dominant culture. The terms *co-culture* and *subculture* have similar meaning, but *co-culture* implies that multiple cultures can exist together in the same geographic space, whereas *subculture* could imply that some cultures are necessarily subsumed into, or are inferior to, other cultures. The term *co-culture* emphasizes that, even though we can identify with a dominant culture, there may be another culture with which you identify more closely and feel best represents who you are and how you behave. For example, you might identify yourself as an American, but have a particular co-culture, such as a religious affiliation, geographic region, or occupation that you also strongly identify with and that is an important component of who you are.

There are various U.S. geographic co-cultures that developed because different ethnic groups or nationalities immigrated to specific regions of the United States. These regional co-cultures each have their own customs and traditions, dialects of the English language, and foods. Regional cuisines, from cheesesteaks and water ice in Philadelphia to green chile stew in New Mexico, grits and sweet tea in the South, and sushi in the West are examples of the influence of different cultural groups in parts of the United States (United States of America, 2010). Customs, traditions, and foods once unique to certain co-cultures also can become part of the dominant culture over time. The holiday of Cinco de Mayo, May 5th, for instance, commemorates the victory of the Mexican militia over the French army at the Battle of Puebla in 1862. The holiday is widely celebrated in the United States (though it is not celebrated in Mexico), especially in cities that have a significant Mexican population, and Mexican food is popular throughout the year in the United States.

Co-cultures also develop in groups other than those who share ethnic backgrounds. You are likely a member of any number of co-cultures, based in part on your gender, religion, political and social beliefs, occupation, school affiliation, athletic team preferences, and hobbies or interests. For example, attending San Diego Comic-Con, the annual convention that celebrates comic books and related aspects of science fiction, fantasy, and popular culture, can make someone who is not a part of the co-culture feel as if he is in a foreign country. There are characters, outfits, customs, phrases, and objects at Comic-Con that you might not understand if you are not a member of the comic book co-culture. Though the comic book co-culture seems like a small co-culture within the dominant U.S. culture, it has actually influenced, and is influenced by, multiple cultures in a meaningful way. Comic book superheroes are now a driving force behind several blockbuster movies. The Avengers, for example, is a multi-movie franchise based on characters and storylines originally developed in Marvel comics. Indeed, one researcher argues that superheroes often represent an ideal American identity and contribute to the narrative of "good American citizenship" (Wanzo, 2009, p. 93).

Another example of a co-culture's potential influence is the proliferation of National Breast Cancer Awareness Month (NBACM), held in October of each

Some co-cultures develop in groups with shared hobbies or interests. Similar to other co-cultures, such groups have unique customs and patterns of behavior.

year. Originally a health campaign started in 1985 by the American Cancer Society and a pharmaceutical company, breast cancer advocates and survivors emerged as members of an influential co-culture that gradually shifted the dominant culture's focus to fundraising and research on this specific form of cancer. The pink ribbon that symbolizes breast cancer awareness became an important marketing tool for showing support for fighting this disease, and for women in general. Eventually, companies such as Estée Lauder, national magazines such as *Self*, and major organizations such as the National Football League became involved in the event. In October 2013, the White House went pink for breast cancer awareness. This shift from small-scale campaign to nationwide co-culture illustrates the significant effects co-cultures can have on the dominant culture.

But some co-cultures have customs and behaviors that are dramatically different from those of the dominant culture; sometimes they are criticized or forbidden if they veer too far afield from conventional norms. For example, organized gangs are prolific in many urban areas in America and often engage in illegal, destructive activities. To combat the influence of gang co-culture, cities may adopt laws prohibiting graffiti, or "tagging," or schools may adopt dress codes that prohibit the wearing of gang colors.

In addition, one of the responsibilities of the Federal Communications Commission (FCC) is to ensure that individuals or groups do not behave in an obscene manner on television. When TV broadcasts do include content that is classified by the FCC as obscene, profane, or indecent, the FCC has the legal authority to levy a fine or even revoke a television station's license. The threat of such punishments prompts many stations (especially those that air live broadcasts with potentially controversial material, such as MTV's Video Music Awards) to use a 5- or 10-second delay. This short delay will allow the station to censor itself before profanity or nudity is broadcast to viewers. The dominant culture of a society, then, can exert a great deal of pressure on those co-cultures it perceives as being troublesome or possibly deviant, so much so that the co-culture may begin to self-regulate to prevent punishment from the dominant culture.

Culture and Media

Communication scholars agree that the media, including social media and emerging technology, is not only a primary tool for information transmission but is also a reflection of culture (e.g., Bybee, 2008). Today, due to its growing and ever-changing nature, media are more central to and interdependent with culture than ever before. Culture and the media are interrelated in three ways:

- Media can provide a range of details about the issues that matter to a specific society.

- Media can reflect dominant cultures and co-cultures.
- Media can help individuals learn about their cultures and others' cultures.

First, we learn about our own culture's politics, social issues, health information, popular movies, television shows, websites, and products and services via the media. As media consumers, we are discerning about which form of media we prefer as sources of information for particular cultural issues. For example, U.S. adults' preferred source of information about the 2010 Patient Protection and Affordable Care Act (also known as healthcare reform) was magazine articles, whereas interpersonal information from sources such as friends and family members was viewed as less satisfying and more difficult to obtain (Bevan, Sparks, Ernst, Francies, & Santora, 2013). Second, though the dominant culture, by definition, has the greatest control and influence over the media (consider the FCC example discussed in the previous section), aspects of any number of co-cultures can also be portrayed in the media. For example, many residents of southern states were upset about how their co-culture was being depicted on television programs such as MTV's *Buckwild* (now canceled) and TLC's *Here Comes Honey Boo Boo*. Third, media globalization means that individuals can use various forms of media to learn about and adapt to different cultures (e.g., Croucher, 2011). The 35% growth in international box office profits from 2006 to 2011 is an example of how U.S. pop culture is growing in size and influence worldwide (Motion Picture Association of America, 2011).

Social media also uniquely transmit and reflect culture. Individuals can use social media sites to communicate with other members of their culture, interact with their dominant culture, and learn about and acculturate to new cultures (Croucher, 2011). For example, some researchers (Johnson, Tudor, & Nuseibeh, 2013) argue that Twitter is a useful form of social media for engaging in political protest for five reasons; Twitter is

1. Quick, providing real-time information in 140 characters or less
2. Free
3. Personal
4. Highly mobile and resistant to government control
5. Capable of providing users with anonymity (p. 129)

Indeed, Ginger Johnson and her colleagues (2013) conclude from their findings that Twitter was an important platform and tool that protesters used when organizing and executing the Egyptian revolution in 2011.

A dominant culture can also strategically use social media to shape its identity; one example of this is the country of Turkey, which utilizes Twitter to communicate its national identity and exercise its cultural influence to followers (Uysal, Schroeder, & Taylor, 2012). Similarly, the White House (@whitehouse), and President Barack Obama (@barackobama) each have their own Twitter accounts, and the tweets signed "- bo" are directly posted by the president. Whether we use social media or other platforms, the media provide access to information and tools that we can use to learn about and participate in our culture and others' cultures. (See *IPC in the Digital Age* to read about the impact of using social media while studying abroad.)

CULTURAL IDENTITY AND COMMUNICATION

As we have seen thus far in this chapter, cultures and co-cultures serve important functions in maintaining a society and establishing norms and practices

IPC IN THE DIGITAL AGE

Does Use of Social Media While Studying Abroad Impact Adjustment?

Many high school and university students experience another culture in depth when they study abroad or take part in a foreign exchange program. Students gain a greater insight into a particular culture through such programs, but it can also be a stressful and lonely experience, especially as students first arrive and learn to adjust to their new surroundings. One study (Lee, Kim, Lee, & Kim, 2012) examined how social media can be used while studying abroad and the impact this use had on students' cultural adjustment. This study focused on 15 Malaysian students' experiences with social media while studying abroad. Specifically, the researchers analyzed students' status updates on Facebook while they were studying in North America and also considered their Facebook friends' responses. They focused on status updates because such updates are an example of a relatively unstructured online interaction, which means there is not an established format but an unspoken procedure that determines how, when, or what information should be posted. The researchers call status updates "the digital equivalence of a short conversation between friends" (Lee et al., 2012, p. 63). In addition, status updates are archived and thus easily retrieved: 917 status updates were collected from the 15 students and then examined for consistent themes. The student participants were interviewed before and after their study abroad experience and also completed a survey approximately 18 months after they had returned home.

The study findings first revealed that students used their Facebook status updates to cope with the stress of studying abroad, to provide information about their experiences in a new culture, and even to engage in social comparisons with other study abroad participants. The students' Facebook friends offered positive social support in response to the status updates that described negative emotions. Friends also offered humor, encouragement, and motivation when the students' updates indicated that they were having a difficult time. The study abroad students were also able to describe their experiences in the new cultures, thus allowing them to explore their new cultural identities while also maintaining ties with their old culture via connections with Facebook friends. The researchers concluded that Facebook was a useful psychological adjustment tool for study abroad students (Lee et al., 2012).

Apply these findings to your own experiences. Even if you haven't studied abroad, if you traveled to a new culture, think about how much you used social media while you were there and how your social media use may have influenced how well you adjusted to your surroundings. Now consider the critical thinking questions provided.

Critical Thinking Questions

1. If you have spent time traveling in another country, what types of social media did you prefer to use and why?
2. To what extent do you think that your use of social media to stay connected impacted how you adjusted to your new culture?
3. Could you use social media too much to stay connected with home and thus not experience as much of your new culture?

for its members. These practices may represent important events in the society's history and can provide a sense of communal pride, bringing people together with shared values, symbols, holidays, and traditions. Culture also helps create a perspective, or worldview, that influences how its members think about the world, themselves, and other people. Your dominant culture is so pervasive in your life that it influences your communication in significant ways. Culture gives you a sense of identity (Novinger, 2001).

Identity is a consistent set of attitudes that defines who you are and shapes how you view and describe yourself. It is your subjective self-image, what you

Nick White/Digital Vision/Thinkstock.

Identity can influence how we communicate with others, but our interactions with others can also influence our identities.

tell yourself, and what psychologists sometimes refer to as a self-schema (Johnson, 1986). For example, a person responding to the "Who am I?" activity from Chapter 2 might describe herself as an American, a southerner, an African American, a Baptist, a mother, a sister, a Girl Scout leader, and a New Orleans Saints fan. Each of these groups in which she claims membership tells others something about how she sees herself, how she defines her racial and ethnic heritage, what she believes and values, and what interests her.

Primary and Secondary Identities

Your identity can include both a primary and secondary identity. **Primary identity** encompasses consistent aspects of your identity, including your biological sex, race or ethnicity, nationality, religion, and age. In other words, an individual's primary identity rarely changes because it is difficult to permanently alter it. As we saw in the beginning of the chapter, the different aspects of one's primary identity can significantly influence how he or she communicates—the first officers described by Malcolm Gladwell were so swayed by their primary ethnic identities that they chose indirect messages even in emergency situations. We can, however, choose to ignore or downplay certain parts of our primary identities. For example, you may be a member of a particular religion, but you choose not to attend its services or follow its customs. People can also ignore their age limitations; Fauja Singh, for example, ran marathons until the age of 101 (BBC News, 2013)! In this way, we do not need to be defined by all aspects of our primary identities.

A **secondary identity** includes the more malleable roles and characteristics of your identity, such as your socioeconomic status, occupation, or relationship status. Your secondary identity can be just as important or central as any aspect of your primary identity but is more likely to change over time. For example, as you move up the ladder in your career, your job title and responsibilities will change, and this will alter part of your secondary identity. Shifting from full-time student to full-time employee, or vice versa, will also alter part of your secondary identity. But some secondary identities can be dangerous, especially when considered a significant part of one's identity. An individual who strongly identifies himself as a smoker, for example, is less likely to consider quitting and may find it more difficult to stop even if he tries (Harwood & Sparks, 2003). This strong identification with smoking thus might also increase his odds of developing smoking-related health issues.

Though primary and secondary identities differ, everybody has both a primary and secondary identity, and no two sets of identities are alike. The identities of individuals in an interaction can sometimes clash. In one study that explored the communication between grandchildren and their grandparents, young adulthood and old age are times when one's primary identity is particularly salient (Kam & Hecht, 2009). Specifically, young adults are negotiating their identities, and older adults who are grandparents view that particular relational identity as being particularly central to them. Jennifer Kam and Michael Hecht (2009) found that the presence of **identity gaps**, or discrepancies between the authentic self and the self that you believe another person finds more appealing, between young adult grandchildren and their grandparents was related to decreased satisfaction with the relationship and the interaction. Our interactions with others can thus shape and shift both our primary and secondary identities because communication can alter how we see ourselves and those roles or groups with which we most closely identify.

Membership, Interests, and Cultural Identities

Who you are not only includes your primary and secondary identities, but also what you enjoy doing and the important groups with which you seek to align yourself. Culture often has a hand in shaping which groups and interests are important. For example, the television show *Friday Night Lights* depicted high school football as an integral activity in Texas, with towns rallying around, and individuals strongly identifying with, their towns' teams and players. On the show, football players' families proudly displayed team signs in their front yards; wealthy and influential boosters provided the team financial support and perks, such as a Jumbotron screen; and most of the businesses in town closed down during games. A male growing up in this culture may want (or at least feel pressured) to be a member of this group to reap the many benefits of its membership, including elevated status in this particular culture. The reverse can also be true: An individual may shy away from a group or interest because it is negatively perceived by a culture. The same male may not want to be characterized as a "band geek," for example, and decide not to join the marching band, even though he loves playing a musical instrument.

How you choose to describe yourself enables you to highlight what you think is important about you, and this can include your memberships and interests as well as your primary and secondary identities. But your identity can also cause others to create a stereotype about you before they get to know you. **Stereotypes** are fixed opinions or preconceptions about someone based on perceived characteristics or expectations of a group rather than factual information about the specific person. In other words, stereotypes are exaggerated perceptions of similarities or differences among people. People in certain groups have some shared experiences, so some stereotypes might contain a grain of truth. To some degree, we need certain stereotypes to cognitively organize all of the information we can receive at any given time via our senses. However, stereotypes become problematic when they cause us to look at all members of a group as similar and to ignore the unique differences among individuals. It is best never to rely only on stereotypes when making judgments or forming an opinion because many stereotypes are negative judgments or are based on ignorance or misinformation about a culture and its members.

Try the following exercise: Picture someone named Garcia. Now picture someone named Claire. What do these two people look like? The people you pictured are based on your stereotypes of what those names signify. Would you be surprised if Garcia was a 5-year-old girl with blond hair and Claire was a 66-year-old man? Table 7.2 contains some stereotypes about U.S. culture and some common American interpretations. In your interactions with other

Table 7.2 Stereotypes of American culture and common American interpretations

Stereotype of American Culture	Common American Interpretation
Americans are self-centered and uncaring or disinterested in others because they rarely ask them personal questions.	It is rude to ask personal questions of people such as their age or how much money they make.
Americans are insincere; they are always smiling and are unrelentingly enthusiastic.	Americans are optimistic, and it is polite to appear happy, even when they are not.
Americans are loud, crass, and effusive. They assertively introduce themselves to others.	Americans value being sociable and friendly.
Americans maintain a large physical distance from one another compared to many other cultures, and yawning, passing gas, and openly breast-feeding are frowned on.	Americans express bodily restraint to avoid offending others by standing too close, touching others, or engaging in behaviors that may make others uncomfortable.
Americans are competitive, and, unlike soccer, American football games can never end in a tie. Football also reflects cultural ideals about sex and gender; the attire of players and cheerleaders exaggerates male and female sex characteristics.	Americans connect with one another through sports. Football expresses an important American value of competition. The attire of football players is primarily for protection from injury rather than to exaggerate male characteristics. However, Americans admit to accenting female sexual characteristics with cheerleader outfits.
The word *American* conjures up an image of a white, middle-class person. All other residents, including the area's indigenous inhabitants, are hyphenated or identified with an adjective: Native American, African-American, Asian-American, Mexican-American. The national census does not hyphenate Americans of European descent.	Hyphenation of names is commonly the preference of the group itself and distinguishes their cultural heritage.
Americans have food rituals to accompany many occasions. Waking up is accompanied by coffee. Social occasions usually include alcohol. Hot dogs and beer are served at sporting events, and popcorn and candy are consumed at movie theaters.	Americans do associate certain foods with certain occasions. However, no pressure is put on people to conform; people are free to avoid eating on these occasions or to substitute other foods and beverages.
Americans celebrate several national holidays, but they are regarded more as family holidays than as celebrations of patriotism. The Fourth of July marks the Declaration of Independence from Britain in 1776, but it is also a time for summer picnics and camping trips for friends and family. Thanksgiving is an annual feast that celebrates the hardships of early colonists, and, according to legend, the American Indians who came to their aid, sharing indigenous foods such as maize and turkey. However, Thanksgiving is important not primarily because of its symbolism but because it is a significant family holiday, and one of the few large and elaborate meals that families prepare.	Many Americans consider national holidays to be times in which families come together. However, they like to think that they celebrate both the family fellowship and the significance of the holiday itself. Americans have a proud military tradition, and flying the American flag, for example, is common on the Fourth of July to celebrate the country's independence. Giving thanks for their blessings around the table before the Thanksgiving dinner is traditional among many American families to show gratitude for the occasion, the food, and the family.
Americans are generally not opposed to social benefits such as pensions, Social Security, and insurance of bank deposits. However, relief programs for the poor, known as welfare, are controversial. In a country where many believe that all its citizens have an equal chance, where opportunity is unlimited, and where only the lazy are poor, programs for the indigent have been vulnerable to cutbacks.	Americans generally believe in providing a safety net for those in the society who are unable to help themselves. However, they also strongly value self-reliance and believe that people have a personal responsibility to care for themselves and their families if they are able to do so. The conflict between these two values is a major political issue in the United States.
Americans have an uncomfortable relationship with their own mortality. Although most residents are Christian, the value placed on youth, vigor, and worldly goods is so great that death is considered a sad and solemn occasion. It is difficult for Americans to talk about, and at funerals it is customary to wear black and to speak in hushed tones. Graveyards are solemn and quiet places.	Americans often have difficulty accepting the inevitability of death. However, they believe that this problem stems more from their enjoyment of life rather than the placement of value on youth or worldly goods. While it is true that Americans admire youth and vigor, they also care for their elders and value them as important family members.

Source: Adapted from United States of America. (2010). *Countries and their cultures: Culture of United States of America.* www.everyculture.com.

people, have you encountered any of these stereotypes, or other stereotypes based on your cultural heritage, memberships, and interests?

Communication Accommodation Theory

A number of communication theories can help us understand and improve how individuals from different groups or cultures interact with one another. The most significant of these theories is **communication accommodation theory (CAT)**, developed 40 years ago by communication studies scholar Howard Giles. CAT aims to provide possible explanations for how and why people adapt their communications with those who are different from them and the social and cultural outcomes of such adaptations (McGlone & Giles, 2011). Specifically, CAT describes how communicators from different social groups or cultures choose to modify or adapt their nonverbal and verbal messages to accommodate, or adjust to, one another (Shepard, Giles, & LePoire, 2001).

According to CAT, **convergence** occurs when we alter our messages towards those used by other communicators in an interaction. For example, we might speak at the same rate, use a similar tone or accent, or self-disclose similar levels of information. Convergence is more likely when individuals seek to be like the person they are interacting with, and it is usually perceived as a positive communication strategy. However, there is also a risk of **overaccommodation** when a communicator goes beyond what is necessary to mitigate differences between communicators, and such accommodations might be perceived as insincere, offensive, or condescending (Sparks, Bevan, & Rogers, 2012). Speaking slowly and loudly to someone from a different culture is one example of overaccommodation, especially if a language difference, not an auditory impairment, is the true barrier to shared meaning.

We can also exercise communication **divergence** if we shift our verbal and nonverbal communication away from other communicators in an interaction. Divergent messages emphasize social distance from others and whether or not one is a member of a particular group. Using divergent communication is often negatively perceived and is considered a signal that the communicator dislikes or is uninterested in the interaction (Sparks et al., 2012). An example of cultural divergence is refusing to learn the language or customs of a foreign country, where you are a visitor, and instead behaving as if yours is the dominant culture.

How can CAT help you improve your intercultural communication? First, it is important to consider altering or accommodating your communication when you interact with members of other cultures or co-cultures. Trying to encode convergent messages when you interact with others will increase communication competence. But be careful not to overaccommodate because then your messages could be perceived as an insult, imitation, or overzealous attempt to gain acceptance. Instead, let the conversation naturally flow. At the same time, monitor the other communicator's responses to your messages and be mindful of how the person adjusts his or her messages.

CULTURAL MEMBERSHIP AND INTERPERSONAL COMMUNICATION

In his classic book *The Silent Language*, anthropologist Edward T. Hall states, "culture is communication and communication is culture," suggesting that culture and communication necessarily go hand in hand (1959, p.186). In his view, culture governs our communication, and communication creates and reinforces culture by transmitting it through language and nonverbal communication. Your culture is the framework that tells you what is important to attend to, how to organize what you see, and how to interpret it. For example, suppose that someone in a room holds up an index finger. If you are from the United States, you may or may not notice the gesture. However, if the person were, instead, to hold up the middle finger of his or her hand, it would probably get your attention. This second gesture communicates a specific shared message to members of American culture, and if you are familiar with that culture you would quickly make sense of and interpret the gesture based on cultural norms.

Both verbal and nonverbal messages reflect your social background and heritage, as well as the experiences, beliefs, values, attitudes, and role expectations supplied by your dominant culture and the co-cultures that are important to your identity. The language that you learn and use in your everyday communication with others is culturally bound, as are the nonverbal communication that you use or do not use. For example, though Americans and British both speak English, certain words have different meanings depending on these specific cultures—elevator versus lift, or chips versus crisps, for example. Americans also frequently make direct eye contact with their conversational partners, whereas members of a number of Asian cultures shy away from direct eye contact, believing that eye contact is disrespectful.

XiXinXing/Thinkstock.

Both verbal and nonverbal messages can reflect one's social background and heritage.

When you come into contact with people from other cultures, you cannot assume they will encode and decode messages the same way you do. Indeed, the cultural, social, and historical context in which the message occurs must be considered to increase the likelihood that meaning will be shared (Hall, 1976). You can certainly encounter communication difficulties with people from your own culture, but the incidence of such problems increases when you interact with people from entirely different cultures. In the personal, professional, and mediated arenas, cultural differences can cause communication difficulties, as can different languages and different interpretations of nonverbal messages. Some of these potential communication challenges are discussed next.

Low-Context and High-Context Cultures

All cultures incorporate both verbal and nonverbal elements into their communication. However, some cultures depend more on words, while other cultures rely more on nonverbal elements such as body language, factors in the environment, or the communication situation itself. One way to understand these communication differences, introduced by Edward Hall in his 1976 book *Beyond Culture*, is to determine a culture's context. *Context*, according to Hall (1976), is a function of culture that "designates what we pay attention to and what we ignore" (p. 85). Context, in relation to communication, is a cultural factor that determines the degree to which the intention or meaning of communication is explicit or implicit. A particular culture, as it relates to Hall's conceptualization, can thus be placed along the continuum ranging from low context to high context.

The meaning of messages in a **low-context culture** tends to be clear, direct, and is typically derived from words. The United States, for example, is a low-context culture. A great deal of emphasis is placed on the words someone uses when they speak, and in U.S. culture phrases such as "I give you my word" and "My word is my bond" reflect the value placed on people's words. A great deal of significance is also placed on explicit, written messages, including formal contracts, meeting agendas, and even course syllabi, to provide necessary information and details. Nonverbal messages such as silence, eye contact, or gestures are generally used to reinforce words. A **high-context culture**, however, emphasizes the implicit and indirect meaning of messages, and thus communicators rely more on nonverbal elements. For example, in some high-context cultures a raised eyebrow might mean "yes," as in France and Polynesia, or it might mean "no," as in Greece (Novinger, 2001). Words are not as important as the way they are said, or the context in which the communication takes place, so members of high-context cultures are better at "reading between the lines." Much of the important information in a high-context message is contained in the nonverbal elements, in a ritualized response, or in the context of the communication.

To help illustrate differences between high- and low-context cultures, consider how individuals might engage in conflict with one another. Stephen Croucher and his colleagues (2012) found that members of the high-context cultures of India and Thailand would either avoid conflict or give in during conflict, whereas members of U.S. and Ireland low-context cultures would be direct and dominating during a conflict. But it is important to note that cultures do not rank as "low" or "high" in an absolute sense. Instead, such distinctions occur on a continuum, or scale, from lower to higher. Greek culture, for example, may depend more on context in a communication (higher on the continuum) than the English culture but depend less on context (lower on the continuum) than Japanese or Chinese. It is also important to remember that people within a particular culture may be extremely diverse and that various co-cultures exist within each dominant culture. For example, even though someone may be from a low-context culture such as the United States, that person's central co-culture could be higher context than the dominant U.S. culture.

Low- and high-context categorizations do not apply to all people in a specific country, but it is important to understand the general tendencies of the dominant culture because this knowledge can help you communicate better with those from cultures different from your own (Copeland & Griggs, 1985). Every culture is unique, and when you interact or do business with people from other cultures, you must become familiar not only with the language of the other country but also with its culture. In some high-context cultures, for example, it is considered rude to directly say "no" if someone makes a request of you, and people instead prefer to communicate the "no" without actually saying the words. They might say, "maybe" or "I will try," but it is clearly understood to mean "no" to someone who is familiar with that culture. The "maybe" or "I will try" answers are simply ritualized responses, much like when we ask someone "How are you?" and they respond "fine" (even when they are not).

People from low-context cultures such as the United States are used to focusing on being precise and using verbal communication. So, when an American makes a request of a person from a higher-context society who responds with an indirect, ambiguous message such as "I will try," the American will typically ignore the ritual and the context, take the words literally, and expect the person to try to accommodate the request. Then the American may become upset when the other person makes no attempt to do so. If the American protests, the high-context person may have difficulty understanding and believe the American is trying to force a rude response (Novinger, 2001). When engaging in an intercultural communication, you may have a tendency to be **ethnocentric**, that is, to believe that your own culture or method of communication is best or does things "the right way" and that others are wrong. One of the most important skills of competent communicators in this multicultural and globalized world is to recognize that cultures are not right or wrong; they are merely different from one another. Figure 7.1 summarizes the different characteristics of communication in low-context and high-context cultures.

Individualistic and Collectivistic Cultures

In addition to differences between low- and high-context communication in cultures, another fundamental way in which cultures differ is their tendency toward individualism or collectivism. In **individualistic cultures**, there is a tendency to focus on individual rights, identity, and achievements. The United States, for example, is an individualistic culture. Americans generally value a strong sense of personal identity and promote individual goals, rights, choices,

Low-Context Cultures	High-Context Cultures
• Rules are clearly stated.	• Rules are not often verbalized.
• Expectations are spelled out.	• Expected behavior is understood.
• Directions are clearly stated.	• Directions are assumed to be understood.
• Instructions are explicit.	• Communicators use their own instincts.
• Acceptable behavior is not assumed.	• It is assumed that people know how to behave.
• Knowledge is made public.	• Knowledge is internalized.
• Behavior is governed by rules.	• Behavior is conditioned by the relationship or by ritual.

Figure 7.1
Communication in low-context and high-context cultures
Every culture is unique, but there are some general factors that we can keep in mind when we interact with individuals from high-context and low-context cultures.
Source: Based on information from Novinger, T. (2001). *Intercultural communication: A practical guide*. Austin, TX: University of Texas Press.

and freedoms. People in the United States, as well as in other individualistic cultures such as Australia and the Netherlands, are encouraged to be unique and self-reliant. They are generally stimulated by individual competition, place personal goals over others' motivations, and often attribute their achievements to their individual strengths. In an individualistic culture, meeting new people often involves questions about accomplishments such as "What do you do for a living?" Many believe that they create their own identity, and they are proud of their personal success.

Members of **collectivistic cultures**, however, focus more on group obligations, identity, and concerns. Collectivistic cultures such as China, Costa Rica, and Indonesia tend to value a strong sense of group identity and promote group goals and values. Such cultures also value close ties, cooperation and harmony, conforming to the group, and relying on others for support. The group, family, or community a person belongs to is of high importance in the culture, and people are more interdependent and closely associated with their social network that includes their family, coworkers, and fellow group members. What is best for the group is the overriding factor in decision making. In Japanese business situations, for instance, decisions are made within the group, with little or no personal recognition for individuals (Morrison & Conaway, 2006).

One significant difference between individualistic and collectivistic cultures is how members of the cultures save face. The term **face** refers to the standing or position a person has in the eyes of others, or "an individual's claimed sense of positive image in the context of social interaction" (Oetzel & Ting-Toomey, 2003, p. 600). When we attempt to "save face," we strive to maintain a positive position in the eyes of other people with whom we communicate or to respect the position of others. When we "lose face," we are embarrassed or humiliated, and we believe that our position in the eyes of others is diminished.

The concept of face appears in most cultures, but it manifests itself in different ways. Intercultural communication researchers John Oetzel and Stella Ting-Toomey (2003) have studied face in relation to culture and found that those in collectivistic cultures place more emphasis on the face of others. In an individualistic culture, face is often the source of one's personal pride or self-respect, and saving face is a personal goal. It is one reason why one may make excuses, rationalize, laugh, or excuse her behavior rather than admit she is wrong. For example, the first officers discussed in Malcolm Gladwell's book *Outliers* likely were swayed by their perspectives about face, meaning that they chose not to threaten the captain's or air traffic controller's face when they made a request or offered a suggestion, even when lives were at stake. But U.S. air traffic controllers were more interested in accomplishing tasks rather than saving face, which the first officers could have viewed as a threat to their own face.

In a collectivistic culture, face influences a person's status in the social group or in society as a whole, and people feel an obligation not only to save face themselves but also to help others save face and not to bring shame on their group (FitzGerald, 2003). In China's collectivistic culture, for instance, the Chinese word for "politeness" includes four components: respectfulness, modesty, a warm attitude, and meeting standards. In this culture saving face means first respecting others by showing appreciation and admiration for them. Second, one must be modest, which is demonstrated by not calling attention to oneself or elevating oneself. Third, an attitude of warmth requires that people show consideration, kindness, and hospitality to others. Finally, one must behave in ways that are appropriate and that meet society's standards. To meet these goals in conversation, Chinese people often present themselves in a modest or self-deprecating way and will avoid saying what they actually think if it might hurt others (Cheng, 2004).

Like low-context and high-context communication characteristics, the differences between individualistic and collectivistic cultures are not absolute but exist on a continuum. There are elements of individualism and collectivism in all cultures, but to greater or lesser degrees. For example, Germany is classified as a moderately individualistic culture, whereas Japan is moderately collectivistic (Oetzel & Ting-Toomey, 2003). Nearly three fourths of the world's cultures can be described as collectivistic (Triandis, 1989). (Read *Everyday Communication Challenges* to get a further view of the issues involved when e-mailing in different cultures.)

Based on what we have discussed about the differences between individualistic and collectivistic cultures, you probably understand how conflicts can occur when people interact closely with others who have different values on issues such as what is best for the group versus what is best for the individual, being unique versus fitting in, and self-reliance versus cooperation. If you want to be a competent communicator when interacting with individuals from other cultures, you must strive to understand the social norms of people from other cultural backgrounds. Figure 7.2 summarizes some differences in the characteristics of individualistic and collectivistic cultures that can influence communication between people in these two types of cultures.

Time Orientation and Culture

Time is a finite concept; we measure it in seconds, minutes, hours, days, months, and years or by cycles of the moon and tides, the weather, the movement of

Individualistic Cultures	Collectivistic Cultures
• Independent	• Interdependent
• Self-reliant	• Reliant on the group
• Competitive	• Cooperative
• Personal achievement valued	• Group achievement valued
• Personal identity prized	• Identity tied to social network
• Loosely associated with groups	• Strongly associated with groups
• Self-assertion and autonomy valued	• Confrontation avoided and harmony valued

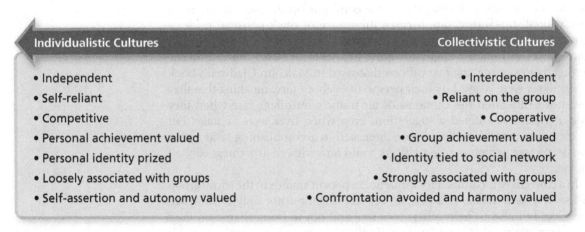

Figure 7.2
Communication in individualistic versus collectivistic cultures
Similar to context, a culture can have a tendency toward individualism or collectivism. There are elements of both in all cultures, but to greater or lesser degrees.
Source: Based on information from Novinger, T. (2001). *Intercultural communication: A practical guide*. Austin, TX: University of Texas Press.

EVERYDAY COMMUNICATION CHALLENGES

"Reply-All" and Individual Correction: To Send or Not to Send?

Have you ever received an e-mail that contained a mistake? If it was a significant mistake such as the time or location of an upcoming and important meeting, it may need to be fixed. You might feel that it is helpful to inform the person who sent the message so that she doesn't get embarrassed or miss an opportunity. However, what if the message was sent to a large group of people? You'll need to decide if you should point out the mistake to that one person or to the group as a whole. Or, what if the mistake isn't that important, like a simple misspelling? Is it important to fix every mistake that you find, or should you correct it to the group on their behalf?

Regardless of what type of culture you come from, you probably don't like being embarrassed. Depending on the sender's culture, it may cause more problems if you try to correct the e-mail than if you simply let the mistake go. In highly individualistic cultures like the United States, it's probably wise to directly contact only the sender so that she doesn't make the same mistake again, since self-respect is often tied so closely to performance and individual ability. The sender may want to acknowledge the mistake herself. However, in a collectivistic culture, like those found throughout Asia, everyone works to help others in their group "save face." In that situation, you probably shouldn't point out an unimportant mistake, as long as that sender's mistake isn't going to create future problems. Instead, by remaining silent on the matter (and by other group members also remaining silent), everyone avoids the potential public embarrassment.

And if you are the sender, remember that it is easiest to avoid embarrassment by not making mistakes in the first place. So always proofread before you hit "send"!

Critical Thinking Questions

1. Think about a professional situation that you have experienced where there were multiple senders and receivers on an e-mail and a mistake was made. How was it handled?
2. Regarding your own e-mail example, were there cultural implications that factored into how the people on the e-mail responded to one another?
3. If a mistake is made in an e-mail that must be corrected, how can you do so in a way that saves the face of the sender, while also conveying the correct information?

planets and stars in the solar system. Time is also a form of nonverbal communication that is structured formally and informally by a culture. According to Edward Hall (1976), "time is so thoroughly woven into the fabric of existence that we are hardly aware of the degree to which it determines and coordinates everything we do, including the molding of relationships with others in many subtle ways" (p. 18). Perception of time is very subjective. A minute waiting for something exciting can seem like forever, and an hour when you are doing something enjoyable can pass quickly.

Chronemics is the study of how a culture structures and uses time, including how individuals perceive, structure, emphasize, and respond to time, as well as how they interpret messages about time. Though time is a structured and formalized entity within and across cultures now, it was not always this way. For example, standard time in the United States did not commence until the spread of railroads as a popular form of human transportation in the mid-1800s made it necessary to establish cultural agreement about exact time. Trains were the first method of transportation that could move passengers from place to place in a relatively short amount of time. Unless 2 p.m. was the same time for every station, it would be difficult for passengers to arrive at the station on time and board the trains before departure. Even today, despite the different time zones around the world, there is agreement that the hours change, but the minutes stay consistent. Issues such as the importance of punctuality, the timing and duration of business and social visits, and the amount of time you should wait for someone who is late all vary from culture to culture. For example, arriving five minutes late for a business appointment in the United States would usually require a brief apology, but it may not be considered important in another country.

When you communicate with people of different cultures, variations in how you structure and use time can cause people to take offense when none was intended. However, time can also be used to send intentional messages to another person, and the person who has more power or influence in the interaction typically uses it for that purpose. For example, former U.S. President Harry Truman reportedly once kept a newspaper editor waiting for an appointment for more than 45 minutes. Finally, the editor asked the president's aide to check with the president about the long wait. Truman is said to have replied that when he had been a junior senator, the editor had kept him waiting for an hour and a half so, as far as Truman was concerned, the editor still had "45 minutes to go" (Sowell, 1994). Since Truman was president, and had more power than he did as a junior senator, he chose to and was permitted to use time in this intentional way. Time can, of course, be used to send a positive message as well—arriving very early for a presentation or submitting a project early can indicate great interest.

Hall (1959) introduced one important relationship between time and culture when he described monochronic and polychronic systems of time. In **monochronic time system cultures**, members prefer to attend to or schedule one task at a time. Time is viewed as a tangible and valuable item that can be gained or lost, and individuals adhere to formal time, which is regulated by a clock. Sayings such as "Time is money" and "I'm out of time" are expressions of a monochronic time system. In the United States, for example, people tend to be punctual about appointments, to focus on one thing at a time, and to get to the point quickly in conversation, interrupting others, if necessary, to move the conversation along. Such behaviors reflect an emphasis on concentration, commitment to a task, promptness, and compartmentalization, which are characteristic of a monochronic time system culture.

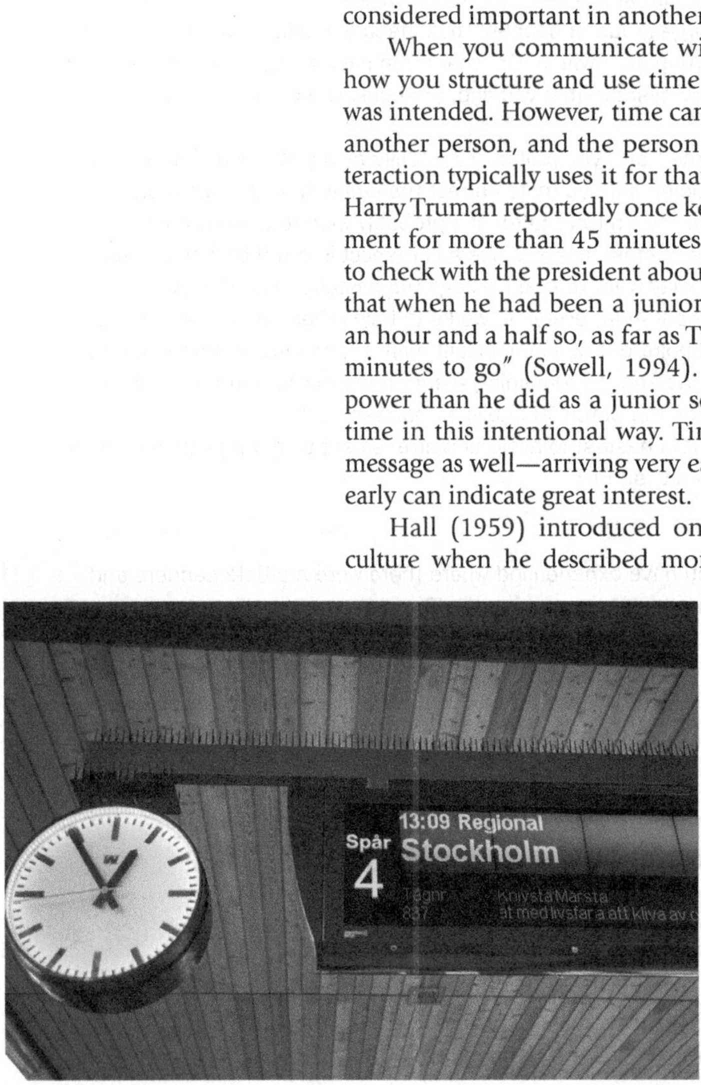

Keith Levit Photography/Thinkstock.

Though time is a finite concept, it is a form of nonverbal communication that differs across cultures. Chronemics is the study of how cultures structure and use time.

In contrast, individuals in **polychronic time system cultures** prefer to focus on and schedule multiple tasks at once. Time, according to this system, is ever changing and flexible and is based more on events rather than actual time. For example, Latin American and Mediterranean countries take much more time to establish a point in a conversation and to establish a relationship with someone. People in these cultures may carry on more than one conversation at a time and often consider it offensive to interrupt others when they are speaking (Novinger, 2001). Such characteristics reflect a culture's emphasis on commitment during interactions and interpersonal relationships and on acceptance of interruptions.

Monochronic and polychronic time are not just a product of dominant cultures; there can be differences between dominant and co-cultures and also between contexts. For example, though the United States as a whole tends to be a monochronic time system culture, residents of regions such as the South and California have a looser, more polychronic time system. In contrast, those from the Northeast typically adhere to a more monochronic time system. In addition, business and organizational contexts are more likely to be monochronic, and personal relationship contexts tend more toward polychronic time (Hall, 1990).

Monochronic and polychronic time can also vary depending on the individual communicator's temporal preferences. Dawna Ballard and David Seibold (2000) identify three **organizational temporal dimensions**, which are the different ways members of an organization believe that time should be structured:

- **Separation**: A temporal orientation that emphasizes an individual's desire to be separate or intermeshed with tasks and individuals in space and time.
- **Concurrency**: A temporal orientation that emphasizes an individual's preference to do either fewer tasks or more tasks at once.
- **Flexibility**: A temporal orientation that emphasizes an individual's desire to have either a more or less flexible schedule.

Monochronic individuals may prefer to be more separate, and less concurrent and flexible, and polychronic individuals may prefer less separation, and greater concurrency and flexibility. You can determine your own temporal orientation using Ballard and Seibold's (2000) scale.

DEVELOPING INTERCULTURAL COMMUNICATION COMPETENCE

You live and work in a multicultural world. To communicate well with someone whose cultural background may be very different from your own, you must understand the customs, values, and characteristics of that person's cultural heritage. One of the first requirements for understanding others is to be open-minded about foreign cultures and eager to learn how another person's perceptions and behaviors may differ from yours. The sections below identify a few specific steps to help you improve your intercultural communication competence, which is defined as "the ability to communicate effectively and appropriately in intercultural situations based on one's intercultural knowledge, skills, and attitudes" (Deardorff, 2006, p. 249). As with interpersonal communication competence, intercultural communication competence involves acknowledging and balancing effectiveness and appropriateness, with a special consideration and appreciation of the different cultures needed to accomplish this delicate balance.

Understand Your Own and Others' Cultures

The first step in improved effectiveness and appropriateness is understanding your culture, as well as the cultures of those with whom you frequently interact or in which you spend time. Refer again to Table 7.2, Figures 7.2 and 7.3, and the organizational temporal dimensions self-test provided in this chapter. Now consider and explore the unique combination of dominant and co-cultures that are part of your background and heritage, and then evaluate your interactions with others from different cultural backgrounds. Do you express an interest in learning about others' cultures? For example, when you have booked a trip to visit a foreign country, do you attempt to learn more about its culture before you visit? While there, do you make an effort to chat with the locals and spend time in areas that are not visited by as many tourists? Are you open to the specific traditions and preferences of that culture, or do you behave entirely as you would if you were home in your dominant culture? Most people are eager to share information about their heritage and the unique features of their cultures, and you will learn a great deal not only about the other culture but about yourself as well. When you engage in communication with people from other cultures, remember to also keep in mind the aspects and characteristics of intercultural communication discussed in this chapter.

Acknowledge and Accept Cultural Differences

Whether you interact with different cultural values where you live or when you are traveling abroad, it is important to recognize that you will encounter cultural differences. Basic information about different cultures—which can be accessed online or in travel guides—can help you anticipate and accept intercultural communication differences that may arise during your interactions with others. For example, when in a country where a language that is foreign to you is spoken, learning to say "hello," "goodbye," "please," and "thank you" in that language is always a good place to start. Also keep in mind the principles of CAT described in this chapter and be conscious of how you adjust your verbal and nonverbal messages.

These efforts help decrease negative perceptions people sometimes have of cultures other than their own. For instance, the expression "ugly American," coined from a 1958 novel of the same name, by Eugene Burdick and William J. Lederer, has been used to describe Americans traveling abroad who act offensively with their arrogance and privilege. What factors advanced this stereotype of Americans traveling abroad? It may be tied to the strongly individualistic culture in the United States, but it is primarily the result of specific travelers who act inappropriately in a new place. The lesson here is that you can facilitate your communication competence and change preconceptions by acknowledging and accepting the inevitable differences between cultures. The *Web Field Trip* feature offers more tips on how to deal with the culture shock involved in traveling abroad.

Strive to Overcome Ethnocentrism

As discussed earlier, resist the tendency to think "mine is better" when comparing your culture to that of others. We are inclined to evaluate other cultures on

> **WEB FIELD TRIP**
>
> ### *Managing Culture Shock*
>
> The U. S. Department of State offers educational, professional, and cultural exchange programs for individuals who are interested in extended immersions in other countries. There are several different programs available for applicants (including arts, technology, and youth programs) that focus on specific topic areas. Visit the website (http://exchanges.state.gov/us) and locate the article "Adjusting to a New Culture" (http://exchanges.state.gov/us/adjusting-new-culture), located under the Exchange Experience tab. This information provides an in-depth look at culture shock, a period of adjustment that visitors often encounter when living in culture that is different from their own. Review the content and consider the following questions.
>
> **Critical Thinking Questions**
>
> **1.** Compare and contrast the three phases of culture shock. How might the suggestions for diminishing culture shock help address the symptoms associated with each of these three phases?
> **2.** If you were to host an exchange program participant, what could you do to help him or her manage their culture shock?

the basis of our own society's dominant culture, and too often people conclude that our way of doing things is superior. We occasionally convey an ethnocentric attitude, without realizing it, through our language choices. Instead of saying, for example, "In Britain, they drive on the wrong side of the road," say, "In Britain, they drive on the left side of the road." Remember that other cultures can be (and frequently are) different. These differences are not wrong or strange, and we can learn to recognize the importance and value of other people's cultures.

One specific way to do this is to apply the concepts in this chapter to a culture that is different than yours. For example, is that culture low or high context? Individualistic or collectivistic? Monochronic or polychronic? Identifying these cultural characteristics can help you understand why members of that culture behave and communicate the way that they do. Understanding the source of the differences between your culture and another culture can shift your thinking away from evaluating other cultures as "good" or "bad." As we discussed earlier in the chapter, one of the most important skills of competent communicators in today's multicultural and globalized world is the ability to recognize that cultures are not right or wrong; they are merely different from one another.

Recognize the Unique Importance of Nonverbal Communication

As individuals in a dominant, low-context culture, most Americans rely more on verbal communication to communicate with one another, but nonverbal communication sometimes is more helpful for intercultural communication. On a wider scale, nonverbal communication includes aspects of the environment and appearance, so observe your surroundings and monitor what people are wearing to better understand and adjust to different cultures that you might visit. Though it is difficult to understand someone who speaks a different language, there are also many nonverbal messages that have the same, or similar, meanings across cultures, and using such messages in an intercultural interaction can help you achieve shared meaning with someone, even if you do not share the same language. For example, nodding one's head is a nearly universal nonverbal gesture that indicates yes—though in certain areas of central Europe, such as Bulgaria, Albania, and Macedonia, a single head nod upward may also communicate disagreement. Though there is no official universal language or nonverbal way to communicate with others, acknowledging and accepting that each culture is unique can motivate you to learn about other cultures and teach you to be flexible, accepting the differences that may arise between your culture and another culture.

SUMMARY AND RESOURCES

Every society has a unique culture which embodies the specialized set of traditions, beliefs, values, norms, and rules of that society. People are often unaware how much their culture and the various subcultures to which they belong influence their behavior and their communication. Culture affects every aspect of your life: how you dress and adorn your body, how you behave, what you eat, what you celebrate, how you raise and educate your children, and how you view life and death. It also dictates how you use physical space, how you conceive of time, and other aspects of your perception of the world through your physical senses. When individuals from different cultures come into direct contact with one another, intercultural communication occurs. You carry elements of culture with you into interactions with members of your own and other cultures, and these remnants of your cultural heritage strongly influence your communication and relationships with others.

Most societies have a dominant culture, which may or may not represent the majority of the population. A culture is considered dominant when it reflects social institutions such as the media, educational institutions, law, political processes, business, and artistic expression. Immigrant groups must become socialized to the dominant culture of the country to which they immigrate because this culture reflects the norms of the society.

In addition to a dominant culture, societies have various co-cultures—regional, economic, social, religious, or ethnic groups—that also exert influence over people in that society. The co-cultures have their own patterns of behavior that may differ from the dominant culture. Cultures and co-cultures exert a great deal of subtle pressure on their members to conform to the cultural norms because these norms perform important functions in maintaining the society. The media also influences, and is influenced by, both the dominant culture and co-cultures.

Culture also assists in creating a perspective that impacts how its members view the world. Your dominant culture is so central that it influences your communication in significant ways. In addition, culture provides identity, which is a consistent set of attitudes that defines who you are and shapes how you view and describe yourself. Your primary identity includes consistent aspects of your identity, such as biological sex, race or ethnicity, and age. One's primary identity is difficult to permanently alter. In contrast, your secondary identity includes more malleable aspects of your identity, such as your socioeconomic status or occupation. Though secondary identity can be just as important as an aspect of primary identity, it can change over time.

All cultures incorporate both verbal and nonverbal elements in their communication. Misunderstandings often arise because cultures can be very different in the emphasis they place on these verbal and nonverbal elements. Some cultures, such as the United States, are considered low-context communication cultures and place a great deal of emphasis on the words used in communication. High-context communication cultures such as Japan, on the other hand, rely more on nonverbal context or behavior than on verbal symbols. In a high-context message, much of the information is contained in the nonverbal elements, in a ritualized response, or in the context in which the communication takes place.

Another fundamental way in which cultures differ is their tendency toward individualism or collectivism. Individualistic cultures value self-reliance and self-motivation and are stimulated by individual competition. Collectivistic cultures, on the other hand, tend to value the needs of the group over the needs of the individual and place a premium on cooperation and harmony. A specific aspect of distinctions between individualism and collectivism are the concept of saving face, acknowledging status, or respecting the position of other people. The concept of face appears in most cultures, but it manifests itself in different ways in different cultures. In an individualistic culture, face is often a source of personal pride or self-respect, but in a collectivistic culture, people want to preserve group pride and respect.

A final aspect of cultural membership that is important to interpersonal communication is time. Specifically, chronemics is the study of a culture's structure and use of time, including how individuals perceive, structure, emphasize, and respond to time, and how they interpret time messages. Cultures can range on a continuum of monochronic (focusing upon one task at a time and viewing time as tangible) to polychronic (focusing upon multiple tasks at one time and seeing time as flexible) time systems. These time systems can also relate to temporal dimensions, which are beliefs about how time should be structured.

Improving your intercultural communication skills requires that you recognize that cultures are different and not "right" or "wrong" in the ways in which their members behave. You must also understand your own culture, be interested in learning about other cultures, strive to overcome the ethnocentrism and negative stereotypes that can hinder your ability to interact in a positive way, and acknowledge the importance of nonverbal communication in intercultural communication situations.

Critical Thinking and Discussion Questions

1. Which is your dominant culture and with which co-cultures do you identify? Which of these cultures is most central in shaping your identity and why?

2. Recall an intercultural interaction in which you were involved that you felt went well, and another that went poorly. Using the terms in this chapter, what do you think was the difference between these interactions that led to these different outcomes?

3. Using the descriptions from this chapter, how would you classify yourself regarding cultural context, individualism/collectivism, and time

orientation? Are your classifications similar to or different from your dominant culture?

4. Have you ever experienced a situation where you felt as if you were stereotyped? How did it impact your communication?
5. How do you use technology and social media in your intercultural interactions? How do you think your online persona reflects your dominant culture or co-cultures?

chapter 8

Interpersonal Communication
Part 1: Initiating Relationships

OBJECTIVES

- Identify three categories used to describe the nature of our relationships with others
- Explore four primary reasons people initiate interpersonal relationships
- Identify three types of attraction: physical, social, and task
- Understand the impact of age, gender, and culture on differences in perceptions of attraction
- Distinguish among social and task goals for relationship initiation
- Understand the three dimensions of similarity and four considerations that individuals make in assessing similarity to self
- Explore goals sought on a first date
- Understand the role of disclosure and reciprocal disclosure on relationship initiation
- Explore the relationship between social penetration and self-disclosure
- Identify the role of question-asking in reducing uncertainty in relationship initiation
- Explore the use of affinity-testing strategies in relationship initiation
- Identify five stages in the process of forming relationships
- Understand the impact of context on relationship initiation
- Explore the impact of technology on communication during relationship initiation
- Understand the four stages experienced by interracial couples in the relationship initiation process

KEY TERMS

relationship
obligatory/involuntary
voluntary
duration
context
rules
role
interpersonal attraction
physical attractiveness
social attractiveness
impression management
self-monitoring
task attractiveness
proximity
similarity/homophily
demographic similarity
background similarity
attitude similarity
similarity to current self
complementarity
attachment security
similarity to ideal view of self
false homophily
goals

© MaxFX, 2007, Shutterstock.

---

social goals
task goals
self-disclosure
reciprocal self-disclosure
social penetration theory
uncertainty reduction theory
predicted outcome value theory
liking
affinity-seeking strategies
social exchange theory
rewards
costs
initiation
experimenting
intensifying
integrating
bonding

OVERVIEW

Many of you have probably heard of the movie *Jerry McGuire* and the line made famous by Renee Zellweger's character, "You had me at 'Hello.'" If only the process of initiating relationships with others was usually that easy! All of our relationships require a significant amount of time and energy. Consider the fact that *every* relationship we are involved in had to start somewhere. In this chapter we take a close look at how we define the term relationship, and how and why relationships are initially established. We also look at the communication behaviors and strategies used early in a relationship's development.

THE ROLE OF COMMUNICATION IN RELATIONSHIP DEVELOPMENT

The decision to begin a new relationship is filled with a myriad of emotions—confusion, excitement, anxiety, and anticipation. Consider the role played by many of the elements of interpersonal communication we have discussed up to this point. First, a person must decide whether to approach another person to initiate a relationship. Then the challenge involves figuring out how to make the initial approach. What opening line or verbal message should be used to make the all-important first impression? Let us not forget the impact of nonverbal messages as well; they have a tremendous impact on every stage of the relationship initiation process. We form assumptions about others based on such nonverbal clues as how they are dressed, whether they are standing with their arms crossed to communicate a closed body position, and whether they engage in eye contact with us. Of course, we also need to consider the role that self perception plays in the process. As discussed in Chapter Two, someone with a low level of self-esteem will face unique challenges when engaging in the relationship initiation process, as opposed to a person who has a positive self image.

As we begin our discussion of relationship development, it is important to first define what we mean by the term relationship. If you are involved in a relationship at this very moment, please raise your hand. Do you have your hand up? If not, you should probably reconsider how you define this term. When we have asked this question in our interpersonal communication classes, only a few students initially raise their hands. But after much prompting with questions such as, "Are you *sure* you're not involved in *any* relationships right now?" every member of the class has a hand up in the air. Our culture causes us to formulate stereotypes about what it means to be "in a relationship." Immediately, most people think of a "relationship" as involving romance. However, we are all involved in a number of different types of relationships at any given time.

RELATIONSHIP DEFINED

Messages about relationships surround us. A trip to the magazine section of a grocery store often involves exposure to multiple statements about the status of celebrity relationships. In the last two years writers for magazines have provided the public with the intimate details of budding relationships referred to only as, "TomKat" (Tom Cruise and Katie Holmes) and "Brangelina" (Brad Pitt and Angelina Jolie). The magazines *Cosmopolitan, People, Oprah,* and *Entertainment Weekly* also beckon you to learn how to attract members of the opposite sex with a sensuous new hairstyle, hip outfit, or clever banter. Even if you do not venture near the magazine sections or notice the magazine covers as you check out, take a moment to consider the most common themes of the songs played over the store loudspeakers while you shop. Many popular songs contain references to relationships. Messages about relationships are everywhere! While numerous magazine articles, movies and Web sites devote a lot of attention to romantic relationships, we encounter a variety of relationships throughout our lifetime. From family relationships to friendships and even work relationships, we form communicative bonds with people across a variety of contexts. But how exactly do we define the term relationship? A **relationship** is a connection between two individuals that results in mutual interaction with the intent of achieving shared meaning. In this chapter, we focus primarily on voluntary relationships, which differ greatly from those described as either obligatory or involuntary. Relationships with family members and co-workers are often defined as **obligatory/involuntary** because they often occur by chance and not by choice. Our relationships with friends, roommates, and romantic partners are considered **voluntary** because we enter into them of our own volition. Some relationships, like those we form with co-workers, may start out as obligatory and transform into voluntary ones. We begin by describing important elements of voluntary relationships.

Could this work relationship transform into a voluntary friendship?

The Nature of Relationships

We often use referents to describe the numerous relationships in which we are involved. Three categories often used to describe the nature of a relationship include references to duration, context, and roles.

Duration. **Duration** references are used to describe the length of time we have known the other person. Statements such as, "my friend from kindergarten," "my new co-worker," and "an acquaintance I met last week" are used to describe the duration of the relationship. These terms provide insight as to the amount of time that the relational partners have had to share information about one another.

Context. In some instances, relationships are described by referring to the **context,** or setting, in which the relationship was initiated. "Friends from the soccer team," "committee members from the PTO," or "co-workers on a project team," provide information about the environment in which the relationship exists. By making reference to the relationship context, clues are offered with regard to the **rules** or expectations for communication. Rules may be explicitly stated. A boss may openly state to employees that there is an "open door" policy in the office, indicating that employees should feel comfortable walking in without an appointment to discuss issues. Some rules are implicitly understood. Teammates have a mutual understanding that emotions have an impact on how messages are created and interpreted on game day. If a teammate has a bad game, the unspoken rule is that it is probably not wise to discuss the errors that were made. It is important to note that rules regarding the appropriateness of topics and the acceptable depth of discussions may differ from context to context. While an individual may be comfortable disclosing her intimate feelings about her newest romantic partner with a family member, such information could be viewed as highly inappropriate in the workplace.

What role does the coach play on the team?

Role. Finally, references to a person's **role** may be used to describe the nature of a relationship. Terms such as *mother, teacher, supervisor, colleague,* or *coach* are used to describe the role an individual plays in a particular relationship. It is important to note that role terms can also provide insight into the contextual nature of the relationship, and to shed light on the rules and expectations for interactions. More formality is needed when a student engages in an interaction with a teacher than when calling up a family member to discuss a bad grade on an assignment. By making reference to our relationships in terms of duration, context, or roles, we let others know what our initial expectations are for communication.

Deciding to Make the First Move: *Why* We Initiate Relationships

Think back to your first day in this class. As you walked through the door, you scanned the classroom and were faced with the decision of where to sit. Were there any familiar faces in the room? If not, you ended up sitting next to someone you had never met before. At that point, you had two decisions to make. Should you (a) initiate a conversation with that person, and if so, (b) how should you begin the interaction? As you reflect on that first day of class, consider how quickly some of these decisions were made. Even if the decision of where to sit was influenced by the fact that there were a limited number of seats available, you still had to choose whether to initiate a conversation, and thus, initiate a relationship with a fellow classmate. Every relationship has a unique history that includes an explanation of why we chose to initiate the relationship in the first place.

Over the years, scholars in the fields of communication, psychology and sociology have been fascinated by the question of *why* we initiate relationships. For example, when writing about why people initiate long-term romantic relationships, interpersonal communication researcher Anita Vangelisti (2002) describes the number of factors that contribute to mate selection as "daunting." Some research even indicates that the process of mate selection occurs by chance

(Lykken and Tellegen 1993). While there appear to be many different reasons, years of research have identified four common explanations for why humans begin relationships. The four primary reasons we establish relationships with others are attraction, proximity, similarity, and purpose.

Not surprisingly, many decisions to initiate relationships are based on the attractiveness of another person. Second, scholars have discovered that we tend to initiate relationships with others on the basis of proximity. After all, it is much easier to begin a conversation with those who are physically close to us as opposed to those who are geographically distant. Third, relationships are typically initiated with those we perceive to be similar to us in some way. How we define similarity may differ from person to person. Relationships between adults may form because their children play on the same sports team. Students may form relationships because they are taking the same class or are in the same major. Finally, some relationships are initiated because they fulfill a purpose or a need. Consider the relationships that you have formed with co-workers or clients to fulfill a need at work. In the next sections, we take a closer look at each of the reasons for beginning a relationship.

Will these two students more likely become friends because they sit near each other in class?

DEFINING INTERPERSONAL ATTRACTION

Identifying the reasons for being attracted to one person and not to another is perhaps one of the greatest mysteries in life. Researchers have dedicated countless studies to exploring the phenomenon of initial attraction. After all, attraction is perhaps one of the most influential factors in setting the relationship initiation process into motion. While references to attractiveness are often assumed to be directed toward physical characteristics, **interpersonal attraction** refers to a general feeling or desire that impacts our decision to approach and initiate a relationship with another person. Many different forms of attraction influence our decision to begin relationships.

Attraction is one of the primary determining factors for choosing to initiate relationships, and it is the basis for forming initial impressions of others. While most people are quick to argue that forming first impressions of others based on their appearance is superficial and trivial, the fact remains that in the U.S. many of our decisions to initiate romantic relationships are rooted in our perceptions of the physical attractiveness of the other person. Consider a time when you were told that someone was beautiful. While you could argue that this could refer to either physical attractiveness or inner beauty, our first instinct is to assume that the statement is being made in reference to the individual's physical characteristics.

When asked to define attractiveness, most people tend to list physical characteristics associated with perceptions of attraction. While our initial impressions typically focus on the physical features associated with attractiveness, other factors can come into play as well. McCroskey and McCain (1974) identified three dimensions of attractiveness used when deciding whether to initiate relationships. These dimensions include: physical, social, and task attractiveness.

Physical Attractiveness

The dimension of attractiveness most often used in deciding whether to pursue a relationship is physical attractiveness. More often than not, we decide whether to initiate conversations with a potential relationship partner based on our perceptions of the partners' physical attractiveness (Vangelisti 2002). According to research by Reis and his colleagues (1980), we are more likely to perceive interactions as pleasant when we view the person we interact with as physically attractive. How do we determine whether someone is physically attractive? Judgments about what constitutes physical attractiveness are often answered by asking the question, "What do I think makes someone pretty or handsome?" When characteristics such as body shape or size, hair color or length, and facial features are used in making a determination of whether to initiate a relationship, this dimension is referred to as **physical attractiveness.** Aristotle recognized the value of physical attractiveness when he stated, "Personal beauty is a greater recommendation than any letter of reference."

Why is physical attractiveness important early in a relationship?

Recall the discussion of perception in Chapter Five. The phrase "beauty is in the eye of the beholder" addresses the perceptual nature of physical attraction and provides insight as to why one person may be attracted to blondes while another is attracted to brunettes. Sometimes we are baffled as to how individuals who appear to be so completely opposite with regard to their physical appearance, could be attracted to one another. Our perception causes us to view physical characteristics in unique ways. Extensive research has concluded that romantic attraction is frequently related to the extent to which partners are physically attracted to one another initially (Curran and Lippold 1975; Goode 1996; Walster, Aronson, Abrahams, and Rottman 1966; Wilson, Cousins, and Fink 2006; Woll 1986). While some studies report that men may value physical attractiveness more than women (Buss 1989; Sprecher, Sullivan, and Hatfield 1994), it is clear that both men and women report physical attractiveness as a factor influencing their decision to initiate relationships (Hatfield and Sprecher 1986).

But why does physical attractiveness play such an important role in the early stages of relationship development? One explanation is that people tend to associate other positive and favorable characteristics with physical attractiveness. Take a moment to think about how much emphasis our culture places on physical attractiveness. An overwhelming amount of research (see, for example, Eagly et al. 1991) seems to support the bias that individuals have towards those perceived as physically attractive. One study found that people described as attractive were also perceived as kind, sexual, responsive, social, and sensitive (Dion, Berscheid and Walster 1972). In this same study, participants predicted that physically attractive individuals would experience more success in life, both personally and professionally. Other factors, such as age, gender and culture, influence our perceptions of physical attractiveness.

Age and Attractiveness. Beginning at a very young age, we are taught that physical attractiveness is often rewarded or valued. After all, the princesses in Disney movies are always beautiful young women, while the evil characters are portrayed as being ugly. Hasbro's Barbie doll is presented to young children as an ideal image of female attractiveness. She has long, blonde hair and blue eyes, is big-breasted, tall and thin. Young children are able to identify her and many idolize her. But let's get real. Barbie's bra size has been estimated to be a DDD compared to the average C cup size of most women, and her body dimensions have been translated to the equivalent of 38-18-34 if she were a real woman. In fact, her tiny feet would not be able to support her busty upper body if she were a real woman. Nonetheless, young girls adore Barbie! They receive the message that being physically attractive, like Barbie, is associated with having friends and receiving more attention, not to mention a host of other rewards: cool clothes, cars, beach houses, and a "cool" life-style.

Even in the classroom, children receive messages regarding the importance of physical attractiveness. Research has shown that attractive children are perceived as being more popular with both classmates and teachers. Richmond (1992) states that elementary age students who are perceived as being physically attractive receive more attention from their teachers, while attractive high school and college age students receive higher grades than those who are perceived to be less attractive. Studies show that teachers provide higher evaluations and establish higher expectations for attractive students. Attractive people are perceived as being happier, more likeable, popular, and friendly (Berscheid and Reis 1998).

Even as we get older, physical attractiveness impacts our perception as well as the perceptions others have of us. Research has found that people under the age of thirty have been rated as being more physically attractive than people over the age of fifty (McClellan and McKelvie 1993), and faces perceived as being younger have been judged as being more pleasant compared to faces viewed as being older. Johnson and Pittinger (1984) discovered that physically attractive males and females aged 60 to 93 were rated more positively than those in the same age group who were perceived to be less attractive. Another study grouped males and females into age categories. These categories included participants aged 20 to 29, 30 to 39, 40 to 49, 50 to 59, and 60 to 69 years. Participants in the study were shown photographs of members of the opposite sex from the same age range categories and were asked to rate their physical attractiveness. Results of the study indicated that as males increased in age, they rated younger women as being more attractive than older women. However, the same was not true for women. Women in the older age categories rated males similar in age to be more physically attractive (Mathes, Brennen, Haugen, and Rice 1985).

Gender and Attractiveness. While both men and women indicate that they view physical attractiveness as important in the initiation of romantic relationships, the intensity that each sex values attractiveness differs. For example, in a study by Hewitt and German (1987), women indicated a strong preference for men who were dressed more formally compared to those who were dressed informally. In the reality show *Queer Eye for the Straight Guy,* male participants receive a significant makeover that might include a new haircut, body waxing, grooming tips, a new wardrobe, and an apartment makeover. Friends, family members, and co-workers are asked to comment on the participant's new look. At the end of the show, relationship partners, who also happen to be women, typically respond very favorably to their partner's new hip, stylish and more formal clothing.

While many research studies point to the positive aspects of physical attractiveness, others have discovered potential pitfalls. In the workplace, physically attractive women often encounter biases *against* them when applying for administrative or executive positions (Zebrowitz 1997). The same is true of women who run for political office. While physically attractive women are often penalized for their appearance in these situations, the opposite was found to be true for attractive males seeking similar opportunities. Because of the increased attention on women's voting behavior in political elections, Lewis and Bierly (1990) examined the impact of female perceptions of male political candidates' attractiveness. Women rated physically attractive political candidates as being more competent than less attractive candidates.

Decisions to initiate dates are most often based on physical attractiveness. In a content analysis of more than 800 personal ads, Harrison and Saeed (1977) found that males are more likely to include descriptors of physical attractiveness as criteria for potential dates. In addition, men tend to indicate a strong preference for women who are younger than themselves. While women also included criteria such as *athletic, tall* or *attractive* in personal ads, references to a partner's status were included more often and emerged as a stronger predictor of attraction (Davis 1990).

To examine the impact of physical attractiveness in homosexual relationships, Sergios and Cody (1985) matched 100 men in dyads (pairs), based on ratings of physical attractiveness. Participants were told that they were being sent on a blind date that was matched through a computer. Physical attractiveness was the biggest predictor of liking and desire to seek a future date. This research is consistent with research on how heterosexual relationship partners select mates. Regardless of whether the relationship is a heterosexual or homosexual one, physical attraction plays a significant role in one's choice of a relationship partner.

Culture and Attraction. Culture is an influential factor in our perception of physical attractiveness. Within our culture, media depict the accepted standards of beauty. Consider the appearance of typical movie villains such as the Joker or the Penguin from the *Batman* movies, and Ursula, the sea witch from *The Little Mermaid.* They are ugly and unattractive, whereas the hero is always handsome or beautiful. As the main characters in *The Exorcist* and *The Fly* turn evil, their external appearances transform from normal to unattractive. The timing of these changes seems to insinuate that there is a direct correlation between turning bad and turning ugly. We do not have to look that far or long to find messages about physical beauty in our culture. Images are found on television and billboards, in magazines, movies and books, and on the Internet.

Perceptions of physical attractiveness can differ across ethnic groups. A very curvaceous figure is often considered to be unattractive among Caucasian women, but African American women may not agree (Hebl and Heatherton 1998). In fact, African American women are perceived as more attractive by African American males if they have a curvaceous bottom, as opposed to being able to fit into a pair of size four jeans.

As we cross cultural boundaries, it becomes apparent that there are universal perceptions of beauty as well. One particular physical feature that has been judged across cultures as a focal point for physical attraction is the human face. In particular, the more "feminine" a face appears the greater its perceived level of attractiveness. In a study comparing the attractiveness of men and women by looking at close-up photographs of their faces, both Caucasian and Japanese participants rated pictures of men and women whose facial features had been "feminized" or softened as being more attractive (Perrett, Lee, and Penton-Voak 1998).

Social Attractiveness

© Galina Barskaya, 2007, Shutterstock.

What questions do you ask to determine your level of social attraction to someone?

Once we initiate a conversation with another person, it is likely that our attention shifts from the physical attributes, which drew us to start talking in the first place, to identifying commonalities. **Social attractiveness** can be defined as common interests or similar patterns of communication that cause individuals to perceive one another as someone they would like to spend time with. Questions used to identify the level of social attraction with another person might include, "Would I like to hang out with this person?" and "Is this someone who would fit in with my friends?"

While physical attraction has a substantial impact on our decision to initiate relationships with others, social attraction is equally important. Some people exert considerable effort to ensure that others perceive their social behavior favorably. **Impression management** is defined as the process of maintaining a positive image of self in the presence of others. Consider the time and energy dedicated to making sure our physical appearance is "just right" when we meet or approach someone for the first time. When interviewing for a job, it is essential that the suit is pressed, the shoes are polished, and the hair is neat and clean.

Individuals vary greatly in the extent to which they are self-aware. **Self-monitoring** refers to a personality construct that causes a person to respond to social and interpersonal cues for appropriate communication behaviors in a variety of situations. High self-monitors are constantly aware of behaviors others perceive to be appropriate in interpersonal situations, and continuously strive to control how they are portraying themselves. By contrast, low self-monitors dedicate little, if any, energy to responding to the cues of social appropriateness. They do not spend a lot of time worrying if they break the social rules by wearing jeans to an event where everyone else is dressed more formally, or by belching in front of a potential romantic partner. To examine the relationship of self-monitoring and relationship initiation, participants were given file folders containing photographs and descriptions of personal attributes of potential dates. High self-monitors dedicated more time to reviewing the photographs in the folders, while low self-monitors spent more time reviewing the personal descriptions (Snyder, Berscheid, and Glick 1985). Thus, it appears that high self-monitors place more emphasis on physical attraction when selecting a potential partner for a date, while low self-monitors focus more on social attractiveness.

Task Attractiveness

While physical and social attributes may be influential in the initiatory phase of relationships, as individuals pursue their professional goals, decisions based on attractiveness may take on a much different perspective. **Task attractiveness** refers to the characteristics or qualities that are perceived as appealing when initiating relationships in which the goal is to complete a task or assignment. Suppose your professor allows you to select the team members you wish to work with on a huge term project. Are you going to select the most physically attractive person to work with on this assignment? Possibly, if your goal is to get a date for Saturday night. Are you going to choose the funniest or most social person in the class to be on your team? Maybe, if your goal is to have plenty of laughs as you work on the project. Most likely, you will seek out people with characteristics and qualities that you know are essential to getting the job done. A question used to identify perceived task attractiveness might be, "Does this person have what it takes to help get the job done?" Depending on the task, the list of qualities used to assess task attractiveness might be very different. If you consider yourself to be "technologically challenged," you may seek someone who you consider to be proficient with computers. Suppose there is a strict timeline for the project. In such a situation, you will probably seek a person who is dependable and organized.

Proximity

Consider our earlier question regarding your decision to initiate a relationship with the person seated next to you in this class. In essence, the decision to begin the relationship was influenced by proximity. **Proximity** refers to the physical distance between two people. The fact that you sit next to the same person for an entire semester increases the chance that you will choose to form a relationship with one another. Segal (1974) supported this notion in a study that examined friendships formed in a college classroom. At the beginning of the term, students were given seat assignments. When asked to indicate the persons whom they considered to be friends in the class, most students reported that they were friends with those who were seated next to them.

So why is proximity such a strong predictor of interpersonal attraction? One explanation may be found in the decreased effort that is required to establish relationships with those who are close in distance. It is just easier to strike up a conversation with the person seated next to you in class, or to share stories with the co-worker whose cubicle is directly adjacent to yours. Much more effort is required to start relationships with those who sit on the other side of the room or who work on different floors. Many people believe that long-distance relationships are doomed, simply based on the physical distance separating relationships partners.

These childhood friends grew up together and share the same background.

Similarity/Homophily

After initiating a conversation, identifying potential topics to discuss can be the next hurdle to overcome. The goal of our discussions at this phase in a relationship is to identify common interests between ourselves and the other person. Remember the phrase, "Birds of a feather flock together?" This phrase refers to an important element of interpersonal attraction known as **similarity**, or **homophily.** Research confirms that we seek out relationships with those who have common interests, backgrounds, and goals, and who are similar in appearance (McCroskey, Richmond, and Daly 1975). This phenomenon might explain why friendships are formed among people who go to the same gym to work out, or how romantic relationships begin between two people who meet in an Internet chat room dedicated to discussions of reality television. Both of these situations provide common topics for discussion. Our similarity with others can be categorized based on demographic, background, or attitude commonalities. **Demographic similarity** is based on physical and social characteristics that are easily identifiable. Consider the relationships that you have initiated with others who are of a similar age or are the same sex. **Background similarity** refers to commonalities that we share as a result of our life experiences. Chances are that many of your friendships began as a result of experiences that you had in common with others—going to the same summer camp, playing on the same athletic team, working in the same organization, or simply growing up in the same hometown. Finally, **attitude similarity** focuses on our perception of the attitudes, beliefs, and values that we hold in common. Some relationships are formed as a result of our cultural, religious or political affiliations. When two friends express similar attitudes towards music, movies, or sports, they are exhibiting attitude similarity.

In their examination of interpersonal attraction and similarity, Klohnen and Luo (2003) identified four dimensions of similarity that individuals consider in initial attraction. These include:

- Similarity to current self
- Complementarity
- Attachment security
- Ideal-self similarity

Similarity to current self refers to the belief that individuals are attracted to those who are similar to themselves. The dimensions we use to identify the congruence between ourselves and others differ from person to person. You may seek someone whose sense of humor is similar to your own, while another person may view similar levels of intelligence as being more important. The **complementarity** hypothesis explains the saying "opposites attract." It predicts that people will be more attracted to those whose personality characteristics complement their own. This may explain why persons who have a high level of communication apprehension seek romantic relationships with those who have low levels of apprehension. To someone who is apprehensive about communicating, it is attractive to have someone who will initiate and carry out interactions. **Attachment security** predicts that individuals will be most attracted to those who are secure. Thus, we find individuals who are confident and trusting more attractive than individuals who are preoccupied by emotions of jealousy, neediness, or worry. Finally, some individuals are most attracted to those whom they perceive to be **similar to the ideal view of self** (as opposed to their actual or current self). Those who are similar to our view of how we would ultimately like to be are rated more favorably.

While creating a favorable impression is a primary conversational goal during the initiation phase of a relationship, it is important to establish realistic expectations. Have you ever experienced the "Me, too!" phenomenon in a romantic relationship or friendship? In a recent episode of the situation comedy *'Til Death*, Jeff is angry with his wife Steph because she lied to him about her interest in ice hockey. Steph finally reveals that she does not like ice hockey and does not want to go to ice hockey games with him anymore. Jeff is angry and wonders what else Steph has lied about and whether he really knows her at all. In one scene, Jeff enters the kitchen and says, "Hi Steph—if that is your real name!" Steph realizes that Jeff is upset about the lie and tries to explain her actions. She tells him that when he asked her out for the first time he also questioned whether she liked ice hockey, to which she enthusiastically replied "Yes!" Steph explains that if she had not said yes, they may have never dated at all because he might prefer someone with more similar interests. Rather than continue to perpetuate the lie, Steph chose to tell Jeff the truth. How often does a situation like this occur in relationships?

When we attempt to portray ourselves as being more similar to the other person than we really are simply to appear more attractive, we run the risk of encountering a relationship pitfall known as false homophily. **False homophily** refers to the presentation of a deceptive image of self that appears to be more similar than it actually is. Claiming that you have interests or beliefs in common with another person just to appear more attractive creates unrealistic expectations in the relationship. While this strategy may be effective for gaining attention in the initial stages of the relationship, eventually the differences will emerge and could cause potential problems, as illustrated in the Steph and Jeff example from *'Til Death.*

One interpersonal context that places considerable emphasis on similarity as a reason for initiating relationships is the Internet. In the absence of the more obvious physical clues that are often used to decide whether to initiate a relationship, information about commonalities is sought to decide whether to interact with the other person. Baker (2005) points out that couples who initially meet via the Internet are explicit in delineating their interests in an attempt to find others with common interests. Typically they go to virtual chat rooms which focus on a specified topic to ensure that they will have something in common with others in the online community. Think about the process of posting information in an online personal ad. Match.com *(www.match.com)* provides several options to search for the ideal partner. Of course, some of the criteria that can be used to search for the ideal mate include physical characteristics, but additional criteria are available to narrow the focus on the basis of similarities. Questions regarding interests (sports, hobbies), lifestyle (job, smoking, drinking), and personal values (faith, education, politics) are included to identify similarities in relational partners.

Goals

© PhotoCreate, 2007, Shutterstock.

What social and task goals do you find in classroom relationships?

A fourth reason people choose to initiate relationships with others is to fulfill a purpose, or goal. Charles Berger (1995) defines **goals** as "desired end states toward which persons strive" (143). Many of our interpersonal interactions are initiated to fulfill two primary goals: social and task. **Social goals** refer to desired end states that fulfill the need for inclusion or affection. Both parties involved in the initial relationship can experience the fulfilled need. Consider the new kid in school. In order to ease some of the anxiety of starting a new school, the student might approach a table of students in the cafeteria and ask, "Is this seat taken?" One explanation for the initiation of this interaction is to fulfill a social goal—the student seeks to fulfill the need for inclusion at school. **Task goals** are defined as desired end states that fulfill the need for the completion of a task. Consider your current relationship with your hair stylist or barber. You initiated the relationship because the task of getting your hair cut needed to be fulfilled. A phone call was made to a local hair salon with the goal of finding a competent stylist to complete the task. As you initiated a conversation with the stylist, the initial task goal was to describe the hair cut you desired. Consider all of the relationships you have initiated to fulfill task goals. Relationships are initiated with teachers to fulfill the task goal of achieving your educational objectives, and teachers form relationships with colleagues to accomplish tasks associated with the job. Interpersonal communication is instrumental in achieving our goals.

Dillard (1990) points out that our goals serve three functions in interpersonal relationships. First, goals are used to take action and fulfill an interpersonal need. Individuals determine what need to fulfill, and the goal prompts the initiation of the relationship. If your social goal is to form new friendships at school, you will introduce yourself in an attempt to take action to fulfill the need. Second, goals assist us in defining the purpose for the interaction or behaviors. Suppose a woman asks a colleague to join her for a cup of coffee to discuss the upcoming presentation for an important client. She realizes that the purpose for the interaction is to accomplish a task goal. However, if she had a romantic interest in the colleague the ulterior motive for the meeting may have been prompted by social goals. Finally, goals provide us with a standard to judge the behaviors and outcomes of interpersonal interactions. We evaluate our interpersonal interactions with others and judge their effectiveness based on whether or not we accomplish our goals. After a blind date we typically evaluate the date as being *good* or *bad,* based on the interaction that took place. If conversation was forced and awkward, we are likely to evaluate the date negatively.

In a study of first date goals, college students identified eight primary reasons for going on a first date (Mongeau, Serewicz, and Therrien 2004). This study compares the responses offered by men and women for their decision for first dates.

It is interesting to note the gender differences in the goals behind asking a person out for a first date. Males were more likely than women to pursue the goal of sexual activity during a first date, while women exclusively reported that their goal for going on the date was due to hedonistic reasons or guilt. Overall, women appeared to focus more attention on relational goals for the first date compared to men. In the past, our culture taught us that first dates should be initiated by men. "Nice girls" were supposed to sit patiently and wait for the male to contact them and arrange for a date. But this trend is changing. Mongeau and his colleagues (1993) reported that approximately eighty percent of men and sixty percent of women went on a date initiated by the female.

Online interactions can also be initiated to fulfill goals. Katz and Rice (2002) pointed out that sometimes Indian parents use the Internet as a source to seek suitable mates for their children as a modern extension of their traditional matchmaking processes. Signing up to post and browse online personal ads signals a social goal—the intent to form a romantic relationship.

INTERPERSONAL COMMUNICATION THEORIES: *HOW* WE INITIATE RELATIONSHIPS

While the decision to initiate a relationship may be based on attraction, proximity, similarity, or purpose, one of the key factors in beginning the interaction and taking the relationship to the next level can be explained by examining prominent communication theories. Theories and concepts such as social penetration theory, uncertainty reduction theory, predicted outcome value theory, liking, and social exchange theory address *how* we initiate relationships with others. Before we address relevant interpersonal theories and concepts, we address the importance of initial impressions and self-disclosure in establishing a relationship.

Starting the Conversation

To identify commonalities, we must first initiate a conversation. For some people, this is one of the most difficult tasks in a relationship. After all, we are often reminded that, "You never get a second chance to make a good first impression." Consider the last time you attempted to start a conversation. Figuring out the most appropriate way to break the ice and create a positive initial impression can be intimidating. Over the years, many of our students have shared "pick-up lines" or relational openers that have been used to initiate conversations with a potential romantic partner. Table 8.1 includes a list of the most interesting. It is important to note that they are not necessarily the most effective conversation starters, although they do succeed in getting one's attention. Our advice is that the next time you think about using one of these pick-up lines to begin a conversation, don't. Informal surveys of our students have revealed that the vast majority feel a simple and sincere introduction is the most effective way to initiate a conversation.

Table 8.1 Notorious Pick-Up Lines/Relational Openers

Excuse me, do you have a quarter? I want to call my mother and tell her I just met the girl of my dreams.
Do you have a map? Because I keep getting lost in your eyes.
You must be tired because you've been running through my mind all night!
Your eyes are blue like the ocean and I'm lost at sea!
Do you know karate because your body is really kickin'!
Is there a rainbow today? I've just found the treasure I've been searching for.
Are you from Tennessee? Cause you're the only "ten" I see!
Do you believe in love at first sight or should I walk by again?
Hey, I like a girl with some meat on her! **(We STRONGLY discourage use of this relational opener!)
Somebody better call God because he's missing an angel.
If I could rearrange the alphabet I'd put U and I together.
You must be a Snickers because you satisfy me.
Your lips look so lonely. Would they like to meet mine?
Do you know how much a polar bear weighs? Enough to break the ice. Hi! My name is ____________.
Were you in the Boy Scouts? Because you've sure tied my heart in a knot.
You're so sweet, you could put Hershey's out of business.
Apart from being beautiful, what do you do for a living?
Are you a parking ticket? Cause you've got "fine" written all over you.
So how does it feel to be the most beautiful girl in this room?
You must be a broom because you just swept me off my feet.

Self-Disclosure. While it is difficult to determine which opening line should be used to initiate a conversation, taking the next step in the conversation can be an even greater challenge. Deciding what information to share about yourself, and what information you should seek from the other person can be viewed as a daunting task. During the early stages of relationship formation, partners will often self-disclose information in an effort to increase intimacy (Reis and Shaver 1988; Reis and Patrick 1996; Sprecher and Hendrick 2004). **Self-disclosure** is "the process of revealing personal information about oneself to another" (Sprecher and Hendrick 2004, 858). Self-disclosing is essential to relationship success and stability because it helps others learn who we are and what we want in a relationship. Aron (2003) validates this statement by noting that much of the process of becoming intimate with others involves disclosing information about the self and connecting the self to relevant others.

Typically, we disclose information more freely to those with whom we feel we have a close relationship. We are most likely to divulge information about ourselves to individuals we like and, as a result of this, tend to come to like those individuals even more (Kowalski 1999). However, in initial interactions the rules for disclosure are a bit more restrictive; we are more guarded in our disclosures. The task involves deciding what, and how much, information we should share. Have you ever heard a horror story of a first date where one person disclosed their deepest secrets or declared their undying affection for the other person? Needless to say, the recipient typically reports being turned off by such intimate disclosures so early in the relationship. Consider what topics are "safe" when initiating a relationship. Would it be best to discuss and make comparisons to your most recent romantic relationship on a first date? Probably not. Similarly, discussing how much money you earn or asking the other person to discuss their greatest fears in life would be viewed as highly inappropriate. As a general rule, **reciprocal self-disclosure**, the notion that disclosure of information between two people, is best when it is similar in terms of topics discussed and depth of disclosure. Disclosures of information in the initial stages of a relationship are often met with similar disclosures. Consider the following initial disclosures between two classmates on the first day of class:

How much information do you feel comfortable disclosing in a new relationship?

Sabina: Hi, I'm Sabina. Have you ever taken a class with Dr. Yost before?

Natalie: Hey Sabina, I'm Natalie. No, I haven't had a class with her, but my roommate took it last semester.

Sabina: Really, what did he say about it?

Natalie: He said she's tough but fair.

Sabina: Ouch! That's what I was afraid of. I have to take this class for my major and this is the only time that it fit into my schedule. If she's a difficult teacher then why did you take this class?

Natalie: Well, even though she's tough, I've also heard that you learn a lot that will help you down the road in other classes in the major.

Sabina: Oh, are you a communication major?

Natalie: Yes, this is my second year. What year are you?

Sabina: I'm a junior, but I just transferred into the major at the beginning of the semester. I feel like I'm so far behind. Everyone else has their schedules all planned out and they know exactly who and what to take.

Natalie: Don't stress yourself out about it. We've all been there before. If you have any questions about who you should take, just ask me. Have you met with your advisor yet? They're pretty good about helping you map out your long-term schedule.

Consider the reciprocity of disclosure in this initial interaction. Both women share information about their majors as well as their fears about the class. As one asks a question, the other answers it. When one woman discloses information, so does the other. In situations where others fail to disclose similar information, we become uncomfortable and may perceive them to be hiding something, or engaging in deceptive communication.

Cultural Differences in Disclosure. Not all cultures approach or perceive self-disclosure in the same way. Nakanishi (1986) found that Japanese view limited levels of self-disclosure as being more appropriate in initial interactions with others. Most research supports the notion that Japanese individuals tend to engage in less self-disclosure than those from Western cultures. In a study comparing the disclosures of Japanese compared with Americans across a variety of relationships, Japanese were found to engage in fewer disclosures than their American counterparts. However, both Japanese and American students reported they preferred to disclose information to their same-sex friends as opposed to their opposite-sex friends, and members of both cultures reported engaging in more in-depth disclosures in romantic relationships than in friendships (Kito 2005). Consider the rules that your culture has for disclosure. These cultural norms may cause frustration when interacting with a person from a different culture. Recall the earlier discussion of reciprocal disclosures. If a person from the United States was disclosing information about financial difficulties with a friend from Japan, expecting similar disclosures, the result would likely be frustrating for the American. Whereas members of the U.S. culture tend to be very open in disclosures, those from Asian cultures tend to be more reserved.

Even within a particular culture, personal preferences for disclosure exist, depending on how familiar we are with the other person. In particular, bartenders and hair stylists report receiving surprising numbers of unsolicited self-disclosures from their clients. A recent *Newsweek* article described the tendency for individuals to disclose personal information to their hair stylists (Silver-Greenberg 2005). Twanda Hamilton, a cosmetologist from Wichita, Kansas was quoted as saying, "You get a client in the shampoo bowl and they just open up and tell us that they are being beaten. We hear so much in the salon that no one else hears." In response to these unsolicited disclosures, a program called Cut-it-Out was launched to train stylists to recognize the signs of domestic abuse.

Social Penetration Theory

Altman and Taylor (1973) created **social penetration theory** to address how information is exchanged during relationship development. This theory focuses on how self-disclosure changes as relationships move from one level to the next. In essence, their theory explains how and why we move from superficial topics of conversation in the initial stages of relationships to more intimate conversations as the relationship progresses. In the movie *Shrek*, Shrek uses the analogy of an onion to explain to Donkey that even though he is an ogre, he possesses many layers of feelings and emotions that need to be taken into consideration.

Shrek: Ogres are like onions.

Donkey: They stink?

Shrek: Yes. No.

Donkey: Oh, they make you cry.

Shrek: No.

Donkey: Oh, you leave 'em out in the sun, they get all brown, start sproutin' little white hairs.

Shrek: NO. Layers. Onions have layers. Ogres have layers. Onions have layers. You get it? We both have layers. *(sighs)*

Donkey: Oh, you both have layers. Oh. You know, not everybody like onions. (*Shrek* directed by Andrew Adamson and Vicky Jenson, 1 hr. 30 min., DreamWorks Animation, 2001.)

This analogy helps to illustrate Altman and Taylor's explanation of the levels of information we reveal as we move from one stage of a relationship to the next. There are three primary levels of information that we reveal as we progress. These include superficial, personal, and intimate. Superficial information is revealed in initial interactions. Communication focuses on safe topics such as one's major, occupation, or hometown. As the relationship intensifies, a layer of the onion is "peeled" away and more personal information is revealed. Personal communication focuses on topics of a more personal nature such as likes, dislikes, and experiences. As the relationship progresses to a more intimate level, so does the communication. Intimate communication focuses on topics that are personal and private. In order to reveal intimate information, a level of trust must be present. At this innermost core of the onion, topics of discussion include goals, challenges, values, and motivations.

As mentioned previously, it is important to adhere to self-disclosure norms or expectations when sharing information with a potential relationship partner. Some research indicates that individuals who self-disclose inappropriately by sharing private information early in a relationship are perceived as odd, deviant or even dislikable (Werner and Haggard 1985). Table 8.2 on page 200 offers some suggestions for both providing self-disclosure and receiving self-disclosure from others competently.

Uncertainty Reduction Theory

Consider the extensive use of questions throughout the interaction between Sabina and Natalie. **Uncertainty reduction theory** (Berger and Calabrese 1975) identifies questions as a primary communication strategy used for encouraging reciprocal disclosure and reducing levels of uncertainty. To test the relationship between initial attraction and the use of questioning or disclosure, Douglas (1990) asked pairs to engage in a six-minute initial interaction. He found that the majority of questions were asked in the initial two minutes of the conversation, and greater disclosures were made in the final two minutes

Table 8.2 Suggestions for Delivering and Receiving Self-Disclosures

DELIVERING

Begin by self-disclosing information on safe or neutral topics.

During initial conversations, talk about where you went to school, hobbies, talents, etc., before sharing any private information.

If possible, attempt to match your partner's disclosures in depth.

If your partner shares intimate information (e.g., fears, future goals, insecurities), he may expect you to reciprocate. Remember that reciprocal disclosures between partners often indicates trust and liking.

Before disclosing private information, ask yourself if this is someone you can trust.

If you feel you cannot trust this person or feel this person will share this information with others, it is probably not a good idea to share private information.

RECEIVING

Do not overreact when someone shares personal information with you.

Try not to become overly emotional or provide judgmental feedback when someone shares private information with you. For example, screaming, "YOU DID WHAT?" when a friend shares information is not recommended.

Provide verbal and nonverbal support.

Make an attempt to display warm receptive nonverbal cues during your conversation by maintaining eye contact, sitting near the person, nodding your head to indicate listening and, if appropriate, smiling. Engage in active listening behaviors which might include paraphrasing and appropriate empathic responses (e.g., I can see why you would be upset).

If you do not feel comfortable discussing a topic or issue, tell your friend or relationship partner.

Rather than avoid the person and risk damaging your relationship, tell the person why you are uncomfortable discussing the topic.

of the conversation. Partners asked each other fewer questions as their answers required more detailed responses. Question-asking decreases as the questions require more in-depth responses. In the process of reducing uncertainty about the other person, individuals engage in a "strategy selection" process. This procedure requires them to maximize efficiency in gaining information about the other person while utilizing behaviors that are viewed as socially appropriate.

Predicted Outcome Value Theory

Once we have reduced our level of uncertainty about a new relationship, the next step involves deciding what we expect or want from the new relationship. **Predicted outcome value theory** focuses on the perceived rewards or benefits associated with the new relationship (Sunnafrank 1986). There is a shift from focusing on the need for more information about the other person to an analysis of the value obtained from the relationship. Consider when you meet someone for the first time. You probably engage in an analytical process to evaluate the potential for the future of the relationship. At that point a decision is made regarding whether to pursue the relationship, how the relationship should progress, and what type of relationship we should seek with the other person (e.g., friendship, romantic).

Liking

Our earlier discussion of uncertainty reduction theory discussed the strategy of information-seeking to decrease our level of uncertainty about the other person. However, an additional benefit of reducing our uncertainty is to increase liking between individuals. The more we know about a person, the greater the possibility that we will like one another. **Liking** is defined as the level of positive affect, or affinity, we feel toward another person. A critical factor in deciding to initiate a relationship is reciprocal liking—each partner must perceive the other as having mutual positive affect. However, the trick often rests in obtaining information as to whether mutual liking is present. Douglas (1987) conducted a study to identify affinity-testing strategies used to identify the presence or absence of mutual liking. Participants in the study were asked to describe the things they do to find out how much somebody of the opposite sex likes them, being reminded to focus specifically on strategies they would use in initial encounters. Eight different affinity-testing strategies were identified in this study: confronting, withdrawing, sustaining, hazing, diminishing the self, approaching, offering, and networking. Participants were also asked to rate the efficiency and appropriateness of each of the affinity-testing strategies. Confronting, which involved asking the individual direct questions, was viewed as the most efficient strategy followed by approaching and sustaining; in the interest of time, it is best to be up front and direct when determining whether reciprocal liking is present. With regard to appropriateness, sustaining was rated as the most socially appropriate strategy. When individuals used the sustaining strategy they made active attempts to keep the conversation going by getting others to reveal information about themselves. This research supports the use of questions to reduce uncertainty. Hazing and diminishing the self were viewed as socially inappropriate. Both strategies involve "playing games" or using manipulative tactics to determine the level of interest in a relationship. When individuals use these affinity-testing strategies, they may be perceived as deceptive and unacceptable.

While Douglas (1987) examined how individuals determine whether mutual liking exists in romantic relationships, research by Bell and Daly (1984) identified the wide range of strategies used in platonic relationships to gain liking. Bell and Daly describe **affinity-seeking strategies** as verbal and nonverbal communication behaviors that are often used strategically to gain liking from others. In their seminal research they asked college students to identify all of the different tactics they used to gain liking from peers. A total of twenty-five different affinity-seeking strategies were identified from the students' descriptive responses. Examples of affinity-seeking strategies included: altruism, physical attractiveness, facilitate enjoyment, comfortable self, inclusion of other, nonverbal immediacy, and openness. Not surprisingly, affinity-seeking strategies are used in all types of relationships to increase liking. For example, a number of studies indicate that both students and professors use affinity-seeking strategies to improve their relationships (see, for example, Frymier 1994; Wanzer 1995; 1998).

Social Exchange Theory

Have you ever heard the phrase "on the market" to refer to a person who is single and searching for a new romantic relationship? While at first this reference may seem degrading, it actually fits quite well with the strategies used when considering new relationships. The process one experiences when evaluating the pros and cons of initiating a relationship is actually quite similar to shopping—we examine the options available and seek the best "deal" available. **Social exchange theory** (also known as interdependence theory) refers to an assessment of costs and rewards in determining the value of pursuing or continuing a relationship (Thibaut and Kelley 1959). **Rewards** consist of behaviors or things that are desirable, which the recipient perceives as enjoyable or fulfilling. By contrast, **costs** are perceived as undesirable behaviors or outcomes. As we exchange information in the initial stages of a relationship, decisions are made regarding the relative value of continuing to pursue the relationship further. While your initial conversation with the person seated next to you on an airplane may be rewarding in the sense that you felt comfortable discussing topics of interest and it helped pass the time on a three-hour journey, the costs of maintaining the relationship (effort involved in emailing and calling the person) may outweigh the benefits. Thus, you decide to shake hands at the end of the flight, exchange pleasantries, and go your separate ways. But suppose the person seated next to you is employed at the company you've always dreamed of working for. In that instance, the costs involved in continuing to communicate across the distance are minimal compared to the potential reward of having an inside connection when you apply for employment at the company in the future.

Stages of Relationship Development

Now that we have explored the reasons why we initiate relationships and some of the theoretical explanations for how we use communication, we turn our attention to understanding the process of progressing from one stage of a relationship to another.

Mark Knapp (1978) proposes a "staircase" model depicting the interactive stages of relationship development and dissolution. The first five steps of this model, known as Coming Together, will be discussed here. Chapter Nine will discuss Knapp's (1978) stages of relationship disengagement or, Coming Apart. Before discussing the stages of relationship initiation and development, it is important to note the following caveats about the movement from one stage to the next (Knapp and Vangelisti 2003):

- Movement from one stage of the model to the next is typically sequential. Moving sequentially allows us to make predictions regarding the future of the relationship.
- Movement may progress from one stage forward to the next. This movement involves an analysis of the potential benefits of continuing the relationship and increasing the level of intimacy in communication.
- Movement may revert to a previous stage. This is often due to a decline in the communication behaviors prescribed in the present stage.
- Movement through the stages occurs at different paces for each unique relationship. While one relationship may move very quickly from one stage to the next, another relationship may stall at one stage while the partners work through the communication challenges of the phase and make the decision of whether to progress to the next level.

Initiation.

Initiation occurs when one party decides to initiate conversation with another person. Communication during this phase typically consists of the polite formalities of introduction. Statements such as "How are you?" or "Is anyone sitting here?" are used to break the ice. Consider the role that variables discussed earlier in this chapter play in our decision to approach someone and initiate a conversation. For instance, we evaluate the person's attractiveness and scramble to come up with the perfect opening line. During this phase, impression management is essential. After all, we want to present ourselves in the most positive way possible. While some people may be tempted to use one of the pick-up lines discussed earlier in this chapter, the best strategy for making a good first impression is to be confident and sincere.

Experimenting. You know that you have reached the **experimenting** phase when the communication involves excessive questions and discussions about topics such as classes, hobbies, or other demographic information. Whereas physical attraction has a strong influence on the decision to engage in the initiation phase, social attraction is discovered during the experimenting phase. Reciprocal disclosures are common, with one person asking questions such as, "So have you lived in Los Angeles your entire life?" and the other person responding with "No, I grew up in Chicago and moved to L.A. last year to escape the cold winters. Did you grow up in California?" Uncertainty reduction is the primary goal of this stage of relationship development.

Intensifying. As we progress to the **intensifying** stage of the staircase model, our disclosures with one another increase in depth. Whereas in the experimenting stage we disclosed information on a variety of topics (breadth), during this phase the information shared becomes more personal and private (depth). Messages communicated between partners involve a lot of "tests" to determine the intensity or commitment felt by one another. Knapp and Vangelisti (2003) identify specific verbal characteristics that are common during the intensifying stage. These include using nicknames or terms of endearment to refer to one another (think "Hunny" or "Babe"), referring to one another through the use of first person plural pronouns ("*We* should go to the movies with Joe and Cara on Friday,") and making explicit references to the commitment like "I think about you all the time when you're not here."

Integrating. The **integrating** stage is marked by a merging of personalities and identities. Not only do the partners see themselves as a couple, but others recognize and refer to them as a unit as well. Relationship rituals that occur during this stage include exchanging personal items such as clothing, pictures, and rings that can be worn or displayed to communicate their identity as a couple to others, engaging in similar verbal and nonverbal behaviors, and identifying common "property" that is identified as special to the relationship ("our" song or purchasing a pet together).

Getting married demonstrates commitment to a long-term relationship.

Bonding. **Bonding,** the final stage of coming together, is viewed as a formal contractual agreement that declares to the world that the couple has made a serious commitment to one another. This stage can be marked by performing public rituals such as exchanging class rings to show that you are "going steady," or getting engaged, or that you have gotten married. It is important to note that while bonding can be viewed as a contract at any stage of the relationship, the message communicated between a couple during this stage is that there is a serious commitment that implies the goal of pursuing a long-term relationship.

Relationship Initiation Contexts

Another factor impacting the decision to initiate a relationship focuses on the setting in which the initial interaction takes place. In a study of college women, the actual settings where significant relationships began were examined (Jason, Reichler, and Rucker 1981). Five settings were identified by single women as the location where their significant relationships were initiated (see Table 8.3 below). Given that the women were currently enrolled in college classes, it should come as no surprise that they listed school as the place where their most important relationships began. While many would question the quality of a relationship that is initiated in a bar, women reported this as the initial location for nine percent of their significant relationships. In a study of relationship initiation in singles bars, researchers noted that a woman was approached by a man once every ten to twenty minutes. However, the average length of the interaction was approximately seven seconds (Glenwick, Jason, and Elman 1978). So while women may have many opportunities in single bars, it appears as though they choose not to pursue the majority of relationships initiated by men.

A study of preferred meeting places for gays and lesbians reveals a slight difference in setting choices. Gay bars are a popular place for initiating relationships given the fact that patrons of the bars are similar in terms of their sexual preference. Among lesbians, the second most preferred meeting place is at political functions, such as feminist or lesbian rallies (Huston and Schwartz 2003). It is important to note that some environments are not open or welcoming to the initiation of homosexual relationships. Thus, frustration in locating a common place to meet similar others is often reported by gay men and lesbians.

The Role of Technology in Relationship Initiation

Online Relationship Initiation. As the number of people who form relationships online continues to grow, there is a greater need to understand the unique nature of interactions in cyberspace. In face-to-face interactions, the initial

Table 8.3 Settings Where Most Important Relationships Began

Setting	Percentage
School	25
Work	20
Through friends	14
Bar	9
Party	9

Source: From "Characteristics of significant dating relationships: Male versus female initiators, idealized versus actual settings" by L.A. Jason, et al., The Journal of Psychology, 109, 185–190, 1981. Reprinted with permission of the Helen Dwight Reid Educational Foundation. Published by Heldref Publications, 1319 Eighteenth St., NW, Washington, DC 20036-1802. Copyright © 1981.

decision to approach another person is often based on physical characteristics. We see the person, make a decision of whether or not to approach him, and subsequently spend time getting to know one another by progressing through the relationship stages identified by Knapp and Vangelisti (2003). Online relationship initiation differs because of the absence of physical cues, which can affect the course of the relationship. Individuals meet via written messages or text. From there, they decide whether to talk with the other person via phone and, ultimately, in person. In essence, online relationship initiation could be considered a "test drive"—we can dedicate as little or as much time as we want getting to know the person before deciding if we want to meet face-to-face.

Baker (2005) developed a model delineating the characteristics of successful versus unsuccessful relationships which were initiated online (see Table 8.4).

While we might doubt the sustainability of relationships that are initiated online, research suggests otherwise. One study examined the stability of a variety of online relationships (acquaintances, friends, and romantic partners) over a two-year period and found seventy-five percent of respondents indicated that they were still involved in a relationship that had initiated online (McKenna, Green, and Gleason 2002).

© Zsolt Nyulaszi, 2007, Shutterstock.

Will this on-line relationship last?

Text-Messaging. If you are a fan of *American Idol*, you have probably seen the commercials for AT&T Wireless in which Ryan Seacrest sends a text message to a woman named Jeanette, across a crowded bar to inquire if she is interested in meeting his friend, Dave. In the end, Jeanette declines the offer to initiate a relationship, but the scene depicted in the commercial is one that is all too familiar to those currently experiencing the dating scene. A popular channel for communicating in Europe and Asia for several years, text-messaging has achieved growing popularity in the United States as a means to communicate with others in relationships. When initiating new relationships, text messaging serves as a "safe" channel for reducing uncertainty and gaining information about the other person before meeting again face-to-face. The term *silent dating*

Table 8.4 **A Model for Successful versus Unsuccessful Online Relationships**

Factor	Positive/Successful	Negative/Unsuccessful
Place met	Sites focused on specific interests	Sites focused on general interests
Physical appearance, degree of importance	Not viewed as being important	Considered very important or crucial
Hyperhonesty	Very honest online	Not honest in online interactions
Cybersex	Never or rarely engaged in cybersex	Frequently engaged in cybersex
Long-time communication before they met in person	Considerable time spent communicating online prior to face-to-face meeting	Little time spent interacting online prior to meeting
Relocation	At least one person willing to relocate	Neither partner is willing to relocate

Source: From *Double Click: Romance and Commitment Among Online Couples* by A. Baker, 2005, Cresskill, NJ: Hampton Press. Reprinted with permission of the publisher.

has been used to discuss the strategy of exchanging text messages for a week or more in the initial stages of a relationship *(http://thescotsman.scotsman.com/index.cfm?id=290812004)*. Anna Close, a twenty-eight-year-old teacher from Glasgow, describes the value of text messages in initial relationships as: "Before text-messaging I'd meet someone and then not hear from him because he'd be too scared to actually go through the process of picking up the phone and having a conversation. But now, if a man is interested in you, he won't call, but he'll definitely text."

Relationship Initiation and Culture

While you might think that perceptions with regard to relationship initiation differ across cultures, you might be surprised to find out that we are more alike than different. Pines (2001) examined the role of gender and culture in initial romantic attraction by comparing Americans with Israelis. She asked participants to describe how they met their romantic partner and indicate what attracted them to the other person initially (see Table 8.5).

The only significant differences occurred when comparing U.S. and Israeli responses to questions relating to status, propinquity, and similarity. Eight percent of Americans reported that they were attracted by the status of their relational partner, while none of the Israeli respondents indicated this was a factor. Propinquity, or the proximity between partners, was listed as being more influential to Americans. Americans report being more attracted to partners who lived, worked, or studied at the same place, as compared to Israeli respondents. Similarity of partners was found to be more important to Americans. Having similar experiences, values, interests, attitudes, and personalities was rated as being far more important to Americans than to Israelis.

Interracial Dating. As the number of interracial relationships increases, so does our need for understanding the stages of progression that are unique to this relationship context. Foeman and Nance (2003) enhance our understanding of these phases by presenting a model of interracial development. In this model, four stages are encountered by the couple. These include:

- Stage 1—Racial awareness
- Stage 2—Coping with social definitions of race

Table 8.5 Attraction Variables (percent) by Country

Attraction Variable	USA	Israel
Appearance	63	70
Status	8	0
Personality	92	94
Need filled	54	6
Propinquity	63	46
Mutual attraction	41	40
Arousal	22	25
Similarity	30	8

Source: From "The Role of Gender and Culture in a Romantic Attraction" by Ayala Malach Pines. Reproduced with permission from *European Psychologist*, Vol. 6, (2), pp. 96–102. © 2001 by Hogrefe & Huber Publishers.

- Stage 3—Identity emergence
- Stage 4—Maintenance

Racial awareness focuses on the existence of multiple perceptions regarding the new relationship. In addition to each partner's perception of the relationship, interracial couples must also deal with the perceptions of the members of one another's racial groups. If the couple decides to move beyond the initiation phase and awareness, the next stage involves coping with society's definitions and reactions to the racially mixed relationship. Several communication strategies are considered during this phase. In addition to identifying how to respond to questions and statements regarding racial differences, the couple needs to decide when to avoid potentially negative interactions with others and when to confront them. During the third stage, identity emergence, the couple begins to define how they see themselves as an "interracial" couple. They work together to develop strategies and skills for addressing problems and often view themselves as being unique or trendsetting. Maintenance, the final stage of the model, involves occasional recycling through the stages of the model as new life events occur (such as the addition of children to the family) that generate new reactions to their status as an interracial couple.

SUMMARY

In this chapter we have answered some of the questions regarding *why* we form interpersonal relationships with others and *how* we use communication to initiate them. While each relationship is unique, the reasons we choose to interact with others are fairly similar. Our hope is that you have gained both an understanding of, and the confidence for, using effective communication behaviors to pursue new relationship journeys. Perhaps the most important piece of advice we could offer as you begin a relationship with another person, whether it is platonic or romantic relationship, is to just be yourself.

APPLICATIONS

Discussion Questions

A. Recall a time when you were successful at initiating a romantic relationship. Offer several suggestions or guidelines for individuals that want to be successful when initiating conversations or beginning a romantic relationship. What types of things should you avoid saying or doing during this critical time period?

B. Based on your experience, how prevalent is the silent dating phenomenon? Discuss several pros and cons of silent dating.

C. In what context or under what circumstances did most of your important relationships begin? Do you initiate different types of relationships in different contexts? Are there similarities and differences in the questions asked/strategies employed during the initiating stages of platonic and romantic relationship development?

D. In your opinion, what is the best way to gain liking from another individual? Bell and Daly identified twenty-five affinity-seeking strategies that individuals use to gain liking. Can you identify at least ten strategies?

REFERENCES

Altman, I., and D. A. Taylor. 1973. *Social penetration: The development of interpersonal relationships.* New York: Holt, Rinehart, & Winston.

Aron, A. 2003. Self and close relationships. In M. R. Leary and J. P. Tangney (Eds.), *Handbook of self and identity.* New York: The Guilford Press.

Baker, A. 2005. *Double click: Romance and commitment among online couples.* Cresskill, NJ: Hampton Press.

Bell, R. A., and J. A. Daly. 1984. The affinity-seeking function of communication. *Communication Monographs, 51,* 91–115.

Berger, C. 1995. A plan-based approach to strategic interaction. In D. E. Hewes (Ed.), *The cognitive bases of interpersonal interaction* (141–180). Hillsdale, NJ: Lawrence Erlbaum.

Berger, C. R., and R. J. Calabrese. 1975. Some explorations in initial interaction and beyond: Toward a developmental theory of interpersonal communication. *Human Communication Research, 1,* 99–112.

Berscheid, E., and H. T. Reis. 1998. Attraction and close relationships. In D. Gilbert, S. Fiske, and G. Lindzey (Eds.), *Handbook of social psychology (4th ed.)* (193–281). New York: McGraw-Hill.

Buss, D. M. 1989. Sex differences in human mate preferences: Evolutionary hypotheses tested in 37 cultures. *Behavioral and Brain Sciences, 12,* 1–49.

Curran, J. P., and S. Lippold. 1975. The effects of physical attraction and attitude similarity on attraction in dating dyads. *Journal of Personality, 43,* 528–539.

Davis, S. 1990. Men as success objects and women as sex objects: A study of personal advertisements. *Sex Roles, 23,* 43–50.

Dillard, J. P. 1990. A goal-driven model of interpersonal influence. In J. P. Dillard (Ed.), *Seeking compliance: The production of interpersonal influence messages* (41–56). Scottsdale, AZ: Gorsuch-Scarisbrick.

Dion, K. K., E. Berscheid, and E. Walster. 1972. What is beautiful is good. *Journal of Personality and Social Psychology, 24,* 285–290.

Douglas, W. 1987. Affinity-testing in initial interactions. *Journal of Social and Personal Relationships, 4,* 3–15.

———. 1990. Uncertainty, information seeking and liking during initial interaction. *Western Journal of Speech Communication, 54,* 66–81.

Eagly, A. H., R. D. Ashmore, M. G. Makhijani, and L. C. Longo. 1991. What is beautiful is good, but . . . A meta-analytic review of research on the physical attractiveness stereotype. *Psychological Bulletin, 110,* 109–128.

Foeman, A., and T. Nance. 2003. From miscegenation to multiculturalism. In K. M. Galvin and P. J. Cooper (Eds.), *Making connections: Readings in interpersonal communication (3rd ed.)* (pp. 166–170). Los Angeles, CA: Roxbury.

Frymier, A. B. 1994. The use of affinity-seeking in producing liking and learning in the classroom. *Journal of Applied Communication Research, 22,* 87–105.

Glenwick, D. S., L. A. Jason, and D. Elman. 1978. Physical attractiveness and social contact in the singles bar. *Journal of Social Psychology, 105,* 311–312.

Goode, E. 1996. Gender and courtship entitlement: Responses to personal ads. *Sex Roles, 34,* 141–168.

Harrison, A. A., and L. Saeed. 1977. Let's make a deal: An analysis of revelations and stipulations in lonely hearts advertisements. *Journal of Personality and Social Psychology, 35,* 257–264.

Hatfield, E., and S. Sprecher. 1986. *Mirror, mirror: The importance of looks in everyday life.* Albany, NY: SUNY Press.

Hebl, M. R., and T. F. Heatherton. 1998. The stigma of obesity in women: The difference is black and white. *Personality and Social Psychology Bulletin, 24,* 417–426.

Hewitt, J., and K. German. 1987. Attire and attractiveness. *Perceptual and Motor Skills, 42,* page 558.

Huston, M., and P. Schwartz. 2003. The relationships of lesbians and of gay men. In K. M. Galvin and P. J. Cooper (Eds.), *Making connections: Readings in interpersonal communication (3rd ed.)* (171–177). Los Angeles, CA: Roxbury.

Jason, L. A., A. Reichler, and W. Rucker. 1981. Characteristics of significant dating relationships: Male versus female initiators, idealized versus actual settings. *The Journal of Psychology, 109,* 185–190.

Johnson, D. F., and J. B. Pittinger. 1984. Attribution, the attractiveness stereotype, and the elderly. *Developmental Psychology, 20,* 1168–1172.

Katz, J. E., and R. E. Rice. 2002. *Social consequences of Internet use: Access, involvement and interaction.* Cambridge, MA: The MIT Press.

Kito, M. 2005. Self-disclosure in romantic relationships and friendships among American and Japanese college students. *The Journal of Social Psychology, 44,* 181–199.

Klohnen, E. C., and S. Luo. 2003. Interpersonal attraction and personality: What is attractive—self similarity, ideal similarity, complementarity, or attachment security? *Journal of Personality and Social Psychology, 85,* 709–722.

Knapp, M. L. 1978. *Social intercourse: From greeting to goodbye.* Boston: Allyn & Bacon.

Knapp, M., and A. Vangelisti. 2003. Relationship stages: A communication perspective. In K. M. Galvin and P. J. Cooper (Eds.), *Making connections: Readings in interpersonal communication (3rd ed.)* (158–165). Los Angeles, CA: Roxbury.

Kowalski, R. M. 1999. Speaking the unspeakable: Self-disclosure and mental health. In B. R. Kowalski and M. R. Leary (Eds.), *The social psychology of emotional and behavioral problems* (225–248). Washington, DC: The American Psychological Association.

Lewis, K. E., and M. Bierly. 1990. Toward a profile of the female voter: Sex differences in perceived physical attractiveness and competence of political candidates. *Sex Roles, 22,* 1–12.

Lykken, D. T., and A. Tellegen. 1993. Is human mating adventitious or the result of lawful choice? A twin study of mate selection. *Journal of Personality and Social Psychology, 65,* 56–68.

Mathes, E. W., S. M. Brennan, P. M. Haugen, and H. B. Rice. 1985. Ratings of physical attractiveness as a function of age. *The Journal of Social Psychology, 125,* 157–168.

McClellan, B., and S. J. McKelvie. 1993. Effects of age and gender on perceived physical attractiveness. *Canadian Journal of Behavioral Science, 25,* 135–142.

McCroskey, J. C., and T. A. McCain. 1974. The measurement of interpersonal attraction. *Speech Monographs, 41,* 261–266.

McCroskey, J. C., V. P. Richmond, and J. A. Daly. 1975. The development of a measure of perceived homophily in interpersonal communication. *Human Communication Research, 1,* 323–332.

McKenna, K. Y. A., A. S. Green, and M. E. J. Gleason. 2002. Relationship formation on the Internet: What's the big attraction? *Journal of Social Issues, 58,* 9–31.

Mongeau, P. A., J. L. Hale, K. L. Johnson, and J. D. Hillis. 1993. "Who's wooing whom?" An investigation of female- initiated dating. In P. J. Kalbfeisch (Ed.), *Interpersonal communication: Evolving interpersonal relationships* (51–68). Hillsdale, NJ: Lawrence Erlbaum.

Mongeau, P. A., M. C. M. Serewicz, and L. F. Therrien. 2004. Goals for cross-sex first dates: Identification, measurement, and the influence of contextual factors. *Communication Monographs, 71,* 121–147.

Nakanishi, M. 1986. Perceptions of self-disclosure in initial interaction: A Japanese sample. *Human Communication Research, 13,* 167–190.

Perrett, D. I., K. J. Lee, and I. Penton-Voak. 1998. Effects of sexual dimorphism on facial attractiveness, *Nature, 394,* August, 27, 884–886.

Pines, A. M. 2001. The role of gender and culture in romantic attraction. *European Psychologist, 6,* 96–102.

Richmond, V. P. 1992. *Nonverbal communication in the classroom.* Edina, MN: Burgess.

Reis, H. T., and B. C. Patrick. 1996. Attachment and intimacy: Component processes. In E. T. Higgins and A. W. Kruglanski (Eds.), *Social psychology: Handbook of basic principles* (523–563). New York: Guilford Press.

Reis, H. T., and P. Shaver. 1988. Intimacy as interpersonal process. In S. Duck (Ed.), *Handbook of personal relationships: Theory, research, and interventions* (367–389). Chichester: John Wiley & Sons Ltd.

Reis, H. T., J. Nezlek, and L. Wheeler. 1980. Physical attractiveness in social interaction. *Journal of Personality and Social Psychology, 38,* 604–617.

Segal, M. W. 1974. Alphabet and attraction: An unobtrusive measure of the effect of propinquity in a field setting. *Journal of Personality and Social Psychology, 30,* 654–657.

Sergios, P., and J. Cody. 1985. Importance of physical attractiveness and social assertiveness skills in male homosexual dating behavior and partner selection. *Journal of Homosexuality, 12,* 71–84.

Silver-Greenberg, J. 2005. Dying to know. *Newsweek, 146,* September, 11.

Snyder, M., E. Berscheid, and P. Glick. 1985. Focusing on the exterior and the interior: Two investigations of the initiation of personal relationships. *Journal of Personality and Social Psychology, 48,* 1427–1439.

Sprecher, S., and S. Hendrick. 2004. Self-disclosure in intimate relationships: Associations with individual and relationship characteristics over time. *Journal of Social and Clinical Psychology, 23,* 857–877.

Sprecher, S., Q. Sullivan, and E. Hatfield. 1994. Mate selection preferences: Gender differences examined in a national sample. *Journal of Personality and Social Psychology, 66,* 1074–1080.

Sunnafrank, M. 1986. Predicted outcome value during initial interactions: A reformulation of uncertainty reduction theory. *Human Communication Research, 13,* 3–33.

Thibaut, J., and H. Kelley. 1959. *The social psychology of groups.* New York, NY: Wiley.

Vangelisti, A. L. 2002. Interpersonal processes in romantic relationships. In M. L. Knapp and J. A. Daly (Eds.), *Handbook of interpersonal communication* (643–679). Thousand Oaks, CA: Sage.

Walster, E., V. Aronson, D. Abrahams, and L. Rottman. 1966. Importance of physical attractiveness in dating behavior. *Journal of Personality and Social Psychology, 4,* 508–516.

Wanzer, M. B. 1995. *Student affinity-seeking messages and teacher liking: Subordinate initiated relationship building in superior-subordinate dyads.* Unpublished doctoral dissertation, West Virginia University, Morgantown, WV.

Wanzer, M. B. 1998. An exploratory investigation of student and teacher perceptions of student-generated affinity-seeking behaviors. *Communication Education, 47,* 373–382.

Werner, C. M., and L. M. Haggard. 1985. Temporal qualities of interpersonal relationships. In M. L. Knapp and G. R. Miller (Eds.), *Handbook of interpersonal communication* (59–99). Beverly Hills, CA: Sage.

Wilson, G. D., J. M. Cousins, and B. Fink. 2006. The CQ as a predictor of speed-date outcomes. *Sexual and Relationship Therapy, 21,* 163–169.

Woll, S. 1986. So many to choose from: Decision strategies in video dating. *Journal of Social and Personal Relationships, 3,* 43–52.

Zebrowitz, L. A. 1997. *Reading faces: Window to the soul?* Boulder, CO: Westview Press.

Part 2: Case Study: A Place for Connecting and Disclosing: Facebook and Friendships at the Dawn of College Life

KEY TERMS

self-disclosure **warranting** **Facebook**
social connection

Ben barely noticed the change in weather as a soft July rainstorm fluttered against his bedroom window. On this late Friday afternoon, Ben knew that many of his high school friends would be gathering together somewhere, doing something social. He'd been to several such gatherings during the summer—this intermission, this pause between the end of high school and the new life of college. Already he had heard his cell phone ring several times, then the chime of a voice mail, then the bleep of a text message. But tonight, as he clutched his Xbox controller, Ben was content to stay home and do some of the things he loved most, perhaps reading part of a novel later tonight. *This game is so much more controllable than my world right now,* he thought.

His mom's familiar knock echoed from his bedroom door. "Come in," Ben yelled as he paused his game.

She cracked open the door. "Got the mail, and there's a letter for you from Lasher State."

"Really?" Ben said as his mom handed him the envelope. As he opened it, he sized it up—it looked official, like everything else from Lasher State, but felt thin, unlike the huge amount of promotional material they sent. During senior year. *Every. Single. Week.*

His eyes scanned the single sheet of paper inside. "What is it?" his mom asked.

"Looks like information about my roommate." Ben was surprised they'd sent the information this quickly. He had only completed the roommate preference form two weeks ago.

"Who is he?" his mom asked excitedly, stepping through the door and turning to see the paper. "David L. Bradford, from Hill City? I wonder if he knows the Woodsmiths?"

From *Casing Interpersonal Communication: Case Studies in Personal and Social Relationships* by Dawn O. Braithwaite and Julie T. Wood.

"Maybe," Ben shrugged. "Probably. There's only about 5,000 people living there."

"Well, his e-mail address and phone number are right here; maybe you should try to give him a call after dinner."

Ben felt his gut tighten. The last thing he wanted to do tonight was talk to anyone else. Much less talk about college. "We'll see; perhaps later this weekend."

"Just don't wait too long. You'll have to make some plans with him before school starts!"

"I know," Ben said, picking up his Xbox controller again as his mom left. He unpaused, fired another shot, and dodged a missile. But then he paused again, curiosity creeping into his brain. *I wonder . . . what can I find out about this David guy online? Google? Maybe even Facebook?* He moved to his computer, noticing he had new e-mails, but it took a moment for him to realize that one message was from David Bradford! But wait, it wasn't a "real" e-mail; the subject line read, "Dave Bradford added you as a friend on Facebook . . ."

The knot in Ben's stomach tightened a little bit. He had only created his Facebook account about a year ago, and mostly to keep in touch with a few close high school friends. At the time, he hadn't thought about how Facebook might help build friendships at college, but thinking about it now, it made sense that it would. He moved to click "accept," but then hesitated. This felt weird. *Honestly, it's strange to accept a request from someone I don't know . . . but I guess I will know him. But then again, what if we don't get along? Will he be upset if I don't accept the request?* For a moment, he stared at the screen, hovering in indecision. Then, with firm finality, he clicked the button. *Now, let's see what my new roommate is about.*

In Dave's profile picture, he was wearing a football uniform, hoisting a medium-sized trophy above his head, enthusiastic teammates and students cheering around him. Ben's eyes moved further down the left side of the page. *What? He has 732 friends? How did he get that many?* Last time he checked, Ben's friends barely numbered 100. *Obviously David likes football . . . U2, of course . . . in a relationship but "it's complicated?"* Ben skipped reading the list of brainless comedy movies Dave seemed to like and started reading Dave's wall. The first post was from someone named Annabelle Watkins, a gorgeous girl with what looked like some kind of alcoholic drink in her hand. "Hey man!!! Life of the party last night!! Won't be the same in h-town w/o u!!" The next post was from Jason Vernum, also wearing a football uniform: "What you doing sending me a FB message at 3 AM?? Oh wait, it's you, ha ha." Most posts were written by girls.

Ben leaned back, looked up, and blew air between his lips. In his mind, he saw his dorm room, plastered with Dave's ridiculous football posters. He saw himself trying to get some sleep while Dave partied into the late hours of the night. He saw Dave trying to hit on every girl that passed down the hallway. And he could almost smell the lingering scent of beer Dave would surely bring into their room. This had been his nightmare about college life: a roommate who would derail his vision of studying hard and being the first person in his family to earn a college degree. How had the housing office messed up so badly? He had made it so clear he wanted someone who prioritized grades. Did Ben just happen to get the last roommate available?

He navigated back to his own Facebook profile. *I list myself as single, but I think there are still a few pictures up with my girlfriend from junior year. Some of the bands under "Favorite Music" seem a bit dated . . . I still list The Crazy Monkeys?*

That's gotta go. And he's going to think I'm such a big nerd with "reading" as my first listed hobby. And, oh wow, the most recent post on my wall is even from grandma. Looking up, his eyes scanned his "Religious Views" and "Political Views." *I kinda listed those reluctantly. Maybe I should take them down before the fall?*

With a level of intensity that surprised him, Ben closed the browser window and turned back to his video game. This was the last thing he wanted to think about on a summer night.

Ben felt a small burst of glee as he plugged his Xbox 360's video cable into Dave's flat-screen TV. *This is going to be so much better than my old TV! And so far only one ridiculous football poster. Maybe Dave won't be so bad after all.* He heard a knock behind him and turned.

"Hi. Looks like you have quite the TV there?" said a tall girl with straight blond hair.

"Yeah, it's Dave's," Ben replied, setting the cable down. He extended a hand. "I'm Ben Hamilton."

"Allison Wickman," she responded, shaking his hand. "I live across the hall and thought I'd say 'hi.' Have you met my roommate yet? Chloe Martins?"

"I think I saw her bringing some boxes up with her mom."

Allison laughed. "Yeah, wait 'til you see how many shoes she has! But I knew that; we went to high school together. How about your roommate? Don't think I've met him yet."

"Dave? He seems OK, but we don't really know each other—just talked on the phone a few times this summer. He seems pretty athletic; spends a lot of time with the football team."

Allison opened her mouth to reply as a girl with curly dark hair tumbled out of the stairwell. The bulk of her huge cardboard box dwarfed her tiny frame.

"Allison? Um, help?" she asked, bracing herself against the wall.

Ben turned with Allison to help steady the box. As Allison grunted under the weight, she said, "Ben, this is Chloe."

"Nice to meet you," Ben breathed, helping them shove the box through the door frame. It barely fit. He heard his cell phone ring in his own room. "I should probably get that; do you have it handled from here?"

"Think so," Allison said. "Catch you later . . . look you up on Facebook?"

"Sure," Ben nodded, then dashed into his room. The phone had just finished ringing; the missed call was from his mom. Ben rolled his eyes; *third time she's called me today.* As he set the phone down, his hand brushed his laptop. He had been editing his Facebook profile before the urge struck to set up the Xbox 360, and it was still on the screen. *Whoops. I still have The Crazy Monkeys listed. Oh well, I guess Allison will just think I have weird musical tastes.*

"Hey Ben," he heard Dave say behind him.

"Back from the weight room?" Ben asked, turning from the computer.

"Yeah," Dave replied. "Hey, thanks for setting up the Xbox!"

"Oh, I'm not quite done yet. A girl from across the hall stopped by and interrupted me."

"Yeah, I think I saw them when I came in. Pretty good looking chicks!"

Ben felt himself squirm inwardly. *Not exactly how I was raised to think about girls. Time to change the subject.* "What are you doing tonight? I heard some of the other freshmen are going to a late showing of *Titan Wars.* Want to come?"

"Oh man, I've been wanting to see that movie!" Dave closed the door and opened up his closet. "But I've got to hit the sack early tonight; I know class doesn't start until Wednesday, but ROTC starts tomorrow. Gotta be up by six, so I'm going to try to be in bed no later than eleven this semester. Been meaning to talk to you about that; hope that's OK with you."

Ben's brain took a moment to catch up with the sudden change in his expectations. "Wait . . . you're in ROTC? From Facebook, it looked like you stayed up pretty late last year!"

Dave chuckled, pulling some clothes from his closet. "Yeah . . . you probably got a strange mental picture of me from Facebook, huh? Like I'm some party animal or something?"

Ben looked down. "Well, I guess . . . "

"No need to pretend; I didn't realize until I saw your profile how it might look to you. It's pretty clear you care a lot about your grades, and your family." He paused a moment, looking uncomfortable. "I don't really want to go into too much detail right now, but I made some bad choices my junior year. I almost didn't get into Lasher State. But then some tough things happened with my family and on the football team, and I changed a lot my senior year. That's why I requested someone who studies a lot and goes to bed early on that form they sent out. Some of my old friends still post stuff on my wall, trying to make it sound like I drink and party a lot, but I don't even go near alcohol anymore."

"Wow," Ben said, feeling stunned. "Yeah, that's not the impression I had of you from Facebook. But I'm probably not as nerdy as I sounded on Facebook, either."

"I don't know about that, buddy—only a nerd would list Crazy Monkeys on the profile."

"Getting deleted right now," Ben chuckled, turning to his computer. He had a new e-mail: "Allison Wickman added you as a friend on Facebook . . . "

Before he clicked "accept," he wondered: *When she reads my profile, what impression will Allison have of me?* Knowing that accepting friend requests would probably become a routine part of his new life at college, Ben clicked "accept." He began to explore Allison's Facebook profile.

In her profile picture, Allison wore a red and white high school cheerleading uniform; an older couple, perhaps her parents, stood next to her, as well as a few friends and football players. But the most prominent friend in the picture was Chloe, also in a cheerleading uniform, her arm tightly around Allison's shoulders. Except for a new haircut, Chloe looked pretty much like she did now. The picture appeared to be taken just after a team victory. The football players looked exhausted, but happy. Everyone was smiling. Ben looked to the left side of the page—*Wow! 985 friends? Are you kidding me? That's . . .* being a bit of a math and statistics geek, Ben quickly calculated in his head . . . *that's about 250 more than Dave! I don't even think I know that many people in person.* Allison's wall was littered with postings from Chloe: "Hey gurl! I had an awesome time dancing last night. Call me la8er. xoxoxo." Another read, "what party are we going to tonight? Gotta see ya before you head to Lasher!" Ben scrolled up and clicked on the "Info" tab. Under "About Me," it read: "I'm heading to Lasher State in the Fall with my girl, Chloe! Can't wait for college! We're going to be roommates! Yay!!!" *Wow. They seem pretty close. I bet it's going to be so easy for them to live together at college.*

Ben looked up from his midterm study sheet and glanced out the window. "Dave, it's snowing!" he exclaimed, watching thin clusters of flakes fall toward the parking lot below.

He heard Dave blow air between his lips. "Too early, man! Too early!"

Ben chuckled. "I think you're just in denial about midterms."

A small knock sounded from their open door. "Aren't we all?" asked Chloe, peeking her head around the door jamb. "Hey, you guys almost ready for dinner?"

Ben glanced at his watch; it was 5:30. "Wow, it is that time already!" Ben thought about how he expected that, many nights, he would have dinner with Dave, Chloe, and Allison. Since the beginning of the semester, they had become pretty good friends. In addition to lunch or dinner several times each week in the dining hall, they watched movies during the week and chatted often on Facebook. *Or at least, we all did until about a week ago.*

As Ben grabbed his room key, attached to his sporty Lasher State lanyard, he thought about asking the unspoken question that had hovered among the three of them this past week. He was sure Dave and Chloe didn't see him open his mouth and close it in hesitation before he finally opened it to speak. "Hey, Chloe, where's Allison?"

Chloe looked down, shaking her head. "Ya know, Ben, lately I just don't know about that girl. She's just never in the room anymore. She leaves early before I get up. She gets in late, sometimes after I'm asleep. And she never talks to me anymore. Ever. I mean, about anything more than basic stuff. I've been wondering if I pissed her off somehow, but I just don't know."

"Nah, it isn't just you," Dave chimed in, throwing his lanyard around his neck. "Allison's been ignoring me lately too. We used to always meet in the library on Mondays after lunch to study, but she hasn't been there the last two weeks. And get this: I was down at the health center yesterday for an appointment about my knee, and I saw her coming out. I just, like, asked her where she'd been, but she seemed upset and said she was just busy. But she also was talking really fast and hardly looked me in the eyes."

Ben fingered his keys idly, thinking. "Well," Chloe said, "I'm sure it's not a big deal; I'll just try to check in with her tonight, no matter how late she comes in."

"Wait a sec," Ben said, bending back over his laptop. "Have either of you checked her Facebook page recently?"

"Hey—isn't that kind of, like, stalking our friend?" Dave protested. But Ben had already accessed her profile. Allison hadn't updated her status message in about two weeks, and hardly anyone had posted on her wall. The exception was a message posted about two minutes ago by an elderly woman named Donna: "Hi dear—Heard from your parents about what's going on—so sorry—love always." Ben read it out loud to Dave and Chloe as they huddled around him.

"Sounds kinda serious," Dave said, his usual levity gone from his voice.

Chloe shook her head. "Maybe, but I know Donna from home; she's friends with Allison's grandma. She sometimes exaggerates things. She probably just heard about how stressed Allison is about midterms. I mean, Allison and I have been best friends since fourth grade. If it were anything really serious, she'd tell me right away. Maybe before her family."

"Guys, I know this could be important, but the dining hall is going to get crowded soon, and I'm so hungry!" belted out Dave. "I hope they don't have that stinky greenish looking meatloaf again!" Ben returned his Facebook page to the news feed and turned to head for dinner.

By the time they returned to their dorm floor after, fortunately, a non-meatloaf dinner, the unseasonably early snow had stopped. "Watching *The Bachelor* tonight?" Ben asked Chloe.

"Yeah. You guys doing your post-dinner Xbox ritual?"

"Of course!" Dave exclaimed. "Study for the psych test later? About an hour?"

"Sounds good," Chloe replied as she walked past her room toward the stairwell to the basement lounge. As Ben loaded the Xbox 360 game, he saw Dave log in to check Facebook. Just as the game finished loading, Ben heard Dave draw in a sharp, startled breath.

"What is it?" Ben asked.

"Um, it's Allison," Dave replied. "Dude, you've got to read this." Ben bolted from the papassan chair to his desk, shaking his mouse to awaken his computer. Allison's note was at the top of his news feed. As Ben began to read, Dave said softly: "I don't believe it. I feel so . . . " Quickly, Ben snapped back, "Shhh, quiet. I'm reading." He read the first two lines:

"I am writing to share some very sad and very personal news. I've been diagnosed with ovarian cancer. The doctors think they caught it early. So my prognosis is good."

Ben felt stunned, his stomach twisting in knots. "This must be why Allison has been so distant," he said. "Why didn't she just tell us and especially Chloe? I know it's really personal, and we haven't known her that long, but it feels like we're good friends . . . "

"Yeah, I know," Dave replied. "Maybe she didn't tell us because it's a 'girl thing?' "

"But it doesn't sound like she told Chloe, either."

With sudden quickness, Dave dashed across the hall and knocked on Chloe's door. There was no answer. He pulled out his cell phone. "What are you doing?" Ben asked.

"Text message," Dave replied. "Asking if she's seen Allison's Facebook note." When he was done, Dave silently returned to his desk chair and opened his psychology textbook.

Ben stood for a moment, staring at Dave, then back at his laptop, then to the Xbox 360, the game's militaristic theme song droning through the television speakers. *I can't believe how normal things felt earlier tonight,* he thought. Not feeling like playing a game anymore, he turned off the Xbox 360 and the television.

Dave's phone played its text message chime. "What does it say?" Ben asked. He held up the phone to Ben: *huh? No, whats wrong? In the dorm lounge; should I come up?* "Sounds like she doesn't know," Ben said, then feeling stupid for saying the obvious.

"What should we do? You know how she's going to react. Should we tell her?"

"I . . . I don't know. Maybe Allison was going to tell Chloe later tonight? Maybe we should back off and let her share her news when she's ready?"

"But she's going to see this next time she checks Facebook, which will probably be after *The Bachelor*—" Dave stopped as they heard footsteps run down the hall, and then saw Chloe swiftly open her door and enter her room. Ben looked at Dave, and then both followed behind her. She was already bending over her computer, a tear streaming down her cheek.

"S—someone downstairs checked the note on their iPhone—" she stammered as she opened the note. Ben and Dave remained awkwardly silent as she read the first few lines, her eyes filling with fresh tears. "Why—why didn't she tell me?" Chloe breathed in, her voice trembling.

"I'm so sorry," said Dave, trying to comfort her, putting his hand on her shoulder; she violently shrugged it away.

"She should have told me," Chloe spat, tears still in her eyes. "We've been friends since elementary school. We've been through everything together! Why couldn't see just tell me to my face? But no, I get to hear about it from some guy friends after she posts it on Facebook for the whole damn world to see!"

"Well, maybe she just wanted to tell everybody at once," Ben said, not sure what else to say. "I bet it would be hard for her to tell the same story over and over. She must have so much going on in her mind, and I'm sure she didn't mean to hurt you."

Chloe collapsed on her bed. "Ben, just shut up. You have NO IDEA what things we've gone through together! She was there when my parents divorced, and when grandpa passed away suddenly, and so many other times. And I told her EVERYTHING. But—" She buried her face in her pillow, sobbing. Ben and Dave's eyes met for a moment; Dave's face mirrored Ben's concern for Chloe, coupled with an utter sense of futility at understanding her feelings, much less comforting her. Without a further word, they both turned to leave.

But before they could take a step, the door swung open noiselessly. It was Allison.

For Further Thought and Reflection

1. Ben's perception of Dave from Facebook was very different than how Dave presented himself in person. When, if ever, have you experienced a mismatch between someone's online persona and how they communicate when face-toface?

2. Some communication research on the *warranting value of information* suggests that we are more likely to believe a Facebook member's wall posts than their own statements about themselves. Why do you think Ben so easily believed wall posts on Dave's profile? When might we believe a person's statements about themselves rather than those of their Facebook friends?

3. Why do you think Allison shared her personal information with everyone on Facebook, instead of telling Chloe, her close friend, to her face? More generally, what qualities of online communication might help some people feel more comfortable self-disclosing online?

4. Do you think Chloe should ask Allison why she did not directly share her medical problem? Why or why not? What do you think might happen next in this story?

REFERENCES

Donath, J. (2007). Signals in social supernets. *Journal of Computer-Mediated Communication, 13*. Available at: http://jcmc.indiana.edu/vol13/issue1/donath.html.

Ellison, N. B., Steinfield, C., & Lampe, C. (2007). The benefits of Facebook "friends:" Social capital and college students' use of online social network sites. *Journal of Computer-Mediated Communication, 12*. Available at: http://jcmc.indiana.edu/vol12/issue4/ellison.html.

Mazer, J.P., Murphy, R.E., & Simonds, C.J. (2007). I'll see you on "Facebook": The effects of computer-mediated teacher self-disclosure on student motivation, affective learning, and classroom climate. *Communication Education, 56*, 1–17.

Tong, S.T., Van Der Heide, B., Langwell, L., & Walther, J.B. (2008). Too much of a good thing? The relationship between number of friends and interpersonal impressions on Facebook. *Journal of Computer-Mediated Communication, 13,* 531–549.

Walther, J. B. (2008). Social information processing theory: Impressions and relationship development online. In L.A. Baxter & D.O. Braithwaite (Eds.), *Engaging theories in interpersonal communication* (pp. 391–404). Newbury Park, CA: Sage.

Walther, J.B., Van Der Heide, B., Kim, S., Westerman, D., & Tong, S.T. (2008). The role of friends' behavior on evaluations of individuals' Facebook profiles: Are we known by the company we keep? *Human Communication Research, 34,* 28–49.

chapter 9

Group Communication

OBJECTIVES

After reading this chapter, you should understand the following concepts:

- A small group is a collection of people who work together either voluntarily or involuntarily to achieve a goal or solve a problem.
- Voluntary groups come together to achieve goals, solve problems, fulfill needs, or simply to connect with others with the same interests.
- Involuntary groups are formed to solve problems, make decisions, or accomplish necessary tasks.
- Groups offer many benefits, but they also have drawbacks, one of which is groupthink.
- Groups typically progress through five stages: forming, storming, norming, performing, and adjourning.
- Your roles in small groups will vary, depending on the group.
- Tools for handling disruptive members include feedback, perception checking, and group contracts.

KEY TERMS

small group	**forming stage**	**group maintenance roles**
interdependence	**storming stage**	**individual-centered roles**
virtual groups	**norming stage**	**disruptive group roles**
synergy	**performing stage**	**group contract**
brainstorming	**adjourning stage**	**feedback**
norms	**task roles**	
groupthink		

INTRODUCTION

"I hate group work!"

This statement is often heard when college students are told they will be working in groups to complete projects. The same sentiment is expressed across offices and at work sites every day. "Why can't I just do this project myself?" Dissatisfaction with working in groups is so common that the term *grouphate* was coined to describe the negative attitude toward group work.[1] If people hate working in groups so much, then why are groups so often used? The answer to the question is fairly simple: Groups outperform individuals most of the time, and groups are capable of taking on more complex tasks. In fact, many employers are willing to pay the added expense of operating a group to take advantage of a group's ability to creatively solve problems and to make high-quality decisions.

Why do groups have an advantage when it comes to problem solving?

For most of us, our first exposure to groups was as early as elementary school. Perhaps we were asked to collaborate with other students to complete an in-class activity or to play on a sports team. These early exposures to groups provide us with our first instructions about how to play nicely with others, how to share, and how to get along. The collaborative learning process continues through college, where the skills being taught are more complex (e.g., conflict management, patience, and negotiation skills) and the stakes are much higher (e.g., grades in our major, grades influencing the next school we attend, financial aid, and our future professions). The stakes continue to rise in our careers. Our ability to work effectively with others affects our salaries, our upward mobility, and even our job security.

Television has capitalized on just how difficult it is to work with others, which is evidenced by the number of popular group-based reality shows. Although the subject of these shows is not directly related to the process of building an effective group or team, they do require participants to work within the framework of a group to achieve goals. For instance, teams are formed on one show to achieve business goals such as marketing and selling a product. Each group member is judged by his or her individual contribution, approaches to group collaboration, and decision making throughout the process. The selling point of such shows is not only the completion of the task at hand but also the relationships among group members. There is something enjoyable about watching how group members balance their own goals with the group goals, manage conflicts, and how they are able to succeed, or fail, under such circumstances.

How do individual strengths combine to make a group successful?

The way we respond to groups, the roles we play, the understanding we bring to them, and the communication skills we use (or fail to use) combine to influence our group experience. Earlier in this book, we discussed the importance of using communication skills to exercise our democratic rights. Effective group communication skills allow us to foster a free flow and thorough discussion of ideas critical in a democracy.

Take a Closer Look

Working in a Group

Think of the last group in which you worked.

- What was the purpose of the group?
- Was the group voluntary or mandatory?
- What was the best part of the group experience?
- What was the worst part of the group experience?
- If you could repeat the group experience, what would you have done differently?

Controversial issues discussed in the context of a group can move from divisive arguments to productive dialogues when the proper skills are employed.

The purpose of this activity is for you to reflect on this particular group experience when reading about the skills necessary to effectively work in and manage groups. Use this experience as a reference point while reading this chapter and participating in class activities.

WHAT IS THE NATURE OF SMALL GROUPS?

© Miodrag Gajic, 2008, Shutterstock.

Small groups in a work atmosphere often form to solve a particular problem.

Stated simply, a **small group** is a collection of people who work together either voluntarily or involuntarily to achieve a goal or solve a problem. But a small group is actually a complex social and communication phenomenon, so let's expand our definition. If we examine how other scholars have looked at small groups, we can gain some additional insight.

Keyton tells us that a small group is three or more people who work together interdependently on an agreed-upon activity or goal.[2] Forsyth says that a group is made up of "interdependent individuals who influence each other through social interaction."[3]

Wallace etal. suggest that a small group is an interdependent collection of persons engaged in a structured, cooperative, often (but not always) face-to-face, goal-oriented communication; each aware of their own and others' participation in the group; and each getting some satisfaction from participating in the activities of the group.[4]

Finally, Beebe and Masterson define a small group as a "group of people who share a common purpose or goal, who feel a sense of belonging to the group, and who exert influence on one another."[5]

As we look at these definitions, let's focus on the important issues:

Goal Orientation

The small groups being discussed in this chapter are created to solve problems or make decisions. As such, they are driven by a focus on some goal to be achieved. The more clearly this goal is defined, the more likely the group will be able to find a solution to the problem or make a quality decision. Group goals provide focus and direction for small groups.

Size Matters

A small group consists of at least three or more members. When there are fewer than three members, the communication is dyadic. When the third member is added to the mix, things begin to change. With three or more members, it is possible for factions to form and for subgroups of members to exchange information that is not available to the

© 2008, JupiterImages Corporation.

What difficulties would this group likely encounter if it were trying to solve a problem?

whole group. Adding more members to the group can be positive because it means that the group will have more points of view to consider when making a decision.

There is a limit, however, to the size of an effective problem-solving small group. What that specific limit is depends, to a large extent, on the individual personalities in the group, the context in which the group is operating, and the nature of the task or problem the group is trying to solve. A group is too large when every member cannot directly communicate with every other member. If you can't carry on a group conversation, then the group members cannot be interdependent. Although there is no definitive upper limit, groups larger than twelve seem to have troubles with interdependence, cohesion, and mutual influence.

Interdependence

The product of a small group is greater than the sum of its parts because of the communication interaction and the **interdependence** of its members. People draw energy, motivation, and ideas from each other, and they take advantage of one another's talents and expertise. Members combine their talents and resources, which gives them the ability to solve more complex problems than they could as individuals working alone. As a result of interdependence, groups have the potential to make better decisions than individuals.

A collection of people isn't necessarily a small group.

Collection of People

A small group is not just an assembly of individuals, but a dynamic combination of people working together to accomplish some common goal. This shared goal and communication among the members are the major elements that separate groups from random collections of people, and it is responsible for the ability of groups to solve problems. For example, a group of people standing on a street corner waiting on a bus to arrive is a collection of people, but they aren't focused on some common goal. They aren't doing anything but waiting on a bus. They just happen to be doing it in the same place. However, these same people could *become* a small group if they decided to design a bus shelter to make their wait more comfortable or if they tried to figure out a better route so the buses would run on time.

Structure

Even though they might sometimes appear to be chaotic, small groups have structure. Some of the structure is fairly common across nearly every group, like there are usually leaders and there are usually followers. Some structures, however, only emerge in certain groups, and the compositions of those structures depend on the nature of the group task and the individual characteristics of the group members. After the group has been together for a while, these structures become more stable, but they are rarely static. Groups tend to negotiate and then continually renegotiate roles, expectations, cohesiveness, the group identity, the way conflict is managed, and many other structural elements.

WHAT ARE THE TYPES OF GROUPS?

Now and in the future, you will participate in many types of groups; some mediated and some face-to-face, some voluntary and some involuntary. We begin by looking at mediated group participation, followed by voluntary groups, and conclude by examining involuntary groups.

Mediated Groups

Whenever a group meets, but does not meet face-to-face, there is some form of media involved. Mediated groups are becoming more dominant with the emergence of the global economy and the improvement of the communication infrastructure around the world. These groups come in several varieties, including virtual groups (computer mediated), teleconferencing groups (members meet using a telephone connection), and videoconferencing groups (members using a combined video and audio connection).

What advantages do virtual groups offer?

Virtual groups are among the most widely used. Many groups are using the Internet and its virtual space to substitute for live meetings, and people are voluntarily joining groups that meet solely in cyberspace. *Virtual groups* are a gathering of people using chat rooms, blogs, social networking sites, bulletin boards, Web sites, listservs, or any other form of computer-mediated communication to meet and solve problems, achieve goals, or share experiences. Of course, while many groups continue to meet face-to-face, many use a *mixture* of face-to-face and mediated channels to accomplish their goals.

The number of companies using virtual meeting space to conduct business is constantly increasing.[6] Meeting online saves time and money spent on travel. It also enables groups to gather at times when it might not be feasible to do so live (e.g., 6:00 A.M. or 12:00 A.M.), it enables groups to transform travel time to time spent on task,[7] and it also encourages shy or reluctant members to participate more openly than they might in face-to-face meetings.[8]

A challenge to virtual groups is the lack of traditional nonverbal communication cues. During a live meeting, a group member may communicate frustration by using a sarcastic tone of voice, a rolling of the eyes, or an unsettled posture. In a virtual meeting, text is often the only channel, so the use of nonverbal cues is limited. This is changing, however, as more and more computers are equipped with video cameras that enable the addition of audiovisual communication channels.

What communication cues can you see during a live meeting that would be missed in a virtual setting?

Several Web-based, open-source communities have emerged, starting a revolution in not only in the way we do business, but also in how we work in groups. Many of today's best-known Web-based companies (Google, Amazon, and eBay, for example) are using computer languages and Web servers that are the result of community-developed software that is produced by programmers from all over the world who collaborate in virtual environments. These group members participate, enhance, correct, and contribute to the building of Web tools without ever being together physically as a group.

Voluntary Groups

In many instances, we join groups voluntarily to achieve goals, solve problems, fulfill needs, or simply to connect with others who have the same interests. This type of group comes in many forms, including support groups, volunteer groups, and specialized groups.

© Christina Richards, 2008, Shutterstock.

What kinds of volunteer groups do you have in your community?

Support Groups. Support groups are groups of people who have similar life goals, tragedies, or experiences, who come together to talk, help, and generally support one another. Some examples of these types of groups are Weight Watchers, Alcoholics Anonymous, divorce groups, dating groups, and cancer survivor groups. These groups may be large or small in size and function to help individuals psychologically, emotionally, and at times, physically.

Volunteer Groups. With the increased attention paid to the value of giving something back to the community, many people are joining volunteer groups. For example, some individuals join groups that organize people to tutor public school students, build houses, assist the elderly, or plant trees. These groups are often associated with nonprofit organizations such as the American Red Cross, Habitat for Humanity, and Children of the Americans.

Volunteerism has received much attention over the last decade. This attention has manifested itself into new educational and noneducational requirements. In both compulsory education and universities, there exists a strong commitment, and in some cases, a requirement, for students to volunteer. For example, many high school students involved in International Baccalaureate Programs (a special honors program) are required to complete up to 150 hours of community service. In March 2000, the California State University (CSU) Board of Trustees passed a resolution in support of community service and service learning. The intent was to ensure that all CSU students have opportunities to participate in service learning, community service, or both. Several colleges and universities, such as Cal-State Monterey Bay require their students to complete service learning hours to graduate. (http://www.calstate.edu/csl/facts_figures/servlearn.shtml). It could be argued that volunteering to fulfill a requirement moves this type of group work from a voluntary group to an involuntary group. However, not only are students learning valuable group lessons through the practice, but many of them continue to volunteer after they have met the requirement.

© 2008, JupiterImages Corporation.

Specialized groups, such as local senior citizens, share common interests.

Participation in volunteer work is not limited to academia. In the corporate world, employees are encouraged to participate in volunteer groups. For example, many companies (e.g., Cargill, American Express, Minnesota based ADC) are providing staff specifically designated to manage the company's volunteer efforts such as organizing events like paint-a-thons, promoting volunteer opportunities to employees, and providing grants to nonprofit organizations where employees volunteer. (http://www.minnesotagiving.org) Nationally, businesses may join the Corporate Volunteer Council (http://

www.pointsoflight.org/networks/business/cvc/) to find volunteer locations, share effective practices, and address community needs through employee volunteerism.

Specialized Groups. Specialized groups are gatherings of people who work in pursuit of a mutual interest. Participation in campus clubs such as the literary club, the future teachers club, or societies like Phi Theta Kappa is voluntary and involves individuals who work toward the achievement of similar goals, such as the advancement of their skills or the opportunity to network. These types of groups include our hobbies (e.g., scrapbooking groups, book clubs), our place in life (e.g., new mothers club, PTA involvement, senior citizen clubs), our own interests (e.g., stock club, chess club, Lions club, Rotary club), or our career interests (engineers clubs, entrepreneurs' club).

Involuntary Groups

Involuntary groups are groups in which we are required to participate. They are often formed to solve a problem, make decisions, or accomplish other tasks. Involuntary groups include academic groups, professional groups, and civic groups.

Academic Groups. These are groups in which you are required to participate to reach academic goals. For example, when you are asked in a class to collaborate with two or more people to write a paper, conduct an experiment, or present a speech, you are participating in an academic group. This type of group can especially be challenging, as individual member's grades often depend on the performance of other group members.

Professional Groups. Committee work in the professional world also requires involuntary collaboration. For example, teachers are required to sit on various committees such as the budget and planning committee, program review, and safety committee. How individuals conduct themselves in these groups can affect their position in the organization in terms of perception of promotability and leadership assessment.

Civic Groups. We participate in civic groups as part of our public or community responsibility. Some civic groups, such as juries, are mandatory if you are selected. Other civic groups are voluntary and perform services for the community, such as Kiwanis Club, the Rotary Club, and a variety of men's and women's clubs.

Volunteer community firefighters provide valuable service to their area.

WHAT ARE THE BENEFITS OF GROUPS?

Understanding groups is a bit easier if you understand some of the properties or characteristics that are common to most small groups. Some of these properties are positive and help groups' productivity, and some are not so positive and present a challenge to a group's ability to accomplish its goals. Let's look at the more positive properties first.

Take a Closer Look

The Pervasiveness of Groups in Your Life

Take time to think about all the groups in which you are currently involved.

- Which groups are voluntary?
- Which groups are involuntary?
- What did you hope or need to accomplish in each group?
- What function did each group serve in your life?

Synergy

Synergy usually occurs in situations in which people with a variety of talents and skills cooperate. **Synergy** suggests that the end product of a group's efforts is superior to the product of the individuals working independently. In essence, the sum is greater than the total of its parts. If we were to examine this in terms of a math equation, then the comparison would look something like this:

The sum of the group's efforts	The sum of individual efforts
2 + 2 = 7	2 + 2 = 4

The consequences of a synergistic system can be seen in the group product. A simple and easy way to think of it might be when a light bulb blows out in a very high ceiling. One person working alone is not tall enough to replace it, but two people working together could do it. If one person stood on the shoulders of the other, the goal can be accomplished! In terms of the kind of groups we are concerned with, here's another way to consider synergy. Say you were taking a marketing class and one of your assignments was to market a new line of cell phones to fellow college students. The synergy perspective argues that if you and three others were sent off to complete the task individually, you would not come up with a campaign as comprehensive, innovative, or effective as those who were collaborating in a group. Some of the explanation for this phenomenon can be found in the other properties of small groups.

Pooling Talent

Groups allow members to pool their talents, combining the strengths of each group member. Instead of just depending on the knowledge and skills of a single member, a group can take advantage of the knowledge and skills of all its members. This means that groups tend to have better collective memories, a variety of expertise, diversity of strengths (and weaknesses), a variety of perspectives (which is essential to group decision making), and more creativity.

What are the advantages of brainstorming in a group?

Brainstorming

When working with others, ideas are developed further. **Brainstorming** is a free flow of ideas from all participants, and the process can spark initial ideas into new directions and solutions. This process helps to open the group up to original perspectives and ideas with a thinking-outside-the-box mentality. Brainstorming can be a powerful tool for creative decision making, but it can also *fail* to be effective if all the members don't participate or cooperate or if the rules for brainstorming aren't followed. Brainstorming will be discussed in a later chapter as a tool for generating a wide variety of solutions to problems.

Complexity

Small groups of people working together are *complex*. This means that a number of individual and independent people have become interdependent and are interacting together in many ways to accomplish some mutually agreed upon goal.[9] If you think of all the ways that individuals are different from each other, and then you think of five individuals working together in a group, the possible combinations of behaviors, conflicts, and outcomes challenges the imagination!

Complexity explains why groups of experts are commissioned to solve societal problems, make policy, and to analyze disasters and tragedies. We see this in the form of national think tanks, political or organizational committees, and commissions. This property of groups allows them to provide more thorough, more creative, and high-quality decisions.

Complex problems often require the expertise of a group effort.

Self-Organization

Groups have a strong tendency to organize themselves. As we will explore in this chapter, groups experience phases or stages of development with no guidance from rules or outside sources. Sometimes this kind of organization works very well and allows groups to achieve their goals. But sometimes the organization that emerges does not allow the group to be productive. In these cases (and often when the nature of the problem to be solved demands it), many groups choose to follow established decision-making procedures. We will explore these procedures in Chapter 11.

Adaptivity

Complex, self-organizing systems are *adaptive.*[10] This means that small groups interact with their environments or situations and change or reorganize themselves as needed to be able to accomplish their goals. They have the ability to learn from their experiences and to make appropriate changes in their behaviors or problem-solving strategies. This property allows groups to stay on course or focused even when they face distraction, conflicts, or other difficulties that might otherwise prevent goal achievement.

Dynamic

Small groups do not stand still; they are always moving and changing. They are often unpredictable, messy, and strongly inclined toward disorder. You could even think of it as a goal-oriented, living system that just happens to be made up of other goal-oriented living systems. Successful small groups are able to overcome all the messiness and even take advantage of it by bringing it into a kind of balance that allows goals to be achieved.

Norms

A product of group interaction is a shared standard of acceptable behavior. **Norms** *are shared guidelines for beliefs and behavior.*[11] Norms develop as groups reach implicit agreement that certain behaviors are appropriate and other behaviors are inappropriate. Although there will be some deviance within each group, *norms help establish the group identity* and they are have considerable influence on the behavior of the group members.

Take a Closer Look

Group Cohesion

Thinking about one of the groups you listed at the beginning of this chapter, reflect on the following:

- On a scale from 1 to 10, how cohesive was the group? (10 = most cohesive)
- Why did you assign this score to the group?
- How was cohesion built in the group?
- What opportunities were missed to build cohesion?
- If you could change one thing the group did, what would you change?

Cohesiveness

When a group is cohesive, individual group members feel a connection or attraction to each other. They are motivated by the attraction to each other and by their attraction to the task. Members feel a sense of bonding and they experience a feeling of trust and interdependence. This is important to the group's productivity, as those who have a strong sense of cohesion are generally more productive. It is not clear if high cohesion causes high productivity or if high productivity causes high cohesion. Whatever the case, the two appear to be strongly related. When cohesion gets too high, however, there is a strong potential for **groupthink** to exist, and this condition can prevent groups from making quality decisions. Groupthink will be discussed in Chapter 11.

Companies are aware of the value of group cohesiveness and actively promote cohesion among their employees. Some companies send entire departments to volunteer together, not only to help the community, but also to give those employees an opportunity to bond. Other companies have been known to fund beach parties and picnics for their employees.

WHAT ARE THE DRAWBACKS OF GROUPS?

We have discussed the more positive properties of groups; however, groups also have some properties that present significant challenges to group success.

Time Consuming

Groups can be time consuming. There are many factors that cause groups to be more time consuming than individuals working alone. Groups begin with organizing schedules. We are all familiar with the scheduling nightmare of trying to get a group of people with varying work, volunteer, family, and school schedules to meet. Solving logistics problems with five or six people can be more difficult than completing the task itself. In a later chapter we will discuss ways we can preschedule meetings and use computer meeting space to help us with this challenge.

In general, while group decisions often take up more "person-hours," the overall time for a group decision is usually less than an individual working alone. For example, a five-member group might work on a problem for ten hours. If you do the math, you will see that the total time equals fifty hours. The same problem might take an individual thirty hours. If you are employer who has to pay all these people, you can quickly appreciate this difference! There are two important differences, however. One is that the group solved the problem more quickly in real time (i.e., 10 hours vs. 30 hours), but it cost more. The other difference is that the group is more likely to produce a higher-quality solution than the individual working alone. An employer (who needed this problem solved) will have to make a judgment as to whether the difference in solution quality is worth the difference in price.

Difficult Members

Difficult group members can also prove to be a time drain. They come in many forms and use a variety of strategies that cause the group to stall. Their behavior distracts the group from time spent on task. Cooperative group members may need to complete work not completed by a difficult group member, to mediate aggressive behavior, and to talk through unsupported objections. The group may find that the time required to finish the task is greatly extended. This will be explored in more depth in our discussion of conflict.

Difficult group members can diminish productive efforts.

Require a Balance of Task and Social Dimensions

Fostering the social dimensions in groups leads to cohesion and is good for a group as it works to accomplish its task, in moderation. Take, for example, the situation of Samantha, a straight-A student majoring in sociology. When Samantha attended the first meeting of her Sociology 101 group, she found herself incredibly frustrated. After a two-hour meeting, the group had only achieved one thing: deciding on a topic for the project. The meeting was held at a convenient location near the college. When she arrived, she found group members eating pizza, talking about instructors, and debating recent films they had seen. It was not until the last ten minutes of the meeting that the group decided to chat about the project. When they were finally engaged in meaningful discussion, some group members needed to leave, ending the discussion before it really started. Samantha, who had turned down an extra shift at work to attend the meeting, was more frustrated than ever. What happened here?

This example shows a group that is building cohesion without moderation. This group needs self-discipline or a leader who allows time for building cohesion but also keeps the members focused on the task at hand. A balance of both task and social dimensions is necessary. It is critical that we learn how to be tolerant of the social time groups need, yet still balance it with appropriate task time. In Samantha's case, the group was imbalanced and spent far too much time on the social dimension.

Samantha could have done one of two things to address the situation. First, as soon as she realized the group was taking too much time to socialize, she could have talked to the group leader to request the meeting get started. Second, if the group had no specific or appointed leader, Samantha could have taken control by asking the group members to focus on the task at hand with her for the next hour. She could have softened this request by reminding them that those who were able to stay longer could socialize a bit more after the meeting.

Groupthink

Mentioned earlier, the term *groupthink* refers to a phenomenon that very often results in a flawed decision made by groups whose cohesiveness becomes so strong they stop challenging each other's ideas. Political mistakes have been attributed to groupthink such as the Bay of Pigs invasion, the Watergate cover-up,[12] the space shuttle *Challenger* disaster, and the 2003 space shuttle *Columbia* disaster.[13] This disadvantage to groups will be discussed in more depth in Chapter 11.

GROUP DEVELOPMENT: HOW DO COLLECTIONS OF PEOPLE TURN INTO GROUPS?

Educational psychologist Bruce Tuckman studied group behavior in the 1960s and identified five stages that groups progress through before reaching a point of maximum productivity.[14] An understanding of these stages can help us better manage our own group experiences. Before reading through these stages, take a moment to reflect on the group you described in the beginning of this chapter. Use your memory of that group experience to see whether the group followed Tuckman's stages.

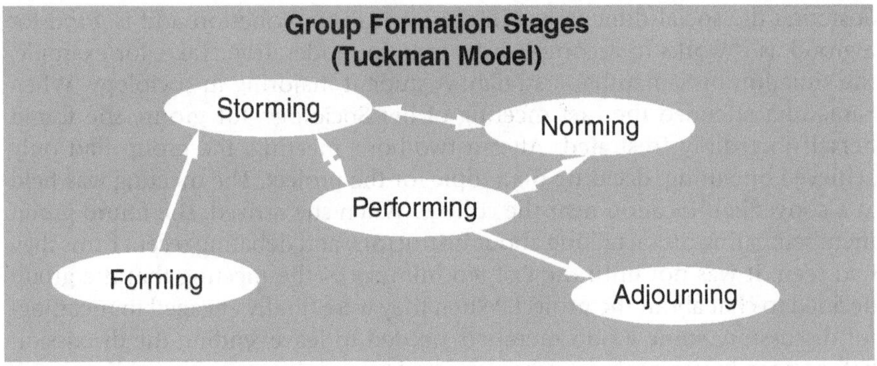

Forming (Orientation)

This initial stage of a group's experience is characterized by a high uncertainty level. Group members are typically quiet and uncomfortable as they attempt to understand the group's goals, member personalities, and overall dynamics. There is an absence of norms of behavior and an absence of clearly defined roles, so there is a lot of uncertainty about how to behave and what to say. The **forming stage** is characterized by group members: (1) attempting to orient themselves, (2) testing each other and the group boundaries, and (3) creating dependence on the group leader or other group members for support during this uncomfortable time. The most important job for the group in this stage is to orient itself to itself.[15] The tension is reduced as members get to know each other better and roles begin to be defined.

Storming (Conflict)

The **storming stage** occurs as a result of interpersonal struggles and polarization inherent in responding to the task at hand. This is where different ideas often compete for consideration, and group members share and challenge each other's ideas. This tension is also a response to struggles for authority and the direction taken by the group that occurs between leaders and the rest of the group. This stage requires active leadership while the group works out its most important dimensions: goals, roles, relationships, likely barriers, and support mechanisms. But as soon as patterns of authority and communication become fairly stable, the conflict is reduced. Until this time, however, the group can be a very active and stormy place! As you might guess, forming and storming are very time consuming, making up about three-fourths the length of Tuckman's five-step process.[16]

What happens during the storming stage?

Norming (Structure)

The **norming stage** happens when group cohesion develops, new standards evolve, and new roles are adopted. The group members have become more unified and more organized. A structure is put into place that enables the group to complete the task at hand.[17] The end results of this stage are that roles are clarified and accepted, a team feeling develops, and information is freely shared among group members.[18] At this stage, members try to make decisions by consensus. Hare says that this is when the group becomes cohesive.[19]

Performing (Work)

It is during the **performing stage** that most of the productive work is accomplished. Group roles become flexible and functional, and group energy is channeled into the task.[20] People are getting their jobs done properly, on time, and in coordinated sequence.[21] Research has demonstrated that this is the point of development, later in the group's life, at which most groups are most productive.[22]

Adjourning (Dissolution)

The **adjourning stage** was added by Tuckman, in collaboration with Mary Ann Jensen,[23] and takes us beyond the time that a group remains productive and functional. This phase involves group dissolution. The group has achieved its goals, solved the problem, or is no longer needed. Roles are abandoned, and participants often experience mourning feelings associated with the loss of a relationship.[24] Care should be taken at this stage because several members of this group could very well become members of another group. Failure to properly handle this stage could jeopardize the success of future groups.

GROUP CULTURE: WHY ARE ALL GROUPS DIFFERENT?

Robert Bales found that members of groups cooperate not only to accomplish some task, but also to create a group culture.[25] Through communication with each other over time, a collective personality and a unique group point of view emerge from the interaction.[26] The emerging culture is based on the values and experiences of all the group members, and it expresses a set of values, behavioral standards, and an identity that influence the way the group members make decisions, respond to each other, and interpret information.

For example, a local water utility was receiving comments about a small group of maintenance technicians who installed and repaired fire hydrants in the city. The comments were all very positive and they came from citizens, the fire department, and from supervisors in other city departments. The members of this group made it their goal to make each repair quickly, neatly, and with a high standard of quality. This kind of group culture was not typical of other work groups in the city. The other groups did generally good work, but the standards of this group were much higher than the norm.

How did this happen? All the members of the group were formerly members of other city work groups and shared general the culture of the city utility. This group found that it actually took less time, but only a little more effort and focus, to do a high-quality job. In addition, the members of the group found that they were getting satisfaction from doing good work! So, in addition to getting a paycheck, they felt good about what they did and they were motivated to come to work and spend the day with the group.

This culture began to develop one day when the group installed a fire hydrant. In addition to the ubiquitous yellow fire plug that we see next to the street, there is always a four- or five-foot pipe reaching below to the main water line. Replacing a hydrant means digging a hole down to the water line, disconnecting the hydrant, and then connecting a new hydrant to the line. When they first started working together, whenever they discovered a hydrant that needed to be replaced, they would call the city office and ask for heavy equipment to be dispatched to dig the hole. The usually had to wait up to two hours for the equipment to arrive and then wait for the hole to be dug. In addition, the use of the equipment made quite a mess in people's yards that was difficult to repair.

One day the crew found a hydrant that required replacement, so they called the city and they were told all the equipment was busy and could not be dispatched. So the crew got out their shovels and began to dig. They were surprised to learn that it took the four of them very little time to dig the hole, and they also discovered that they could do it more neatly than when the heavy equipment was used. They did such a great job that day that the lady whose yard they were digging in brought them cookies and then called the city supervisor to report how happy she was with the quality of the work and the care that was taken by the crew. This experience was only the beginning for this group, who found other high-quality ways to approach their jobs and gained a great deal of satisfaction from working together.

You might think this is a silly example, but the fire departments that depended on the hydrants to work properly when needed and the citizens who retained neat lawns would disagree with you. The city also found that this group made their repairs at lower cost than all the other maintenance crews. They didn't do anything to change the world, but because a culture of quality work evolved in this group, it turned into a true high-performance team.[27]

All groups develop their own unique cultures. Fraternities and sororities, clubs, social groups, and work groups each negotiate their own unique view of reality. The rules that govern your interaction with other group members, your interpretation of events, and the meaning you give to messages and behaviors differ from group to group. The culture of the group provides the frame of reference that tells members how to behave and how to interpret others' behavior.

WHAT SHOULD *MY* ROLE BE IN SMALL GROUPS?

Your specific roles in small groups will very likely be different as you become a member of different groups and as those groups attempt to accomplish different tasks. You and other members in your groups will adapt your behaviors and problems-solving strategies to these different situations. Considerable research has identified typical roles that appear in most groups, and they have been categorized as **task roles, group maintenance roles,** and **individual-centered** (also referred to as disruptive or egocentric) **roles.**

Keep in mind that you can often fulfill more than one role when working in groups, and that the roles you play may change, depending on the group and the group task.

Functional Roles in Small Groups

Earlier we discussed the fact that there are both task and social dimensions to groups. Similarly, the informal roles we play work to fulfill the tasks or the maintenance of our groups. Informal roles differ from formal roles like chairperson, secretary, or sergeant-at-arms because they are not appointed or elected. Informal roles often result from an individual member's personality, knowledge, or talents, or they arise from the problem-solving context itself. Task roles contribute to the group's productivity and are concerned with moving the group toward achieving its goals. Maintenance roles strengthen the group's social and emotional structure and contribute to the group's cohesion. They have a more indirect impact on group productivity than task roles, but are still necessary for group success at making high-quality decisions. Benne & Sheats concluded that for a group to survive and for it to make quality decisions, it must focus on accomplishing its task and it must maintain

Take a Closer Look

What Kind of Group Member Are You?

One of the critical factors determining your success as a communicator is the ability to monitor and reflect on your own behavior. It is through this process that you can discover communication behaviors and skills that can be improved.

To help you do this, think of the last group you worked in and consider the following:

- What do you believe to be your greatest strength as a group member?
- What was your most significant contribution to the group's goal?
- What do you believe to be your greatest weakness as a group member?
- What two aspects of your participation in groups would you like to improve?

Table 9.1 Selected Group Task and Maintenance Roles

Task Roles	Maintenance Roles
Initiator-contributor: Makes suggestions, considers new ways to look at group problem.	*Compromiser:* Tries to find agreements among conflicting points of view. Could change own position to help mediate conflict.
Information seeker: Focused on finding the facts; asks questions.	*Follower:* Serves as audience for the group; goes along with the other members.
Opinion seeker: Looks for expressions of attitudes and opinions of group members.	*Gatekeeper/expediter:* Tries to encourage participation from all group members.
Information giver: The expert of the group. Provides information based on experience.	*Encourager:* Gives positive feedback to others. The encouragement results in an increase in group members' self-esteem, excitement to complete the task at hand, and confidence.
Coordinator: Finds connections in suggestions and possible solutions; pulls information together into a coherent whole.	*Standard setter:* Expresses or begins discussion of standards for evaluating the group process or decisions.
Procedural technician: This person volunteers to complete tasks, help others, takes notes, distributes information, and takes on additional work.	*Harmonizer:* Always willing to listen. Group members often seek this person out to help soothe nerves, mediate interpersonal conflicts, or solve problems not group-related.
The organizer: This person helps to keep the group organized via scheduling, mapping out courses of action, coordinating efforts, etc.	*Observer/commentator:* Calls attention to the group's positive and negative characteristics and advocates change when necessary.

Source: Benne and Sheats, 1948.

What role does the man at the end of the table play?

How is this man's role disruptive to the group?

relationships among the group members.[28] Table 9.1 illustrates a selection of the task and maintenance roles.

Not all group roles contribute to building cohesiveness and solving problems. There are individuals who fulfill *individual-centered*[29] or *disruptive* group roles.[30] This type of role distracts the group or blocks the group from moving forward toward goal or task completion. Individuals exhibiting these roles harm the group's productivity, cohesiveness, and harmony.

Group members who play individual-centered roles might be doing so consciously or unconsciously. Although it is possible that they are trying to prevent the group from accomplishing its goals, it is likely that they just have some strong personal needs to be fulfilled and they use the group to get attention, recognition, or help with their problems. Whatever the cause, the effect is interference with group problem solving. Table 9.2 identifies some specific individual-centered roles.[31]

Disruptive Roles in Small Groups

Mudrack and Farrell identified **disruptive group roles** that are similar in type and function to the individual-centered roles mentioned above.[32] The following roles fit the disruptive definition, and we suggest some communication strategies to help counteract them.

The Nonparticipant. This is a passive group member characterized by not participating in group activities, consistently missing group meetings, and not completing individual group work. When he does attend a group meeting, he either arrives

Table 9.2 Individual-Centered Roles

Aggressor: Communicates disapproval of ideas, attitudes, and opinions of other group members. Attacks the group and other members.
Blocker: Takes advantage of opportunities to oppose group plans or procedures. Says he or she wants no part of the group. Expresses negativity.
Dominator: Manipulates group members and situations; Creates defensiveness with certainty and superiority.
Self-confessor: Wants to talk about his or her own feelings that are unrelated to the group goal.
Help seeker: Seems insecure and confused; asks for personal advice.
Recognition Seeker: Self promoter; wants attention or praise for himself or herself.
Playboy/girl: No interest in being involved in the group; detached; interested in having a good time.
Special interest pleader: Separates self from the group; identifies strongly with another group or interest.

Source: Benne and Sheats, 1948.

late or leaves early. There could be many reasons why an individual may be a nonparticipant. Some people are very shy. Their intent may be to be an active group member, only they simply cannot overcome their communication apprehension to the point where they speak up. Others just might not care, do not feel connected to the group, or are bitter toward the group for some reason.

Strategy. Regardless of the cause, a constructive way to approach nonparticipants is with encouragement.

- Gently invite them to participate.
- Ask for their opinions, ideas, and help.
- Notice when they do not attend meetings.
- Try to avoid assuming that their behavior is intentional. Rather, give them the benefit of the doubt and make a strong effort to include them.

The Bulldozer. This person takes control of the group without paying much attention to the desires, opinions, or ideas of others. A bulldozer monopolizes conversations, imposes courses of action, and discourages the participation of others. Individuals might bulldoze as a result of (1) a past experience in which they were not listened to or heard, (2) a lack of awareness of *bulldozing,* or (3) a desire to be the group's leader, but without the knowledge of how to approach the role constructively.

Strategy. One way to respond to bulldozers is with an intentional description of group norms. To prevent them from monopolizing the group, set up expectations for balanced participation, such as asking every group member to contribute at least one idea at each group meeting or by using an agenda to impose time limits on any one individual's *floor time.*

The Controller. This group member wants to make all of the decisions for the group. He or she appears to have a self-perception of superiority above the other group members and a belief that his or her ideas and plans are the best. An individual may feel a need to control the group due to insecurity, fear, or hunger for power. Whatever the reason, it is important to avoid making assumptions and to approach this behavior positively.

You can use communication strategies to balance the power in the group. This may be achieved in a variety of ways: by rotating group roles, by assigning tasks by pulling names from a hat, or by creating a meeting agenda. Whichever approach is used, first try to understand the reason for the disruptive communication choices and then do your best to respond in a way that helps the group to continue moving toward its goal.

© 2008, JupiterImages Corporation.

Some gossip is inevitable in a group, but it can become a problem.

The Gossiper. Although some gossip is inevitable in all groups, it becomes a problem when it hurts the feelings of others or undermines the group's goal achievement. An individual may do this to get back at a group member in retaliation, to be popular, to control the group, or to intentionally sabotage the group.

Strategy. Group members should work to create a climate of trust and mutual support when the group is in the early stages of formation. This can be done through increased social time (hosting a barbeque at one of the group member's houses, for example) or by utilizing team-building activities such as paper airplane contests, working through puzzles together, or volunteering to help with a campus club drive.

To respond to the gossiper, constructively confront the person. Discuss not necessarily the content of the gossip, but more importantly, the reason for it. Many times dissatisfaction is expressed in a passive-aggressive fashion. After confronting the group member, use the collaborating conflict management style (see the Interpersonal Communication chapter for additional information about conflict management styles) to unearth the real problem and work toward finding a mutually satisfactory solution.

The Social Loafer. This is one of the most troublesome of group members. The social loafer is an individual who loves working in groups because it means a *free ride* for the project's duration. The loafer does not complete assignments, is generally unreliable, and often submits inferior work. A loafer is often perceived to be someone who simply does not care, is not skilled, is lazy, or is a low achiever. However, some loafers are not lazy at all; rather, they loaf because they can. Other group members allow them to loaf by completing work for them that they do not finish.[33]

Strategy. This is a good time to practice your leadership skills. Most individuals will work when there is motivation to do so. It is important that the loafer feel valued and that his or her contributions are needed and are important. It is critical that other group members *do not* complete the work for them, as this only allows loafers to continue in that role. Instead, loafers can be mentored by being paired with another group member who is willing to mentor. In extreme cases, you can resort to the **group contract** (explained later in this chapter).

Coping with Disruptive Members

There are a number of strategies we may use to respond to disruptive or egocentric members. In addition to those already mentioned, we have included some strategies for coping with more generalized types of egocentric and disruptive behaviors.

What Would You Do in These Situations?

Reflection

It is the beginning of the semester; you are ready and eager to dive into school, work on projects, expand your mind, and successfully complete another semester, getting closer to achieving your goal of becoming a teacher. You attend your history class and learn that you will soon be placed in groups with four other classmates to complete a semester-long project.

At the next class meeting, you learn who your group mates will be:

- **Candy:** A twenty-two-year-old single mother of two. Candy works part-time, is enrolled in twelve units, and is maintaining a 3.9 G.P.A.
- **Dawn:** An eighteen-year-old freshman. Dawn is not quite used to the college environment and feels a bit lost on campus, in this class, and in the group.
- **Mike:** A twenty-one-year-old water polo player. He is a C student with a very active social life.
- **Kevin:** A thirty-year-old student who is back in school to change careers. He works full-time, is married, and has two children.

The group selects you as the leader. Thus, the onus is on you to organize meetings, motivate individuals, and monitor the group process. You do not mind the role until you run into some difficult situations.

Situation one: Dawn cannot seem to make it to group meetings on time. Your last meeting was across the street from campus at Starbucks and she was responsible for bringing a laptop for the group to begin typing out the assignment. She arrived thirty minutes late without the laptop. The group's frustration is growing and they look to you to solve the problem.

Situation two: Kevin not only completes all of his group work, but does so with perfection. He approaches schoolwork with the utmost professionalism. With this professionalism comes a low tolerance for those who do not approach their schoolwork with the same zeal. Subsequently, Kevin often becomes annoyed and even verbally aggressive with members who do not "pull their weight." He seems to feel the need to control as much of the group work and process as possible so as to ensure a good grade.

Situation three: Mike is the socialite of the group. Everyone loves his personality but loathes his approach to group work. He does not meet deadlines and turns in little to no work. The group members are beginning to feel taken advantage of. When he does arrive to a group meeting, he only wants to talk and socialize, not to work. Kevin views him as setting out to sabotage the group's performance.

Situation four: Candy is a hardworking group member, but simply does not have much time to devote to the group meetings and work. Subsequently, she has very little tolerance for those who arrive to group meetings late, do not spend time on task, or waste the group's time in any way. She is becoming especially intolerant of Mike and Dawn and frequently discusses her dissatisfaction without talking directly to Mike or Dawn.

- How would you characterize the roles these group members play?
- How would you address each of these situations so as to achieve the group's goals while still maintaining cohesion?

(After answering these questions, compare your answers with the discussion later in this chapter about the communication strategies to use with disruptive members.)

How could he convey his disappointment constructively?

Feedback Sessions. A **feedback** session is the act of communicating to the disruptive group member how his behavior is affecting the group. Many students who have experienced trouble working in their groups go to their instructor for help. When asked if they have discussed the issue with the troublesome group member, the usual answer is that they have not. Before approaching a supervisor, manager, or teacher, group members should first try to solve the situation using *feedback.*

Negative or corrective feedback is not always easy to give to others. If you are not careful about the manner in which the feedback is given, then relationships could be damaged. However, when used effectively, it is one of the most powerful communication tools available. The feedback process involves the following:

1. *Describe the problem as clearly, neutrally, and specifically as possible.* (See discussion on group decision making for a discussion of description versus evaluation.) Point out the similar interests you have with the group member, such as earning a good grade on the assignment or the satisfaction of a job well-done.
2. *Resist the temptation to place blame.* Instead try to take a *mutual problem approach* in which you use language such as, "How can *we* work to remedy this situation?" The use of *we* shows a sense of mutual responsibility and commitment to solving the problem as a team.
3. *Take ownership of your feelings and avoid blaming or attacking the disruptive member.* This can be achieved by using "I" messages instead of "you" messages.
4. *Stick to one issue at a time.* Bringing up more than one concern complicates the discussion and makes resolution more difficult.
5. *Do not gang up on the disruptive person with the other group members.* Those receiving the feedback need to be sent the message that it is fair, unbiased, and that your goal is *not to criticize,* but to work together to solve the problem.

Perception Checking. Imagine the following situation:

> You are in Athens, Greece, on vacation and decide to go to the flea market, the *plaka,* to buy some souvenirs. You find yourself in a negotiation with a merchant for an item. As you keep insisting on a price, the merchant nods his head from left to right and says "ne." You interpret this as a rejection, are disappointed, and are ready to leave when he interjects and keeps repeating the same phrase "ne, ne." You perceive his behavior to mean "no."

Before leaving the market and missing out on an opportunity to buy a great souvenir, it would be a good time to use some perception checking. You find a translator and go through the perception checking process as follows:

1. *Describe* the behavior: "I am trying to buy this item from the merchant over there. When I offered him a price, he nodded his head from left to right and said 'ne.' "

2. *Interpret* the behavior: "I thought he did not want to negotiate. However, he kept at me. I am not sure whether I have misunderstood his rejection or if I have offended him in some way."
3. *Ask:* "Can you tell me what is going on?"

Through this perception checking and with the translator's help, you find that "ne" means "yes" and his headshaking is, in fact, a sign of confirmation.

You do not need to be in a foreign country to experience misunderstandings like this. When group members communicate with each other, differences in perception occur often. Try using the three-step perception-checking process when you suspect that your perception may be inaccurate.

Utilize a Group Contract. Since we often do not know if we are going to encounter disruptive group members until we are in the middle of a group task, it is wise to use some preemptive strategies to handle problems before they arise. This can be done by writing up a group agreement, or contract, that outlines group norms and consequences for breaking them. Although the

CASE STUDY

What Would You Do?

You have been asked to help out in a freshman class at the local high school. You are responsible for organizing student work groups (teams), introducing the student's group assignment, and monitoring the students as they discuss their approach to the task. Most students in this class are hardworking, motivated, and ambitious. However, there are a few class members who are known to engage in loafing and troublemaking.

You consider your options:

1. Mixing them into the group with the students who are hardworking, knowing that those students will more than likely do the work for them.
2. Speaking with them ahead of time to ask them to be "good" to their group members.
3. Group all the loafers and troublemakers together to work as a team, taking the risk that they will either meet the challenge or fail miserably.

What would you do?

A teacher faced this very challenge while teaching high school. She did not want to burden the hardworking students with the loafers and troublemakers. She did not think it would be fair to the dedicated, hardworking students. This was especially true given the fact that these disruptive students had already been talked to about their behavior, only to have it continue. She opted for the third choice and put them in a group together.

Through this experience, she learned a great deal about these types of troublesome group members who knew they were loafers and troublemakers and responded to the teacher's decision with attitudes reflecting, "How can you put us all together? We will fail." Ironically, they did not fail. As a matter of fact, it was with this project that the teacher was able to get them to work the hardest. They rose to the occasion and completed the task; it met all the requirements, was submitted on time, and helped participants feel better about themselves and the class.

contract is usually a preemptive tactic, group members will still misbehave and problems will still come up. So you could draw up a contract even when your group is fairly mature. The contract is something a group should resort to only when all communication attempts fail.

Group contracts should have these elements:

- All group members are involved in the writing of the contract.
- Responsibilities and behaviors expected of all members are clearly defined.
- Consequences for misbehavior behavior are clearly specified.
- All group members sign the contract and receive a copy.

SUMMARY

Though many people remain resistant to working in groups, extensive experience and research show us, again and again, that the product of group collaboration is worth all the effort. Groups are messy, complex, and a constant challenge to control. But we tolerate these conditions because the quality and creativity of group solutions to difficult problems are nearly always superior to solutions produced by individuals working alone. The key to successful and productive small groups is managing the "messiness" and keeping the members motivated and focused on group goals.

The next chapter, "Leadership and Power," is designed to help you gain some insight into how you can influence and manage groups that you belong to. Following that chapter, we provide some specific decision-making steps you can follow to help your group make the best use of its time and produce high-quality decisions.

NOTES

1. S. Sorensen, "Grouphate," paper presented at the International Communication Association, Minneapolis, Minnesota, 1981.
2. J. Keyton, *Communicating in Groups: Building Relationships for Group Effectiveness* (New York: Oxford University Press, 2006).
3. D. Forsyth, *Group Dynamics.* (Belmont, CA: Wadsworth, 1999).
4. S. Wallace, L. Yoder, L. Hungenberg and C. Horvath, *Creating Competent Communication: Small Groups* (Dubuque: Kendall/Hunt, 2006).
5. S. Beebe and J. Masterson, *Communicating in Small Groups: Principles and Practices.* 8th ed. (Boston: Allyn and Bacon, 2006), p.4.
6. L. Rosencrance, "Meet Me in CYBERSPACE," *Computer World* 39 (8) (February 21, 2005): p.23–24.
7. A. Cohen, "Virtual Sales Meetings: On the Rise," *Sales and Marketing Management* 155(8) August, 2003: 12.
8. B.J. Carducci and K.W. Klaphaak, "Shyness and Internet Usage," poster session presented at the annual meeting of the American Psychological Association, Boston, August 21, 1999.
9. M. Waldrop, *Complexity: The Emerging Science at the Edge of Order and Chaos* (New York: Simon & Schuster, 1992).
10. Ibid.
11. S. Kiesler, *Interpersonal Processes in Groups and Organizations* (Arlington Heights, IL: Harlan-Davidson, 1978).
12. R. Cline, "Small Group Dynamics and the Watergate Coverup: A Case Study in Groupthink," paper presented at the annual meeting of the Eastern Communication Association, Ocean City, MD, April 27–30, 1983.
13. J. Schwartz and M.L. Wald, "'Groupthink' Is 30 Years Old, and Still Going Strong," *New York Times,* March 9, 2003, p.5.
14. B.W. Tuckman, "Developmental Sequence in Small Groups," *Psychological Bulletin* 63 (1965): 384–399. Also B.W. Tuckman and M.A. Jensen, "Stages of Small Group Development Revisited," *Group and Organizational Studies* 2 (1977): 419–427.

15. H. Robbins and M. Finley, *The New Why Teams Work: What Goes Wrong and How to Make It Right* (California: Berrett-Koehler Publishers, 2000).
16. Ibid.
17. B.W. Tuckman (1965).
18. Robbins and Finley.
19. A.P. Hare, *Handbook of Small Group Research* (New York: The Free Press, 1976).
20. B.W. Tuckman (1965).
21. Robbins and Finley.
22. R.F. Bales and F. Strodtbeck, "Phases in Group Problem Solving," *Journal of Abnormal and Social Psychology* 46 (1951): 485–495. Also, A.P. Hare and D. Nevah, "Conformity and Creativity: Camp David, 1978." *Small Group Behavior* 17 (1986): 243–268.
23. Tuckman and Jensen.
24. Ibid.
25. R. Bales. *Personality and Interpersonal Behavior.* (New York: Holt, Rinehart, and Winston, 1970).
26. E. Bormann, Fantasy and Rhetorical Vision: The Rhetorical Criticism of Social Reality. *Quarterly Journal of Speech,* 58 (1970): 306–407.
27. J.R. Katzenback and D. Smith, *The Wisdom of Teams: Creating the High Performance Organization* (New York: Harper Business, 1993).
28. K. Benne and P. Sheats, "Functional Roles of Group Members," *Journal of Social Issues,* 4 (1948): 41–49.
29. Ibid.
30. P.E. Mudrack and G.M. Farrell, "An Examination of Functional Role Behavior and Its Consequences for Individuals in Group Settings," *Small Group Behavior,* 26 (1995): 542–571.
31. Benne and Sheats.
32. Mudrack and Farrell.
33. D.R. Comer, "A Model of Social Loafing in Real Work Groups," *Human Relations* 48 (1995): 647–667. K. Williams, S. Harkins and B. Latane, "Identifiability as a Deterrent of Social Loafing: Two Cheering Experiments," *Journal of Personality and Social Psychology,* 40 (1981): 303–311.

chapter

10

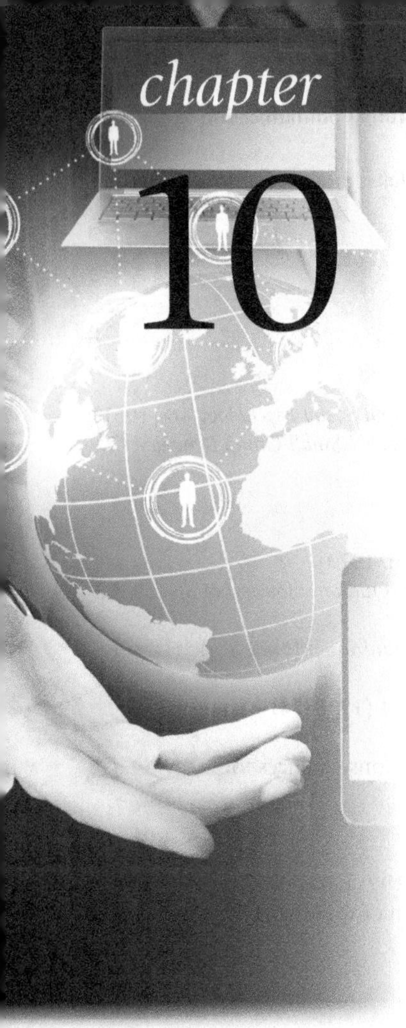

Organizational Communication

OBJECTIVES

Upon completion of the chapter, the student should be able to:

- Define and explain the role of culture in the creation of an organization.
- Explain how Social Identity Theory comes to inform the creation and manifestation of an organization's culture.
- Describe the artifacts that are part and parcel of an organization and give an example of the role that each artifact plays in the organizing process.
- Differentiate among the three stages of organizational socialization and explain the role of communication in each.
- Explain how organizational cultures can be framed as both enabling and constraining.

KEY TERMS

Anticipatory stage	**Ideology**	**Organizational socialization**
Artifact	**Metamorphosis stage**	**Social identity theory**
Corporate we	**Metaphor**	**Symbol**
Encounter stage	**Organizational culture**	

DEFINING ORGANIZATIONAL CULTURE

As both personal history and historical fact attest, no two organizations are the same. In light of this statement, we have to pose the following question: What differentiates one organization from another? Anyone who has held several jobs can say, with certainty, that some organizations are better to work for than others. But what makes one organization better and another worse in terms of employment experience? Edgar Schein, a prominent management and leadership scholar, claims that it's an organization's culture that differentiates it from others (Schein, 1985). **Organizational culture** can be defined as a socially constructed way of thinking, feeling, and doing that provides a blueprint for employee action, and that has both psychological and behavioral effects. If an employee claims that she does not like working for a particular organization because of the leadership style, the way that feedback is offered, the way that rewards and incentives are distributed, the design of office spaces, or the level of mentorship, then she is speaking about the negative implications of an organization's culture, as all these factors are outcomes of the practices that are created, recreated, and maintained by the organization.

Organizational culture
A socially constructed way of thinking, feeling, and doing that provides a blueprint for employee action and that has both psychological and behavioral effects.

This chapter highlights the role of culture in an organization, including the elements that are part of an organization's culture, the effects of an organization's culture on the employee base, the processes by which employees are socialized into an organization's culture, the existence of potential subcultures, and reasons why a culture can be framed as both enabling and constraining.

To truly understand an organization, we must understand its culture (Schein, 1996). A culture can be considered a constellation of rules, regulations, mission, symbols, and the effect(s) that each has on employee well-being. Simply put, it is important to conduct studies *in* organizations, not studies *of* organizations. As Schein points out, an organization's culture is something that gives common meaning and common understanding to a group of interconnected beings, making an organization a collective unit. This closely aligns with Kenneth Burke's (1950) discussion of employee identification, whereby an organization's culture becomes one of the variables necessary for organizational unity and provides a sense of collective membership (see Chapter 13). Perhaps the greatest contribution provided by Burke (1950) to the study of organizations was his notion of the "**corporate we**," symbolizing a unified identity among employees. Much scholarship since has framed an organization's culture as the independent variable that predicts such unification (Denison & Mishra, 1995). That is, it's the organization that predicts the collective identity, not the collective identity that predicts the organization.

corporate we
A unified sense of identity among employees.

Think for a moment about the culture that has emerged among your closest group of friends. There are clearly certain cultural elements that define your group that promote as well as inhibit membership. For example, perhaps your group of friends likes sports, fast food restaurants, video games, carbonated soft drinks, comedy movies, and romance novels. Henri Tajfel and John Turner (1986) are prominent social psychologists who are perhaps best known for the development of **Social Identity Theory**. This theory argues that people construct a certain sense of self based on the groups in which they find themselves embedded. They claim that such small group characteristics play a large role in the creation and maintenance of group membership (Tajfel & Turner, 1986). Given the previous example, one would only be part of this group if, in fact, he or she enjoyed sports, fast food restaurants, video games, carbonated soft drinks, comedy movies, and romance novels. This provides a sense of in-group membership. At the same time, however, this also bars membership to those who dislike sports, dislike fast food restaurants, dislike video games, dislike carbonated soft drinks, prefer horror movies, and read historical autobiographies. This, according to Tajfel and Turner (1986), creates an out-group. This in-group/out-group partition is exactly what creates and inhibits group membership (Mael & Ashforth, 1992). In essence, we are in groups where people enjoy and dislike similar things. There exists a longstanding joke in the New York City area whereby fans of the New York Mets root for two teams: the Mets and whichever team is playing against the New York Yankees. In other words, Mets fans clearly want the Mets to win, but they also want the Yankees to lose, as this rivalry has come to define what part of the city you are from as well as a host of other characteristics that separate one New York sports fan from another. This idea of team allegiance illustrates and promotes the idea of group membership. Those who are part of the group like and dislike the same things, creating psychological and behavioral contagion. **Contagion** is the process through which attitudes and/or behaviors are either adopted or barred by people, based on the number of others who have created similar attitudes or engaged in similar behaviors, as they make both collective and individual decisions.

Social Identity Theory
The idea that individuals construct a certain sense of self based on the groups in which they find themselves embedded.

This QR code will take you to an article on the role of culture in an organization's social existence.

http://www.organizationalculture101.com/

Organizations, too, foster a sense of in-group mentality through culture (Martin & Siehl, 1983). Imagine a world without rules or norms. At first glance, it might sound luxurious. There would be no such thing as a legal drinking age, no such thing as a speed limit, no such thing as cheating on an exam, no such thing as wearing too much cologne, etc. However, it is likely that, over time, the nonexistence of rules and norms would prove challenging, perhaps so much so that we would be faced with too much ambiguity about the difference between right and wrong to the point that we would be ill equipped to navigate our social worlds. We might not like a particular speed limit, but we feel comfort in the fact that we know what such a limit is and why it was put in place. We might not like that the drinking age is so high, but we feel comfort knowing what is legal and illegal. We might not like that cheating is banned, but we feel comfort knowing that it is a punishable offense. In other words, we live in a social world rife with rules, rites, regulations, and policies that dictate human behavior.

Organizations are no exception. They, too, have rules, rites, regulations, and policies that drive employee action. That is, organizations have cultures. Consider perhaps the largest organization in the United States, the U.S. government. In the United States, home ownership is considered a positive practice for social, moral, and civic order. How can the government create or influence a culture to strongly believe that home ownership is something that is sought by its citizens? Some ways include offering tax breaks for first-time homebuyers, low-interest federal loans, tax savings for home improvement, etc. All of these "organizational practices" serve to influence the culture in terms of how people view home ownership and, as a result, have both attitudinal and behavioral implications.

FACTORS ASSOCIATED WITH AN ORGANIZATION'S CULTURE

ideology
A set of ideas that inform employees about their organization's goals, practices, aspirations, needs, and expectations.

artifact
A symbolic element that comes to shape and create employee knowledge and understanding.

An organization's culture provides an **ideology**, or set of ideas, that informs employees of its goals, practices, aspirations, needs, and expectations (Mumby, 1989). According to Schein (1985), the foremost ideological indicator is the collection of an organization's artifacts, which are those elements that shape and create employee knowledge and understanding. In fact, the term **artifact** comes from the anthropological world, wherein paleontologists attempt to discover information about ancient cultures by digging up remains and fossils to better understand a life that once was. For example, we know about dinosaurs because of the fossils that remain and we know about ancient man because of the bones that have been unearthed. These, in essence, are cultural artifacts that provide anthropologists with information about once-existing cultures. The same would be true if an anthropologist visited an organization.

One artifact this anthropologist would be interested in studying would be an organization's dress code, which, according to Schein (1985), is among the many organizational artifacts. Like fossils and bones, a dress code provides much information about an organization. Assume, for example, that an anthropologist enters an organization where the dress code is extremely formal. In a not-so-popular movie from the 1980s called *The Secret of My Success,* Michael J. Fox's character, Brantley Foster, is hired as a mailroom clerk, and he and his fellow mailroom employees refer to those in administrative positions as "the

Table 10.1 **Artifacts Associated with an Organization's Culture**

Artifact	Cultural Effect
Dress Code	Formality/Informality
Office Space	Reliance on Hierarchy/Flattened Structure
Mission Statement	Organizational Purpose
Symbol	Organizational Representation
Metaphor	Organizational Analogy

suits." The suits were those in the marketing, finance, and operations departments. In organizations, if those in such hierarchical positions, or the "suits," are dressed in formal garb, this speaks a lot about the organization's culture. Compare this with an organization that fosters less formal dress, or what is today termed business casual. It is likely that an organization with a formal dress code is more vertically structured and more formal in terms of communication and the construction of interpersonal relationships (see Chapter 7). On the other hand, it is likely that an organization with an informal dress code is more horizontally structured and more informal in terms of communication practices and relationship development (Pratt & Rafaeli, 1997). Just as bones and fossils serve as an indicator about a life that once was, dress code can serve as an indicator of an organizational life that currently is being lived (see Chapter 9 for a discussion of nonverbal aspects of organizational life).

In addition to dress code, another cultural artifact within an organization is the physical layout of the office spaces (Schein, 1985). An organization that has a lock-and-key office for every employee communicates something quite different when compared to the organization that has offices for only those in administrative positions, the organization that forces employees to share offices, or the organization that has employee cubicles. This is not to say that having an office for each employee is preferred. It is to say, however, that an organization's physical layout depends on the culture that it wants to create. A formal organizational culture would probably have a more formal dress code and individual offices (likely larger for those in more superior positions), whereas an informal organizational culture would likely have a more relaxed, informal dress code with perhaps a more open layout (such as cubicles) (Deal & Kennedy, 1982). In fact, architects and interior designers have become very important in terms of aesthetics that are consistent with the organization's mission. For example, consider the architectural layout of new hospitals geared toward children, cancer patients, or other specialized populations. The environment is carefully manipulated to communicate the organization's vision and purpose. Thus, both dress code and physical layout say a lot about the culture of an organization.

This QR code will take you to the website of *Johnson & Johnson*, where you will be able to locate their organizational credo.

http://www.jnj.com/connect/

In addition to dress code and physical layout, another cultural artifact about which Schein (1990) speaks is an organization's **mission statement**. Mission statements provide both employees and consumers with information about what the organization in question deems most important (Fairhurst, Jordan, & Neuwirth, 1997). A prime example of a mission statement that is extremely informing of its organizational practices is that of *Johnson and Johnson*, one of the world's leading pharmaceutical companies. Their organizational mission statement, or Credo, includes the information about the employees being "respected" and "recognized," meaning that they truly are the ties that bind *Johnson and Johnson* together. What does this credo say about the organization and its culture? As is likely evident from even the quickest, cursory read of this mission statement, the organization is very attuned to the needs of its employees. Think about an organization that fosters dignity, recognition, mindfulness, opportunity, advancement, and competency, and does so in written form. Such a mission statement eliminates guesswork and provides direction and understanding (Pearce, 1982). Like bones and fossils, and dress code and physical layout, mission statements provide much information about organizations and how they function.

symbol
A type of sign that is human made or an artificial phenomenon.

Another interesting cultural artifact that speaks volumes about an organization is its **symbol** (logo), or the socially constructed representation of its organizational image (Pettigrew, 1979). Organizations have long understood the importance of symbols to promote an organization and to inform its employees and consumers. For example, the Nike swoosh, the golden arches of McDonald's, Disney's Mickey Mouse ears, Mercedes Benz' three-pointed star, Audi's four interlocking circles, Geico's gecko, and Starbucks' long-haired female siren all inform both employees and consumers about the organization's culture and what the organization stands for.

As Linstead and Grafton-Small (1992) claim, however, it is exponentially more difficult to decipher and decode an organization's symbol than it is to create it. For example, what does the Nike swoosh truly mean? In other words, what is the symbolic meaning of this organization's logo? Is the symbol arbitrary and meaningless? Does it come to represent a check mark, indicating that no matter what, the Nike organization has what you want? Does it mean, similar to the check mark that appears when a text message is sent from one cellular device to another, that this company delivers? Those who are well-versed in the historical trajectory of Nike might know that Carolyn Davidson, the 1971 creator and designer of the company's logo, meant for it to represent the wing of Nike, the Greek goddess of victory. What is important, however, is not why or how the symbol is encoded, but rather how it is decoded (Feldman, 1986). In other words, how does the employee or consumer translate this symbol and create meaning from it. This, in essence, highlights the role of an organization's symbol in the creation of its culture and how it comes to represent its mission, goals, purpose, and values. To illustrate this point further, assume two people look at the same Nike swoosh logo and attempt to garner meaning from it. One person conjures a warm and happy thought of his time on the college basketball team, where Nike was one of the team's sponsors, while the other person conjures a vision of her pair of Air Jordan sneakers that were less than ideal for competitive tennis matches. Clearly, this presents problems in terms of decoding an organization's symbol.

metaphor
A term that comes to symbolically and comparatively represent, by association, something else.

A fifth cultural indicator within an organization is its **metaphor.** A metaphor is defined as a term that comes to symbolically and comparatively represent, by association, something else. For example, if your dorm roommate tells you that your side of the room is a pigsty, he or she is implying that it is time to clean up. Within organizations, a metaphor comes to symbolically represent the way employees communicate and engage in their work practices (Morgan, 1980). An organization metaphorically analogous to a machine is strikingly different from the organization that is metaphorically analogous to a family, a circus, a prison, or a group. What, however, is different? The difference, according to Dose (1997) and Putnam (1998), is that metaphors are emblematic of an organization's set of work values or the norms by which an organization operates. Gareth Morgan, an organizational behaviorist best known for his research on metaphor analysis, concurs. He claims that metaphors give both organizations and employees direction, definition, and a sense of group membership (Morgan, 1983). Recall in Chapter 1 that we discussed Morgan's (1986) multiple perspectives, which consist of nine metaphors commonly used to characterize organizations.

Kendall and Kendall (1993) offer different categories of metaphors consisting of the following: organization as game, as machine, as journey, as jungle, as family, as zoo, as society, as war, and as organism. Each of the nine metaphors carries with it a different connotation about an organization and the practices and processes that accompany it.

The organization metaphorically analogous to a:

- *game* connotes the idea that an organization works as a collective group of people, all having a different role or position, attempting to win.
- *machine* connotes the idea that each part of an organization must work together as well as independently. If even one part of the organization fails to produce, the machine stops working and failure results.
- *journey* connotes both the possibilities and troubles associated with tackling the unknown, starting at one point and having a clearly defined goal.
- *jungle* is one where there is an "every man for himself" mentality, where chaos is not only omnipresent, but is also highly endorsed and valued.
- *zoo* connotes an organization that partitions employees based on departmental membership, where a leader is necessary to keep the livelihood of the collection of workers.
- *society* is one with its own set of rules and makes certain to adhere to the needs, desires, and wants of internal members, paying particular attention to politics and the communication and behavioral processes that accompany them.
- *war* is one that seems to always be in battle, where leaders must stand at the front line and have their employees ready, willing, and able to attack if and when necessary.
- *organism* is one that understands the importance of birth, development, and death, paying particular attention to the role of innovation, change, and adaptation in organizational success.

Table 10.2 Organizational Metaphors

Metaphor	Implication
Game	Need to win at all costs
Machine	All parts work together
Journey	Must move from Point A to Point B
Jungle	Chaos and elements of individuality
Family	All in it together
Zoo	Partitioning based on departmental membership
Society	Politics are governed by leaders
War	Potential battle is always possible
Organism	Birth development and death are inevitable

In the end, an organization's metaphor, which is both produced and enacted by employees, explains how it runs and provides an organizational blueprint for employee action and communication (Morgan, 1980).

Collectively, the combination of an organization's artifacts, including its dress code, its office layout, its mission statement, its symbol, and its metaphor, is indicative of its character, and truly provides employees with a way of doing, a way of thinking, and most importantly, a way of communicating (Wilkins, 1983). All organizations have artifacts and, according to Schein (1990), these are instrumental in differentiating one from another. From an effects perspective, an organization's culture provides uniform expectations, uniform understanding, and a collective, uniform identity, all of which are linked to such things as employee productivity, employee well-being, employee motivation, job satisfaction, and organizational tenure.

ORGANIZATIONAL SOCIALIZATION

Up to this point we have discussed many aspects of an organization's culture and its importance. Now we discuss how employees learn about an organization's culture. If you have ever visited a different college or university, travelled to another country, attended a ceremony for a religion you are unfamiliar with, gone to see a sports event at an opposing team's stadium, or had dinner at a friend's house, you have encountered a cross-cultural situation. Such cross-cultural experiences are both exciting and anxiety producing. They are exciting because of the novelty, though they are anxiety producing because of the potential lack of information about behavioral norms and social rules needed to successfully behave in this new culture.

Organizations are no exception, as they, too, have embedded cultures that are both novel and exciting. Such practices must be taught to new employees as they begin their organizational experiences. Frederic Jablin, an influential and well-established researcher in the field of organizational communication, spent most of his academic career studying the many processes involved in **organizational socialization**, or the process by which newcomers learn the ropes of their organization's culture (Jablin, 1987). Even though artifacts, such as those mentioned in the previous section, exist, there is not much information about them in any form of written correspondence or house organ. Therefore, there is a need to teach new employees about the organization's culture and its way of doing things. This is primarily achieved through verbal dialogue with veteran employees. While a person can read about an organization, its mission statement, its earnings, etc., it is through communication that the learning of an organization's culture really takes place. According to Jablin (1987), the process of organizational socialization includes three stages, appropriately termed *anticipatory, encounter,* and *metamorphosis.*

organizational socialization
The process by which newcomers learn the ropes of their organization's culture.

As Jablin (1987) notes, there are times in one's childhood, adolescence, and young adulthood when he or she develops an interest in a particular area of work. This is not to say that children, adolescents, or young adults know, at an early age, that they want to work for Apple or Pfizer or Dannon or Starbucks. This is to say, however, that it is not uncommon to hear teachers, construction workers, police officers, doctors, or military personnel claim that they knew from an early age that this vocation/career was exactly what they wanted to do. With such knowledge comes expectation. Although every organizational culture is different, there are certain expectations that accompany professional membership. For example, teachers will not be surprised to learn that their workday begins at 7:45 a.m.; police officers will not be surprised to learn that they will have periodic weekend commitments; and construction workers will not be surprised to learn that certain holidays do not warrant time off. According to Jablin (1982), the reason there is little surprise is because such employees have been able to (knowingly or not) anticipate life in their organization.

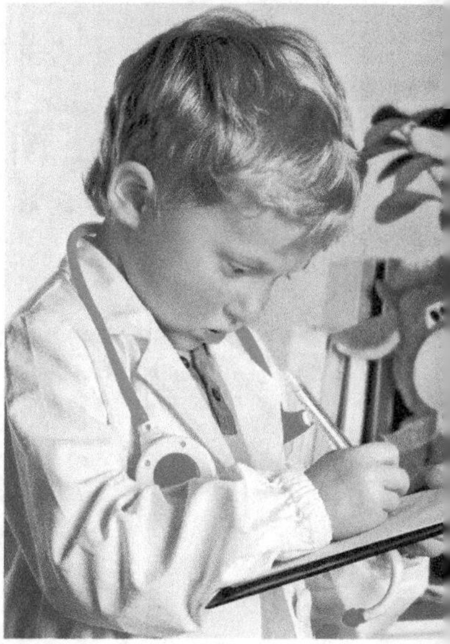

Think for a moment about your choice to attend your college or university. Did you know for certain what was in store for you regarding the reality of attending your institution? Probably not. But merely by being provided information about the population of the school, the male/female ratio, the average SAT/ACT scores of students admitted, the percentage of students who graduate in four years, the percentage of students who are commuters, the percentage of students who participate in extracurricular activities, and the number of students per major, you learned a great deal about the institution. In addition, you probably visited the school and were able to ask current students about their experiences and what they liked and disliked about being there. You may have even been fortunate enough to have a friend or family member attend the same school to give you useful, practical advice. These are examples of the types of information provided during the **anticipatory stage** of socialization, before you even entered the college or university.

anticipatory stage
The first stage of the socialization process within which employees begin to anticipate life within the organization.

The same things occur in organizations, where newcomers enter with a lot of information about such things as its practices, its culture, and its employee base. Gaining a lot of important and valid information about an organization prior to entry, according to Van Maanen and Schein (1979), is a strong predictor of job satisfaction. It is likely that if you know someone who transferred from your school before graduation, he or she said, in one form or another, that the reality of being there did not match their expectations. Valid expectations, according to Jablin (1982), are a key ingredient for organizational success.

The second stage of the organizational socialization process is known as the **encounter stage**, or what Jablin (1982) and Van Maanen (1975) call the **breaking-in period**. If one was able to appropriately and adequately gain enough information during the anticipatory stage, then much of the information provided from more experienced employees during the **encounter stage** would be repetitive. If, for one reason or another, one was not able to gain much valid, explanatory data prior to joining the organization, then much about the organization's goals, mission, culture, rules, behaviors, and norms would probably be a surprise. However, as mentioned previously, newcomers enter with much information about both the organization and the profession within which the organization is embedded. Most importantly, it is during this second stage of the socialization process that expectations are learned and sense making occurs (Jablin, 1987). A good example of the encounter stage is

encounter stage
The second stage of the socialization process within which employees begin to learn the ropes and experience the realities of the organization.

Table 10.3 Stages of Organizational Socialization

Stage	Effects
Anticipatory	Expectations are created
Encounter	Norms are taught
Metamorphosis	Employees become organizational insiders

when a person experiences corporate training (see Chapter 11). The majority of organizations have training programs, either informal or formal, wherein new employees are taught norms about such things as formal correspondence with superiors, how to deal with negative feedback, the role of technology in organizational practices, how to deal with multiculturalism, how to effectively manage interpersonal conflict, how to delegate responsibilities, how to work and excel in small-group situations, and how to deal with troubled coworkers. Clearly, these are not things that will surface informally during the anticipatory stage, though they are important for on-the-job decisions and understanding an organization's cultural norms (Falcione & Wilson, 1988). Most of the research in this area has concluded that much of what an employee learns during the encounter stage occurs during communication with the newcomer's supervisor (Jablin, 1982). Research also points to the important role that coworkers play in the process of newcomer learning.

Assume that you have an exam forthcoming in one of your advanced communication courses, but have never before had the instructor and become worried about the nature of the exam (e.g. how much material is covered, how difficult the exam will be, how much of the exam will be devoted to the outside readings, etc.). From a communication perspective, it seems as though there are two ways to gain such necessary information. The first option, which is likely something that some undergraduate students take advantage of, is to speak to the instructor directly. This, clearly, would provide the most useful and valid information. However, there is oftentimes something inherent in such a situation that discourages students from approaching the information-gathering process this way. As a result, this student might choose a less direct strategy, such as speaking to friends about the instructor's exams. This information would come from students who have already taken the course with the same instructor, so that such academic testimony is based on a "been there, done that" mentality. The first example, where the student speaks directly to the instructor, would be similar to the employee who gains information from his or her supervisor (Jablin, 1994). Although this is very important, and probably optimal for accurate information, engaging in such a social situation is filled with feelings of inequality and nervousness on the part of the student. If such inequality and nervousness trump the need for direct, valid information, then students might speak to friends who have either taken the course, studied with the instructor, or, in a perfect world, both. This would be similar to an employee gaining salient organizational information from coworkers using evidence-based testimony (Jablin, 1987). Although such information is valuable, it is perhaps prejudiced because of differences in individual needs and individual perceptions. For example, the student who wants to take an "easy" class will likely claim that the instructor's exams are difficult merely because of the density and difficulty of the material. This friend will likely create nerves in the mind of the student and, in the end, this information could prove disadvantageous for exam preparation. Given this example, the student would be provided a biased perspective because of the cognitive perception of his/her friend. In the end, there are both opportunities and problems associated with gaining information from supervisors and coworkers during the encounter stage of socialization, though it is important to do both if one is to get a well-rounded, comprehensive view of an organization and its cultural artifacts.

This QR code will take you to a YouTube clip highlighting the benefits of successful and effective organizational cultures.

http://www.youtube.com/watch?v=wSZ3IPDmqCg&feature=related

The final stage of the organizational socialization process, according to Jablin (1982), is metamorphosis, which is analogous to the caterpillar that turns into a butterfly. From an organizational perspective, then, the employee turns, communicatively and behaviorally speaking, from an outsider to an insider by not only learning the values, norms, expectations, rules, regulations, and standards of the organization, but also by behaving in ways illustrative of them (Falcione & Wilson, 1988). For example, it is not only learning that an organization deals with conflict through cooperative, rather than competitive strategies. It is also enacting the cooperative strategy during the conflict resolution process. In essence, the anticipatory stage might best be defined as the "expectation stage," the encounter stage might best be defined as the "understanding stage," and the **metamorphosis stage** might best be defined as the "change stage." A good example of the metamorphosis stage is formal recognition of a new brother or sister into a collegiate fraternity or sorority. Students decide to pledge a particular Greek organization because of the inherent value of such membership. That is, one decides to pledge a fraternity or sorority because they anticipate that the rewards that come with membership will not only be great, but also will be greater than joining any other Greek organization. This is an example of *anticipation*. During the pledge process, potential organizational members learn about the organization, including its mission, its history, what its Greek letters stand for, its philanthropic duties, as well as the sisters or brothers who are members of the local chapter. This is an example of **encounter**. Finally comes the pin ceremony, a momentous event for most fraternities and sororities, during which time new members are officially "sworn in" by the existing sisterhood or brotherhood. This is emblematic of the formal acceptance of new members based on knowledge of and appreciation for the organization's mission and goals, and the cultural indicators that accompany them. This is an example of metamorphosis. By becoming an organizational insider, and being metamorphosized, employees accept the organization's culture and the practices and processes associated with it.

metamorphosis stage
The third and final stage of the socialization process within which employees begin to accept and manifest organizational norms and become organizational insiders.

In the end, the process of organizational socialization is important for organizations and the employees who are part of them. In essence, it is during the anticipatory, encounter, and metamorphosis stages that employees expect, learn, and manifest certain organizational norms. Without such socialization, either formal, informal, or a combination of both, employees might not know or understand their organization's ways of doing things. This, unfortunately, could have serious negative ramifications at both the employee and organizational levels.

ORGANIZATIONAL CULTURES AS ENABLING AND CONSTRAINING

Organizational cultures are necessary for employees to understand how to perform normal, daily, routine tasks. For example, it is an organization's culture that determines how one provides positive and negative feedback, how and when small groups are more conducive than individual efforts, if and how to ask a manager for time off, how one is commended for his or her accomplishments, and how to deal with troubled coworkers (Schein, 1992). As the information in this chapter illustrates, there seem to be two overarching benefits, or enabling factors, that are realized when one properly understands an organization's culture. First, cultures provide a blueprint (Hofsteade, 1998). Simply put, a **blueprint** is a prototype or design that documents the ways in which certain interdependent parts of the organization work together. Just as an architectural blueprint informs the architect about the construction plans for a building or home, a culture provides the employee with a blueprint for organizational operations. For example, an organization's symbol and mission statement provide a blueprint for action. That is, whether it is the golden arches of McDonald's, the bulls-eye of Target, the silver boomerang of Nike, American Express' "we value our people, encourage their development, and reward their performance," Family Dollar Stores' "a compelling place to work ... by providing exceptional opportunities and rewards for achievement," or Amazon's "to build a place where people can come to find and discover anything they might want to buy online," these cultural artifacts are informative. Entering into an organization where the "suits" and the "nonsuits" are geographically dispersed based on office design, where lock-and-key offices are for those in managerial positions and cubicles are for those in nonmanagerial positions, can provide a lot of information about the communicative and behavioral practices of employees. Having an employee of the month program, where achievements are recognized, speaks a lot about an organization's method of reward and acknowledgment. Although these are not things that an employee can necessarily anticipate, such cultural artifacts are learned during the encounter stage, become part of employee life during the metamorphosis stage, and provide a behavioral blueprint for organizational action.

Second, an organization's culture shapes a sense of collective identity among employees (Ravasi & Schultz, 2006). That is, although organizations are composed of people with different backgrounds, genders, expertise, departments, experiences, morals, work ethics, and aspirations, the one attribute that all employees share is organizational membership. Much research on organizational identity concludes that an organization's culture is one of the strongest predictors of collective membership and identification (Tajfel & Turner, 1986). For example, if you have ever been to Johnny Rockets, a franchise best known for its hamburgers, you likely will not be surprised when the wait staff begins to dance at every 15-minute interval. If you have ever been to Cold Stone Creamery, offering what the organization calls "the ultimate ice cream experience," you probably will not be surprised when the staff begins to sing when patrons leave a tip. If you have ever been to TGI Fridays, a casual dining franchise, you likely will not be surprised when the wait staff begins to (perhaps embarrassingly) celebrate your birthday through song and cheer. It is these seemingly small, trivial cultural norms that set organizations apart. Being part of a collective, or what Tajfel and Turner (1986) call the in-group, has been predictive of such things as organizational commitment, job satisfaction, a sense of community, increased involvement, organizational motivation, and feelings of self-worth. It is likely that if you asked the managers of Johnny

Table 10.4 Enabling and Constraining Factors Associated with an Organization's Culture

Enabling Factors	Constraining Factors
Provides an organizational blueprint	Becomes overly restrictive
Promotes a sense of collective identity	Difficult to change
	Potential for subcultures to emerge

Figure 10.1
Examples of Organizational Symbols

Rockets, Cold Stone Creamery, and TFI Fridays why they do these communicative norms, they will say that it is just part of who they are. This sense of organizational self results in a collective sense of identity, created by cultural artifacts that are both understood and performed by all employees (Ashforth & Mael, 1989).

However, organizational cultures are not without problems, as they carry with them constraining factors that might ultimately inhibit certain employee practices. For example, cultures might be seen as constrictive, meaning that as much as they provide a blueprint for action, they also prohibit certain behaviors from occurring. Assume, for example, that Barry is in disagreement about an idea that Brian brought forth at a recent organizational meeting. Rather than speaking to Brian privately after the meeting or sending him an email or speaking to Brian's supervisor, Barry decides to publicly reject Brian's idea. After the meeting, Barry's boss, Sayre, brings him into her office to tell him of her disappointment. In so doing, Sayre tells Barry that "this is not the way that we do things around here." Given this example, as much as an organization's culture provides a blueprint for acceptable behavior and communication, it also implicitly provides a blueprint for behavior and communication that is deemed unacceptable. In a sense, then, culture can be enabling on one hand (e.g., providing necessary organizational information), though constraining on the other (e.g., norms become firm and steadfast).

In addition to organizational cultures being constrictive, they are also difficult to change (Schein, 1985). Much research over the past decade has focused on cultural change during organizational transition in the wake of a **merger** or **acquisition**. A merger is when two organizations combine to create a new entity, whereas an acquisition is when one organization takes control of another. Cartwright and Cooper (1993) argue that a successful cultural "marriage" must occur for successful mergers and acquisitions. For example, the merger of United Airlines and Continental Airlines required that a new organizational culture emerge. It's important to keep in mind that each organization operated as an individual entity prior to the merger in 2010. As such, each operated according to its own cultural norms. What is this new organizational entity to do? Should its administrative body determine which culture should become dominant? Should it combine the two once-existing cultures? Should it create a new culture from scratch? In addition, once such a decision is made, how are employees to be socialized into the new organizational culture? In other words, would employees merely be re-socialized, or will an entirely new training program need to surface? Such decisions, according to Giffords and Dina (2003), are extremely important, yet extremely difficult to make. In the end, cultural change becomes a potential constraining factor for organizations during times of transition.

This QR code will take you to an interactive website that allows you to gain practical knowledge of, and hands-on experience with, organizational mission statements.

http://www.missionstatements.com/

Finally, and perhaps most problematic for employees, is the idea that certain subcultures are likely to emerge within organizations. That is, although an organization has one overarching culture, it's likely that departments have their own minicultures, teams have their own minicultures, and circles of friends have their own minicultures. This is the idea that there exist structures within structures within structures. It is likely that you have at least once said to yourself that you wished you had a different teacher for a course that you took. In fact, it is likely that certain sections of certain courses fill first during the registration process because of the instructor. What does this say about an organization's culture? It says that although courses, departments, instructors, and curricula are all housed within the college or university (the organization), departments and instructors might dance to their own tune. It is probable, therefore, that the history department differs from the communication department, which differs from the anthropology department, which differs from the political science department, which differs from the biology department. What becomes overly problematic about this is when cultures begin to compete. A friendly, democratic department housed within a bureaucratic college or university creates a dialectical tension for employees, meaning that it might be extremely difficult for a faculty member to design his/her own syllabus (democratic) within an organization where administrators make most of the salient decisions (bureaucratic) (see Chapter 5). If multiple cultures exist within a given entity, the likelihood of employee equivocality, or uncertainty, increases, which, according to Weick (1979), can be detrimental for organizations and the employees who are a part of them.

SUMMARY

An organization's culture helps define what the organization is and ultimately provides a sense of shared community and collective identity for all members. Cultural artifacts, such as symbols, mission statements, dress codes, and physical office layouts provide direction and inform employees about behavioral norms. Given that organizational cultures exist before we even encounter them, employees must learn about them through formal training, informal discussions, and/or on-the-job encounters. For some employees, an organization's culture is inconsistent with their personal values and, as a result, they may decide to leave for another organization whose culture is more consistent with their values, desires, and motivations. For most employees, however, cultural understanding and acceptance occur and they become metamorphosized. It becomes clear that there are both enabling and constraining factors associated with an organization's culture, therefore making it important for organizations to harness the benefits and reduce the (potentially) harmful factors produced by culture. Merely by walking into an organization and seeing its cultural artifacts, an outsider can learn a great deal about its norms and practices. As fossils and bones provide the cultural anthropologist with information about a life that once was, an organization's culture provides information about a life and world that currently exists, and one that will likely exist well in the future.

Questions for Discussion and Review

1. Explain what is meant by *cultural artifact*. Give some examples of them within the organizational environment.
2. Create a new mission statement for your organization. Explain its role in informing employees about work practices and behaviors.
3. Choose two organizational symbols and compare and contrast them in terms of the meaning they represent for the organization and its employees.
4. Create a new organizational metaphor. Explain its utility for employees and the behavioral norms by which they operate.
5. Explain the role of the anticipatory, encounter, and metamorphosis stages of organizational socialization. Give examples of what occurs at each stage.
6. Explain what is meant by enabling and constraining factors. Give an example of each as they relate to an organization's culture.

REFERENCES

Ashforth, B. E., & Mael, F. (1989). Social identity theory and the organization. *Academy of Management Review, 14,* 20–39.

Burke, K. (1950). *A rhetoric of motives.* Berkeley, CA: University of California Press.

Cartwright, S., & Cooper, C. L. (1993). The role of culture compatibility in successful organizational marriage. *Academy of Management Executive, 7,* 57–70.

Deal, T. E., & Kennedy, A. A. (1982). *Corporate cultures: The rites and rituals of corporate life.* Reading, MA: Addison-Wesley.

Denison, D. R., & Mishra, A. K. (1995). Toward a theory of organizational culture and effectiveness. *Organization Science, 6,* 204–223.

Dose, J. J. (1997). Work values: An integrative framework and illustrative application to organizational socialization. *Journal of Occupational and Organizational Psychology, 70,* 219–240.

Fairhurst, G. T., Jordan, J. M., & Neuwirth, K. (1997). Why are we here: Managing the meaning of an organizational mission statement. *Journal of Applied Communication Research, 25,* 243–263.

Falcione, R. L., & Wilson, C. E. (1988). Socialization processes in organizations. In G. M. Goldhaber & G. A. Barnett (Eds.), *Handbook of organizational communication* (pp. 151–169). Norwood, NJ: Ablex.

Feldman, S. P. (1986). Managing in context: An essay on the relevance of culture to understanding organizational change. *Journal of Management Studies, 23,* 587–607.
Giffords, E., & Dina, R. (2003). Changing organizational cultures: The challenge in forging successful mergers. *Administration in Social Work, 27,* 69–81.
Hofsteade, G. (1998). Attitudes, values, and organizational culture: Disentangling the concepts. *Organization Studies, 19,* 477–492.
Jablin, F. M. (1982). Organizational communication: An assimilation approach. In M. E. Roloff & C. R. Berger (Eds.), *Social cognition and communication* (pp. 255–286). Beverly Hills, CA: SAGE Publications.
Jablin, F. M. (1987). Organizational entry, assimilation, and exit. In F. M. Jablin, L. L. Putnam, K. Roberts, & L. Porter (Eds.), *Handbook of organizational communication: An interpretive approach* (pp. 679–740). Newbury Park, CA: SAGE Publications.
Jablin, F. M. (1994). Communication competence: An organizational assimilation perspective. In L. Van Waes, E. Woudstra, & P. Van Den Hoven (Eds.), *Functional communication quality* (pp. 28–41). Amsterdam: Rodpoi.
Linstead, S. A., & Grafton-Small, R. (1992). On reading organizational culture. *Organization Studies, 13,* 331–355.
Kendall, J., & Kendall, K. (1993). Metaphors and methodologies: Living beyond the systems machine. *MIS Quarterly, 17,* 149–171.
Mael, F. A., & Ashforth, B. E. (1992). Alumni and their alma mater: A partial test of the reformulated model of organizational identification. *Journal of Organizational Behavior, 13,* 103–123.
Martin, J., & Siehl, C. (1983). Organizational culture and counterculture: An uneasy symbiosis. *Organizational Dynamics, 122,* 52–65.
Morgan, G. (1980). Paradigms, metaphors, and puzzle-solving in organization theory. *Administrative Science Quarterly, 2,* 27–46.
Morgan, G. (1983). More on metaphor: Why we cannot control tropes in administrative science. *Administrative Science Quarterly, 28,* 601–607.
Morgan, G. (1986). *Images of organizations.* Thousand Oaks, CA: SAGE Publications.
Mumby, D. K. (1989). Ideology and the social construction of meaning: A communication perspective. *Communication Quarterly, 37,* 291–304.
Pearce, J. A. (1982). The company mission as a strategic tool. *Sloan Management Review, 23,* 15–24.
Pettigrew, A. M. (1979). On studying organizational cultures. *Administrative Science Quarterly, 24,* 570–581.
Pratt, M., & Rafaeli, A. (1997). Organizational dress as a symbol of multilayered social identities. *Academy of Management Journal, 40,* 862–898.
Putnam, L. L. (1998). Metaphors and images of organizational communication. In J. S. Trent (Ed.), *Communication: Views from the helm for the twenty first century* (pp. 145–161). Boston: Allyn and Bacon.
Ravasi, D., & Schultz, M. (2006). Responding to organizational identity threats: Exploring the role of organizational culture. *Academy of Management Journal, 49,* 433–458.
Schein, E. H. (1985). *Organizational culture and leadership.* San Francisco: Jossey-Bass.
Schein, E. H. (1990). Organizational culture. *American Psychologist, 45,* 109–119.
Schein, E. H. (1992). *Organizational culture and leadership* (2nd Ed.). San Francisco: Jossey-Bass.
Schein, E. H. (1996). Culture: The missing concept in organization studies. *Administrative Science Quarterly, 41,* 229–240.
Tajfel, H., & Turner, J. C. (1986). The social identity theory of intergroup behavior. In S. Worchel & W. G. Austin (Eds.), *The psychology of intergroup relations* (pp. 7–24). Chicago: Nelson-Hall.
Van Maanen, J. (1975). Breaking-in: Socialization to work. In R. Dubin (Ed.), *Handbook of work, organization and society* (pp. 32–103). Chicago: Rand-McNally.
Van Maanen, J., & Schein, E. H. (1979). Toward a theory of organizational socialization. In B. M. Staw (Ed.), *Research in organizational behavior* (pp. 209–264). Greenwich, CT: JAI Press.
Weick, K. E. (1979). *The social psychology of organizing.* Reading, MA: Addison-Wesley.
Wilkins, A. (1983). The culture audit: A tool for understanding organizations. *Organizational Dynamics, 12,* 24–38.

Communication with New Media

OBJECTIVES

What We Will Be Investigating:

- Examine the growing role of information technologies as mediated communication in modern organizational life.
- Identify the variety of low-tech and high-tech communication technologies used in mediated organizational communication.
- Describe the advantages and disadvantages to using mediated channels of organizational communication.
- Identify strategies for building technologically adaptive organizations that are prepared for the development and introduction of new communication media, technologies, and software.
- Examine how to leverage the advantages provided by the use of mediated channels of communication while minimizing the potential disadvantages that can arise when using these channels.

KEY TERMS

Agenda setting
Blogs
Branding
Closure
Computer etiquette
Computer literacy
Computer security
Cyber bullying
Decoding
Encoding
Habituation
Hackers
Hypertext
Impression management
Information authenticity
Information availability
Information confidentiality
Information integrity
Information overload
Intranets
Malware and spyware
Media convergence
Media mix
Mediated channels of communication
Message chunking
Message testing
Panopticon
Scannability
Selective attention
Selective perception process
Small-world phenomenon
Social media
Technology-mediated channels
Telephone etiquette
Usability studies
User-centered design
Video technology

The newest computer can merely compound the oldest problem in the relations between human beings, and in the end the communicator will be confronted with the old problem, of what to say and how to say it.

—Edward R. Murrow

INTRODUCTION

Modern organizations use a wide variety of communication channels. In earlier chapters, we focused primarily on the use of face-to-face (F2F) communication channels. This chapter expands our focus to different **mediated channels of communication** used by organizational participants. Mediated channels include a wide range of *print media* (books, memos, letters, pamphlets, newsletters, etc.), *telephonic media* (landlines, cell phones, smart phones, fax machines, etc.), *computers* (desktop computers, laptops, tablets, networked computer systems, etc.) and *mobile devices* (smart phones). In recent years, organizational communicators have become increasingly dependent on mediated channels of communication to accomplish their organizational goals.

As we have discussed throughout this book, a wide range of messages are exchanged in organizational life. These messages are delivered in numerous ways, with differing levels of influence on their intended audiences. With the rapid advance of new communication technologies, increasing numbers of organizational messages are delivered through **technology-mediated channels** such as phones, computers, and videoconference equipment. Growth in the widespread use of mobile communication technologies has enabled organizational participants to exchange messages wherever they may be at all times of the day. Of course, organization members also continue to use low-tech mediated channels of communication, such as memos, letters, and manuals. Strategic organizational communicators learn how to use these high-tech and low-tech mediated channels of communication together effectively, and they carefully integrate the use of mediated communication with face-to-face human interactions.

This chapter examines the growing dependence on a broad range of traditional and new communication media and technologies in modern organizational life. It examines the relative strengths and weaknesses of using different communication channels and media to guide informed decisions about how to best use communication tools to achieve organizational goals. It also describes strategies for coordinating the use of traditional communication (such as face-to-face, memos and letters, etc.) with newer digital, mobile, and social media (such as email, videoconferencing, intranets, websites, blogs, smart phones, etc.). It also analyzes strategies for building technologically adaptive organizations that are prepared for the development and introduction of new communication media, technologies, and software. The chapter concludes with a case study that illustrates the powerful influence of communication media and information technologies on modern organizations.

MEDIATED CHANNELS

As organizational enterprises become increasingly complex, involving participants from a variety of locations—spread across buildings, cities, regions, nations, and countries—there is an increasing need to use mediated channels of communication to stay in touch with distant organizational partners. In this section, we look at some of the advantages and disadvantages of mediated channels of communication.

Advantages of Mediated Channels

Mediated channels of communication provide many useful information exchange opportunities and advantages to organizations. For example, technology-mediated communication channels often enable users to quickly and efficiently reach many different organizational participants in a variety of locations, making it easier for them to share information and coordinate activities from anywhere in the world. This has led to the **small-world phenomenon**, which refers to the ability to establish and maintain relationships and close coordination with organizational partners in many different locations (Kreps, 1988). The small-world phenomenon has helped increase familiarity and interaction between people who would normally have minimal opportunities for interpersonal contact. It has also led to the growth of interorganizational cooperative ventures, such as multinational corporations, global sporting events, and international government alliances. We'll discuss the small-world phenomenon in more detail in Chapter 10.

What is the small-world phenomenon?

Mobile communication channels are especially convenient in a wide range of places and times, whenever and wherever organizational participants need to be in touch. Such mobile communication channels have helped to extend the range of organizational activities beyond the traditional workplace and workweek. For example, the use of telecommuting has enabled employees to work at organizations that are distant from their homes. In my university department in the Washington, DC, metropolitan area, we employ a research professor from Northern California who works on conducting surveys, analyzing data from studies, and publishing research results, while rarely coming to campus. She conducts virtually all of her work via computer and phone. Furthermore, many technology-mediated communication channels have introduced useful automated features, such as built-in address books, automatic connections, global positioning systems (GPS), and data analysis tools that make them convenient and powerful. A number of technology-mediated channels also have the ability to record (via audio, video, and text) transcripts of communication events, preserving messages for later review.

Disadvantages of Mediated Channels

Unfortunately, some of the advantages provided by mediated channels of communication can also pose significant challenges and limitations. As we have discussed, organizational participants typically operate in complex, multichannel media environments, with a range of media used to convey messages. The interplay between organizational communication across a range of channels and media is often referred to as the **media mix**. Often, the mix of messages in modern organizations is haphazard and uncontrolled, resulting in organizational participants being exposed to an abundance of information, contradictory messages, and unclear messages that can lead to information overload. **Information overload** occurs when so many different messages are impinging on a person that the person has difficulty making sense of all the information available. When experiencing information overload, organizational participants often become confused, frustrated, and even irritable (Kreps, 1990). This is clearly not the best set of conditions for conducting organizational activities. In increasingly fast-paced, multichannel organizational communication contexts, the opportunity for information overload is high. Strategic organizational communicators therefore develop effective strategies to help organization members cope with the competing sources of information available to them and thereby avoid information overload.

Another disadvantage of technology-mediated channels of communication is that organizational participants who do not have access to the latest and most powerful communication technologies due to limited availability, limited organizational technical infrastructure, or to the high expense of advanced equipment may be at a significant disadvantage compared to those who do have the latest and best media tools. Those organizational participants who do not have access to media tools may miss out on important organizational messages and will not have as many opportunities to provide information and input to organizational operations as those who do have the best communication tools.

Meanwhile, those organizational participants who do have access to advanced communication technologies often need training to learn how to effectively operate the tools they wield. It can be challenging to use computer technologies or advanced software to achieve organizational goals, yet with the swift advances in technology, there is increasing demand for organizational participants to quickly learn how to use the latest media tools effectively. The constant and rapid introduction of new information technologies has spawned the development and introduction of technology training programs in many organizations to help members keep abreast of the correct use of the latest media tools. The introduction of new information tools has also led to the introduction of technology development and maintenance departments, whose personnel keep busy installing, updating, and repairing organizational media.

Another drawback of certain mediated channels of communication is their limited capacity to send and receive the full range of relevant messages, which can constrain communication. For example, text messaging, although convenient, is limited to the expression of short written messages. Similarly, conventional telephones enable users to exchange only auditory cues, limiting

ORGANIZATIONS IN ACTION

Introducing Tablets to Cockpits at United Continental

The Problem: Airline pilots were increasingly being forced to carry around, from airport to airport, a weighty suitcase full of paper maps, charts, and schedules. A pilot's "flight bag" was filled with logbooks, weather forecasts, operating manuals, reference books, flight checklists, navigation charts, and other materials that pilots had to have at the tip of their fingers in the cockpit. A typical pilot carried about 12,000 sheets of paper weighing 38 pounds. Not only was all of this printed material not readily updatable, but also it was hardly a "green" practice. However, Federal Aviation Administration (FAA) regulations prohibited mobile electronics from being a sole information source for airline pilots, out of fear that the devices would fail at higher altitudes.

The Solution: A Boeing subsidiary company called Jeppesen saw a market need waiting to be filled, and, utilizing a tablet application called "FliteDeck," it began digitizing all of that flight bag paper. The FAA engaged in rigorous testing of tablet computers, including simulating rapid decompression at over 50,000 feet. In February 2011, after the tablets were found to perform effectively, the FAA changed its regulations and allowed pilots to use tablets instead of paper. Suddenly, airlines and pilots had the choice of carrying around 38 pounds of paper, or carrying a 1.5-pound tablet computer. The choice was obvious.

How have tablet computers changed the airline industry?

In May 2011, a few months after the FAA ruling, Alaska Airlines began giving its pilots Apple iPads, and by the end of the summer of 2011, United Airlines and Continental Airlines (which were in the process of merging) became the first major airlines to provide iPad technology to all 11,000 of their pilots. Now, United and Continental pilots have the essential information updated in real-time at their fingertips from departure gate to arrival gate for every flight. Parent company United Continental Holdings says it saves 16 million sheets of paper, and, through the reduction in weight, could save over 325,000 gallons of jet fuel annually.

Critical Thinking Questions

1. Can you think of other new communication innovations whose adoption was delayed by regulations? Are regulators being overly cautious or just plain old-fashioned? Should we as a society be willing to forge ahead, or is it best to take a "go-slow" stance in the adoption of some technologies?
2. As a student, have you encountered high school or university regulations that prohibit mobile devices? Why do you think such rules are in place?
3. What do you think the future will hold for replacing paper with mobile communication devices? Can you think of other uses, and what would you need to do to work toward developing the technology app to market such an innovation?

Source

Murray, P. (2011, September 3). United and Continental Airlines go paperless: Give their pilots 11,000 iPads. *Singularity Hub*. Retrieved from http://singularityhub.com/2011/09/03/united-and-continental-airlines-go-paperless-give-their-pilots-11000-ipads/

the expression of a wide range of nonverbal messages. Email, faxes, and websites can often feel overly formal and distant to users. Strategic organizational communicators therefore learn to leverage the advantages provided by such mediated channels of communication while minimizing the potential disadvantages that can arise when using these channels. Let's now turn our attention to a closer look at print and text-based media.

PRINT AND TEXT-BASED MEDIA

The written word is perhaps the most basic form of mediated organizational communication. Memos, notes, letters, manuals, pamphlets, newsletters, press releases, and billboards are among the most commonly used traditional (that is, low-tech) mediated organizational communication channels that depend on the use of the printed word. For example, many organizations depend on newsletters and organizational magazines to communicate with their own members as well as with key external publics. Effectively written and designed newsletters and magazines can therefore perform important *internal and external organizational communication functions* by disseminating relevant organizational information, chronicling organizational accomplishments and milestones, and reinforcing organizational image and culture.

Similarly, carefully prepared media releases can help promote positive media coverage about organizations that can reach broad audiences. Media coverage of organizations can serve an important *branding and agenda-setting function* by raising organizations' public profiles and creating organizational identity with key publics, such as potential customers, supporters, and regulators. **Branding** involves establishing a clear image for the organization through the ways the organization communicates, such as the use of organizational taglines (such as Nike's "Just Do It"), logos, and advertising. **Agenda setting** involves raising public consciousness about key organizational issues, activities, and products, typically involving the use of news stories about the organization carried by both organizational media (such as websites and brochures) and external media (such as newspapers and television), media releases, and organizational advertising. Of course, more advanced electronic organizational communication technologies, such as websites, email, and text messaging, also rely on the written word (text) to communicate with organizational participants.

What are some organizational communication functions of mobile technology?

It is almost impossible to participate actively in modern organizational life without developing good reading and writing skills. Consider your experiences as a student. You have undoubtedly depended on your reading and writing skills to apply for admission to school, to enroll in classes, to learn about course requirements, to study course materials, to prepare your assignments, and to take exams. And now, as you review this chapter, you are using your reading skills to learn about organizational communication. Similarly, participants in most organizations depend on their ability to read and write messages conveyed via a variety of low-tech and high-tech communication channels in order to perform their jobs.

Encoding and Decoding

Two primary communication processes are involved in the effective use of print and text-based media in organizational life: the *encoding* and *decoding* processes.

- **Encoding** refers to the important *message development* challenges facing organizational participants who prepare memos, letters, press releases, advertising copy, reports, newsletters, and other text-based media. Message developers such as writers and editors must carefully compose written materials to meet the needs of key audiences.
- **Decoding** refers to the important *audience interpretation* challenges confronting organizational participants who need to make sense of the written word in print and other text-based media. Organizational participants who are the consumers of written materials must take care to attend to and accurately interpret important written texts.

Those organizational participants who encode organizational messages must make strategic choices regarding the best media to use (i.e., reports, email, faxes, memos, pamphlets, web pages, etc.), the best design features for these media (i.e., graphics, layout, font style and size, colors, etc.), and the most effective written messages to prepare for distinct organizational situations and audiences. To reach different audiences, organizational representatives need to select the right media that these audiences are likely to use and pay attention to. For example, when trying to reach a teenage audience, it would be a good idea to use popular websites and social media to send messages. However, to reach wealthy retired individuals, these channels would not likely work as well. It might be better to use the *Wall Street Journal* and television news shows to reach this audience. The following are a few of the many questions those who encode messages must ask:

- Which print media are most likely to effectively convey written messages to my targeted audience?
- Which print media are targeted audience members most likely to use?
- How much time and energy are organizational participants likely to expend on attending to specific written materials?
- Which messages are likely to resonate with specific audiences, eliciting the development of rich and influential meanings?

Based on the answers to these questions, strategic organizational communicators make informed choices about the best media channels, messages, and design features to use to reach and influence key audience members.

Time and Attention

The issues of time, attention, communication capacity, and message exposure have become increasingly important criteria when designing print media. Since organizational participants are busy with a variety of organizational demands, they may not take the time and effort to pay attention to all the written messages they receive. For example, they may settle for rapidly scanning written messages to get a general picture of what is being expressed instead of engaging in a detailed review of written materials to develop a clear understanding of these written texts. This tendency to *scan* rather than *read* documents generally leads to organizational members missing important information and making mistakes that may have serious organizational consequences.

Think about your own attention to the email, text messages, and other forms of written communication you receive each day. Do you carefully review all these messages? How much of the content of these messages do you miss? To overcome this problem, organizational writers must do the following:

- Make their written documents distinctive, interesting, and provocative to capture audience members' attention.
- Make their written documents brief, clear, and to-the-point so audience members can make sense of the main issues covered quickly and easily.
- Consider using an outline format, short declarative sentences, and/or bulleted points to more effectively convey key messages to busy organizational participants.

Selective Perception

Earlier in this book, we discussed the **selective perception process**, in which strategic organizational communicators make active decisions every moment to help them make sense of all the messages available to them. In selective perception, organizational participants focus in on key messages (**selective attention**), block out of their consciousness less important messages (**habituation**), and interpret the messages they have attended to (**closure**).

This selective perception process is most relevant to the strategic interpretation of written messages. Organizational communicators therefore need to carefully determine which written messages to focus on and which ones to skim. They must make good decisions about what the written documents mean and how they should respond to the content in these documents. Organizational participants who spend limited energy on selective perception may miss a good deal of important information. These communicators often habituate key messages and reach premature closure about the texts they need to understand. This can be dangerous and lead to serious mistakes.

As consumers of written messages in organizational life, we must carefully process written information so we can use it to guide our activities. Many of us receive hundreds of email, memos, letters, and other written materials in a given day. We need to quickly prioritize which of these messages are most important to attend to right away, and which can wait until we have more time to carefully review them. It is important to distinguish between which messages are most organizationally relevant (such as directives for immediate action from your boss) and which messages may be less critical to the accomplishment of your job (such as advertisements and spam).

The Importance of Reading Skills

Earlier in this book we described listening as an important communication competency in modern organizational life. Similarly, *reading* is a critical organizational communication competency. Organizational participants with limited literacy levels may need training to enhance their reading skills. In fact, the U.S. Department of Education recently found that a significant proportion of the adult American public has problems with reading, suggesting that many organizational participants have problems reading organizational texts and accessing relevant organizational information (Baer, Kutner, & Sabatini, 2009).

Even organizational participants with strong reading skills may need help making sense of written organizational messages. These participants must invest time and energy to carefully review written materials, and sometimes the sheer amount of materials that organization members need to review can be overwhelming, especially for top executives, scientists, and other professionals. In these cases, it may be wise to hire specialists, such as librarians and content editors, to review and condense written materials into executive summaries for key organization members. As a college student, you most likely relate to this as you may be overwhelmed by the amount of written materials you need to read. You therefore must develop attention and time-management strategies to tackle the reading demands that come with taking college classes.

The Importance of Design and Message Testing

Message developers must also make strategic choices about how print media are designed and how written messages are composed. Too often, the print materials we encounter do not communicate their intended messages effectively. For example, the pharmaceutical industry has relied for many years on medication package inserts—the small slips of paper placed in medication boxes that list the ingredients, correct uses, and potential side effects of medications—to communicate about prescribed medications with consumers. Have you ever read a medication package insert? Many medication users do not pay close attention to these inserts because they are not easy to read. First of all, the print is usually extremely small. Next, the language is often very complicated and technical, making the information difficult to understand. Finally, the inserts are written in a style that appears to meet legal requirements for informed consent but not in a manner that is appropriate to the information needs of most consumers.

Is it any wonder that many patients do not understand basic information about the medications they have been prescribed? In fact, evidence suggests that as many as half of all consumers fail to take their medications as prescribed, with many of these consumers saying they do not understand why they need to take their medications at all (Kreps et al., 2011). This is obviously not a wise communication decision by pharmaceutical companies, which need to communicate information about their medications to consumers to promote the correct use of the drugs as well as to encourage consumer adherence to prescription recommendations.

Similarly, many technology manufacturers have not done a good job designing and writing the instruction manuals they provide to consumers with new computers and other products. Have you tried to read an instruction manual only to find it confusing, boring, and cumbersome? This common problem leads to many errors in setting up and using new computer equipment. How do you think this affects consumer satisfaction with the new equipment and satisfaction with the equipment manufacturers (Schriver, 1997)?

Organizational participants must therefore take care to use clear and appropriate written language for their intended audiences. Using relevant examples that speak to readers' experiences and interests, and including clear diagrams can help clarify complex topics. Text must be formatted so that it is easy for key audiences to see and read. This not only means that the words are easily understood but that the design is attractive and that the text is brief enough to minimize information overload but complete enough to provide readers with all the information they need.

How might you use message testing in your organizations?

The best way to determine whether written messages are likely to communicate effectively to targeted audience members is to conduct **message testing**. Message testing is a form of user-centered research that involves presenting written texts to samples of readers representing the audiences the texts are being developed for, asking these readers to provide feedback about their interpretation of the messages, and encouraging them to provide suggestions about the best message strategies to convey the intended information to them. Data from message testing can help organizational members make sure they develop appropriate and effective written texts.

Improving Organizational Writing

Good writers are in high demand in modern organizational life. For example, the ability to write a clear and concise memo, a well-organized and complete report, and an interesting and compelling proposal are important communication skills for many organizational participants.

Writing is an important part of using organizational media. This is especially true for organizations that depend on written text for their websites, advertising materials, and electronic correspondence. Organizational participants with strong writing skills can perform important functions in organizations as writers and editors. The demand for effective writing skills is especially important for formal organizational leaders. Yet good writing skills are not widespread in many organizations. Such writing skills do not come naturally to most people; they must be carefully nurtured and developed.

Writing experts recommend that the first step to good organizational writing is careful analysis of the information needs, reading characteristics, and communication orientations of intended audiences. As in all forms of communication, it is a good strategy in written communication to adapt messages to specific audiences to insure that the messages meet audience expectations and communication competencies. The following are some questions that should guide message development:

- Does the target audience need the information being presented?
- Will target audience members be receptive to the messages being sent?
- Are the messages written using language that the target audience members will understand?
- Are the messages written in a way that will be interesting to the target audience?
- Do the messages provide target audience members with information they can use in organizational life?

As noted earlier, message developers should also pay close attention to the overall design of documents. Some key print design features include strategic use of color and of typeface styles and sizes. Message developers must ensure the legibility of text and establish appropriate sentence and paragraph lengths. They must also make decisions about the use of bullets and numbering, the spacing of text on the page, as well as the use of examples, charts, diagrams, and pictures.

A great deal of attention has been given in recent years to promoting the use of plain language in both print and web-based texts. The plain language movement developed in recognition of the limited literacy levels of many audience members. Plain language involves writing text on a basic (usually no higher than a sixth grade) reading level that will be understood by most audiences. However, many organizational materials—particularly academic, scientific, technical, and health-related information—are written in ways that are far too complex for most readers to understand.

Similarly, numbers and statistics should be used appropriately to match the numeracy levels (the ability to understand numerical information) of targeted audiences. Message developers must take care to use appropriate and easy-to-understand language and numerical examples if they want their written materials to be effective forms of organizational communication.

TELEPHONIC MEDIA

The telephone—from landlines, to cell phones, to fax machines, and so on—has become an essential tool for many organizational participants, especially for those holding jobs concerning survey research, sales, telemarketing, customer service, technical support, and reception. Although most people assume that speaking with others over the phone involves the same communication dynamics as speaking with others in person, this is not true. There are a number of key differences between telephone and face-to-face communication. Some of these differences can afford telephone communicators with certain advantages over those communicating in person, which we'll discuss next. However, some of the unique features of telephonic communication can lead to disadvantages for organizational communicators in comparison to face-to-face interaction.

Advantages to Telephonic Communication

One clear advantage provided by telephonic communication is the ability to easily span geographic distances—to connect with others in different locations around the globe. With conference calling features, organizational communicators can interact simultaneously over the phone with many different people in different locations. Using the telephone to communicate with distant organizational participants can be much more convenient and far less expensive than visiting people in person who are located far away. This can also save a lot of time.

Another potential advantage to telephonic communication is the privacy and partial anonymity it can afford communicators. In most telephone interactions, the person you are speaking to can't see you. That person can't tell what you look like, how you are dressed, how old you are, and what other visual nonverbal cues you are providing. This enables communicators to conceal certain aspects of their identity relatively easily over the phone. This can be very useful for **impression management**—influencing the ways that other people perceive you.

For example, in certain situations, communicators may want the person they are speaking with on the phone to perceive them in certain ways, perhaps as well educated, mature, and trustworthy. Over the phone, a communicator can mask some of the visual cues that might not support these personal perceptions, such as the way the speaker is dressed or the speaker's age. Furthermore, skilled telephone communicators can adapt their speaking voices while on the phone to reinforce impressions about their personal characteristics. They can also adjust their speech to match the vocal characteristics of the individuals they are speaking with to help establish a personal bond with them. Telemarketers often use this strategy to influence customers over the phone. Similarly, executives, salespeople, and customer relations specialists do their best to build identification between themselves and the individuals they are working with. Matching nonverbal cues is a powerful way to build identification, and it is often easier to match the limited number of nonverbal cues available when communicating over the telephone and other electronic media.

What are the pros and cons of using phones as means of organizational communication?

Disadvantages to Telephonic Communication

On the other hand, telephonic communication can be a less immediate (i.e., less dynamic, exciting, and involving) and a less personal channel for communication than face-to-face communication. The reason for this loss of immediacy is the absence of visual cues such as eye contact and facial expressions that cannot be conveyed via the phone. Skilled telephone communicators learn how to use their vocal cues to lend excitement and interest to telephone interactions. They use vocal expression, pacing (how quickly they speak and respond), volume, vivid language, and emphasis to increase the immediacy of phone conversations.

Another disadvantage to telephonic communication is the tendency for misunderstandings to occur between communicators. Without the normal visual cues available to them, telephonic communicators depend entirely on what they hear to interpret messages from their partners. Sometimes, particularly when the telephone connection is not very strong or when complex information is conveyed quickly over the phone, messages can become jumbled, and mistakes in interpretation often occur. Unless communicators carefully repeat important information, there is limited opportunity to review information exchanged during phone calls to help clarify messages and enhance understanding.

Telephone Etiquette

Learning how to communicate effectively over the phone may take training. Telephone communicators need to learn how to express themselves concisely, clearly, and emphatically. Some organizations have established systems of **telephone etiquette**, composed of cultural norms, for strategic telephone communication. The following are a number of these common telephone etiquette norms:

- Announce yourself when speaking on the phone (especially on group conference calls); your telephonic partners can't see who is talking (unless, of course, you are using a video phone or a technology like Skype).
- Express yourself concisely, with short, clear sentences.
- Use strategically varied paralinguistic cues, such as tone, expression, and volume, to enhance listener interest and increase communication dynamism.
- Use vocal cues to coordinate turn taking so that communicators can avoid interrupting others on the phone. This can be especially tricky when participating in a conference call with a number of participants.
- Remember to communicate politely, sensitively, and clearly.

There are also rules about the appropriate length of telephone calls. Savvy organizational communicators make appointments ahead of time for business calls and schedule the calls for convenient times and durations with the individuals with whom they would like to speak. Violations of telephone etiquette can alienate communicators from one another and undermine the cooperation needed for effective organizing.

VIDEO-BASED MEDIA

The use of **video technology**—that is, the use of moving video footage on websites, smart phones, teleconferencing, and other electronic media—is becoming increasingly popular in many organizations. Video-based programs are used often in modern organizations for consumer education and employee training purposes. For example, organizations that use advanced technologies to build products are likely to use specialized video programs to train workers about how to correctly use specialized equipment. Similarly, video programs are used by many organizations to provide ethics training to employees as well as training related to topics such as privacy, race relations, sexual harassment, conflict of interest, and credit card uses and reconciliation.

Video programs are also used by many organizations to educate consumers about how to set up and use their products. Health care delivery systems often show video programs to patients to explain complex medical procedures, to prepare them for surgery, and to teach them how to follow complex therapeutic protocols after leaving the hospital. It has become relatively common for organizations to show video promotion programs as a form of publicity at internal and external stakeholder meetings. These video promotion programs are often produced to share information about organizational products, services, events, and milestones.

The use of promotional videos grows out of the long-standing external organizational communication practice of producing video-based commercials for advertising purposes. Many large for-profit, not-for-profit, and government organizations have established their own video production units that script and produce video programs, record meetings, and provide organizational (in-house) video services. These production units often have significant communication budgets dedicated to covering the costs of producing video-based advertising and promotion programs. For example, most hospitals and medical centers have their own audio-visual departments capable of executing a wide range of video production tasks. A number of organizations also hire independent communication companies (such as production houses and advertising agencies) to handle video production work.

Videoconferencing

When is videoconferencing an adequate alternative to in-person meetings? When is it not?

Videoconferencing has also become a popular organizational application of video technology. In traditional videoconferencing, participants gathered in two or more specially equipped videoconference studios. Newer technologies such as Skype have made it easier for organizational participants to teleconference without complex video technology infrastructures. Group member activities are captured on sound and picture signals that are sent back and forth instantly so all participants can hear and see each other in real time. Obviously, the use of videoconferencing can save a great deal of time and expense for organization members who do not have to travel to remote locations to participate in important meetings. On the other hand, group members lose some of the immediacy of having all the meeting participants in the same room at the same time. It is important for participants in these videoconferences to actively engage the remote members, encourage active interaction and exchange, and follow up with remote participants on group decisions and tasks.

The Effectiveness of Video Programs

Numerous issues influence the effectiveness of the use of video technologies in organizational life. Similar to the issues we discussed earlier regarding print media, video media programs must be designed to meet the communication needs, expectations, and competencies of the organizational participants who will use these media products. The following are some questions creators of video programs must ask:

- How well are the video programs scripted to meet the information needs, communication skill levels, and interests of their intended audiences?
- How easy will it be for targeted audiences to access and use these video technologies?
- Are the video programs engaging, interesting, clear, and persuasive?

As in all forms of organizational communication, strategic organizational communicators must design video programs with target audiences in mind. Messages conveyed on videos must be clear, relevant, interesting, and compelling. Video equipment also must be easily accessible to users and easy for organizational participants to operate.

The effectiveness of video programs as forms of organizational communication is also dependent largely on the *quality* of media production. How good are the production values of the video programs, including the use of interesting and relevant visuals, clear and compelling sound, and editing that captures and keeps audience attention? High quality video production can be time consuming and expensive. Keeping organizational video programs up-to-date is also a challenge, since many things change in organizational life. For example, a video program describing the correct operation of technical equipment can quickly become obsolete when new equipment models are introduced and adopted within organizations. There are also limited opportunities for interaction and feedback with audiences when using video programs to increase understanding and to answer any questions that might arise. That is why some organizations provide live support and feedback sessions when they show videos to answer questions and increase audience understanding.

COMPUTER MEDIA

Many organizational participants spend the majority of their time each day logged on to computer systems. Computers serve a wide range of organizational functions. Organizational participants use their computers to communicate with others via email, discussion boards, and blogs. They also use specialized software to perform complex and tedious organizational tasks, such as filling out and maintaining forms for purchasing, budgeting, and inventory control. The ability for computers to automate many of these functions has helped to improve task efficiency and effectiveness in organizations. Many organizations have developed their own **intranets**—specialized in-house computer portals that provide organization members, certain suppliers and customers, and other key constituents with access to specialized organizational information and support. Computers therefore provide organizational participants with an invaluable range of tools to support their accomplishment of critical organizational activities.

Company Websites

Most organizations use company websites as a primary channel for communicating with their internal employees and customers. Typically, company websites provide information about the organizational mission, goals, history, products, and personnel. Such websites may also provide customers with information about products and services and organization members with information about organizational activities, processes, and regulations. Well-designed websites can be effective channels for organizational communication. However, many organizational websites are not well designed or easy to navigate. In addition, the language used on some websites is difficult to understand. When creating organizational websites, strategic communicators must take into account these and other important website features.

Several web-based communication theorists have recommended the use of **message chunking**—providing information in short bulleted sections surrounded by white space—as a strategy for increasing the understandability of information on websites and minimizing information overload for users. The best way to determine whether websites are meeting the needs of organizational users is to conduct **usability studies** on the websites. Usability studies involve observing typical users navigating the website, asking them to find information on the website, and asking them questions about what they like and don't like about the website. Usability studies help to promote **user-centered**

design that can guide the development of websites that meet user needs and abilities.

There are a number of established strategies for designing the presentation of information on websites so the information can be easily understood. Computer usability theorist Jakob Nielson (1999) makes the following suggestions for writing for the web:

- Be succinct: write no more than 50% of the text you would normally have used in a hardcopy print publication.
- Write for **scannability** (text that is chunked for easy skimming): don't ask users to read long continuous blocks of text.
- Use **hypertext** (text displayed with references, or hyperlinks, to other text that the reader can immediately access) to split long information into multiple pages.

How effective is your school's website at providing you with information? Is it easy to read and understand? Is it interesting and engaging? How might the website be improved?

Special Issues Related to Organizational Computing

Modern organizational computing is a complex technological process that demands specialized knowledge. A great deal of time and energy is spent in many organizations on purchasing the best computer equipment to meet organizational needs. Care must also be taken to design appropriate and usable software to address specific organizational tasks (such as purchasing, accounting, budgeting, and ordering functions).

As computer technologies have advanced and older equipment and programs have become obsolete, it has become necessary to introduce new equipment and software into organizations on a regular basis. It is crucial to provide computer training for organizational participants so they can use computer systems and software correctly. Specialized technical staff members are also often needed to maintain, install, repair, and upgrade computer systems. Technical staff members must be able to communicate well with a broad range of computer users to help these users debug the different problems they encounter when using computers and to help these users learn how to use their computers effectively. It is often a complex process for organizations and organizational participants to keep up with the advances in computer technologies.

Computer systems are designed to provide organizational participants with sophisticated technical tools to help them quickly access information, accomplish organizational tasks, and enable electronic communication. However, computers are also a source of problems in organizational life. For example, computer systems are not always used in the ways that organization leaders wish for them to be used. In some organizations, workers spend a great deal of time engaging in non-work-related activities via computer, such as exchanging personal email with family and friends, watching YouTube videos, and shopping online. In some cases, workers spend more time and effort on these non-work-related activities than they do using their computers to work on organizational business. This has become a growing problem in many organizations.

Some workers also use their office computers to communicate inappropriately with others via computer. In fact, there have been growing numbers of violations of communication ethics and etiquette with the use of computers in modern organizational life. Worse, some organizational participants share and download inappropriate and even illegal materials via their office computers. There have also been serious incidents reported where organizational participants have used their computers to send intimidating and manipulating messages to others, sometimes referred to as **cyber bullying**.

Do you know what all of these computer risks are?

Meanwhile, computer **hackers** have breached the security of organizational computer systems, including government computer systems, to access and steal proprietary information. Malicious computer programs (**malware** and **spyware**) and viruses have been introduced into organizational computers to infect computer systems and to spy on the activities and private information of computer users. Scam artists have been using computers to trick computer users into buying false and sometimes dangerous products and services online. There is definitely a darker side to computer use in modern organizational life that has challenged the ethics of appropriate organizational communication.

Computer Etiquette and Security

It has become increasingly important for organizations to provide computer and email protocol training for organization members to teach **computer etiquette** for users. These training programs recommend the appropriate use of email, including appropriate uses of language and images, tactful decision making about whom to copy messages to, and acceptable topics for electronic communication. Moreover, computer training programs can help organization members develop **computer literacy**, so they can evaluate the credibility of information obtained via computer, avoid malicious computer infections and computer scams, and effectively interpret information obtained online.

Increasingly, modern organizations are employing computer surveillance services and technologies to help maintain **computer security**. Surveillance systems are used to track the use of computer systems by organizational participants, a process that has become known as **panopticon** (Botan, 1996; Taekke, 2011). These computer surveillance activities have been justified as a way to protect organizations from illegal uses of their computer systems, but others have been concerned about the growth in organizational computer panopticon as an invasion of individual privacy (Botan, 1996). However, there are compelling needs in organizational life for maintaining computer security to promote information confidentiality, integrity, availability and authenticity. Effective computer security systems do the following:

- They help to preserve **information confidentiality** to prevent disclosure of organizational information to unauthorized individuals.

- They maintain **information integrity** to make sure that organizational data cannot be undetectably modified.
- They preserve **information availability** for users by making sure that systems are not shut down due to unforeseen or malicious events.
- They ensure **information authenticity** to make sure that all computer-based transactions are genuine and not fraudulent.

Many organizational participants fail to recognize that their online computer activities can be monitored by their organizations with the use of computer surveillance systems. They often engage in communication activities online, such as visiting inappropriate websites, sending personal email, and representing their organizations in an unfavorable light, that they would not like their supervisors to know about. Online surveillance can readily detect these computer-based communication infractions, which can lead to serious problems for organization members who use their computers inappropriately. Electronic surveillance can also result in reduced trust between organization members and organizational leadership. The clear lesson here for strategic organizational communicators is to be judicious about their use of organizational computers.

Social Media

In recent years, many organizations have begun to deliver written messages via **social media** (such as Facebook and Twitter) to provide organizational participants with organizational updates, invitations, and instructions. Social media have become increasingly popular and trusted sources of information for many people because of the similarities and shared interests between members of these social networks. Yet, it is important to determine whether the intended audiences for key messages are regular social network users and are likely to have easy access to these media programs. Do they use computers for business purposes outside of the office? Are these social media networks the channels of communication that they want to use to access official organizational information?

Similarly, **blogs** have become popular sources for information in organizational life. Blogs are websites that display linked user commentaries (such as Twitter), descriptions of events, or other material, such as videos online. Specialized blogs examine organizational activities, political events, and other public issues, providing organizational participants with access to a wide range of relevant information. However, care must be taken to carefully assess the accuracy of information accessed on blogs since the sources of information presented may have hidden agendas or limited expertise about the subjects they are writing about.

MOBILE MEDIA

As we discussed earlier in the chapter, with advances in mobile communication technologies, it has become easier for organizational participants to access and use relevant communication media wherever they may be. For example, cell phones have liberated organization members from their dependence on landlines located in their homes and offices. They can reach others and others can reach them no matter where they travel, as long as they have their cell phones with them. Similarly, the growing use of networked laptops, netbooks, tablets, and smartphones has enabled organizational participants to access websites, exchange email and text messages, and engage in other organizational activities wherever they go. This means that organization participants can now conduct many tasks outside of the office, beyond normal business hours, and at virtually any time and in any place.

However, mobile communication has also tended to expand the work hours for many organizational participants and increased organizational expectations about how much work they can accomplish. There has been a growing loss of privacy for many organizational participants, who can now be easily reached outside of the office. It has become increasingly challenging for modern organizational participants to maintain a balance between their work and personal lives due to increased access and demand for interaction via electronic media. Care must be taken to maximize the benefits of mobile communication, while minimizing its detriments.

MEDIA CONVERGENCE

Technological advances have also led to **media convergence**, where a number of powerful communication technologies have been miniaturized and integrated into small mobile organizational communication devices. There are now also ways to blend media used together, such as using the Internet to conduct surveys and interviews that might have been conducted in person or via telephone in the past. Modern mobile computing technologies, such as laptops, netbooks, and tablets, are being designed to integrate a broad range of computing and media activities, including audio-video playback, recording, and editing; word processing and publishing functions, phone and fax capabilities, printing capabilities, and advanced data processing. Organizational participants can carry an entire suite of organizational communication functions with them in one small advanced mobile communication device. Computer-based presentation software now allows organizational participants to make presentations at meetings that integrate projected slides of text, images, sounds, music, and video clips, providing audience members with rich multimedia messages.

This convergence of communication technologies has the potential to revolutionize organizational communication by

- increasing interaction between organizational participants,
- enabling advanced production of organizational communication media (text, audio, video, and web-based media), and
- enhancing the productivity of organization members in accomplishing important tasks.

However, like other forms of mediated organizational communication, there are challenges to the effective use of these new media devices. Organization members must be carefully trained to use these modern devices effectively and appropriately. Technical support is needed to help install, maintain, repair, and debug new communication equipment. Communication devices must also be judiciously updated and introduced to users as media changes are warranted by developing technological advances.

Organizational members must also learn that the use of new media devices does not replace the need for personal, face-to-face communication with other organizational participants. The use of new media channels is a powerful supplement to more traditional channels for organizational communication. They are not a substitute for the strategic and integrated use of multiple important channels for organizational communication. It is important for modern organizations to encourage organizational participants to use the wide range of media available to them to make sure they are connecting with everyone they need to interact with and that their messages are being paid attention to. Some organizational participants spend all their time on the computer, even communicating with coworkers down the hall via email. It might be a good idea to actually walk down the hall and say hello to these coworkers from time to time. Additionally, the use of the phone in combination with email to follow up on written messages is often an effective strategy to make sure that others have received and are acting on your electronic communication. Sometimes, the use of older media, such as written notes sent via land mail, can elicit greater attention than the use of more commonly used electronic communication channels. Combining the use of different communication media can be a very effective organizational communication strategy.

CASE STUDY

Big Brother and the Holding Company

Samantha (Sam) Jones was recently promoted to a newly created professional position, director of information security, at ABC Holding Company, a large distributed national corporate real estate management firm with headquarters in New York City and a regional West Coast office in Los Angeles. Sam had worked for ABC Holding at its corporate headquarters for the past seven years, ever since her graduation from Queens College with a bachelor's degree in information technology. During her first year at ABC Holding, she served as a computer systems installer. For the next four years, she served as a computer systems repair technician, and for the past two years, she served as the supervisor of computer system technical operations for the company. In her new job, she was charged with maintaining computer system security for the company, which included minimizing security risks to the company's computer systems, promoting appropriate use of company computer systems, and identifying and correcting any computer system and information risk problems.

This new job posed significant challenges for Sam. Although she had a good educational background in computer technology, she had minimal experience with computer systems security. She prepared for her new job challenges by gathering background information about computer security from online sources. She found particularly useful the information provided by the National Institute for Standards and Technology's (NIST) Computer Security Division website about standards, metrics, tests, and guidelines to increase secure information technology planning, implementation, management, and operation. She also consulted the website for the Information Security Forum (ISF), a global professional association that examines computer security practices. She was so impressed with the information she found on the ISF website that she joined the organization and ordered several relevant publications and related materials from the organization concerning computer security standards and practices. Based on the information she collected from her online research, she prepared a computer security plan report that outlined the recommended steps for implementing the new security plan for the company.

She arranged for a meeting with the ABC Holding corporate leadership team to present her computer security plan and to get their approval to implement it. She emailed a summary of the plan to all the meeting participants prior to the meeting to allow them to review it ahead of time. Most of the local company leaders were able to attend the meeting in person at the corporate offices. A few leaders who were out of town called in via conference call to participate, and the management team from the ABC Holding Los Angeles office participated in the meeting via a video conferencing system.

The meeting went well. Sam began by showing a short video program that she had ordered from the ISF about computer security needs and guidelines. Then she gave a digital media presentation to the assembled group describing her new computer security program, which followed ISF security guidelines. The presentation integrated text, visuals, background music, and video to illustrate her implementation strategy. Finally, she distributed print materials from the ISF, answered questions, and solicited advice from the group. She received unanimous support from the senior management team for the computer security implementation plan.

A first step in the security plan implementation was the installation of surveillance software that tracked computer usage on all of the company's computers. The software was designed to identify risky or illegal communication practices. Sam was surprised at how many computer communication risks were identified in the first week the software was in operation at the company. She found that many company computers were being used to visit risky websites and that a number of computers were infected with malware and spyware viruses that posed serious risks to the confidentiality of proprietary company information and even had the potential to shut down the company's entire computer network. Actions were taken to correct these problems. Warnings were provided to problematic computer users about the dire consequences of continued inappropriate use of company computer systems. Technical staff cleansed viruses from infected computers and updated antivirus software on company computers.

Sam arranged to have an online computer security training program installed on the company's computer server. The training program was delivered to all organization members via the company's intranet. Every organization member was required to take the training program and pass a test demonstrating his or her understanding of key computer security guidelines. Any organization member who did not pass the computer security training program test was prohibited from logging on to company computers. However, they were allowed to retake the test until they were able to pass it.

Sam arranged to have the company Internet and computer usage policy statement posted on the entry page of every company computer automatically whenever anyone logged on to one of the computers. The policy statement informed all computer users about the appropriate business use of company computers, identified strategies for maintaining password and file security, and warned users that all computer and email usage might be monitored. In addition, the policy statement clearly stated that the use of computers for sexual and any other forms of harassment, as well as for the display or transmission of sexually explicit images, messages, ethnic or racial jokes or cartoons, or anything that could be construed as harassing or disrespectful to others was strictly prohibited. It informed users about the proprietary and correct use of all software. It provided guidelines for responsible and appropriate Internet and email usage. It warned against unauthorized copying of copyrighted materials. It informed users of the company's right to monitor all Internet traffic, and retrieve and read any data composed, sent, or received through online connections and/or stored in computer systems. It advised that all users were required to take all necessary antivirus precautions and that any abuse of the computer system in violation of law or any company policy would result in strict disciplinary action. The policy statement also provided specific examples of computer activities that were prohibited. Employees were also asked in the statement to notify their immediate supervisor, the Information Security Department, or any member of company management upon learning of violations of the policy.

In addition, Sam arranged for an email reflecting company computer security guidelines to be sent out from the company president to every employee at ABC Holding. The email clearly listed the key rules and regulations for correct computer use and warned of serious consequences for those who violated any of these regulations. Employees were instructed that, after reading the email, they should respond by clicking on the "I Agree" link at the bottom of the email. This link registered the users that clicked it with the Information Security Department. Any employee who was not registered was barred from logging on to a company computer.

Furthermore, the company Internet and computer usage policy was included in the online and print versions of the ABC Holding Company handbook. Updates to the policy were designed to be provided quarterly in emails to all employees. All members of the company's information technology support staff were trained to identify any breaches in the computer usage policy when they worked on company computers as well as to help employees comply with policy guidelines. Within a few months on the job, the number of computer risks identified by the new surveillance software had decreased dramatically. There were fewer viruses detected, and there were no disruptions to computer operations.

Critical Thinking Questions

1. How effectively were different media used in this case? Give examples about the use of print media, telephonic media, video media, and computer media.
2. How effectively were the various low-tech and high-tech communication technologies used in this case? Give examples of their uses.
3. Describe the media mix described at ABC Holding in this case study. How well balanced was the use of different communication media and channels? How effectively did Sam balance the use of face-to-face and mediated communication channels?
4. Were there examples of media convergence and the use of mobile communication in this case? How could media convergence and the use of mobile organizational communication affect information security at the ABC Holding?

5. How does this case illustrate communication strategies for building technologically adaptive organizations that are prepared for the development and introduction of new communication media, technologies, and software?
6. What are the unique ethical issues illustrated in this case about the use of computer-mediated channels of communication? Evaluate the effectiveness of Sam's computer security policy statement for addressing these ethical issues. Would you have added or deleted anything to this policy statement? Why?
7. How did Sam incorporate the use of media training programs into this case? How effective do you think the media training programs described in the case would be for promoting information security?
8. Describe the use of panopticon by the ABC Holding Company in this case. Was the use of panopticon appropriate? What were the effects of panopticon for promoting information security at the company?

SUMMARY

In recent years, organizational communicators have become increasingly dependent on mediated channels of communication to accomplish their organizational goals. Such technology includes videoconferencing, computer-mediated messages and websites, and mobile devices such as smart phones. Technology-mediated communication enables users to reach many different organizational participants in a variety of locations quickly and efficiently, making it easier for them to share information and coordinate activities from anywhere in the world. This has led to the small-world phenomenon, which refers to the ability to establish and maintain relationships and close coordination with organizational partners in many different locations. However, like any type of communication, technology-mediated communication has its advantages as well as its drawbacks.

But potential benefits and potential weaknesses exist with any medium of communication, whether it be memos, notes, letters, manuals, pamphlets, newsletters, press releases, billboards, or telephone conversations. In the end, organizations must find the right media mix to maximize the advantages and minimize the disadvantages of each communication channel. Within organizations, doing so requires excellent writing and reading skills, along with a good sense of timing, design, and awareness of one's audience. The use of message-testing—presenting written texts to samples of potential readers for feedback and suggestions—is one way to help ensure that organizational messages are achieving their intended purpose.

Discussion Questions

1. Do you think that modern technology-mediated communication is really an improvement over more traditional communication channels, or are we using new technology simply because it's there and it's "new"?

2. Given that many older people have had less exposure to new technology, how should organizations deal with employees and customers who are less experienced in the skills of the digital age?

3. Is telecommuting—working from home on your computer—an organizational practice that you find to be appealing? What problems and issues might be connected to telecommuting?
4. This chapter discusses both telephone etiquette and computer messaging etiquette. Do you believe that people use their phones and email in ways that reflect good manners?
5. With principles of good communication in mind, how would you assess the websites of organizations of which you are a member? What do their websites do well, and what needs improvement?
6. The use of social media such as Facebook is always tempting for anyone who's sitting at their desk and feeling a little bored. How should organizations handle non-work-related uses of social media during the normal workday?
7. Various social critics—the late Neil Postman, for example, in his book *Technopoly*—have argued that with every new gain which comes from an advance in technology, there are also corresponding losses. With respect to the computer, what do you regard as those gains and losses?
8. Do you see a day when we will actually have a true "paperless" society—that is, a situation where organizations basically eliminate paper and do virtually everything electronically?

The Internet versus Traditional Media

OBJECTIVES

- Discuss the early history of computer systems and the purpose they served in the 1960s and 1970s
- Explain how the concept of connecting computer networks became the Internet
- Discuss the roles Vinton Cerf and Tim Berners-Lee had in creating the modern Internet
- Identify the challenges and opportunities the Internet introduced to traditional media outlets
- Explain the difference between one-to-many and many-to-many media
- Discuss how citizen journalism affects the way we receive and interpret news and information
- List four major concerns regarding the Internet
- Explain the role of social networking Web sites in society

KEY TERMS

ARPANet
citizen journalism
e-commerce
hypertext transfer protocol (HTTP)
many-to-many model
modem
network
one-to-many model
open architecture networking
packet switching
social networking
streaming
transmission-control protocol (TCP)
uniform resource locator (URL)
viral videos

INTRODUCTION

When was the last time you picked up a newspaper to check the weather forecast, purchased a CD in a music store, or sent a handwritten letter to an out-of-state friend? Chances are you have not participated in one of these activities in quite sometime. For members of generations X and Y, and even some tech savvy baby boomers, most of these tasks are performed using the Internet. With Web sites that allow users to track weather patterns and get up-to-the-minute predictions, Internet-based e-mail that lets individuals send messages to acquaintances across the country instantly, and online retailers that permit

© Monkey Business Images/Shutterstock.

How has the Internet changed the way you get information?

consumers to purchase and acquire products on demand, it's no wonder why more than 70% of the U.S. population is connected to the Internet. That means more than 212 million people, in urban and rural areas alike, are able to search for and acquire information 24 hours a day, seven days a week. Internet usage is not exclusive to populous and highly developed countries. Internet rates are even higher in smaller countries such as Iceland (86%), New Zealand (75%), and Portugal (74%).[1]

As an international juggernaut, the Internet has changed the way the world sends and receives information. It has created a subculture of interconnected individuals with fervor for around-the-clock access to news, sports, and entertainment. But does more information mean we are better informed? Does faster access to information mean more accuracy? Does more communication create a united world? While there are no definitive answers to these questions, they certainly evoke an interesting discussion. In this chapter we will touch on these subjects as well as the emergence of the Internet, how it affects other forms of mass media, and how we will adapt to a digitally dominated society in the future.

WEAVING "THE NET"

network
a number of interconnected computers that are able to share data electronically

As the Internet has become a popular medium for social networking, digital media, and shopping, it is sometimes forgotten that the Internet was created and developed mainly for strategic military purposes. In fact, the British Colossus system, one of the first computers invented, was created to crack German military codes during World War II. Similar proto-computers such as the famous Enigma machine were also used in WWII to decrypt secret messages and track the movement of troops, warships, bombers, and missiles. During the 1960s and 1970s, the United States military started to realize the full potential of computer systems by connecting each unit together through a system called a network. A **network** is a number of interconnected computers that are able to share data electronically. The AUTODIN I, a defense command-and-control system, was one of the first computer networks created. Like most networks of its time, the AUTODIN I was a special-purpose system that was created with very clear strategic goals in mind.

© markrhiggins/Shutterstock.

The Enigma machine helped decrypt secret messages and track troops during World War II.

The Primary Purpose

The Internet as we know it today was preceded by one of the first general purpose networks called the ARPANet, which was created in 1969 by the Advanced Research Projects Agency (ARPA) of the U.S. Department of Defense. The **ARPANET** was a network that connected computers at government-supported research sites, such as universities and government laboratories and allowed information and computational resources to be shared. A group of ARPA scientists invented the basic packet switching technology that is still one of the main pillars of the Internet. **Packet switching** takes large chunks of computer data and breaks them up into smaller, more manageable pieces, or packets, that can move through any open circuit to a specific destination. Once the packets

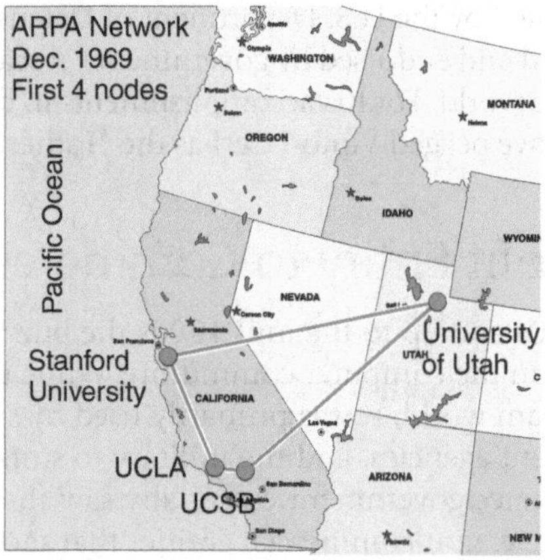

Figure 12.1
The first four nodes of the ARPA Network connected Stanford University, University of California Los Angeles, University of California Santa Barbara, and University of Utah

ARPANet
a network that connected computers at government-supported research sites, such as universities and government laboratories and allowed information and computational resources to be shared

packet switching
a form of technology that takes large chunks of computer data and breaks them up into smaller, more manageable pieces, or packets, that can move through any open circuit to a specific destination

modem
a device that allows computers to "talk" and exchange data by using existing telephone networks

open architecture networking
a process in which networks with fixed standard interfaces would be interconnected by open "gateways"

reach the destination, the pieces are reassembled into readable data. Because packet switching does not require a single dedicated circuit between each pair of computers for communication, through the use of a **modem,** computers can "talk" and exchange data by using existing telephone networks.

During the 1970s the ARPA, later renamed the Defense Advanced Research Project Agency (DARPA), investigated other methods of connecting computer systems such as satellite-based and ground-based packet networks.[2] The satellite-based packet networks allowed the United States to connect with several European countries and other remote regions, while the ground-based packet radio network allowed computers to connect to mobile terminals. Soon it was clear that in order to connect to the greatest amount of systems in the most efficient ways, the networks would need to be connected to one another. Thus, the concept of the Internet was born.

The idea of the Internet was embraced by the DARPA. They established a program called Internetting, which was based on the concept of **open architecture networking.** In open architecture networking, networks with fixed standard interfaces would be interconnected by open "gateways." However, the concept was easier on paper than in practice. In order for the system to work, new protocol and system architecture had to be designed and developed. In 1974, a Los Angeles-raised mathematician Vinton Cerf from Stanford University in California collaborated with the DARPA on a report that established the proper protocol and system architecture for this type of networking—namely the **transmission-control protocol (TCP)**—which allowed computers to communicate efficiently and consequently be joined in a coherent network of servers. The TCP also included the Internet protocol (IP), which was a global addressing device that permitted routers to transmit data packets to their end user. By the early 1980s this system of open architecture

Vinton Cerf is considered by many to be the Father of the Internet.

transmission-control protocol (TCP)
an official procedure, which allowed computers to communicate efficiently and consequently be joined in a coherent network of servers

networking was adopted by the U.S. Department of Defense, and later the TCP/IP system was accepted and endorsed by governments, researchers, and businessman from around the world. For his accomplishments in constructing the TCP/IP approach, many have pegged Vinton Cerf as the "Father of the Internet."[3]

From Non-Profit Entity to Commercial Behemoth

Throughout the 1980s and up to the mid-1990s the buzz surrounding the Internet stayed mainly in the computer community. While the system was accessible to the mainstream world, it was primarily used by scientists, researchers, academics, government agencies, and the military to store and exchange data. In fact, the United States government essentially saw the ARPANet, and then the Internet, as strategic, non-commercial entities that should be regulated and managed by non-profit agencies. To that effect, in 1988 the U.S. Department of Defense (DoD) founded the Internet Assigned Numbers Authority (IANA), a non-profit agency created by a contract between the ARPA and the University of Southern California to administer and manage the daily operations of this incipient network. It was up to the IANA, for example, to keep a registry of addresses, servers, and top-level domains.

While still under some government control, the Internet inevitably experienced rapid commercialization. The introduction of the personal computer in the mid-1980s made mainstream citizens more comfortable with computer technology and by the end of the decade opened the door for the Internet phenomenon. One of the first commercial movements was through the connection of commercial e-mail services to the Internet. In 1988 the Corporation for National Research Initiatives connected MCI mail to the Internet. It was the first connection with a provider outside of the research community. By 1993, federal legislations opened up space in government-sponsored networks for commercial users. The transition from a researched-based Internet to a commercial-based Internet was eased by the introduction of a computer program known as a browser. Tim Berner-Lee, an Oxford-educated Englishmen who worked for the European Organization of Nuclear Research (CERN), created one of the first Internet browsers known as the World Wide Web (WWW). The WWW was a virtual "space" in which scientists could store information that could be retrieved by colleagues throughout the world. In addition, Berners-Lee also invented **Hypertext Transfer Protocol (HTTP)**, the "language" computers would use to send and receive documents over the Internet. What's more, Berners-Lee also created the **Uniform Resource Locator (URL)** address system to store and locate information. Berners-Lee's achievements gave the world their first glimpse of the modern Internet and ignited a commercial explosion.

hypertext transfer protocol (HTTP)
the "language" computers use to send and receive documents over the Internet

uniform resource locator (URL)
an address system to store and locate information

Piggybacking on the access protocols and standards developed by Berners-Lee, researchers at the University of Illinois created a user-friendly browser called Mosaic. The browser allowed users to point-and-click through the interface, an action previously unavailable to Internet users. In 1994, the Netscape Communications Corporation streamlined the Mosaic program and made it available for commercial use. Soon after, software titan Microsoft developed a Web browser called Internet Explorer, which was also based off of the Mosaic program. By the late 1990s there were approximately 10,000 Internet service providers in the world, with the majority located in the United States.[4] To create more efficient and profitable services many small- and moderately-sized providers merged and created industry leaders such as America Online, Inc. (AOL) and Yahoo. With a virtually endless arena in which to sell advertising space, Internet providers saw sky rocketing advertising revenues into the year 2000. Businesses with Internet connections saw sales and consumer traffic increase at an exponential rate. By the turn of the century more than ten million businesses and government agencies had Web sites. Today that number has increased to more than 70 million active Web sites and 175 million hostnames.[5]

© Feverpitch/Shutterstock.

The Internet is where people go now to get information.

The Internet phenomenon hit its peak with the introduction of search technology. Search engines such as Google took the vast amount of information on the Web and organized it based on keywords and Web hits. So something that once served as a carrying case for the world's information was now a virtual answer machine. The Internet is often the place people look for answers. What's the best driving route to take to work? What year was *War and Peace* first published? What is the president's position on immigration? With a few clicks of a mouse this information can be displayed in front of us almost instantly, a process unmatched by any other form of media. So how does the Internet affect other types of media like books, radio, newspapers, and television? And how does using the Internet as a primary source of information affect society? We will discuss these topics in the following sections.

CONSEQUENCES TO OTHER MASS MEDIA

What are the implications of this Internet revolution, and in what way does it affect traditional mass media operations? In previous sections of this book, we have examined how digital production and distribution are changing the media. In fact, digital production and distribution of mass media content have become the cornerstones of the whole industry. Nowadays, most, if not all, media outlets participate in some type of digital distribution. While digital media enables traditional media sources to reach a larger audience and expand business, the transition can stir up uncharted issues.

For example, from November 2007 to February 2008 members of the Writer's Guild of America (WGA), a union that represents writers working for the entertainment industry, battled with TV and movie producers for more control of media content produced and distributed electronically. After a 14-week standoff an agreement was reached that gave writers an increase in the residual rate for all movies and TV shows sold online and assured the union's authority over content created specifically for the Internet.[6] However, the writers' strike was about much more than being paid for media content streamed online—it was about how to adapt to this new electronic reality, and how writers and other content producers can keep control of (and be compensated for) the products they create for a media market that is in a huge state of flux. The strike also highlighted the fact that electronic distribution of entertainment will come to play a major role in the way we receive our favorite music, movies, news, and TV shows.

Let's now see in more detail some of the challenges and opportunities posed by the Internet to traditional media.

© Zsolt Nyulaszi/Shutterstock.

Readers still enjoy the feel of a real book in today's digital world.

Books

Book publishing has been big business for over five hundred years. From the Gutenberg Bible to the Harry Potter series, readers have long enjoyed the feel of soft paper on their fingertips as they flip through pages and the sense of accomplishment they acquire when the back cover is finally closed. It's these tangible aspects of a printed book that have kept book publishers from surrendering to the digital era completely. With their cumbersome size and expensive production cost, you would think that books would be the first form of traditional media to go completely digital, however printed books still account for the majority of revenue acquired by book publishers. Since the early 90s, companies have tried to market digital readers to consumers. Companies such as Adobe, Microsoft, Palm, and Franklin Electronic Publishers have tried to sell digital readers that mock the look of an actual book and give consumers the ability to purchase thousands of titles online, but the public didn't bite. In 2002, less than 500,000 electronic books were sold in the United States, far less than the 1.5 billion printed books sold in that same year.[7] However, new products and initiatives have helped push books in the digital direction.

While recreational readers are still more likely to purchase the latest title from Tom Clancy in hard cover than as an e-book, digital books are becoming extremely useful for researchers and students. Initiatives like The Internet Public Library and Project Gutenberg have brought all the information that was once only available in a bound book to the computer screen. Project Gutenberg is the first and single largest collection of free electronic books. Hundreds of volunteers work to convert printed works from the public domain into digital form and make them available online.[8] This process eliminates the need to go to a library and search through the stacks for classic works such as Shakespeare's *The Comedy of Errors.* However, most online libraries only have a fraction of published works available, requiring people to log off the Internet and flip through some pages.

Bringing works from the past into the future may be a slow-moving process, but the book publishing industry is not shying away from the electronic revolution. Kindle, an electronic reading device created by Amazon, is the latest gadget to attempt to convert print book readers to e-book readers. With sales toping 240,000 units in 2008, the moderate success of the product is a sign that hard covers and paperbacks may make a slow retreat in the future.

Radio

Since the emergence of companies like XM Satellite and Sirius Satellite Radio, it has been well publicized that standard AM/FM radio stations have been losing listeners to popular satellite radio stations, but traditional radio has also been losing listeners to Internet music and broadcasting sites. While 90% of people in the United States still listen to traditional radio, even avid listeners spend 14% less time listening to their radios than they

Books Gone Cellular

In 2007, five out of the ten best-selling books in Japan were "cell phone novels"—books written by authors on their mobile phones as text messages and uploaded, one message at a time, to Web sites and blogs. The way they were produced and delivered is not the only different thing about these "text-messaging books." Most of them were written by young, female, first time authors, as they rode the subway to school or work, or killed time between other activities. The serialized character of these novels, partial chapters, or short sentences is uploaded as they become available. The completed book is then published in hard or soft cover. The characters and plot development of these novels are more like soap operas and Harlequin novels than complex, rich literary achievements, but popular just the same.[9]

have in previous decades.[10] The cause of radio's diminishing audiences is a combination of listeners choosing to replace traditional broadcasting programs with those found on the Internet and seeking new music from digital-music Web sites.

Since the late 90s, **podcasting** has become a popular form of Internet broadcasting. The phrase podcasting comes from a combination of *iPod* and *broadcasting,* as many podcast files are downloaded onto portable digital music players such as iPods. Although the essence of podcasts existed before Apple released the iPod in 2001, the medium was not as popular before that time.[11] Podcast programs can range in format from that of a traditional radio program featuring a well-known figure to a simple rant expelled by an ordinary person. Through this medium virtually any person with a computer and webcam or microphone has the ability to create and share their thoughts, opinions, or music tastes with the entire Internet community.

Since the Internet has the ability reach farther than radio waves, many radio stations have opted to stream their programs through a station-sponsored Web site in addition to the airwaves. **Streaming** is a method of relaying video or audio material over the Internet. Streaming corporate radio programs online has become a popular choice for many listeners. A 2007 study by Credit Suisse evaluated the performance of the twelve leading Web-radio sites and found that the amount of Internet radio listeners increased by 33.5% since the previous year.[12] These streamed programs not only allow radio station to cultivate an audience outside of their local listeners, it keeps them competitive in a changing market. The inclusion of the Internet is vital to radio's survival as the amount of money spent by corporations on online advertising is expected to surpass the amount spent on radio advertising in the next year.[13]

streaming
a method of relaying video or audio material over the Internet

In order to stay relevant in the digital world it seems that the radio industry needs to change some of its signature characteristics—like being heard but not seen. Taking a cue from popular radio hosts like Howard Stern, Don Imus, and Danny Bonaduce, many radio programs set up webcams in the studio and broadcast video on the Internet. This new format combines the Internet's innovative form of communications with radio's traditional strength of using on-air personalities and local flavor to interest listener.[14] Whether or not this new format can still be considered "radio" is up for debate, nevertheless the medium has accepted that traditional radio needs to change and adapt in order to survive in the twenty-first century.

Newspapers

The Internet and the digital revolution have profoundly affected the way newspapers work. On the editorial side, online media affects the way writers and editors gather information and designers layout and produce their pages. On the business side, executives must change the way advertising space is sold, subscriptions are marketed, and circulation numbers are measured to adapt to the Internet era. While these changes may deviate from the traditional methods used in newspaper work, they often serve as an opportunity to increase readership. Still, the Internet poses some enormous challenges to other aspects of the newspaper industry, forcing many newspapers to maintain a shaky balance between print and digital mediums.

During a six-month period in 2007, the *Denver Post* and the *Rocky Mountain News*, popular regional daily papers based in Colorado, saw their paid circulation numbers drop an astounding 12%. The dramatic drop puzzled newspaper executives, as the periodical's level of quality and trustworthiness had not changed. What did change, however, was the character of the newspaper business.[15] The two respected Colorado papers are not alone. As more and more readers migrate to the online versions of their favorite newspapers, dailies from coast to coast are struggling to maintain their paid circulation numbers. Lost circulation numbers means fewer paid advertisers, and that is a lethal combination that translates to lost revenue. While each of the top fifty most read newspapers in the United States offer an online version, the print versions of newspapers are still viewed as the mainstay of the industry.[16] Realizing the obvious impact of the Internet, the Audit Bureau of Circulations (ABC), an industry non-profit that computes newspapers' circulation, measured the reach of newspapers by combining both paid circulation and Web site readership for the first time in 2007. This new rating system legitimized online versions of newspapers and gave industry executives and advertisers a more accurate look at a changing market.

Not only do online versions offer newspaper companies the ability to update information twenty-four hours a day, fill a virtually unlimited amount of ad space, and save money on print production and delivery costs, it also allows the publication to reach a wider audience. A man from Topeka, Kansas can read the Miami Herald and a woman in New York City can read the Birmingham News. But with this increased reach, comes an increase in competition. Because the Internet has created an open market for online news outlets, newspapers have significantly expanded their local coverage and gone out of their way to convince readers (online or otherwise) that they remain an essential local news delivery outlet that is tailored to the local reader's needs. One of the newspaper industries' main tasks, right now, is to nurture a new generation of faithful readers who will trust, rely on, and stay loyal to their local dailies even as their digital options expand.

Will printed newspapers soon become a thing of the past?

"Innovate or become extinct" has become the mantra for newspapers large and small. The addition of online versions has kept newspapers alive for now, but one must wonder what the future holds. The young, highly sought after audience that online versions attract, are luring advertisers away from print versions.[17] This natural progress may cause newspaper companies to abandon what was once their bread and butter and go completely digital.

Television

Digital video production and editing, high definition television, digital cable, satellite delivery, and digital video recording devices such as TiVo are not the only technological advancements that are affecting the television industry. As we discussed earlier, the Hollywood writers' strike shed some light on how important digital delivery (and control of the delivery) has become to television and cable.

A new generation of mass media consumers, who have grown up with the Internet, seems to have no problems conforming to this new reality, watching shows on their laptops, desktops, phones, PDAs, and iPods; legally or illegally downloading movies, shows, and clips on the Internet; or streaming podcasts, radio shows, or even live TV as soon as they become available. However, as broadcast and cable channels watch their audiences shrink, they worry that Internet delivery might be threatening their very survival. A study in England found that young adults, ages 16–25, spend on average 40% more time online than they do watching TV (19.3 hours per week online, compared to 13.5 hours watching TV). Online use also topped other forms of media such as radio (8 hours) and newspapers (5.1 hours).[18]

To keep up with the lifestyle of the cyber generation, most major networks allow viewers to stream full episodes of select programs for free. This offering has the potential to attract views that may not otherwise tune in to a particular program, but it also has the potential to pull viewers away from their TV sets and push them towards the convenience of online viewing. Networks are forced to closely monitor the ever-changing balance between TV and online viewership, as online broadcasts are less profitable than the traditional method. While some networks have trouble maintaining that balance (see

Viewers Must Flip on the TV to Get the "Gossip"

In 2008, the CW, a television network owned by CBS corp. and Warner Bros., found out just how hard it is to maintain a profitable balance between online and on-air audiences with their hit program "Gossip Girl." Originally the network offered viewers the ability to watch full episodes of the show for free via the CW's Web site. However, after the show saw its TV ratings drop 20%, network executives decided to pull the online viewing options, forcing audiences to watch the program the old fashioned way: on a television set. The decision came with a dose of irony, as the Internet is integral to the plot of the show (episodes are narrated by an anonymous blogger), and the target audience is 18–34 year olds, which is a demographic that is most comfortable watching online entertainment.[19] Executives admitted to making a risky and myopic decision, but hoped it would not alienate its key audience. To keep the Internet audience's interest, the network offered free behind-the-scenes footage and two-minute recaps on its Web site and the ability to purchase full episodes on Apple's iTunes. The removal of free online streaming may have annoyed faithful viewers, but it did not deter them, as the second session of "Gossip Girl" brought in 3.4 million viewers, giving the CW its best Monday night ratings in two years.[20]

Changing the Game for Advertisers

Big changes in mass media mean big changes in the world of advertising. The introduction of the Internet has created a new medium on which advertisers can reach potential customers. While advertisers can still follow familiar advertising methods by purchasing banner ads or commercial space online, they are also presented with new options such as search related advertising and product focused viral videos. Search related advertising gives companies the option of putting their Web site at the top of a search engine list and increases the chance that Internet users will visit the company's Web site. It is not surprising that search engine giant Google controls about 75% of all search-related Internet advertising.[21] **Viral videos,** digital videos that are passed on from user to user, have also emerged as a unique way for advertisers to reach potential customers. They even created a new marketing method called viral marketing. In 2004, Burger King created a viral video called the Subservient Chicken, which features a person dressed in a chicken suit taking commands from an off camera man. The ad was to promote the idea that you can get "Chicken the way you like it" at Burger King. More than 385 million people have viewed the ad. While this new form of advertising may be bizarre to some, they can generate $100 million to $150 million dollars a year for advertisers.[22]

viral videos
videos that are passed on from user to user

below), other networks are tipping the scale and proactively developing new methods of reaching a larger Internet audience. In 2007, ABC, CBS, NBC, and Fox all announced initiatives to make more programs and materials available online. ABC partnered with America Online (AOL) to offer full episodes via AOL; CBS launched the CBS Audience Network, which delivers content worldwide through multiple partners such as Yahoo, MSN, Comcast, and YouTube; and NBC and Fox worked together to create hulu.com, a Web site that allows viewers access to videos from more than 90 content providers.[23] These types of partnerships have allowed networks to maintain their brand and have more control over copyrighted content.

© junjie/Shutterstock.

Will the Internet surpass television as a source of entertainment programming?

For now, network television seems to be adapting well to the Internet age and succeeding in staying relevant in the industry, but there is no certainty that traditional television broadcasting can maintain that relevancy in the future. Soon, watching live television may be considered passé. Since the market is in a state of disequilibrium, it is hard to determine if and when the Internet will surpass the television as a source of entertainment programming, but television networks seem determined to evolve and adjust their business models rather than become obsolete.[24]

ONE-TO-MANY, MANY-TO-MANY

one-to-many model
a model in which a centralized cluster of producers tightly controls the content that is created and distributed to consumers

many-to-many model
a model in which information flows in a decentralized way

As we have discussed, in some ways the Internet and other forms of mass media work hand-and-hand: you can stream radio through a Web site, read a book online, or watch a network news program via an online media player. But when Web pages break away from traditional media sources the connection is lost and concerns over content arise. As we saw in previous chapters, a communications model in which a centralized cluster of producers tightly controls the content that is created and distributed to consumers characterizes traditional mass media. This communication system has been called a **one-to-many model.** However, the Internet has created a **many-to-many model** in which information flows in a much more decentralized way. Content, in the form of Web sites, search engines, blogs, discussion groups, multiplayer universes, and

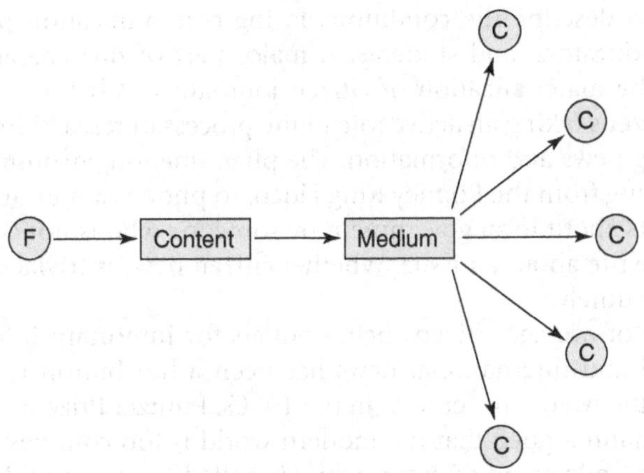

Figure 12.2
Traditional Mass Media Model (One-to-Many)

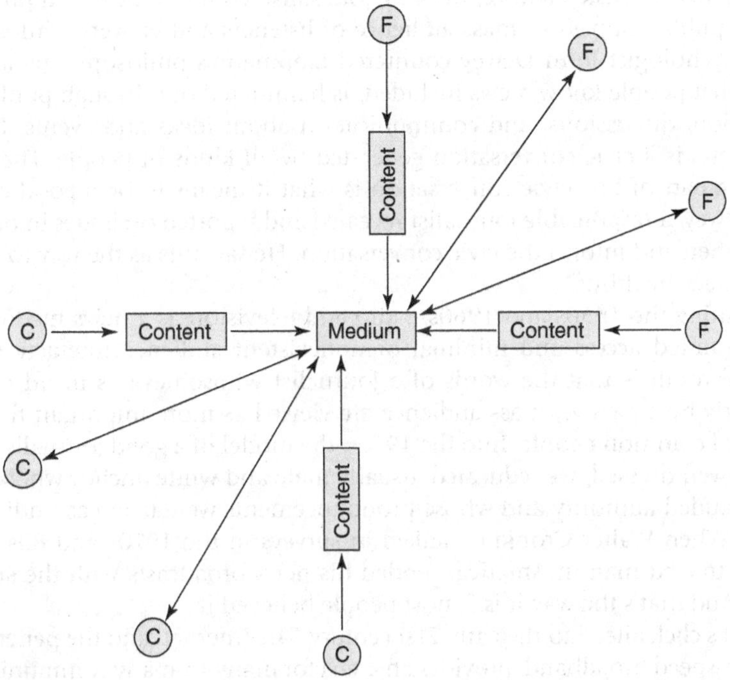

Figure 12.3
Internet Mass Media Model (Many-to-Many)

even e-mail is easily created by millions of users and dispersed to millions of other users, without any need for centralization or control. Technology has allowed for the extreme democratization of information and turned everyone with access to a computer and basic content-production skills into a potential mass media mogul and raises concerns about citizen journalism.[25]

Citizen Journalism

Currently, the media ecosystem is as stressed as our natural environment as it heads toward the second decade of the 21st century. "Media climate change"

citizen journalism
the act of citizens taking an active role in the process of researching, collecting, and reporting news and information

is one way to describe the conditions facing communication professionals, journalists, educators, and students. A major part of this change can be attributed to the materialization of citizen journalism. **Citizen journalism** is the act of citizens taking an active role in the process of researching, collecting, and reporting news and information. The phenomenon encompasses "news" features ranging from the Rodney King video, to phone cam photos of celebrities, to reports about local government by someone who is not a reporter, but is moved to write about an issue. Whether citizen news is trivial or tragic, it is typically very timely.

The idea of average citizens being outlets for important information regarding local and international news has been a hot button issue since the early part of the twentieth century. In the 1920s, Pulitzer Prize winning author Walter Lippmann argued that the modern world is too complex for the average citizen to understand without help. He called for a "journalistic elite" to analyze complex issues facing the nation and boil down complexity for the common person. He felt that the news is so important to our democracy that only a special trusted source, the elite journalist, could frame it and present it to the public—a passive mass audience of listeners and viewers. Philosopher and psychologist John Dewey countered Lippmann's philosophy by arguing that what people know, news included, is hammered out through public participation, discussions, and communication about ideas and events. He felt that news is a civic conversation generated by all kinds of people. Therefore, being a part of this civic conversation is what it means to be a good citizen. For Dewey, a responsible journalist revealed and reported on issues in order to strengthen and inform the civic conversation. He saw this as the way to keep a democracy healthy.[26]

During the 1950s and 1960s, radio and television as a news medium offered limited access and minimal or nonexistent audience interaction. The natural result is that the words of a journalist whose news is heard or seen regularly by a passive, mass audience are viewed as more important than the views of common people. Into the 1970s, the model of a good journalist was a sober, well-dressed, welleducated, usually male and white anchor whose presence exuded authority and whose pronouncements were taken as undisputed truth. When Walter Cronkite, ranked in surveys in the 1970s and 80s as the "most trusted man in America," ended his news broadcasts with the sign-off line, "And that's the way it is," most people believed it.

Let's click ahead to the early 21st century. The Internet, and the penetration of high-speed broadband, provides an arena for many-to-many communication media. Today, being connected in the developed world allows inexpensive public conversation between everyone. With very few barriers, more people have a chance to be heard and get their ideas into the global conversation, including the news. Though Walter Lippmann successfully promoted his model of the journalist as an elite news provider, the model contained the seeds of its own demise. Becoming part of an elite brings with it pressure to serve those in power. The journalist gets distanced from the public he or she is supposed to serve.

In 2000, Christopher Locke, Rick Levine, Doc Searls, and David Weinberger put the Cluetrain Manifesto online. It was signed by thousands of people and became the best-selling business book of 2001. Ironically, the entire text was available for free, online. They opened the Cluetrain Manifesto, with these words, "A powerful global conversation has begun. Through the Internet, people are discovering and inventing new ways to share relevant knowledge with blinding speed."[27] Similarly, knowledge-sharing Web sites such as Wikipedia, established in 2001, allow any person to share their expertise in various subjects and basically create an online database for the world's knowledge.

As the 21st century opens, there are tools to talk to one another live, forums for debate, and video-casting tools, podcasts, and audio, video, and text blogs that maintain an open global dialog. These are some of the many-to-many communication tools available to everyone—school children, soccer moms, and senior citizens—not just corporate news outlets. But eliminating the corporations from the news delivery process also eliminates accountability. What stops a teenage blogger from spreading a nasty rumor about a celebrity or a World War II enthusiast from unintentionally providing false information on a knowledge-sharing Web site? These types of issues fuel many of the concerns and controversies surrounding the Internet.

CONTROVERSY AND CONCERNS

The Internet's ability to reach a wide audience and that audience's ability to create, change, and access its contents can create many concerns. While the severity of these concerns is gauged by personal opinion, they are still issues that affect all Internet users. Let's take a closer look at some of these concerns.

Credibility

With the wealth of information available on the Internet it is hard to distinguish facts from fiction. Putting information on Web pages is relatively cheap, easy, and unmonitored, and there is no authorized authorities to remove false information. This forces Internet users to determine legitimacy on their own. Is a blog a good place to find information about the government's role in a foreign conflict? Is a knowledge-sharing Web site a good source for a research paper? Since reliability is a subjective term, determining what is a reliable source and what is not can create gray areas. Typically a domain type of .edu or .gov indicates that there is some content supervision by a respected institution, however there is no guarantee. Many educational institutions, as well as business, have created their own criteria for evaluating online sources. This is an attempt to take advantage of the easily accessible knowledge on the Internet without sacrificing the quality of information.

Table 12.1 Domain Types and Their Meanings

Domain Type	What It Means
.com	a company, commercial business, or organization
.edu	an academic institution, such as a college or university
.int	an international organization
.gov	a non-military government entity, such as state park
.mil	a military organization
.net	other organizations: nonprofit, nonacademic
.uk, .au, ca, jp, etc.	country codes indicating servers found in other countries

Copyright Infringement

Napster, the pioneer of digital music, was also the pioneer of copyright infringement laws involving the Internet. As a Web site that allowed users to exchange digital music files for free, Napster and its founder Shawn Fanning came under fire after record companies and recording artists claimed the Web site was illegally distributing copyrighted materials. Do to a lawsuit filed by the Recording Industry Association of America against Napster, the Web site eventually had to convert to a paid subscription format.[28]

More recently YouTube, a video sharing Web site, has been at the forefront of the copyright controversy. YouTube regularly removes a large amount of material that infringes copyright, but because Internet users mostly control the site, many copyrighted videos still manage to sneak through. Hollywood has a love-hate relationship with YouTube: marketers love it, legal staffs hate it. A media organization may have a relationship with YouTube in which it is promoting its own content while at the same time going after infringers posting material without its consent.[29]

Some critics argue that media companies are having such a hard time with the digital age because the decentralized, tough-to-control character of the Internet has threatened the well established, commercially driven media model. Others say that an intense emphasis on short-term profits has blinded media companies to the long-term (positive) effects the Internet might bring. Media companies, on the other hand, counter argue that the commercial, private model that we have come to know and cherish is what allows for creativity and innovation to thrive. If movie, TV, and music studios are not collecting the profits, how can they keep financing expensive movies, shows, and other media products? If artists, writers, directors, and stars are not being paid for what they do, what incentive will they have to create?

It can be said that when it comes to the Internet, media companies want to "have it both ways"—while they are not shy to use the free-for-all, chaotic character of the Internet to generate buzz and hype and to freely promote their movies, shows, records, and stars, conglomerates become eager to draw a line when they sense that this "free publicity" might be eating into their profits.

Cybercrime

The Internet offers a new gateway for criminal activity. **Cybercrimes,** crimes committed through the use of digital technology, can range from selling illegal prescription drugs to identity theft. Now, criminals no longer have to stand in dark alleyways to solicit customers, they can do it anonymously from a computer. As of 2005, the U.S. Drug Enforcement Administration (DEA) has investigated 236 cases of illegal drug trafficking on the Internet and seized more than $14 million in cash.[30] Identity theft is also a crime that has been accelerated by the Internet. In 2003, the U.S. Federal Trade Commission released the first national survey on identity theft. The report estimated that 3.3 million Americans had their identities fraudulently used to open financial accounts such as bank accounts and credit cards. The crimes caused a loss of $32.9 billion to businesses and $3.8 billion to individuals.[31] These types of crimes generate concern over what information is safe to offer on the Internet. It also forces Internet users to decide between the convenience of storing personal information online and the security of keeping your identity safe.

Internet Addiction

It may seem bizarre, but it is certainly not farfetched to claim that many people struggle to step away from their computer screens. In South Korea, two-thirds of the population is on the Internet, and most of them have fast broadband connections, making South Korea one of the most wired countries in the world. Consequently, it is also a country with the highest rates of Internet addiction.[32]

In November 2007, a story in the *New York Times* reported on the popularity of Internet "rehab centers" in South Korea. These rehab centers receive mostly teenage boys whose parents worry that the long hours spent by their children online have begun to have serious negative effects on their daily activities and school work, not to mention their social lives and even their health.[33]

© iofoto/Shutterstock.

Are you constantly connected to your PDA?

Internet addiction does not only affect teenagers. Since the introduction of personal digital assistants (PDA) and portable browsers such as the BlackBerry and iPhone, young professionals have problems stepping away from the Internet and resisting the need to continuously check e-mail. The MIT Sloan School of Management conducted a study that showed 90% of participants felt some degree of compulsion in their BlackBerry usage.[34] This type of compulsion can lead to increased stress and anxiety at work and at home. While one of the many advantages to the Internet is that it helps us stay connected to friends, work, and various other entities, we have to wonder, is that always a good thing?

Overall many critics of the Internet are concerned about a potential "dumbing down" effect, in which new generations of users might abandon more rigorous entertainment or research procedures in favor of fast, superficial, pre-digested content. Defenders of the Internet are quick to point out that some of those same criticisms were raised when new media such as television or comic books came about. They note that, historically, whenever a new mass medium surfaces, there is always a period of confusion and adjustment, as society and traditional media struggle to understand it and adapt to the new reality. Furthermore, some critics contend that in essence, the Internet is only a neutral new delivery system, and that it will be up to society and all of us to determine how this new technology is used.

SOCIAL ASPECT OF THE INTERNET

While issues and concerns may circulate about the positive and negative effects the Internet has on mass media and society, there is no denying that the Internet has brought the world closer together and created its own unique culture. Social Web sites are a key part of this developing culture. If you have a personal page on a Web site like MySpace or a Facebook page you are one of millions to do so. You are also participating in a phenomenon called **social networking,** a trend in which users connect with one another based on shared interests, geography, history, or other factors. Early social network sites such as Classmates.com, created in 1995, focused on reconnecting with high school classmates. Other social networking Web sites catering to young adults soon followed.

social networking
a trend in which users connect with one another based on shared interests, geography, history, or other factors

Table 12.2 Worldwide Growth of Selected Social Networking Sites June 2007 vs. June 2006

Total Worldwide Home/Work Locations Among Internet Users Age 15+			
	Total Unique Visitors		
Social Networking Site	June 2006	June 2007	% Change
MySpace	66,401,000	114,147,000	72
Facebook	14,083,000	52,167,000	270
Hi5	18,098,000	28,174,000	56
Friendster	14,917,000	24,675,000	65
Orkut	13,588,000	24,120,000	78
Bebo	6,694,000	18,200,000	172
Tagged	1,506,000	13,167,000	774

Source: comScore World Metrix, http://www.comscore.com/press/release.asp?press=1555.

Social Networking

MySpace and Facebook are the sixth and seventh most-visited Web sites respectively, according to Alexa, an online traffic-monitoring site. Users can customize personal Web pages to their own tastes, post pictures or blogs, and chat or leave messages for friends. According to Facebook, two million people establish accounts every two weeks. In May 2007, Facebook created a utility that permits individuals to program third-party extra applications for the site. These utilities include trivia contests, video games, puzzles, and more—over 10,000 such applications existed as of December 2007. Users can also create customized groups to gather together online in support of a person, purpose, or event.

YouTube is also another form of a social networking site. Owned by Google (purchased in 2006 for $1.7 billion), YouTube permits users to upload and view videos on its site and currently hosts about 6.1 million videos. While YouTube is often used to post humorous videos and entertaining TV and movie clips, it is also used for more serious purposes. Political parties have been using YouTube to advertise their candidates. Users can see statements from the candidates and respond to them by uploading their own videos. In the fall of 2007, YouTube partnered with CNN to televise debates by the Democratic and Republican presidential hopefuls featuring questions submitted by YouTube users.[35]

Personal Privacy

The enormous popularity of social networking sites makes issues of privacy and identity protection even bigger. According to several 2007 reports from the Pew Internet and American Life Project, 64% of online teens ages 12–17 have participated in content-creating activities, like social networking sites, picture or video posting, or standalone Web sites. Although 66% of those teens do restrict access to their personal information, 32% report that strangers online in some way have contacted them. A majority use their first names on their sites (82%), their city or town (61%), and photos of themselves (69%). Twenty-nine percent include an e-mail address, and 2% post a cell phone number.[36]

A Social Networking Page Could Cost You a Job

Public information is not just a problem for teenagers; many employers report that they surf social networking pages to find details about potential employees that may not be discussed in an interview. As one career developer points out, employers are looking at more than just the resumes of their prospective employees; they are concerned about all publicly available information: "The term they've used over and over is red flags. Is there something about [a prospective employee's] lifestyle that we might find questionable or that we might find goes against the core values of our corporation?"[37]

For most users, social networking and other participatory sites are ways to keep in touch with old friends, make new ones, market goods and services, and be entertained. They allow individuals to be creative, connect with people from different cultures, and become involved with social issues. Whether the content on social networking sites is trite or imaginative, exclusive or inclusive, lackluster or inspirational it all contributes to the global conversation and brings us closer together as a world.

Throughout this chapter we have discovered how the Internet was born and developed. Overtime the simple idea of sharing information has morphed into something that has changed the world. The Internet is a piece of technology that transcends social, economical, and demographic lines and, for better or worse, changes the way people live their lives. If you don't think that the Internet greatly affects your existence, just imagine your life without it. In a few years, many people will not have to. To future generations the Internet will no longer be a revolutionary form of media; it will be as common as the radio and TV, and perhaps we will have a new form of media to which to adapt.

e-commerce
the act of buying or selling of goods or services over an electric system such as the Internet

CAREERS IN THE FIELD

As we have learned, the Internet has changed the way corporations do business and the way people work, it has also created new career choices. Electric commerce, or **e-commerce** is the buying or selling of goods or services over an electric system such as the Internet. E-commerce professionals can work in various facets of the industry. Web site design and development, content development, Web programming and application development, and database administration are just a few options. Naturally, as the Internet becomes a more popular way for consumers to purchase goods and services, the more in-demand the field becomes. E-commerce is offered as a major at many colleges, universities, and through some MBA programs.

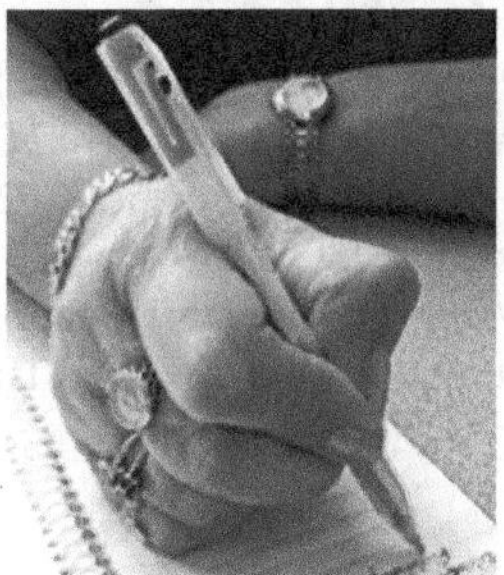

SUMMARY

- The Internet was originally developed for strategic military purposes, before the technology was made available for commercial use.
- Vinton Cerf created the transmission-control protocol (TCP), which allowed networks to connect. Tim Berners-Lee created the World Wide Web, which allowed users to browse the contents of the Internet.

- Books, radio, newspapers, and TV are all positively and negatively affected by the Internet. Each media outlet has changed its traditional business model to adapt to new technology.
- Traditional media sources are represented by the one-to-many model, which is a centralized cluster of producers that tightly control the content that is created and distributed to consumers. The Internet is represented by the many-to-many model, which involves information that flows in a much more decentralized way.
- Citizen journalism has taken the responsibility of reporting news and information away from the "journalistic elite" and placed it in the hands of the common citizen.
- Concerns regarding the Internet include content quality, copyright infringement, cybercrime, and Internet addiction.
- Social networking sites allow groups of individuals to communicate with one another and contribute to the global conversation.

DISCUSSION QUESTIONS

1. During the 1960s and 1970s who were the primary users of computer networks? What purpose did they serve?
2. Does the Internet offer more opportunities than challenges for radio? Newspapers? TV?
3. How do you personally participate in the many-to-many media model?
4. Does citizen journalism help or hinder the global conversation?
5. What other concerns does the Internet generate? What issues concern or affect you the most?

REFERENCES

"Citizen Journalism" at Online Newshour, http://www.pbs.org/newshour/bb/ media/july-dec05/citizen_11-16.html#

Thomas L. Friedman, *The World Is Flat 3.0: A Brief History of the Twenty-first Century* (2007) New York: Picador

Henry Jenkins Convergence Culture: Where Old and New Media Collide http://books.google.com/books?id=RlRVNikT0 6YC&ie=ISO-8859-1

Mark Whipple, The Dewey-Lippmann Debate Today: Communication Distortion, Reflective Agency, and Participatory Democracy. Sociological Theory. 23:2, June, 2005

NOTES

1. Nielsen/NetRatings, December 2007 Global Index Chart at http://www.netratings.com/resources .jsp?section=pr_netv&nav=1. Accessed September 10, 2008.
2. Internet. *Encyclopedia Britannica* at http://www.britannica.com/EBchecked/topic/291494/Internet. Accessed September 10, 2008.
3. "Tim Berners-Lee," *Internet Pioneers* at http://www.ibiblio.org/pioneers/lee.html. Accessed September 10, 2008.
4. Internet service provider. *Encyclopedia Britannica* at http://www.britannica.com/EBchecked/topic/746032/Internet-service-provider. Accessed September 10, 2008.
5. "August 2008 Web Service Survey," *Netcraft* at http://news.netcraft.com/archives/web_server_survey.html. Accessed September 10, 2008.

6. Rebecca Winters Keegan, "Writers Guild Strike Nears End" *Time*, February 10, 2008. Accessed September 8, 2008 at http://www.time.com/time/arts/article/0,8599,1711750,00.html?iid=sphere-inline-sidebar.
7. "E-Books, Once Upon a Future Time," *Wired* September 14, 2003 at http://www.wired.com/techbiz/media/news/2003/09/60435. Accessed September 10, 2008.
8. "Gutenberg: About," *Project Gutenberg* at http://www.gutenberg.org/wiki/Gutenberg:About. Accessed September 10, 2008.
9. Norimitsu Onishi, "Thumbs Race as Japan's Best Seller Go Cellular," *New York Times*, January 20, 2008 at http://www.nytimes.com/2008/01/20/world/asia/20japan.html. Accessed September 10, 2008.
10. Richard Siklos, "Is Radio Still Radio if There's Video?" *New York Times* February 14, 2007 at http://www.nytimes.com/2007/02/14/business/media/14radio.html. Accessed September 10, 2008.
11. Media convergence. *Encyclopedia Britannica* at http://www.britannica.com/EBchecked/topic/1425043/media-convergence. Accessed September 10, 2008.
12. Media and Publishing. *Encyclopedia Britannica* at from http://search.eb .com/eb/article-257962. Accessed September 10, 2008.
13. Catherine Holahan, "Advertising Goes Off the Radio" *Business Week* December 7, 2006 at http://www.businessweek.com/technology/content/dec2006/tc20061207_485162.htm. Accessed September 10, 2008.
14. Richard Siklos, "Is Radio Still Radio if There's Video?" *New York Times* February 14, 2007 at http://www.nytimes.com/2007/02/14/business/media/14radio.html. Accessed September 10, 2008.
15. David Milstead, "Denver papers' Circulation Falls" *Rocky Mountain News* April 28, 2008 at http://www.rockymountainnews.com/news/2008/apr/28/denver-papers-circulation-slide-continues/. Accessed September 10, 2008.
16. Richard Perez-Pena, "More Readers Trading Newspapers for Web Sites" *New York Times* November 6, 2007 at http://www.nytimes.com/2007/11/06/business/media/06adco.html?n=Top/Reference/Times%20Topics/ Organizations/A/Audit%20Bureau%20of%20Circulations. Accessed September 10, 2008.
17. Ibid.
18. "Media Literacy in Regions Revealed," *Association of Online Publishers* at http://www.ukaop.org.uk/cgi-bin/go.pl/research/article.html?uid=952. Accessed September 10, 2008.
19. Meg James, "CW to Stop Free Streaming of 'Gossip Girl' " *Los Angeles Times* April 18, 2008 at http://www.latimes.com/business/la-fi-gossip18apr18,1,1364751.story.
20. Benjamin Toff, "Gossip Girl Rating 3.4 Million Season Premiere Lifts CW to Best Monday Ever," *The Huffington Post* September 2, 2008 at http://www.huffingtonpost.com/2008/09/02/gossip-girl-ratings-34-mi_n_123337.html. Accessed September 10, 2008.
21. "Microsoft Seen Losing Ground In Next-Gen Ad Technologies" 7 February 2008. Dow Jones News Service.
22. Catherine Holahan, "The Web's Most Viral Ads," *Business Week* at http://images.businessweek.com/ss/06/07/viral_marketing/index_01.htm. Accessed September 10, 2008.
23. "In the Growing Market for Online Video, TV Networks Want a Piece of the Action" *Knowledge at Wharton* October 3, 2007 at http://knowledge.wharton.upenn.edu/article.cfm?articleid=1814. Accessed on September 10, 2008.
24. "In the Growing Market for Online Video, TV Networks Want a Piece of the Action" *Knowledge at Wharton* October 3, 2007 at http://knowledge.wharton.upenn.edu/article.cfm?articleid=1814. Accessed on September 10, 2008.
25. "Commercial Scenarios for the Web: Opportunities and Challenges" by Hoffman, Novak and Chatterjee *Journal of Computer-Mediated Communication*, Vol. 1, Issue 3, 1995.
26. Dewey (New Republic May 3, 1922) and in The Public and Its Problems. Also: The Public and Its Problems (New York: Holt, 1927; London: Allen & Unwin, 1927); republished as The Public and Its Problems: An Essay in Political Inquiry (Chicago: Gateway, 1940).
27. Levine, Locke, Searls & Weinberger *The Cluetrain Manifesto: The End of Business as Usual* (2001) at http://www.cluetrain.com/book/index.html. Accessed September 10, 2008.
28. Computers and Information Systems. *Encyclopedia Britannica* at http://search.eb.com/eb/article-215140. Accessed September 10, 2008.
29. Ben Fritz and Michael Learmonth, "Showbiz's site fright: Web seen as both a threat and a gold mine," *Variety*, March 10, 2007 at http://www.variety.com/article/VR1117960880.html?categoryid=13&cs=1. Accessed September 10, 2008.
30. "DEA Congressional Testimony" *U.S. Drug Enforcement Administration* at http://www.usdoj.gov/dea/pubs/cngrtest/ct121305.html. Accessed September 10, 2008.
31. Cybercrime. *Encyclopedia Britannica* at http://search.eb.com/eb/article-235700. Accessed September 10, 2008.
32. Caroline Gluck, "South Korea's Gaming Addicts" *BBC News* November 22, 2002 at http://news.bbc.co.uk/2/hi/asia-pacific/2499957.stm. Accessed September 10, 2008.
33. Martin Fackler, "In Korea, a Boot Camp Cure for Web Obsession" *New York Times* Nov. 18, 2007 at http://www.nytimes.com/2007/11/18/technology/18rehab.html?_r=3&scp=1&sq=korea+internet+addiction&st= nyt&oref=slogin&oref=slogin&oref=slogin. Accessed September 10, 2008.

34. Margaret Locher, "BlackBerry Addiction Starts at the Top," *PC World* March 6, 2007 at http://www.pcworld.com/article/129616/blackberry_addiction_starts_at_the_top.html. Accessed September 10, 2008.
35. "CNN, YouTube To Unveil Presidential Debate Details Thursday" by Caroline McCarthy. CNET News, June 13, 2007.
36. "Internet News Audience Highly Critical of News Organizations Views of Press Values and Performance: 1985-2007," The Pew Research Center for the People and the Press. Released August 9, 2007.
37. Alan Finder, "For Some, Online Persona Undermines a Résumé," New York Times, June 11, 2006. Accessed September 10, 2008.

Chapter 13

Journalism in the Digital Age

Lars Zahner/Shutterstock.com.

OBJECTIVES

What you will learn from this chapter:

- What is journalism in the digital age?
- Why is news important for society to function?
- How has technology changed the way news is written and produced?
- What makes news?
- How can you prepare for a career in news?

WHY JOURNALISM?

It's difficult to read a newspaper, news magazine or a news website lately without finding some kind of article or editorial that pronounces the death of journalism. Pundits and critic cite the decline of newspapers in American cities as every month brings news of news staff cutbacks or closing of newspapers or as is the case with the New Orleans Times-Picayune, a cut in how often the newspaper is published. Since 2012, the daily award-winning newspaper of New Orleans appears only 3 days per week, with a severe cut in staff.

The decline in news reading and advertising revenues has been observed for at least 40 years. Most recently, newsrooms have become less populated, with 30% fewer employees in 2013 than they had in 2000 (Pew, 2013). The Pew survey also found that TV news has also declined; sports, weather and traffic now occupy over 40% of a newscast. News stories are fewer than at any time in history, and the actual length of news stories has decreased a great deal. Time is the only weekly news magazine left standing and even it has experienced recent setbacks.

Of course, the number of readers determines how much a newspaper can charge for advertisements and ad revenues in general have been declining for both television and newspapers as readership declines. But in newsrooms across the country many people are asking "How can a major city survive without news? How can a democracy survive?" The answer is: they cannot. It is the theme of this chapter **that news is alive and well, and it isn't going away.** Whether news is printed on paper or through the Internet, we need news to survive and to operate a complex society.

BELL, CALIFORNIA: AN EXAMPLE

Bell is a town about a 15 minute drive southeast from Los Angeles with a population of approximately 35,000 according to the 2010 census. The population is 93% Hispanic, with a per capita income of $12,500. One in four adults is below the poverty line in annual income.

In 2010, a scandal brought the tiny, relatively poor town to national attention. City council members were making over $100,000 per year! The Assistant City Manager was making over $340,000 per year, a sum that a prosecutor later called "theft by paycheck". The actual beginning of the corruption in Bell was in 1988, when Town Manager Robert Rizzo was hired because he was willing to work for a smaller salary than other candidates (Farham, 2013). By 2010, his salary and benefits amounted to over 12 million dollars a year! He achieved this by buying the silence of everyone in city government; the Police Chief's yearly salary was $457,000. Of course, most of this money came from hugely inflated property taxes, questionable parking tickets and plain old fraud from concealing these huge salaries.

How could such a corrupt town continue to operate? A major reason lies in the fact that Bell had no daily newspaper of its own. There was no one connecting the dots except for whispered rumors in the streets. In 2010, two investigative reporters from the Los Angeles Times began to look into the town of Bell, because in a related investigation of another town they found that salaries for Bell officials were the highest in the nation. After their publication of the first article, arrests of the corrupt officials began to accumulate. The majority are serving long sentences for a number of convictions of corruption-related crimes including conspiracy, misappropriation of funds, and other crimes.

The case of Bell, California represents a shining example of the *watchdog* function of journalism. If no news agencies, TV stations or reporters are around to investigate corruption, gangs, bad police officers, and other social problems, what will happen to society? What if contaminated food or water threatens a population, who will warn its citizens? Pundits who say we will survive without news organizations are wrong and crusaders against injustice will always need a microphone, a press, a computer or a video camera to bring important news stories to the masses.

But how about our daily lives, when we aren't plagued by disease or victimized by corrupt officials? Why do we need news? News brings us information about science, health and technology that we wouldn't learn in our daily lives unless we are an expert in any one of these specialized fields. When natural disasters strike; tornadoes, droughts, diseases and other threats to our health or lives are on the horizon, it is journalists who warn and inform.

In terms of finances, journalists are there to bring news of changes in interest rates, new products, company mergers, minimum wage issues, the triumphs and failures of industries like fuel, transportation or medicine. What if they aren't present? More often than not, institutions decay and we all suffer.

How about politics? How will we know who or what to vote for in city, state and national elections? How will you participate in a democracy if you don't know what candidates stand for on important issues? But most important, how well will politicians serve your personal, financial, business and other needs if there is no journalism? Bell California is a telling example.

WHAT IS NEWS?

In almost every journalism textbook there are discussions of *news values* or elements that are common to stories that make news. Let's explore them in light of some of the changes in media in the digital age. What are the stories that get to the top of page 1, the first moment of a nightly newscast or the first headline on a news web page?

Everyday, in every place where news originates, there are one or more meetings (either in an office or in cyberspace) where reporters, editors, news bloggers and other professionals discuss what will be featured that day, what will be emphasized and which stories are most important. While news values themselves are not frequently discussed they are aspects of news stories that determine their importance to journalists. They are:

- **Impact**
  Impact means "How many people are affected by the story?" Generally, an outbreak of a disease like Ebola or even difficult strains of influenza which have the potential to sicken or kill thousands of people are considered more newsworthy than a traffic accident that injures two people. Even though those two lives matter, the sheer number of people affected often determines the amount of pace or time will be devoted to the story.
- **Proximity**
  Where are the people featured in or affected by a news story located? News about events unfolding near us is more important than things that happen hundreds or thousands of miles away. Stories about your town, your neighborhood or your country attract your attention more than do stories about people and events far way. But the world is shrinking in terms of how interdependent our lives are with people in other nations. Still, stories about our "turf" usually emerge as more significant in the news. There is also a dimension of "psychological proximity" in that we sometimes feel "close" to a story because people in it bear some similarity to us. An example is a story about fraternity hazing that goes national may be of interest to college students who belong to Greek organizations in a distant campus.
- **Prominence**
  In this context, prominence means that news that happens to or is made by famous people is more newsworthy than people who are not public figures. Anything that a rock star, movie star or politician does becomes major news, whether it involves an arrest, a speech or an award is news, sometimes even to the point of absurdity. In election years, a politician who teams up with an entertainment celebrity for a cause or event is guaranteed to be high up in the newspaper or web page or early in a broadcast.
- **Conflict**
  The news value of conflict means, essentially, that everyone loves to watch a good fight. The war on terror, two hip hop artists calling each other names or experts disagreeing on the cause of an economic recession all

involve some sort of conflict. Newsreaders/viewers are drawn to stories that contain some element of this value. Sometimes it's necessary to cover a town meeting where nothing really happens, no motions of importance are passed or no changes in policy are made. Then, suddenly, a council member says "The Mayor lied to us!" It is common for a reporter to lead with this conflict, even if it wasn't central to the story.

- **Novelty**
  Novelty means unusual, unexpected or weird. In fact, a syndicated column titled "News of the Weird" is featured in many weekly newspapers throughout the United States. As an old journalism proverb frames it "A headline that reads 'Dog bites man!' is not news. 'Man bites dog' IS news!" The news value of weird centers on the unexpected or unfamiliar.
- **Human Interest**
  Stories that make us smile, or bring a tear to our eye, or simply highlight the human condition are human interest stories. Stories about a cat being rescued from a tree, or about a 7-year old who wins a spelling bee or a person with an incurable disease is given a "bucket list" trip somewhere will always part of the news mosaic, perhaps because in a world full of difficulty, war and disappointment, sometime we need an emotional break.
- **News You Can Use**
  In this category are news stories that are utilitarian in that they can help us do something to improve our daily lives. A computer program that helps us count calories, a new app for our mobile phone that helps people to determine whether there is someone nearby who is looking for a romantic partner or a sidebar that recommends what to look for in a new appliance are all stories that characterize this news value that adds value.

So What?

News values are simply categories of stories that have gleaned attention for over two centuries of journalism. Awareness of them helps us understand why some stories have "legs" or ones that go one for days, weeks and sometimes months. And news values help journalists frame arguments for why a story is worth doing when newsroom time and resources are scarce.

It is important to note that often, more than one news value is present in an important story. For example, a famous TV actor is involved in a fight in a bar in a city near your home. The *combined* news values of prominence, conflict and proximity all combine to guarantee that this story will be read and viewed by many.

News Story Structures

One of the most documented aspects of how news stories are structured is the inverted pyramid with the five w's and the "h" which dictates that the *lead* or the first one or two sentences of a news story contain who, what, when where, why (sometimes) and how" (sometimes). The "sometimes" means that "how" and "why" cannot always be explained in an initial news story or at least not in the first sentence. This structure is rumored to have originated in the era of the telegraph, where shortened stories of "just the facts" were necessary due to the time demands of telegraph operators, though the origin is difficult to confirm.

The expression *inverted pyramid* means that, like an upside-down ice cream cone, the most important elements of the story are in the lead, then content narrows down into details which can be eliminated by editors if the story needs to be shortened, while still preserving the initial details. A story about an accident, for example, might lead off with:

> Fargo: A local farmer was struck by an Ampco locomotive yesterday afternoon when a signal failed, according to witnesses in a nearby office building.
>
> (The farmer is *who*, the *when* is "yesterday afternoon" the *what* is "struck by locomotive" the *where* is Fargo and the *why* is "signal failed".)

This is known as a delayed identification lead because the farmer is not a "public figure" or a person who is not famous in the usual sense.

Later, we have:

The farmer, Walter Whitney, escaped without injury. He said he had stopped over the tracks because he feared that he wouldn't hear a train because of the noise coming from his truck cab, which was loaded with live chickens. He was able to open the truck door when he heard a train approaching Railroad officials are investigating the reported signal failure. Chickens surviving the collision were removed to a shelter by local animal protection officials. According to Whitney "I feel real bad about them, but there was nothing I could do."

Although these "details" are important, especially to the farmer's family, the inverted pyramid demands that they appear lower than "just the facts".

An editor will later write a headline for the story that tries to entice the reader and summarizes the elements in the lead: **Fargo Poultry Farmer Survives Collision with Train**. This is an example of a "typical" inverted pyramid story, and though this style of newswriting has many variations, it is still the predominant one today. Busy people still demand "just the facts" and readers who elect to read stories on the web spend even less time on websites than readers do on websites, so the pyramid survives.

NEWS PLATFORMS

To really understand changes in the news business, it is important to consider news as *business*. Just as it was in predigital times, profits come from advertising revenue. The majority of news organizations in the United States exist to make profits for corporations and they compete for readers/viewers and ultimately, for dollars. Even not-for-profit news sources such as National Public Radio (NPR), for years supported by grants from congress, now find that support shrinking so that the burden of income has shifted to viewers and listeners. It is also supported by sponsors including large corporations with on-air name-mentioning that increasingly has the look and feel of traditional advertising.

Central to the issue of platforms, or channels for delivering news to reader/viewers, is "Where is the money coming from?" In recent years, the decline of newspaper circulation has leveled off from the low point of 2007 to 2008, and the revenue from digital sources (Internet and mobile channels have increased by over 12% in the years since (Bazilian, 2013). Digital advertising rose to $3.42 billion in 2013 and produced 19% of advertising revenue. On the other hand, "Local TV audiences were down across every key time slot and all networks in 2012, with overall audiences falling 6.5 percent. The decline was especially sharp among younger viewers."

Traditional

Newspapers, TV stations, radio and newsmagazines are traditional platforms, or media channels that through which Americans have relied on for most of the twentieth century and continue in the present. All of them have suffered significant losses in terms of audience and revenue. Time Magazine is the only weekly newsmagazine which survives where previously there were a half dozen. Radio news is scarce in most areas, except for NPR, which deliver news and news commentaries daily.

New Platforms

The Internet in its present form with usable graphics and other features began to be accessible to most Americans in the mid-1990s (Marsh, 2015). But long before that, in the late 1970s, small pockets of tech savvy computer professionals and hobbyists had access to software that allowed for discussion groups of other skilled users. With the assistance of software called *USENET* journalists from all over the world could research, share and discuss news with others. USENET groups continue to this day, with vast numbers of interest groups sharing information over the Internet.

It is hard for students who were born in the digital age to imagine what the early Internet was like. There was no world wide web, the graphical interface that came much later than the text-only Internet. There were no pictures, colors, movies, audio or any of the features we take for granted today. There was only text—words on a screen—but the promise of a better future for the sharing of information kept journalists interested. I received my first lesson in how to use the software from journalists at the Hartford Courant in 1990. It was thrilling to be able to download press releases from the Whitehouse, for example, a day or two before they were faxed to other readers. No one could imagine the richness of multimedia available in the twenty-first century, or how easy it is to download verbal and visual information from a variety of devices like laptops, mobile phones and virtually anywhere there was a screen.

Boykov/Shutterstock.com.

Today, nearly every news organization has a presence on the web. Apart from the many papers and other media that only publish on the web, all of the major city newspapers have web pages as well as paper ones. As these pages evolve, most newspapers and many smaller regional weeklies and dailies offer enriched content via their web versions. Stories of all kinds are enriched by multimedia, where readers can see, hear and experience stories in real time, during or shortly after they occur. "Digital" includes both online readers using a computer and mobile, those who read on pads of smart phones.

Multimedia

Multimedia means "more than one medium" and it means that it's vehicle, the Internet, can deliver news stories in sound, words, photos, movies, graphics and other media that, unlike their broadcast media counterparts, add the quality of *interactivity* or the ability of the user to control when they want these features or whether they simply skip them and read the summary. Some news professionals have labeled this mix of choices *on demand delivery.*

Boykow/Shutterstock.com.

Some features of multimedia that are driving readers online include:

- **Powerful Visual Content**
  Photos have brought "punch" to news since the early twentieth century. In the multimedia world, slide shows enhance stories by offering content beyond anything involved in captioned still photos. The part of a sideshow (below) covers a Civil War re-enactment from an anniversary of the civil war.

Rigucci/Shutterstock.com.

Demonstration. Sometimes a news story demands an explanation of how things work. A video clip, for example, (below) about how salmon use fish ladders in the Pacific Northwest a "natural" for a conservation feature about the declining numbers of wild salmon.

When the new, technologically sophisticated 100 dollar bill appeared in 2013, news stories offered explanations of why they are difficult—and prohibitively expensive—to counterfeit. A blue ribbon appears in the center, along with alternating liberty bells that appear when the bill is tilted, and these were made clear to readers with a how-it-works graphic.

Maps. Maps help reader/viewers picture the scene of breaking news stories. The "where" of a news lead comes into quick clarity with a map. The location of nuclear waste sites in America and Europe becomes clear very quickly. Another advantage of news maps is that they can become "live" when a cursor drags over parts of them to reveal data and other information. When this happens, they become "information graphics" or "infographics" that offer tremendous advantages in readability over text or still photographs.

guroldinneden/Shutterstock.com.

To see a good example of this trend, visit the website www.newsmap.jp online. According to its creators, "Newsmap is an application that visually reflects the constantly changing landscape of the Google News Aggregator." (Hollings, 2010). The site reveals what news stories are being read in 14 nations in Europe, the Americas and Asia (online) at the time when click into the site in *real time*. The size of the story on the newsmap indicates how important the story is in each nation. Clicking on the story allows readers to go to the site for more information. This information graphic offers readers a chance to compare what makes news in each region of the world, including a choice of categories that include sports, business and entertainment besides "hard" news.

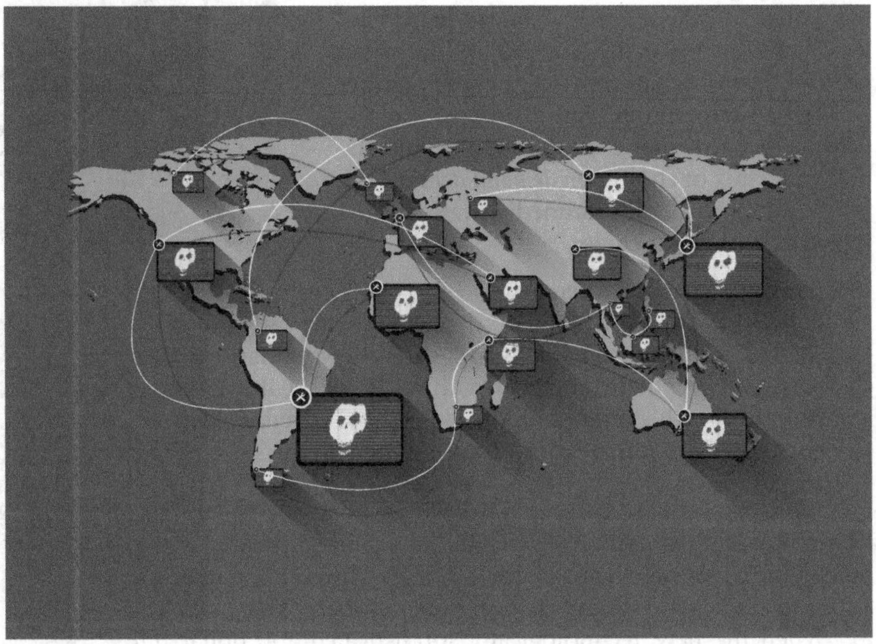

Crystal Eye Studio/Shutterstock.com.

Video. Video clips offer the benefit of showing movement and with on-demand delivery there are no worries about sacrificing the text of a story by forcing it to occupy valuable television time. Now that smart phones can take web quality photos and videos readers/viewers can supply unique on-the-scene photos and movies for use by online news media.

Audio. The decision on when to use audio in news stories requires news professionals to ask "What can sound add to this story?" Certainly interviews that offer someone saying something in a unique way make audio a necessity in storytelling. A news source speaking from the scene of a disaster or battlefield can convey the panic, surprise or any kind of emotion some stories require. Stories about a new singe or band can feature clips of an actual performance to either build an entire story or underline one. NPR stories are entirely audio, and they are as "newsy" or sometimes even better than their verbal or graphic counterparts. *Ambient Sound* adds depth and a sense of presence in a way no other medium can. A story about a restaurant can, for example, include the sound of dishes rattling in a kitchen in a powerful manner that makes the listener feel like they are present on the scene.

MOBILE NEWS PLATFORMS

Mobile devices including smartphones, tablets and computer-equipped cars offer all of the benefits of Internet platforms, along with go anywhere convenience. The world of *mobile* platforms offers promise of the future of revenue for advertising-supported news. Users of mobile devices reading news from newspaper sources increased 73% from January 2014 to January 2015, more than 68 million readers who use only these devices (Newspaper Association of America, 2015). A 2014 Pew Foundation survey of readers who use smartphones or tablets to receive news reveals the growing implications of mobile platforms for news (Mullin, 2014):

"The survey also finds that a substantial number of smartphone owners use their phone to follow along with news events near and far, to share details of local happenings with others, and to navigate the world around them:

- 68% of smartphone owners use their phone at least occasionally to follow along with breaking news events, with 33% saying that they do this "frequently."
- 67% use their phone to share pictures, videos, or commentary about events happening in their community, with 35% doing so frequently.
- 56% use their phone at least occasionally to learn about community events or activities, with 18% doing this "frequently."
- 67% of smartphone owners use their phone at least occasionally for turn-by-turn navigation while driving, with 31% saying that they do this "frequently."
- 25% use their phone at least occasionally to get public transit information, with 10% doing this "frequently.""

For these reasons, mobile platforms are now in great demand by readers. As advertising revenue continues to grow, news organizations that fail to develop them will probably regret that neglects as news appears on increasingly smaller screens than ever before.

THE ROLE OF REPORTER IN THE DIGITAL AGE

Since almost all the major newspapers in most nations now have online editions (or have gone completely online) multimedia allow the reader total control of how much depth or detail they want, as well as a universe of supplemental information. A story about the drug wars in Mexico can add maps tracing the location of major crime organizations, play interviews with law enforcement individuals and, using hyperlinks, get instant reports of the progress of attempts to interfere with illegal operations. For students of journalism, it means that some capability with photography, videography, video and audio editing and other technologies are as necessary today as notebooks and typewriters were to earlier "cub" reporters. Because so many news organizations have cut staff from newsrooms, reporters are now often "backpack journalists" operating alone, without the assistance of photographer and video editors to capture the scenes where news happens.

grynold/Shutterstock.com

Among the items in their backpacks are smartphones, so that reporters can not only take pictures, but also relay information to editors in an office or receive eyewitness accounts of events anywhere in the world. As the use of these devices multiply, readers also want to share instant information rather than waiting for the evening news. What this means for news providers is that information that once came on paper, or on TV, must now be available for audiences on smart phones, and this means a shift in strategy. Online news editors must think about how a story will look and "feel" on a 5 inch screen, and that includes advertisers who continue to provide revenue for the majority of news companies.

CONTENT-BEYOND BELLS AND WHISTLES

While the web offers enormous potential for journalists, in the end it is the stories that matter. News content is what readers/viewers want and it is content, after all, that serves all of the public's interest. What is new about the shift in delivery from paper to cyberspace are the countless opportunities that multimedia with on-demand accessibility offer for editing, updating and fact-checking that are so vital to today's news operations. What haven't changed are the basic functions that journalism performs.

Editor Stephen Busemeyer offers excellent arguments for the primacy of *stories.* He does not believe that the transition to online is a death knell for journalism, as long as news professionals preserve the values that made it the unreplaceable resource that it is today.

The Hartford Courant

Courtesy of Roger Desmond.

Stephen Busemeyer

After spending five years as breaking news editor, Stephen Busemeyer became The Courant's data editor in 2014. Since joining The Courant's in 2000, he's been an editor in the Avon, Middletown, Enfield and New Britain news bureaus. Before coming to The Courant, he was the editor of the Daily Press in Craig, CO, and the city editor at the Star-Tribune in Casper, WY. He teaches journalism regularly at the University of Hartford and has also taught at the University of Connecticut and the University of Colorado.

He explains:

I work for a newspaper that has been publishing for more than 250 years, one of many venerable papers in the nation that are hanging on despite changes to a business model that helped us thrive for centuries.

We are adapting to this new digital world everyday, even though new challenges appear around every corner. We've had to make tough decisions about how best to cover our world with the resources at hand, and with new products and a healthy approach to digital revenue, many are well-positioned for the future.

But, as one might expect during turbulent times, some companies have made fatal mistakes along the way.

In the hysteria to be "Digital First," they've focused on shiny new tools and de-emphasized the "content." Reporters tweet furiously on iPhones, take videos and dutifully upload them, and stumble into the web trying to be the first to send a text alert. The accuracy, the richness, the context of the report sometimes gets lost in the haste. Now that we have tools that allow us to act with speed, we feel like we must use them.

I look at our web traffic everyday. The stories that get the most hits are *the best stories*—the revelations about a politician's peccadillos, the breaking news, the investigative work, the interactive maps and charts that give the reader access to the underlying data. Of course photo galleries and other easily-digestible items get lots of clicks, but it's gratifying to see that people honestly do care about fascinating stories. Good investigations, well-written tales, stories that our relevant to our lives -- they are still our main attraction. People want to read, and share, good journalism.

Newspapers in general still make most of their money from the print product. Millions of people buy and enjoy the print version of newspapers everyday. Presses have been working in American newsrooms for 250 years, and journalism has survived more challenging circumstances than we find ourselves in at the moment.

In fact, despite the predictions that the Internet would lead to a loss of readers of mainstream newspapers, the opposite came true. More people are reading our work than ever before. Our reach is longer, our impact is harder, our reporting is often better and our relevance is higher than at any time in our history. Readers can plumb deeper into the facts behind the news by interacting with raw data in ways never before possible. They can easily share their discoveries with their friends. They can form or argue public policy well-armed for battle.

And it's all thanks to the Internet, the best tool ever invented to commit high-quality journalism. Since newspapers went online in the late 1990s, we have regained our immediacy, we break news as fast or faster than anyone, and we remain the only source for deep, rich, contextual reporting.

Journalism won't simply *survive* the fading printed page. Thanks to technology, journalism is at the dawn of a golden age.

The challenge is solving the revenue picture—figuring out what readers want to pay for and how to make it easy for them to pay for it.

That means it's more important than ever to make the news attractive to consume and easy to digest.

A "story" (what some people mistakenly call "the content") is so much more than a bunch of written words. Everything is a story. Pictures, graphs, videos and interactive data visualizations are all different ways to tell different types of stories, and our job is to use the best tools at our disposal.

Witness the latest sexy thing: data journalism. This is simple story-telling at its root, but its practitioners (me included) are learning how to use the latest computer tools to show people what their world is like from a different point of view. We uncover stories simply by learning how to gather databases and manipulate them.

But does the future of journalism really depend on our ability to use Excel?

Our lives are increasingly quantified. The government knows how much money we make, who our neighbors are, what color our skin is, where we go to church and where we work.

Google tracks how fast you drive and knows when you leave for work everyday. Twitter knows what sports teams you root for. Target knows what you eat for breakfast. Facebook knows whom you love (probably better than you do).

Our quantified selves—our human experiences—are now recorded and archived in databases.

Who will analyze all of this? Scientists, statisticians, mathematicians, marketers, politicians, anyone who can use the data to their advantage. And "data journalists" must keep up.

We're doing it already. Some of the best investigative work done at my newspaper in the last 15 years has come from careful analysis of databases. Take the great work done at politifact.com, propublica.org, fivethirtyeight.com, factcheck.org and so many more. They plumb reams of data, use clever analysis, uncover high-impact stories highly relevant to public policy and share them in ways that just couldn't be done in the Watergate era of old-school investigative journalism.

In that way, moving away from the print product could be a blessing in disguise. We could focus more on interactive offerings and throw open more doors for the readers. Being able to curate the massive collection of government and other data and make it transparently available to everyone is like Prometheus stealing fire from the gods.

And we will grow.

Journalism is talking to people, making sources, earning their trust, gathering information, learning how the world works and being able to share those discoveries in a way that people understand. We find a good story and tell it in a simple, compelling way—whether that's with words, a map, a database, a video, a graph, a song, a haiku.

That's good journalism, and it is valuable stuff. People want to read this, and people like to interact with data online when it's presented properly. And more and more, they are willing to pay for it.

Journalism, once again, is a growth industry.

INVESTIGATIVE REPORTING

Primary among the functions of news is the "watchdog" function, where journalists investigate problems in government, the military, business and virtually all of our institutions. Just as the illegal and unethical problems in Bell, California (alluded to at the beginning of this chapter) a great many of society's ills continue on and fester until someone in the news business investigates. The problem for today's news organizations with rapidly decreasing budgets and staff is that it is really expensive and labor-intensive to do solid investigations that require enormous amounts of legal, financial, and plain old detective-style research in order to make sure that the effort will tell the truth about the focus of the query. What has happened is that many major national news organizations can only do a few serious investigations in a year. One organization, Propublica, exists to help with investigations.

A good example of how investigative journalism is conducted today, the web-based organization is an assembly of investigative reporters and support staff who exist to expose wrongdoing at every level of society. Their stated mission is to use investigative journalism to expose wrongdoing in all corners of society. (Propublica, 2015).

Founded in 2007 by a former managing editor of the *Wall St. Journal* and now headed by a former managing editor of *The Oregonian,* Propublica operates a newsroom in Manhattan with about 45 professional journalists. Because it is funded by a foundation, grants, advertising and public donations, Propublica offers many of its best investigative stories for free to any news organization that wants the material. A visit their website (www.propublica.com) reveals the quality, depth and scope of their research.

Recent topics for investigation include a probe about a series of alleged rapes by an NFL star, the demolition of worker's compensation in a number of states, the shooting mistreatment of black Americans in several police departments, problems in regulation of Wall Street loopholes that rob investors of money and numerous other endeavors. Propublica is responsible for ongoing investigations in "Big Tobacco," "invisible" payments to physicians and researchers by drug companies seeking to increase revenues by pressuring physicians to prescribe its products, erosion of natural resources by natural gas "fracking" operations and virtually every corner of suspicious misdeeds by officials in the public trust. Because it spreads the new of these projects online it has no expenses involved in running a daily news company and can move efficiently to tackle new investigations. Propublica boasts that it invests 85% of its budget on actual news and investigation which indicates that economically it is more efficient than the majority of newspapers and TV stations.

But television can, and does, conduct investigations of enormous importance. *60 Minutes*, the award-winning Sunday evening CBS news magazine, is also a major provider of important investigative stories. Now in its 47th year, the program is seen weekly by over 12 million viewers. It has won nearly every award for broadcast journalism with investigations of federal government in virtually all functions, corruption in the pharmaceutical industry, US roles in surveillance of foreign governments and vice-versa, and myriads of other vitally important stories.

Local newspapers, TV stations and online news sites also conduct investigations that focus on the city, state or even the neighborhoods of their readers/viewers. The highest award for journalists is, of course, the Pulitzer Prize. The category titled "Investigative Reporting" (in the past, by a variety of other titles) has been awarded for over 50 years. The prize is administered by a board of journalists and the Columbia University School of Journalism.

According to the prize website, "In journalism the major newspapers, such as *The New York Times, The Wall Street Journal,* and *The Washington Post,* have harvested many of the awards, but the board also has often reached out to work done by small, little-known papers. The Public Service award in 1995 went to The Virgin Islands Daily News, St. Thomas, for its disclosure of the links between the region's rampant crime rate and corruption in the local criminal justice system. In 2005, the investigative reporting award went to *Willamette Week,* an alternative newspaper in Portland, Oregon, for its exposure of a former governor's long concealed sexual misconduct with a 14-year-old" (Pulitzer.org, 2015). The prize is administered by a board of journalists and the Columbia University School of Journalism.

What the list of previous winners reveals is that size of a newspaper and quality are *not related,* at least as defined by the size of previous award winners' organizations. In every city, town and even island, the job of investigation is carried out without regard to the time involved or the paper's resources.

OTHER CATEGORIES OF NEWS

- Breaking News

  Where was the fire last night? Is the highway closed because of an accident? Has the burglar in the area been arrested? These are the kinds of questions that are answered by breaking news, or news of immediate interest. There is no formal definition except that breaking news is today's, this minute's or this week's event that might be relevant to a segment of reader/viewers. Before the digital revolution, this type of news was a prisoner of deadlines: a newspaper's final moment before it went to print or a radio station's music program. Today, breaking news is "24/7" in that the web allows for a deadline every second; there is no real deadline.

  Most TV, newspaper and online news company features updateable brief headlines and perhaps only two or three sentences of bare bones outline of an important news story. In a fire story, for example, a first report might give location, and most important, whether anyone is known to have died or been injured. In any story about an emergency human life must be first in the lead. In an update several hours later, details such as possible cause of the fire, amount of damage, and whether arson is suspected. Major fires, or other disasters, may be updated numerous times over days or weeks as explanations emerge. The immediacy of reporting breaking news demands that editors must use news judgments at lightning speed, yet still beat the competition at the local level. The tension to be first is greater than ever experienced by previous generations of reporters and editors.

National and International News. Except for a few huge daily newspapers and television stations operated by the "big four" networks, the majority of national and international news comes to the local news outlets by news services, organizations that exist to provide news gathered by them around the world. Prior to the 1980s in the United States, two news services dominated the business: United Press International (UPI) and Associated Press (AP). UPI suffered financial losses and sold its broadcast division to AP in 1999, so competition for sources of news text and photos has weakened, with AP the industry leader of this domain.

In most of the twentieth Century and earlier, newspapers in cities like New York, Chicago, Los Angeles all had news bureaus around the world with teams of correspondents reporting first-hand the events and issues in most nations. But even before the digital age, this kind of coverage began to disappear as news companies could no longer support the expense of correspondents, their support staffs, the cost of housing them, and travels costs within the areas of coverage. Today, sources of news are everywhere: news is furnished by news companies in each nation and within the United States. Because of the perpetual amount of news available on the web, most newspapers have cut the amount of this category of news. But the availability of important news has never been greater for news readers/viewers. International news has increased due to the number of news outlets in every nation, and national news, especially in the category of politics, is more available than ever in history. The digital age has made the world seem much smaller than ever, and as nations' interests are increasingly intertwined, the importance of news from everywhere has mushroomed.

Business News. College students (and many others) respond to business sections or web pages by saying "business stories are boring." Sometimes this comes from a lack of familiarity with exactly what they are. **Business** stories, when done well, are dramas of the richest and most entertaining kind, complete with tales of heroes and villains, romance and war. One reason why some readers think that business news is boring is that they think that **earnings stories** are the only thing that are important. Earnings stories are essentially reports of how, for example, a publically held company's stock performed in the last year, 3 months or any period of time although annual and quarterly stories are the most typical. Public companies are those that sell shares of stock on the NY Stock exchange or an exchange in another country outside of the United States. American companies are required by law to report the major events to the government briefly, every 3 months and in more detail every year. The content of these reports are public information, available to anyone and today, are available online. Information included is the amount of money it took in, the amount of money it cost to operate (overhead), changes in management of the company and other details. Because this information is so vital to shareholders, earning stories are often "just the facts" with little or no explanation of the *why*.

Why, for example, did the company earn less money this year than the year before? Did the cost of materials required to produce what the company make go up? Did the company decide to pay fewer dividends to stockholders and invest the difference in future growth? Good business reporting goes beyond the numbers and tries to explain what factors influenced the company's performance since the last period. Other important and interesting business stories include the **CEO profile**, where owners, managers and company leaders are detailed and personalized for readers. Product features offer news consumers information about new developments or products the company has announced. What has the company done that will excite potential customers and what do critics and competitors think if it? Recently, Apple Corp. decided to release many versions of a "smart watch." Many of the business press most prominent reporters told readers that the watches, although technologically sophisticated, weren't going to be popular with consumers because they didn't fulfill a new need; about all they were good for was to remind consumers to check a new message on their smartphone or other devices. But in the first few weeks of release, consumer demand was such so high that most Apple store sold out all inventory within the first day! Some reporters underestimated the demand for anything new from the company, particularly in Asian markets. Some credited the demand to the ease it will bring to paying for retail transactions as methods of digital payment are becoming sophisticated and secure. Business stories can be as exciting and important as any other category of news.

Political News. As many local newspapers and other news organizations cut back on political coverage, what suffer is the day-to-day reports from specialists who are present where laws are made: in the city councils and state legislatures. National political coverage is not as much as a problem, in that coverage of Washington-based coverage is solid and during election season, politics is over-covered. Focus on the "horse-race" aspect of elections dominates news in season but after elections, all but disappears. An exception is in the case of political scandals, where a great deal of coverage of accusers and accused leads the news with lots of detail.

In the case of Connecticut, one solution has emerged in the web based "ctnewsjunkie.com" (www.ctnewsjunkie.com). In 2006, former reporter Christine Stuart and her husband Doug Hardy, also a newsroom veteran, put the publication online. The focus of the publication is on state politics, broadly conceived. Now operating with a small staff of part-time reporters, the focus of the publication is on news about politics, the *people* who make it and the *people* who are affected by it. Supported by banner ads, newsjunkie is impossible to ignore. Every newspaper and TV station in the state, and an increasing number of national organizations, cites and often re-publishes articles and photos from newsjunkie. Because it is based in the state capitol, the news is fresh and complete with photos and videos from the moment of the story. As an article in Time Magazine stated:

"On any given day at CTnewsjunkie.com, there are stories about Connecticut's budget woes, health care issues and Senator Chris Dodd's attempts to reform the credit card industry. Most of the stories are written by Stuart. All the photos are taken by Stuart. And Stuart or her husband, who works as a layout editor at a local paper, handles most of the ads, which are for local unions or the Connecticut Dairy Farmers Association. So far, her best month garnered her site 67,000 page views. But Stuart, 31, who has to have a part-time job to make ends meet, says she is treated, more or less, as an equal by the other reporters in the office." One of them told me, 'You have to make it, because you're the future.'" (Luscombe, 2009).

Science, Technology, Medicine and the Environment. As new planets or stars are discovered (or downgraded), new threats to crops and animals are uncovered and robots perform increasingly more complex tasks, readers/viewers demand explanations. Journalists are challenged to explain and to help readers who aren't physicists understand the importance of scientific developments. The demand for science journalists is one of the greatest personnel needs of today's news companies: people trained in science and technology who can also explain and investigate these complex topics for the public.

In terms of environmental issues, the watchdog function of journalism is at the forefront. How dangerous are storms and weather events in which parts of the country? Are organic vegetables more nutritious than conventionally grown ones? Why are bees, so necessary to growing plants, disappearing more rapidly than ever in the last few years?

Hundreds of new medicines are released every year, as are new surgical practices and cures for diseases. And physicians and other health professionals have become celebrities, appearing on talk shows and news documentaries with more visibility every season. Who should we believe? Journalists need to be investigators of every claim made by science and medicine so that they can accurately interpret technical advances for a curious public.

CONCLUSION: YOUR FUTURE IN JOURNALISM

At the beginning of this chapter there was a statement of strong claim: Journalism is alive and well, and it isn't going anywhere. Hopefully, after reading this survey the new horizon of journalism in the digital age, you are convinced that news is necessary for participating in a society and in a democracy this necessity is absolute. But some of you may even be interested in exploring a journalism career. What do you need to know?

In terms of skills, writing and research ability are the most important skills for any aspect of journalism. A university or community college typically offers courses in these skills, and campus newspapers and TV stations are always in need of skilled writers. Perhaps you didn't major in journalism, or aren't planning to. That's just fine with increasing numbers of employers. They are looking for skills and talent, not specific college majors. Because of the demand for science and technical journalists, many employers want new hires to have an area of expertise beyond journalism. Perhaps it is expertise in physics or engineering that will set you apart. Or it could be a strong interest and background in agriculture or water management. Given the need for political writers, a major or minor in political science might be what opens the door.

Beyond specific educational backgrounds, what most journalism employers want to see is experience. That doesn't necessarily mean on-the-job news experience. Articles written for a campus newspaper or magazine are important, as are resume tapes made up of interviews you have done for your campus TV station or news website. If you need more avenues to develop these, your school's public relations unit might need some video interviews. The world of online news is also a place to gain experience. Search and read news blogs on the web. Find out if you can contribute.

While still in college, take courses in TV production and multimedia production. The more comfortable you are designing websites and informational databases and information graphics the more an employer will be glad to listen. If you can shoot, edit and mount a video story on the web, that's an asset. If your program offers internships, they also count as experience. And even if it doesn't, don't be afraid to ask if you can be of help to news professional. Many will admire your dedication just because you asked. A great source of information about careers, salaries and ads for jobs is available from The Poynter Foundation, a nonprofit school for journalists and students (www.poynter.org). Their online courses, (many are free) can be viewed at www.newsu.org.

Whether you plan a career in journalism or simply want to become a capable citizen in any career, read. Reading everything is a path to having a background of world knowledge. Keeping up with current events will give you knowledge that is valuable no matter what you plan for your future. The world of information in the digital age is available at your fingertips. Use very chance you can to drink from that well.

REFERENCES

Bazilian, E. (3/18/2013). Pew Finds Digital News Consumption Up but Revenue Dwindling. Advertising Week. Available at: http://www.adweek.com/news/advertising-branding/pew-finds-digital-news-consumption-revenue-dwindling-148012.

Farham, A. (3/20/2013). Corruption on Steroids Case Reaches Verdict. Available at: http://abcnews.go.com/Business/guilty-verdict-bell-calif-corruption-scandal/story?id=21164782.

Hollings, R. (2010). NewsMap.jp—The Latest News in a Visual Setting. Available at: www.killerstartups.com/web-app-tools.

Luscombe, B. (2009). As newsrooms cut back, who covers the statehouse? *Time* 7 May 7, 12 (Business).

Mullin, B. (2014). Pew Report: News Consumers are Increasingly Using Smartphones. Available at: http://www.poynter.org/news/mediawire/331511/americans-rely-increasingly-on-smartphones-new-pew-report-shows/.

Marsh, D. (2015). A New Home for the Mind. Available at: http://www.netvalley.com/archives/mirrors/davemarsh-timeline-1.htm/Pew.

Pew (2013). The State of the News Media 2013. Available at: http://www.stateofthemedia.org/2013/overview-5/.

Propublica, 2015. The Mission Statement, Available at: http://www.propublica.org/about/.

Pulitzer.org (2015). The Pulitzer Prizes. Available at: www.pulitzer.org/.

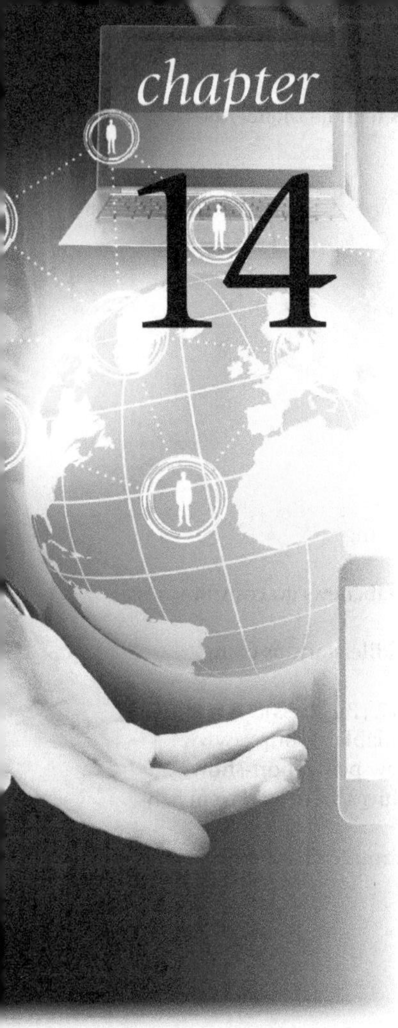

chapter 14 Advertising

OBJECTIVES

- Explain how the advertising industry has evolved over the last three hundred years
- Describe how advertisements are used in mass media
- Explain how advertisements benefit the consumer and media outlets
- Understand how the government regulates advertisers and how advertisers regulate themselves
- List four future trends in the advertising industry

KEY TERMS

advertising
bait and switch
consumerism
direct mail
fairness doctrine
guerrilla marketing
outdoor advertising
paid search
pay-per-click
point-of-sale advertising

INTRODUCTION

From the moment you wake up in the morning until the time you go to sleep at night, how many commercial messages do you think you are exposed to? If you watch TV or read the newspaper regularly, you many think you are exposed to a hundred or so messages. If you rarely give attention to major forms of mass media, you may think the number is even lower. The reality is that the average American is exposed to 3,000 commercial messages a day, that's over one million a year.[1] That number may seem inflated, however, if you really think about the words and images that are communicated to you over the course of a day you can see the truth behind this staggering number. As you get ready to leave the house in the morning you may flip on the radio or morning news and hear numerous broadcast commercials. When you pour your cereal, you may notice a promotion for an unrelated product printed on the back of the box. On your way to work or school you are exposed to hundreds of messages: the billboard for a vacation package alongside the road, a sign for a brand of shampoo on the side of a bus, or a bumper sticker on the car in front of you. You may be exposed to some commercial messages without even noticing: the Nike logo on your friend's shirt, the Starbucks coffee cup on your neighbor's desk, or the Jansport label on your backpack.

Commercial messages are all around us, and corporations are making it increasingly difficult to avoid them. Nearly $450 billion is spent annually to lure customers to certain products or services. Promoting commercial messages is called advertising. **Advertising** is essentially the act of calling the public's attention to a product, service, or need. Advertising is commonly found in different types of mass media in the form of radio or television commercials, newspaper spreads, or billboard announcements. However, as we discovered earlier, advertisements can be found almost anywhere.

Advertising
the act of calling the public's attention to a product, service, or need

ADVERTISING BEFORE THE 21ST CENTURY

© Alexey Malashkevich/Shutterstock.

New York's Time Square shows just about every kind of advertising you can imagine.

Advertising has existed in the United States for over three hundred years. The first known advertisement was placed in a newspaper, the *Boston News-Letter*, in 1703. The advertisement, or ad, publicized the sale of an estate in Oyster Bay Long Island. Years later Benjamin Franklin began running advertisements in the *Pennsylvania Gazette*. The first true pioneer of advertising did not emerge until 1833. Printer Benjamin Day found a way to bring advertising to the masses by creating the first successful penny newspaper, the *Sun*, in New York. Within four years of its first edition, the publication's circulation reached 30,000, making it the most widely read newspaper in the world. As the 19th century progressed, advertising became an important part of business development for major companies. Advertising agencies formed, companies hired full time advertising copywriters, and major corporations invested unprecedented amounts of money in ad placements. In 1882, Procter & Gamble Co. started an advertisement campaign for Ivory soap with an $11,000 budget, an amount that was unheard of at the time.

Modern advertising began to emerge in the 1900s with products such as Kellogg's cornflakes. In 1906 WK Kellogg created a widespread campaign by placing its advertisements in six Midwestern magazines. By 1915 Kellogg was spending more than one million dollars a year on national advertising, creating a benchmark for the future of advertising. By 1921, RJ Reynolds was designating $8 million to advertising, most of which was spent on promoting Camel cigarettes. The investment proved to be successful as by 1923 Camel controlled 45% of the U.S. cigarette market.

As advertising became more popular, the government became involved in the process. The Section 5 of the Federal Trade Commission Act, passed in 1914, declared that the Federal Trade Commission (FTC) can issue cease-and-desist orders against any company that engages in dishonest or misleading advertising. Companies were now liable for any claims made in advertisements. Cigarette companies found themselves in hot water because of this act.[2] We will learn more about tobacco advertising and government regulations later on in this chapter.

A Changing Market

As public preference changed, so did the approach of advertisers. During the early part of the 20th century radio emerged as a popular form of media. Soon

Advertisers and Athletes: The Start of a Love Affair

In 1905, three-time National League batting champion Honus Wagner became the first person to sign an endorsement contract. Wagner's deal with bat company Hillerich & Bradsby, Co. allowed the company to engrave his signature on Louisville Slugger bats and sell them to eager fans. Since 1905, more than 7,000 endorsements deals have been created between Louisville Slugger and professional baseball players. Wagner's deal sparked an ongoing trend in endorsement relationships between corporations and professional athletes that is highly prevalent in the advertising world today.[3]

companies opted to spend their advertising dollars on the airwaves rather than print pages. By 1938, radio exceeded magazines in advertising revenue. But again, the market changed. Advertisers turn to television as a new way to reach consumers. On July 1, 1941, NBC's WNBT aired its first telecast. A close-up view of a Bulova watch opened and closed the telecast, marking one of the first instances of product placement on television.

Other changes in advertising occurred around this time. The US government started to use advertising to help build support for World War II. The War Advertising Council gained free advertising for public service messages. Popular campaigns such as "Buy War Bonds" and "Loose Lips Sink Ships" were placed in magazines and radio broadcasts across the United States. After the war, the War Advertising Council was renamed the Advertising Council and proceeded to advertise public service campaigns such as Smokey the Bear, McGruff the crime dog, and "Just Say No" to drugs.[4]

Advertisers' approach to choosing the perfect medium for their products changed with the emergence of AC Nielsen's machine-based rating system for television. The system made it possible to track how many households view certain television programs. Nielsen's machine allowed companies to find out on which programs their advertising dollars would be most wisely spent.

As the 20th century progressed, advertising companies became more methodical about where, when, and how they placed certain ads. Advertisements were no longer just used to persuade consumers to buy a product; they were used to encourage the public to embrace a brand. "The Pepsi Generation" was an advertising campaign initiated in 1963. It projected the image that all those who are young, or young at heart, should drink Pepsi brand cola.[5]

Soon after the MTV era introduced new, flashier forms of advertising during the 1980s, the Internet introduced new, high-tech forms of advertising in the 1990s. By 1993, the Internet enlisted five million users and emerged as a profitable medium for advertisers. Before the end of the century, well over $2 billion was spent on Internet advertising. Today over $24 billion dollars is spent on Internet advertising adding to total of $450 billion spent on advertising worldwide.[6] To understand why so much money is spent on advertising, let's examine why we need it.

A CULTURE OF CONSUMERISM

With billions of dollars being spent every year to convince consumers to buy certain products, one must question the necessity of advertising. Why can't the consumer just decide what products and services to purchase on their own? That question cannot be properly answered without understanding consumerism. **Consumerism** is the theory that an increase in the consumption of goods and services will benefit the economy.[7] In short, the more we buy the more we thrive. Americans adopted a culture of consumerism at the start of the 20th century. People began to work fewer hours, acquire higher paying jobs, invest in the stock market, and buy luxury items like cars, washing machines, and expensive clothing.

Consumerism
the theory that an increase in the consumption of goods and services will benefit the economy

The culture of consumerism is clear in today's society. Americans purchase more than $6 trillion dollars in goods and services each year, and they rely on advertisements to inform them about new products. Gone are "mercantile days" when each shopkeeper waited on every customer by taking and filling their order personally, acting as clerk, cashier and then often as salesman, describing new products and discussing the merits of various goods. How does the consumer today learn about the amazing plethora of goods and services available in today's expanding marketplaces? For better and worse, this is where advertising comes in.

Advertising and the Consumer

Advertising may not seem like a benefit because of the negative connotations connected to the practice. Consumers sometimes feel that advertisers are always trying to sell them something they don't need. However, in many cases advertisers are promoting goods and services that support our basic needs. Food, clothing, shelter, and other goods that aid us in our daily lives are products that are advertised. Sure, we may not need brand name clothing, but a Gore-tex jacket may help you keep warm in the winter. Without advertising, consumers may never learn about new product that can improve their health and well being.

© Jim Barber/Shutterstock.

How does advertising financially benefit the consumer?

Advertising also has financial benefits for the consumer. Advertising promotes competition within the market, which drives down prices and increases product availability. It also helps consumers decide where to get the best price and what products have the best value.

Advertising and the Media

Advertising is the foundation of the economic health of our nation's media. Broadcast television and radio are solely supported by the revenue brought in by advertising. Newspapers, magazines, cable television, and Internet outlets rely on subscription fees as well as advertising revenue to support their businesses. Without revenue from advertising many media outlets would not exist and those that could survive would come at a substantially higher cost to the consumer.

Because advertisers allow media outlets to function with little to no cost to the consumer, more outlets are able to flourish, giving consumers more choices in news and entertainment. For example, in the 1950s television viewers were only offered three broadcast networks. Today, they have their choice of six broadcast networks and hundreds of cable channels. Advertising had the same effect on print media. In 1960 there were 312 morning newspapers, and today there are over 700. The number of consumer magazines has increased as well. In 1988 there were almost 13,000 publications, and today that number is more than 18,000.[8]

Advertising is also an integral part of the Internet. Paid advertisements make many of the most popular sites such as Google, Mapquest, and YouTube free to Internet users. Without revenue from advertisers there would be little incentive for Web site administrators to develop new Web sites. But when it comes to advertising and the Internet, the benefits run both ways. As we will discuss later on in the chapter, the Internet has become a large part of the future of advertising.

Now that we know why advertising is important to the consumer and the media, let's see how it is used.

THE MANY FACES OF ADVERTISING

Traditionally, advertisements appear in media in the form of print or broadcast. Print advertisements usually contain pictures or photos, catchy headlines, and occasionally coupons and can appear in newspapers, magazines, or flyers. Broadcast advertisements consist of brief 15-20 second audio and/or video pieces designed for television or radio. In addition to traditional advertising, methods such as direct mail, outdoor signage, and point-of-sale advertising can also make a big impact on consumers.

Direct Mail

Direct mail
a type of advertisement sent through the postal service

Direct mail, sometimes referred to by consumers as junk mail, consists of advertisements sent through the postal service. Direct mail advertisements typically promote special sales or offers to select consumers. It can be a very useful form of advertising because companies can create mailing lists that only target consumers that are most likely to purchase their goods or services. Grocery store circulars and "pre-approved" credit card offers are common direct mail pieces. While direct mail pieces often receive a bulk rate for postage costs, it can still be rather expensive. The advertisements can also be viewed as a nuisance and be thrown away unopened.

© GWImages/Shutterstock.

Direct mail advertisements can be sent to mailing lists that target specific consumers.

Point-of-Sale

Point-of-sale advertising
the placement of products, promotions, or other offers on or near a checkout counter

Point-of-sale advertising is the placement of products, promotions, or other offers on or near a checkout counter. The candy in a grocery store checkout line and the flyer asking you to try a new style of burger on the counter of a fast food restaurant are both forms of point-of-sale advertising. Point-of-sale advertising has become high tech in the last few years. At coffee retailer Aroma Espresso Bar, customers who approach the counter may be greeted by a cashier and video screen that displays images of the various breakfast items available for purchase. Through this type of advertising, customers who entered the shop with the intention of only purchasing a cup of coffee may be encouraged to also pick up a croissant or muffin.

Point-of-sale advertising can be very beneficial to advertisers because most purchasing decisions are made in the store and advertisers have a chance to appeal to consumers' impulses.[9] However, point-of-sale-advertisements, especially the kind that involves technology, can be expensive and sometimes overlooked.

Outdoor Advertising

Outdoor advertising is another way to reach consumers outside of their homes. Traditionally thought of as billboard signs, outdoor advertising has changed a lot in the last ten years. Outdoor media now includes park benches, public transit vehicles, or bus shelters that are wrapped with images and text promoting various products.

Outdoor advertising
the placement of ads outside in the view of the general public, typically on billboards, signs, or other outdoor objects

Some outdoor advertising methods can range from silly to bizarre. In Times Square in New York City a glass elevator was designed and built to simulate an Oreo cookie being dunked into a glass of milk. In London, a group of individuals were paid to walk on to a subway train wearing jackets with video screens in the arm pits. When a person would raise their arm, a video ad for Right Guard deodorant would play for the whole crowd in the train to see. While this method of advertising may sometimes be viewed as precarious, advertisers are willing to spend big, $7.3 billion in 2007 according to the Outdoor Advertising Association of America, in order to get their message out to the public.[10]

© emin kuliyev/ Shutterstock.

Advertisers are willing to do just about anything to get their message out to consumers.

The Internet

While advertisers are getting more creative with the way they execute advertising in traditional mediums, nothing has shaken up the advertising world more than the Internet. As we discussed in Chapter 10, the Internet is becoming a dominate force in media. In many ways the Internet works like a television or a newspaper. Advertisers can place an electronic banner ad, similar to a print ad in a newspaper, on a home page or a select page of a Web site. They can also place a pop-up or side bar video, similar to a television commercial, on a partnering Web site. These types of advertisements are increasing as more people are looking to the Internet to read up on the latest news or watch their favorite TV program.

Paid search
a form of advertising used on a search engine Website, which allows companies to have a brief advertisement placed on top or next to search results when certain keywords are used

Pay-per-click
a form of advertising in which Web page administrators allow outside companies to place advertisements on their Web pages in exchange for a small fee, which is paid to the Web site administrator, when a user clicks on the ad

The Internet also offers advertisers other ways to reach consumers that are unmatched by newspapers or television. Paid search and pay-per click advertising has come forward as one of the fastest growing methods of advertising. **Paid search** is a form of advertising used on a search engine Web site, which allows companies to have a brief advertisement placed on top or next to search results when certain keywords are used. For example, when a user types in the keywords "hair salon Miami" a small add for Gabriella's Unisex Salon in Miami may appear at the top of the search results page under a paid advertisements section. In **pay-per-click** advertising, Web page administrators allow outside companies to place advertisements on their Web pages in exchange for a small fee, which is paid to the Web site administrator, when a user clicks on the ad. For example, Sarah Hawkins has a Web site for her event planning business. To make some extra cash for her business, Sarah allows Larson's Limousine Services to place a small ad on her Web page. Sarah may receive about 10 cents from the limo service every time a user clicks on the ad.

Paid search and pay-per-click were first implemented and mastered by Google founders Sergey Brin and Larry Page. Called AdWord (paid search) and AdSense (pay-per-click), these forms of advertisements are a key part of what has made Google the multi-billion dollar company it is today.[11] In 2007, Google made over $16 billion in advertising revenue and that number is projected to grow even larger in the next few years.[12]

Companies are drawn to this type of advertising because it allows advertisers to more accurately measure how many potential customers they are reaching, and it also guarantees that consumers are actively viewing the advertisement. Unlike a television commercial that can be missed when a viewer leaves the room or a print ad that can easily be passed by, paid search and pay-per-click advertising is actually initiated by the consumer, increasing the chances that the ad will be thoroughly viewed.

In a 2010 Supreme Court decision called "Citizens United," the justices removed limits on corporations' independent spending during campaigns for the Presidency and Congress. The decision will have an important impact on political advertising in future elections.[13]

Political Advertising: The Living Room Candidate

During election season in the United States, television viewers may notice more ads for political candidates than ads for fast food restaurants. Since the 1950s, television has changed the game for political candidates. Through television, candidates can enter voters' homes and influence their decision making through images, slogans, and rhetoric. The use of television ads for political advertisings was not in vogue until the 1952 election between Dwight D. Eisenhower and Adlai Stevenson. Previous candidates such as Governor Thomas Dewey viewed political television ads as "undignified" and refused to use them in his 1948 campaign.

Diverging from this view, Eisenhower embraced television ads, creating several 30 seconds spots titled "Ike for President" that featured animated characters, songs, and the now famous slogan, "I like Ike." Eisenhower's campaign merchandised the candidate just as a corporation would merchandise a new product. So it is not surprising that the same ad agency that created M&M's slogan "melts in your mouth not in your hand," developed the "Eisenhower Answers America" ad series. In these television ads Eisenhower responded to questions from ordinary citizens. Forty spots, recorded in one day and then broadcast throughout the campaign season, aired before popular shows such as I Love Lucy. The spots helped Eisenhower enter his constituents' living rooms on a nightly basis and be viewed as a man of the people.

Stevenson never warmed up to the idea of using television to market a candidate. He publicized his disapproval of the process with the statement: "I think the American people will be shocked by such contempt for their intelligence. This isn't Ivory Soap versus Palmolive." Stevenson created television spots promoting his campaign; however they were often long and dull and aired during late hours. Viewed as nothing more than on-camera radio spots, Stevenson's television ads did little for his campaign.[14]

Dwight D. Eisenhower won the 1952 election by a large margin. His campaign changed the way Americans view their candidates, but also the way candidates make their appeal to the American people. In the 2008 presidential campaign, candidates spent nearly $3 billion on political television ads.[15] Whether they are used to promote a candidate's views and proposed policies or to portray competitors in negative light, political television ads have become an important part of the election processes.

Advertising Agencies

The forerunner of the advertising agency as we know it today was founded in 1841 by Volney Palmer, whose Philadelphia brokerage service specialized in buying advertising space from newspapers at a volume discount, then selling parts of that space to individual advertisers at a markup. To this day advertising agencies gain part or all of their compensation through the discount they receive from publishers bringing in ads. It is a service to the publishers to have large blocks of ads coming in without having to work with individual merchants or manufacturers.

It was not until the 1870s that advertising agencies emerged to serve manufacturers who needed advice on how to package their products and promote them to consumers. The N. W. Ayer and Son Agency, also of Philadelphia, was among the first to provide the service of studying a product and developing a "campaign" or strategy, for making that product familiar and desirable. The Ayer agency is responsible for many of the advertising slogans that have become part of our cultural lexicon, like "Diamonds are forever," and "When it rains it pours."[16]

MONITORING ADVERTISING INFORMATION

As we discovered earlier in this chapter, advertisers will go to great lengths to draw consumers to their products. However extreme, silly, or idiotic the ploy, advertisers still have to adhere to certain standards set by the advertising community and the federal government. Unscrupulous advertising is a major concern for media outlets and consumers alike. Publishers, networks, and other communication companies must be sure not to align themselves with companies that make false claims or promote dangerous products. False advertising cannot only damage the reputation of a media outlet, it can also harm the consumer. In the following section we will look at how Americans have monitored advertising using a mixture of government surveillance, consumer advocacy, media self-regulation, and industry self-regulation.

Government Regulations

The first casualty of government regulations in advertising was the pharmaceutical industry. Fed up with false claims and dangerous ingredients, the medical community joined with consumers and publishers to press Congress for the passage of the Pure Food and Drug Act in 1906. The law prohibited claims of undocumented cures, forbade manufacturers to misrepresent the efficacy of their products, and required all ingredients to be identified on the product label. This act particularly exposed the use of alcohol and drugs such as morphine in many pharmaceuticals. While these products apparently produced miraculous effects, more serious problems of addiction or complications were likely to follow the initial relief.

Soon after the Pure Food and Drug Act, the Federal Trade Commission (FTC) was established in 1914. The agency was authorized to regulate advertising and prevent deceptive practices. The FTC monitors and corrects claims of products that "cure" the common cold, guarantee "permanent weight loss," or "reverse baldness." As the FTC grew stronger, it became more proactive in its supervision of advertising practices; rather than merely handling complaints, the agency studied abuses and issued reports that attacked deception and the dissemination of misleading information.

Bait and switch
a method of fraudulent advertising in which a company advertises a product at an unprofitable price then reveals to a potential customer that the product is unavailable

In the 1950s, the FTC began to crack down on "bait and switch" ads that lure consumers with a "low-ball" price. **Bait and switch** is a method of fraudulent advertising in which a company advertises a product at an unprofitable price then reveals to a potential customer that the product is unavailable. The FTC charged that many merchants used pressure sales tactics to convince the consumer to "move up" to higher-priced products after claiming that the advertised items were out of stock or not really of satisfactory quality. The FTC also investigated the misuse of the word free in advertisements for products that weren't really free but required the purchase of other goods.

Beginning in the 1970s, the FTC took a hard look at "Brand X" ads, which compared a sponsor's product with an unnamed competitor. The government agency pushed advertisers to (1) name the competitor so the consumer would know which two products were being compared; and (2) cite impartial research data as proof that one product is better or more effective than another.

In order to protect the rights of companies and consumers, the FTC can issue a cease-and-desist order or can levy a fine against advertisers whose messages it feels have injured another firm or a consumer. In the 1970s, the agency began to require "corrective advertising" to offset the effects of long-running campaigns that had misled the public. Profile bread was required to explain to consumers that its claim of having fewer calories per slice was true only because its slices were thinner than those of the competitor, and that using the product would not cause weight loss. The FTC forced Profile to spend one fourth of the company's advertising budget to correct this misleading claim. Some companies have used sneaky maneuvers to sidestep FTC rulings. Ocean Spray, the maker of various juices, was ordered to spend a portion of its advertising budget one year to correct a false claim. The company simply decided not to advertise that year. They rested on the claim that one quarter of zero dollars is zero dollars.[17]

More than 20 U.S. government agencies are empowered to regulate one or more forms of advertising. The U.S. Postal Service screens catalogs and other direct mail advertising for information that would constitute "using the U.S. mail to defraud." The Securities and Exchange Commission keeps an eye on any claims that would tend to create undue expectations for the rise in the value of a stock. The Food and Drug Administration oversees the dissemination of any information concerning foodstuffs, health care products, cosmetics, and drugs. A current area of concern for the FDA is the proliferation of health claims that seek to take advantage of the public's concern about fitness and dieting. In 1991, the agency announced new rules that would curb claims like that of Quaker Oat Bran, which allege to "reduces cholesterol," unless such claims could be substantiated by independent authorities such as the Surgeon General or the National Academy of Sciences.

Manufacturers and the advertising industry constantly pressure government agencies to ease up on regulations for fear that regulations will become as stringent as they are in some other countries. In Malaysia, television ads that show a car driving fast and even flying through the air—a common way of demonstrating the handling of an automobile in American ads—are prohibited because uneducated viewers might attempt to emulate the behavior. Malaysia's strict code controlling TV ads also stipulates that speakers in commercials must use the correct pronunciation of the official Maylay language, not dialects of Chinese or Indian.

Subliminal Messages

Surely one of the most pervasive hoaxes of the twentieth century was the notion that "subliminal" advertising was used to make people desire an alcoholic drink, buy a certain make of car, or dash off to a restaurant lusting for a plate of clams. Gullible people with little understanding of psychology—including some state legislators who have introduced bills that would ban "subliminal" ads—fall prey to books and articles suggesting that words hidden in ice cubes, shapes concealed in the folds of a garment, or symbols worked into pictures of food have the power to make the consumer jump up and rush to the store, controlled by some unknown force.

In fact, in certain New Jersey theaters in the 1950s, movie audiences were exposed to images superimposed over the last scenes of films, exhorting them to "Drink Coca-Cola" and "eat popcorn." That caused newspaper editorialists to raise a hue and cry against the "alarming and outrageous" mind-fooling technique they supposed would put consumers in a trance. But it doesn't take much to stimulate a movie audience to get up and move to the refreshment stand during intermission. The "subliminal" trickery was hardly necessary.

Psychological research indicates that intense stimuli have a much greater effect than subtle stimuli. Messages hidden within other images certainly are far too subtle to equal the effects of obvious and overt advertising techniques. Despite these findings, legislators in the U.S. government proposed a ban on subliminal advertising in all forms of media.[18]

Most Americans value their right to receive information without interference. They would not welcome or tolerate government control of entertainment or educational information for reasons of cultural purity or governmental preference. On the other hand, they place great value on receiving accurate information, especially about health and personal products. That is why there has been little or no protest from citizens as legislative and regulatory bodies have become more stringent with advertisers.

The Attack on Cigarette and Liquor Advertising

Because of the wealth of information regarding the health problems caused by cigarette smoking and second hand smoke, cigarettes have been under attack in the United States for nearly half a century. In 1965, a series of findings by the Surgeon General led to required warnings on all cigarette packages and advertisements.

In 1971, after a long congressional debate, cigarette advertising was prohibited from the broadcast media by the federal government, which has more direct control over broadcast media than over print media. The tobacco industry and the broadcast industry maintained—and continued to argue—that the ban was unconstitutional. The temporary setback in advertising revenues for the broadcasters was a gold mine for the print media, which had lost billions of dollars to television over the preceding decade.

Pushed by the American Medical Association in the mid-1980s, Congress debated whether cigarette ads should be banned from the print media as well. The growing number of regulations imposed by the industry on smoking in the workplace and the decision by the military to restrict smoking helped fuel the spread of anti-smoking information. The industry responded with its own arguments that smokers should be allowed to choose whether to use the product and whether to receive information about it.

© Netrun78/Shutterstock.

What demographic do cigarette ads appeal to the most?

Lawyers for the RJ Reynolds Tobacco Company, for example, successfully fought the Federal Trade Commission's decision that one of the firm's advertisements misrepresented the results of a government study of smoking. The ad said that the results of the study were inconclusive. RJ Reynolds contended that the company's interpretation of the study was corporate opinion, and was thus protected by the First Amendment. The FTC simply saw the ad as one of many false claims about a scientific study by the tobacco industry.

Research shows that today more college women than college men smoke cigarettes, which researchers attribute to the fact that the tobacco industry is successfully linking smoking by women with images of glamour, success, and equality, as well as a means of staying thin and attractive. All of these charges are denied by the tobacco industry, which maintains that cigarette advertising is now directed only at people who already smoke.

The drive to prohibit all advertising of harmful substances such as tobacco and alcoholic beverages is being spearheaded by the medical community. Ironically, it came shortly after the medical professional societies finally altered their own ethical standards to permit "tasteful and restrained" advertising for doctors and medical institutions—a practice long prohibited by the profession.

The national debate over the effects of advertising on people who abuse substances has become heated and emotional. A former "Winston man" quit smoking and testified before Congress stating: "My job was to encourage, entice, and lure. I became a high-priced accessory to murder." The National Association to Prevent Impaired Driving, a coalition of a hundred traffic safety, health, and public policy groups, issued a study titled "Beer and Fast Cars" that criticized the brewing companies for sponsoring auto races and putting their emblems on cars. The practice, said the report, targets young blue-collar men,

Joe Camel

During the 1990s, Joe Camel, the cartoon spokesman for Camel brand cigarettes, was one of the most recognizable characters in American culture. With his dark sunglasses, slick clothes, and entourage of gorgeous friends, Joe Camel stood for all things cool. The Camel cigarette dangling from the corner of his mouth connected the cigarette brand to a favorable image. The fact that Joe Camel was an animated character concerned many consumers. Opponents of the character felt RJ Reynolds Tobacco Company, maker of Camel cigarettes, was using Joe Camel to appeal to children and young teens. A study conducted in 1991 by *The Journal of the American Medical Association* showed that 6-year-old children were just as familiar with Joe Camel as with Mickey Mouse.[19] The study also showed a connection between the Joe Camel campaign and an increase in teenage smoking. RJ Reynolds denied that it tailored its advertisements to children and conducted its own studies that contradicted those of the American Medical Association.

Still, in 1997 the FFC declared that the Joe Camel campaign violated federal law because of its harmful effects on minors. RJ Reynolds decided not to fight the ruling and chose to replace Joe Camel with a realistic non-animated outline of a camel.[20] Today the stylish image of Joe Camel can only be seen in back issues of magazines or faded billboards; however, the character's impact is still visible in the demographics of today's smokers.

the group with the highest incidence of auto accidents and arrests for driving under the influence of alcohol.

A study conducted for *The Wall Street Journal* showed that U.S. citizens overwhelmingly opposed the illegalization of alcoholic beverages and tobacco products, but their attitudes toward dissemination of information about the substances are quite different. By a substantial majority, the respondents favored banning beer and wine ads from television (hard liquor was already banned) and banning all alcohol and tobacco advertising from print media as well.

Consumers with a Voice

In 1989 advertisers including Ralston Purina, General Mills, and Domino's Pizza canceled their advertising on NBC's controversial sketch comedy show "Saturday Night Live" at the urging of a religious group that viewed the show as objectionable. "It's a difficult time for advertisers," said an NBC spokesperson. "There are a lot of pressure groups out there."

Pepsi discovered that statement to be true when it presented a commercial featuring recording artist Madonna shortly after the controversial music video for her song "Like a Prayer" hit the airwaves. Some religious groups opposed Madonna's use of Christian symbols and deemed the video and the artist distasteful and offensive. Pepsi canceled the Madonna ad feeling its association with the artist would create negative publicity. Pepsi found itself in the same situation again in 2002. However, it only took a complaint by one person to cause the company to change its advertising campaign.

On his news show *The O'Reilly Factor* political commentator Bill O'Reilly questioned Pepsi's use of rapper Ludacris as a company spokesperson, claiming the rapper espouses violence, degrades women, and promotes substance abuse.[21] Pepsi later dropped Ludacris as its spokesperson, but still received negative responses from consumers, and the rapper, who were disappointed that the company gave into pressure from one conservative figure.

It is not the opinions of well know figures that truly concern advertisers, it is the opinion of the American people. Irate individual consumers have always fired off letters and e-mails complaining about ads, but it is when special interest groups get involved that advertisers begin to worry. Groups such as the American Family Association's OneMillionMoms.com often participate in large-scale letter writing campaigns that aim to encourage advertisers to pull spots from television or radio shows that are considered immoral, violent, vulgar, or profane. The group takes credit for convincing large retail chains such as Lowe's to pull advertising from popular, but morally questionable, shows such as ABC's *Desperate Housewives*.[22] Organizations such as the American Family Association petition the advertisers of "distasteful" entertainment in attempt to pull funding from shows the organization finds offensive. A reduction in the number of paid advertisers may cause the entertainment industry to remove certain content from their products.

Today more than ever, advertisers have to walk a fine line in order to avoid offending one or another side of almost any issue. Advertisers must sometimes choose to alienate one segment of the population in order to appeal to their target audience. Still advertisers keep their ear to the ground when it comes to the opinion of the American consumer. A tarnished brand image can result in a major loss in revenue for advertisers.

ACT Against Predator Advertising

Action for Children's Television (ACT), a grass-roots organization formed by Peggy Charren in 1968, was created out of concern regarding the lack of suitable television programs for children. The group also had concerns about the type of advertising shown within children's programming. In 1989, ACT served as a consultant to the Consumers Union's holiday special, a program aimed to educate parents and children on the seduction of toy advertisements around the holiday season. "Buy Me That!", broadcasted on HBO, dissected several misleading techniques, including the implication that toys can walk and talk, the suggestion that a toy house or gas station comes with all the people and cars shown in the ad, and the failure to make clear that "some assembly required" may mean that an adult has to build a toy from parts before a child can play with it. The program also revealed how ads that show children happily bouncing around on Pogo Balls and tossing Flip Balls with the ease of Olympic athletes are the results of editing, and it is unlikely that most kids will be able to perform with the same happy satisfaction as those depicted on the screen.[23]

ACTs most successful campaign occurred when the organization helped pass the Children's Television Act of 1990, which increased the quality of educational and informational television. Shortly after the act was passed, Charren closed ACT and suggested that it was now up to parents to police the airwaves and decide for themselves what type of programs are best for their children.[24]

Media Self-Regulation

Mass media producers usually exercise their rights to refuse advertising that is in bad taste or that makes questionable claims and they are also in the position to reject spots that touch on controversial political issues. On the night of the 1984 presidential election, the WR Grace Company began running an "issues" spot on network television that depicted a baby crying when it was handed a bill for $50,000—the child's share of the national deficit. Two of the networks accepted the ad, but one rejected it. In 1986, the company submitted a new version of the ad to the networks depicting an elderly man on trial in the year 2017 for failing to do anything to halt the growing national debt. This time all three networks would not accept the ad, stating that it was too controversial and exposed the networks to possible complaints under the **Fairness Doctrine**, a policy created by the FCC that required the coverage of all controversial issues to be fair and balanced.

Fairness Doctrine
a policy created by the FCC that required the coverage of all controversial issues to be fair and balanced

J. Peter Grace, chairman and chief executive officer of the firm, responded: "They sell commercial time to advertise detergents, lingerie, hamburgers, appliances, and beer. Can it really be argued that selling time for conveying facts or ideas on important public issues will be detrimental to the interests of the country or the three networks?" Grace scoffed at the networks' contention that their news departments could do a better job of covering political issues than could business interests using advertising as a tool of information.

Most of the American advertising industry agreed with Grace and saw the network move as an attempt to pressure the Congress to do away with the Fairness Doctrine. In other words, the issues ads were being used as bargaining chips by the networks in their quest for less regulation. In 1987, the FCC finally did abolish most provisions of the Fairness Doctrine, but the regulatory body announced that it would continue to enforce the provision stating that issues currently the subject of voter referenda come under the Fairness Doctrine. Thus, opponents have to be given free air time to respond to statements made by another side on the issue.

For a long time the National Association of Broadcasters code was another media mechanism that affected what advertisers could do. First drafted in 1929, the code did not have the force of law; it was accepted by individual stations as a condition of membership in the NAB. When a suit resulted in the 1982 court decision that such a code unduly restricted the freedom to communicate information through advertising, the NAB withdrew it. Nevertheless, many of its provisions had been adopted as part of the standards and practices followed by individual stations, and thus they survive today.

The NAB code prohibited or limited the presentation of some products, which is why you never see hard liquor in commercials, and nobody actually *drinks* the beer or wine being advertised. Actors in commercials are permitted to be shown only lifting the glass or bottle toward or away from their lips. The film editor cuts away from the action during the moment when the liquid ostensibly is being guzzled.

© iofoto/Shutterstock.

Did you ever wonder why you never see anyone actually DRINK the wine they're advertising?

Without the authority of the NAB code, broadcast stations are finding it more and more difficult to explain what messages are acceptable for commercials or public service announcements, and why. For example, a station had a long-standing policy of refusing messages advocating birth control, explaining that "controversial issues" were not suitable for ads and were more properly covered by public affairs discussion programs. The station decided to accept condom ads, however, if they were presented as part of a campaign to slow the spread of HIV/AIDS or other sexually transmitted diseases.

Most media will not accept an anonymous advertisement that discusses a public issue or in any way takes a political stand. The name of at least one sponsoring person must be placed in the ad. The media will refuse the ad if they cannot verify that the sponsoring name is a valid one. The media also rejects advertisements they feel may open them to libel suits; in the eyes of the law it is the media who publish the defamation and thus share the responsibility for it, even if the damaging words were written by the sponsor.

Industry Self-Regulation

In order to forestall regulation, the business community and the advertising industry try to prevent abuses that might lead to public outrage and government interference. Most advertisers support their local Better Business Bureaus in the campaign to warn consumers about fraudulent claims and deceptive practices. The local telephone company's yellow pages will not accept advertising it deems to be misleading, and merchants must prove claims they are the "best" or the "only" before the telephone book will carry those words.

The National Advertising Review Council (NARC) was formed by the national Better Business Bureau, the American Advertising Federation, the American Association of Advertising Agencies, and the Association of National Advertisers—in short, the major forces in the advertising industry—for the purpose of self-regulating advertising. The investigative body of the NARC is the National Advertising Division (NAD), which is empowered to initiate inquiries into deceptive or misleading advertising and to hear complaints from both consumers and advertisers.

In a typical complaint to the NAD, Orville Redenbacher popcorn charged that General Mills' Pop Secret cheese flavored microwave popcorn claimed consumers preferred its product to Orville Redenbacher's cheese flavored popcorn, but the test was taken before Redenbacher had reformulated its product and the ad was run after the new product was on the market. In a later test, Redenbacher claimed, its popcorn scored higher. General Mills said its ad had completed its run, and new ads would not be run until after further testing. Case closed.

A more exotic complaint was lodged by the Children's Advertising Review Unit of the NAD against a copying machine company whose ads showed frustrated business people throwing their copiers out of windows. The complaint said that the dangerous act of throwing things out windows might lead impressionable children to imitate the practice, and the scenes of copying machines crashing on the sidewalk might cause anxiety in young children. The sponsoring firm agreed to consider those concerns when planning new ads.

The NAD does not have the power to censor ads, impose fines, or bring any other sanctions. But both the act of review and the publication of the results in the leading trade publications are instructive to the advertising community and help prevent future abuses or excesses. In practice, the NARC and NAD have been effective forces in serving the information needs of the consumer.

THE FUTURE OF ADVERTISING: KEEPING CURRENT

© Monkey Business Images/Shutterstock.

Advertisers may start sending full length commercials to consumers' PDAs.

With the introduction and expansion of new media, the advertising industry will have to continue to evolve. While traditional media such as television, newspapers, and radio will still be important outlets, advertisers must look at the cultural trends to determine the best way to reach consumers.

New Technology

Since a growing number of people are looking to the Internet to stay up-to-date on news and entertainment, advertisers are going to look to the Internet to spend large portions of their budgets. Paid search and pay-per-click advertising is just the beginning. Viral videos and blogs will emerge as an effective way to reach consumers.

Mobile phones have also changed the game for advertising. As a device that people rarely leave home without, mobile advertising is riding on the heels of the Internet as the newest way to deliver commercial messages to consumers 24 hours a day. Today's mobile phones are far more advanced than the two-pound clunkers introduced in the 1980s. With the ability to browse Web pages and send e-mails, mobile phones are like handheld computers. Now that many cell phone makers are creating phones with flash technology, it can be possible to send full length commercials to thousands of consumers via their mobile phones.

Product Placement

When you watch episodes of your favorite TV show or movie you may notice the main character is drinking a Vitamin Water and wearing a Ralph Lauren Polo shirt. Those items were not randomly placed in the scene; they were put there by advertisers. Advertisers hope that consumers see a character wearing or using a certain product then want to emulate that character's choices.

The practice of inserting advertising into film and television entertainment came under scrutiny when consumers started to take notice. The executive director of the Center for Science in the Public Interest used the op-ed page of *The New York Times* as a forum for alerting the public to the amount of advertising that is finding its way into the movies we pay to see. In one movie, "Bull Durham," he counted the presence of Miller beer products or signs 21 times, along with obvious plugs for a soft drink, a brand of bourbon, and even Oscar Mayer wieners—a total of 50 brand names on screen for an average of one every two minutes.

Today, some television shows can have up to 7,500 instances of product placement in a single season. TV executives may worry that too much product placement may harm the integrity of a show, but as more and more advertisers are choosing the Internet over TV, they welcome the revenue. For advertisers looking to continue marketing products on television, product placement will be an increasing force.

Guerrilla Marketing

Traditional advertisements like the 30 second commercial and the newspaper insert will soon take a back seat to more exciting and cost-effective forms of advertising formulated by guerrilla marketing. **Guerrilla marketing** is an unconventional form of advertising that attempts to get the maximum result from minimal resources. Examples of this type of advertising could involve a person running the New York City Marathon in a chicken suit and signs advertising a new fast food restaurant chain. The gimmick may cost a few hundred dollars, but the message could reach over one million spectators and possibly get news coverage.

Guerrilla marketing
an unconventional form of advertising that attempts to get the maximum result from minimal resources

Guerrilla marketing is not always used for a cheap laugh; it can sometimes call attention to serious issues. At Taiba Hospital in Kuwait, administrators painted pink strips on a speed bump at the entrance of the hospital. A sign next to the speed bump said, "Feel the bump? Have your breasts checked." The ad was a high impact way to remind women to get a yearly breast examination.[25]

In the next decade we will see a lot of changes in the way advertisers deliver their commercial messages and the number of commercial messages we are exposed to will continue to grow. Whether these changes and increases will benefit us as consumers or saturate our lives with unneeded products is unclear. However, good or bad advertising will still remain an integral part of our economy and culture.

Social networking and social media are upending some ideas about how advertising works because people often hear about products from friends via Twitter or Facebook, and bypass advertising agencies and media organizations altogether. This is a new phenomenon and its full impact on advertising and messaging is as yet unknown.

Predictions about Advertising

- The 30-Second Spot will finally die. The funeral will be attended by the 60-Second Spot, the Radio Ad, the Infomercial, and the Bumper Sticker.
- Blogs will change everything. For marketers, the blogosphere will prompt them to think very seriously about their business models.

- The consumer will be boss.
- The FDA will crack down on illegal drug marketing via the Internet.
- Advertising "one-stop shops" will thrive. As marketers are pressed to find ways to reach consumers, advertising holding companies like WPP and Interpublic will continue to evolve into "one-stop shops" for everything from advertising to guerrilla marketing to package design.
- The Hispanic consumer will arrive. After years of treating the Hispanic segment as an afterthought, marketers will shift more money to addressing the demographic with a much greater amount of TV, print, and online ads featuring Latinos.
- Marketers will continue to fear Google.

Todd Wasserman

CAREERS IN THE FIELD

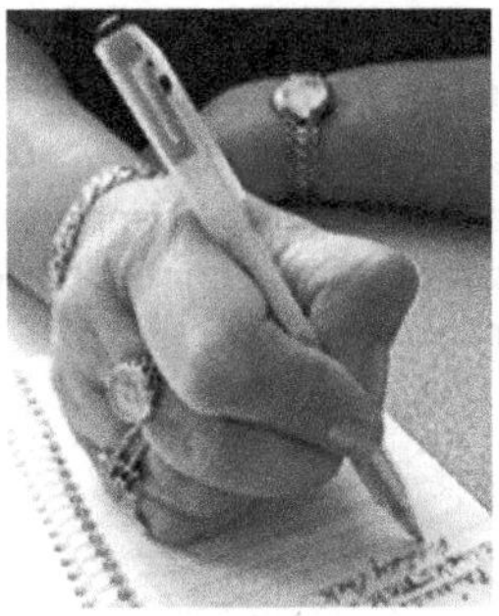

After seeing a commercial have you ever thought to yourself, I could come up with a better way to deliver that message? If so, perhaps you should consider a career in advertising. The field of advertising can be very exciting for creative and managerial types alike. However, advertising involves more than just coming up with catchy jingles or clever slogans. It involves a high level of research, analysis, and at the heart of it all, salesmanship. There are different facets of advertising that job seekers might find interesting. On the administrative side, positions include account management, media planning, and market research. When hiring for these positions, agencies look for candidates with a strong business mind, effective communication skills, and leadership experience. On the creative side, openings are in copywriting and art direction. Agencies typically look for copywriters and art directors with the ability to think outside of the box and come up with innovative ideas that will benefit the client and the consumer. Jobs in advertising are a bit scarce and competition for positions, especially on the creative side, can be tough. However, if you have the right combination of business sense and creativity, you might just stand out in the crowd.[26]

SUMMARY

- Americans are exposed to thousands of commercial messages a day from various types of media outlets.
- Advertising has evolved over the years to adapt to the changes in mass media.
- Advertisers go beyond standard television and radio commercials to advertise products. They use methods such as direct mail, point-of-sale advertising, outdoor signage, and the Internet to promote their message.
- Government agency, community groups, and the media regulate advertisements to ensure they are not dishonest, misleading, or distasteful.
- Advertising is a continuous force in our economy, and advertisers are finding new and inventive ways to reach consumers.

DISCUSSION QUESTIONS

1. How aware are you of the advertising in your environment? Do you think you have ever been swayed to purchase a product without being aware of the commercial message that prompted your purchase?
2. Do you think you benefit from advertising? Do you use it to help make decisions about what products to buy?
3. Do you think that banning tobacco advertising is against the first amendment? Should tobacco companies have the same rights as other companies?
4. Do you think advertising has become too intrusive? Would you be willing to pay more money to media outlets if they removed advertising?
5. What examples of guerrilla marketing have you noticed in the last few years?

NOTES

1. Brenda O'Neill, "Can you feel sorry for an ad man?" *BBC News* November 21, 2005 at http://news.bbc.co.uk/ 2/hi/uk_news/magazine/4456176.stm.
2. "Advertising Age: The Advertising Century" *Ad Age* at http://adage.com/century/timeline/index.html.
3. Scot Mondore "One Hundred Years of Player Endorsements: Honus Wagner and Louisville Slugger" The National Baseball Hall of Fame and Museum February 19, 2007 at http://www.baseballhalloffame.org/news/ article.jsp?ymd=20070219&content_id=859&vkey=hof_news.
4. The Advertising Council, "Ad Council: The Story of the Ad Council" at http://www.adcouncil.org/timeline.html. Retrieved October 10, 2008.
5. http://wehner.tamu.edu/mgmt.www/v-buenger/466/Coke_and_Pepsi.pdf.
6. "Mobile Advertising" *The Economist* October 4, 2007 at http://www.economist.com/business/displaystory.cfm?story_id=9912455.
7. Merriam-Webster at http://www.merriam-webster.com/dictionary/consumerism.
8. "The Role of Advertising in America" Association of National Advertisers at http://www.ana.net/advocacy2/
9. Jennifer L. Schenker, "Point-of-Sale Advertising Goes High Tech" *BusinessWeek* September 22, 2008 at http://www.businessweek.com/globalbiz/content/sep2008/gb20080922_109810.htm.
10. Stephanie Clifford, "Summer Silliness Brings a Pizza Field and a Giant Oreo" *The New York Times* August 1, 2008 at http://www.nytimes.com/2008/08/01/business/media/01adco.html?pagewanted=1&_r=1.
11. Google Web site at http://www.google.com/ads/.
12. Google Web site Investors' information at http://investor.google.com/fin_data.html.
13. http://www.scotuswiki.com/index.php?title=Citizens_United_v._Federal_Election_Commission.
14. "The Living Room Candidate: 1952 Eisenhower vs. Stevenson" Museum of the Moving Image at http://www.livingroomcandidate.org/commercials/1952.
15. Mark Preston, "Political television advertising to reach $3 billion" CNN October 15, 2008 at http://www.cnn.com/2007/POLITICS/10/15/ad.spending/.
16. N.W. Ayer & Son. *Encyclopedia Britannica* at http://www.britannica.com/EBchecked/topic/1349123/ NW-Ayer-Son. Retrieved October 17, 2008.
17. *Age of Propaganda: The Everyday Use and Abuse of Persuasion* by Anthony Pratkanis and Elliot Aronson. New York: W. H. Freeman (2001).
18. Chris Sharp, "Subliminal Messaging: A life changing phenomenon" Helium at http://www.helium.com/items/383493-subliminal-messaging-a-life-changing-phenomenom.
19. Jane E. Brody, "Study Ties Women's Brands To Smoking Increase for Girls" *The New York Times* February 23, 1994 at http://query.nytimes.com/gst/fullpage.html?res=9405E5DB113BF930A15751C0A962958260&sec=health&spon=&pagewanted=all.
20. "Joe Camel Advertising Campaign Violates Federal Law, FTC Says" Federal Trade Commission Press Release May 28, 1997 at http://www.ftc.gov/opa/1997/05/joecamel.shtm.

21. Bill O'Reilly "Challenging Pepsi" *The O'Reilly Factor* August 28, 2002 at http://www.foxnews.com/story/0,2933, 61546,00.html.
22. Frank Rich "The Great Indecency Hoax" *The New York Times* November 28, 2004 at http://www.nytimes.com/2004/ 11/28/arts/28rich.html?pagewanted=print&position.
23. Walter Goodman, "TV VIEW; A Cautionary Guide for Little Customers" *The New York Times* December 3, 1989 at http://query.nytimes.com/gst/fullpage.html?res=950DE1D61030F930A35751C1A96F948260&sec=&spon=&page wanted=all.
24. William Richter, "Action for Children's Television" The Museum of Broadcast Communication at http://www .museum.tv/archives/etv/A/htmlA/actionforch/actionforch.htm.
25. "Taiba Hospital: Feel the bump? Have your breasts checked" www.Jazzarh.net March 18, 2008 at http://www.jazarah .net/blog/taiba-hospital-felt-the-bump-have-your-breasts-checked/.
26. "Guide to Careers in Advertising" Advertising Educational Foundation at http://www.aef.com/industry/ careers/1422#3.

chapter 15

Public Relations

OBJECTIVES

- Trace the development of the public relations industry, from inception to present day
- Discuss the contributions of pioneering figures in the field of public relations, including P.T. Barnum, Ivy Lee, and Edward Bernays
- Identify the four PR models, and outline their major elements
- Discuss the components involved in implementing a PR plan
- Identify and discuss the varied roles and functions of public relations in the contemporary global marketplace
- Understand the skills necessary for professionals to succeed in the public relations industry

KEY TERMS

corporate social responsibility (CSR)
damage control
focus group interview
greenwashing
issues management
MBO
media facilitators
press agent/publicity model
propaganda
public information model
public opinion poll
public relations (PR)
RACE formula
rebranding
spin
subpublics
two-way asymmetric model
two-way symmetric model

INTRODUCTION

In 2000, Turkcell, one of the three main mobile phone providers in Turkey, learned from a customer survey that its subscribers wanted to see the company more involved in the community, particularly when it came to supporting educational projects. As a result, the company joined nonprofit organizations in launching a campaign, "Contemporary Girls of Contemporary Turkey," that aimed to increase educational opportunities for Turkish girls, especially in impoverished rural areas.

As part of this ongoing public relations campaign, scholarships were offered in the first year to 5,000 girls in 28 rural areas. Because of the campaign's dramatic success, those numbers were increased in successive years, reaching 35 areas and benefiting thousands of girls who would have not been otherwise able to attend primary and secondary schools.

For Turkcell, the campaign changed people's general views of the company, earned them three major social responsibility awards in the program's first three years, and generated not only positive publicity, but also popular support and goodwill toward the organization.[1] In 2007, the program won the prestigious Golden World Award from the Institute of Public Relations.[2] This campaign provides an excellent example of how companies are using public relations—that is, the business of bringing about public understanding and goodwill toward a person or organization—to improve their image and build a more positive relationship with consumers.

© Panos Karapanagiotis/Shutterstock.

Aristotle's Rhetoric is considered by some to be one of the earliest volumes on public relations.

public relations (PR)
the business of bringing about public awareness, understanding, and goodwill toward a person or organization

EARLY PUBLIC RELATIONS: A HISTORICAL OVERVIEW

The Origins of Public Relations

While the term **public relations** probably is barely over a century old, one finds ample instances of such activity among the ancients. Aristotle's *Rhetoric,* for example, is considered by some to be one of the earliest volumes on public relations. In this work, the ancient Greek defined rhetoric as the "art of oratory, especially persuasive use of language to influence the thoughts and actions of listeners"—a primary concern in any public relations campaign, past or present. Moreover, the authors of the first major public relations textbook indicate that "Caesar carefully prepared the Romans for his crossing of the Rubicon in 49 B.C. by sending reports to Rome on his epic achievements as governor of Gaul.[3] Others suggest that the gospels (*gospel* means "good news") were written "more to propagate the faith than to provide a historical account of Jesus' life."[4]

The groundwork for much of modern public relations thought can likewise be traced to the American colonial era. Founding fathers, including Benjamin Franklin, Thomas Jefferson, and John Adams, used propaganda techniques familiar to today's public relations practitioners. Samuel Adams spelled them out:

- Formation of an activist organization
- Using many media
- Creating events and slogans
- Orchestrating conflict
- Sustaining an information campaign over time until the minds of the public were won over to the cause.[5]

Although conceived of during the eighteenth century, these public relations tenets remain relevant today, particularly within the political arena.

From Press Agentry to Public Policy

Politics remained an integral venue for the development of public relations throughout the 1800s. Andrew Jackson, the first "common man" to assume the presidency (from 1829–1837), felt more responsible to the masses than had previous presidents. Distrustful of those who traditionally held power, he surrounded himself with a "kitchen cabinet" of advisors more in tune with his populist views. Among his confidants was Amos Kendall, a former newspaper editor who took on many of the duties now associated with the White House press secretary.

Kendall's approach was that of a press agent—catering to the needs of the press. He wrote speeches for Jackson to deliver, conducted straw polls on public opinion, and built Jackson's image as an honest and resourceful president. By shaping the way Jackson was represented in the press through words, action, and the strategic release of information, Kendall became a model for public relations practitioners to follow for years to come.[6]

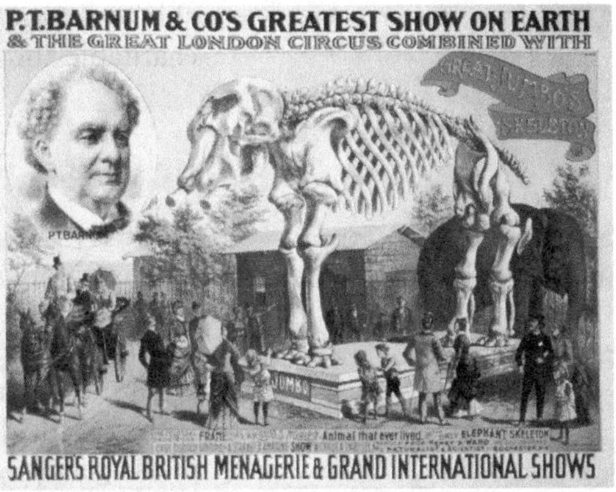

© CORBIS.

P.T. Barnum became a master of publicity with his "Greatest Show on Earth."

P.T. Barnum can be credited with translating the emerging public relations industry, and its reliance on press agentry, into the world of entertainment. Barnum not only catered to the press, but in fact courted them with bold, sensational stunts and spectacles meant to capture the world's attention. And he became, indeed, a master of publicity: exhibitions at his American Museum sold millions of tickets.[7] And he is perhaps best known for proclaiming his eponymous circus to be "the greatest show on earth."

By the beginning of the twentieth century, the term public relations had come into use. It generally was interpreted to mean the way business explained itself to the people and attempted to convince them that it was working for their general welfare. American Telephone & Telegraph Company (AT&T) president Theodore Vail gave the term legitimacy when he directed that the company's 1908 annual report be titled "Public Relations." The publication focused on the firm's responsibility to make a fair profit, to treat its employees well, and to answer any questions that could reduce conflicts between itself and its publics.[8]

Ivy Lee: Informing the Public

As the twentieth century began, American business was under attack as a force that dominated society and trammeled individuals. Magazine muckrakers took industry to task for dehumanizing the workplace and putting worker comfort and safety second to profits. As a result, unions organized and legislators began to enact laws to limit business practices. A former New York newspaper business reporter, Ivy Ledbetter Lee, saw the need for industry to do a better job explaining itself to society. Lee's message to business was: "Let the public be informed!"

Business had always tended toward secrecy, but Lee advised business leaders that openness could help win the support of distrustful publics, including legislators. Lee opened one of the first publicity agencies specializing in providing information about business to the media. Lee centered his agency's services around his Declaration of Principles, which spelled out how his firm intended to give editors accurate, complete information and to answer inquiries from the press as swiftly as possible.[9]

One of Lee's greatest PR successes occurred within the coal industry. Lee provided news on behalf of the coal operators to counter information supplied by local labor unions. He convinced John D. Rockefeller to visit the family's mines in Colorado to offset criticism in a labor dispute. Eventually he was able to change the senior Rockefeller's image of detached aloofness to one of a charitable and concerned leader of business.

Edward Bernays: Shaper of the Profession

While Ivy Lee is considered a pioneer in the PR field, the name Edward L. Bernays is synonymous with the shaping of public relations as we know it today. More than any other work, his *Crystallizing Public Opinion*, published in 1923, ushered in the era of scientific persuasion within the public relations realm. Scientific persuasion effectively replaced Ivy Lee's construct of public relations as the simple dissemination of information, which had previously supplanted press agentry—the hype and hoopla associated with P. T. Barnum.

Born in Vienna and a nephew of Freud, Bernays once was a press agent—the person who contacts the media to promote theatrical events—for the great tenor Enrico Caruso. A journalist by training, he was called to serve on the American government's Creel Committee for Public Information during World War I, which gave him a better understanding of the workings of **propaganda**—information deliberately spread to help or harm the reputation of an individual, organization, or country.

propaganda
information deliberately spread to help or hurt the reputation of an individual, organization, or country

His second book, *Propaganda*, published in 1928, was based on the concept that "the conscious and intelligent manipulation of the organized habits and opinions of the masses is an important element in democratic society. Those who manipulate this unseen mechanism of society constitute an invisible government which is the true ruling power of our country."[10]

Bernays coined the phrase "engineering public consent" as a synonym for proactive public relations. He argued that facts and events could be arranged and presented to convince an audience that one course of action was preferable to another. His textbook *Public Relations* was published in 1952, and he continued as a spokesperson and advocate for public relations past his hundredth birthday in 1991.

Bernays, who died in 1995, also coined the phrase "public relations counsel" and suggested that it was a profession, not merely a craft or trade.[11] Unlike press agents and publicists, who care only about getting publicity for their clients, Bernays suggested that the public relations counsel should use the techniques of the social sciences to understand how public opinion is created and thus how public opinions can be swayed through scientific, ethical, and socially responsible techniques.

MODERN PUBLIC RELATIONS: MODELS, CONCEPTS, AND PROGRAM BASICS

PR Models

As with many subfields of mass communication, it can be helpful to conceptualize public relations in terms of theoretical models. Two leading public relations scholars and theorists, James E. Grunig and Todd Hunt, characterize Edward Bernays as responsible for developing two new models of public relations, which joined two earlier models.[12] P. T. Barnum personified the **press agent/publicity model**, with his shameless promotions based more on fancy

press agent/publicity model
a PR model, favored by P.T. Barnum, that emphasizes promotion and publicity with little regard for facts

than fact. Ivy Lee, in contrast, represented the **public information model**, with his emphasis on one-way (source-receiver, or producer-consumer) dissemination of truthful information.

The writing and practice of Bernays led to the development of what Grunig calls the **two-way asymmetric model.** This model uses formative research—research conducted before beginning an information campaign—to ascertain the attitudes of the target publics. While the flow of information is imbalanced in favor of the producer, feedback from the consumer can and does influence the producer. The two-way model represents a necessary way of conceiving public relations when the actions and behaviors of consumer publics affect the actions and behaviors of producers in the competitive business system.

As Bernays worked with educators and professional leaders, he came to realize that in businesses subject to heavy government regulation, or where the activist consumer has as much influence as the producer, balanced communication is necessary to adapt the organization to the realities of society. Grunig calls this fourth situation the **two-way symmetric model.** Examples might include an energy utility wishing to open a nuclear power plant, or a pharmaceutical company hoping to introduce an experimental drug. Consumer feedback and, ultimately, approval, is critical in such situations in order to ensure success for the business.

With the popularization of the Internet and other media technologies that facilitate the speedy dissemination of information, it is possible to say that consumers and clients have attained a new level of power over all realms—business, politics, and entertainment. Nowadays, it is virtually impossible for most industry sectors to succeed without fully taking into account the opinions, needs, and desires of their target publics. In this sense, the two-way symmetric model has become the most important and widely used public relations model.

Table 15.1 summarizes the characteristics of the four models of public relations. Note that the development of the models follows public relations history over the last century.

Although the two-way symmetric model tends to dominate the field in today's age of information, all four models still coexist. The astute public relations practitioner is the one who knows how to choose the correct one to fit the situation at hand. Your own college or university, for example, might use publicity to promote the institution and its offerings to prospective students, public information to tell about a research project, two-way asymmetric public relations when dealing with student protesters, and the two-way symmetric model when trying to convince a foundation to fund a major grant.

public information model
a PR model, favored by Ivy Lee, that emphasizes one-way (source-receiver, or producer-consumer) dissemination of truthful information

two-way asymmetric model
A PR model in which formative research is used to ascertain the attitudes of the target publics before a PR plan is implemented; it recognizes that the actions and behaviors of consumer publics affect the actions and behaviors of producers in the competitive business system

two-way symmetric model
A PR model most often applied to businesses subject to heavy government regulation, or where the activist consumer has as much influence as the producer; it recognizes that balanced communication is necessary to adapt the organization to the realities of society.

Table 15.1 Four Models of Public Relations

Model	Characteristics
Press agent/publicity	Emphasis on promotion, sensationalism, persuasion and/or manipulation of public, sometimes at the expense of facts
Public Information	Emphasis on one-way dissemination of truthful information
One-way asymmetrical model	Emphasis on formative research to determine wants, needs, and attitudes of target consumers
Two-way symmetrical model	Emphasis on balanced communication between producer and consumer

Facilitating the Flow of Information

Preceding chapters have examined the functions of specific news and entertainment media. However, the subject of this chapter, public relations, as well as the topic of Chapter 13, advertising, are not media in themselves. Instead, they may be conceptualized as **facilitators** and they also utilize media to disseminate their messages. That is, public relations and advertising make the creation and distribution of mass media possible because, directly or indirectly, they underwrite the cost of disseminating information cheaply to large audiences.

media facilitators
industries, such as public relations and advertising, that make the creation and distribution of mass media possible because, directly or indirectly, they underwrite the cost of disseminating information cheaply to large audiences

Advertisers, as we shall see in the next chapter, provide the cornerstone of financial support by purchasing time or space in the mass media. Public relations, on the other hand, bestows what some have called a "subsidy" because it involves the supply of information, which the media otherwise would have to pay to gather, for free. In fact, without the financial support of public relations and advertising, the forms of media that we consume on a daily basis would be astoundingly expensive—a newspaper might cost a couple of dollars, instead of 25 or 50 cents, and magazines might run $15 each.

© arteretum/Shutterstock.

Without the financial support of public relations and advertising, everyday media would be very expensive.

In addition to providing financial support, PR has, over the past few decades, transformed from a "behind the scenes" entity to a powerful, highly visible, and influential industry at the forefront of media, culture, and business. In his 1986 book *Goodbye to the Low Profile,* Herb Schmertz, former vice president of public affairs at Mobil Oil, highlighted and described this rapidly changing role of public relations.[13]

Schmertz had once been considered controversial among public relations practitioners because of his willingness to inject his own forceful personality into the debate on oil companies and their policies. For years, it had been assumed that PR people worked quietly behind the scenes, avoiding conflict and perpetuating the fantasy that events happened naturally without the assistance of public relations. As the title of his book suggests, Schmertz believed it was time to reinvent the popular concept of public relations, acknowledging the role of PR in fostering open and full debate on public issues.

While not all PR professionals agree with his assertive techniques, most appreciate that public relations, once considered an apologist and publicist for big business, has become a force for building alliances, influencing discussion of public issues, and facilitating the flow of information between producers and consumers of products, services, and ideas. Public relations clients in today's global marketplace thus need, and demand, sophisticated, multi-faceted PR programs that require and depend on astute research and novel, persuasive devices.

© Monkey Business Images/Shutterstock.

In order to implement a PR program, you need to tailor the message for a specific audience.

Program Implementation

The implementation of a modern PR program is a complex operation that varies greatly, depending on the account and client. However, a few components tend to remain consistent across all situations.

Identifying Subpublics. These days, PR professionals realize that modern consumers have effects on the producers that are as important as the effects producers hope to have on consumers. The mass public rarely acts in a unified way. As a result, one key component in implementing a PR program for any organization or purpose is to determine the characteristics and behaviors of the target consumer, or **subpublics.** This is not a totally new concept: magazines and radio, responding to the competition from television, learned to tailor their messages for specialized audiences with specialized information needs and interests.

subpublics
specialized audiences with specialized information needs and interests that PR professionals must identify before implementing and specifically targeting a program

Some of the subpublics a large organization such as a corporation must identify and plan communication programs for might include:

- Employees
- Consumers of products or services
- Other individuals or organizations providing raw materials or services to the organization
- The surrounding business community and local chambers of commerce
- Stockholders in a company or members of an association
- Municipal governments and state and federal regulatory and legislative bodies that can pass laws affecting the organization
- Political and activist groups
- Professional groups that determine norms and standards for a field
- Minorities
- Voters
- The news media
- Trade publications serving a particular industry

Each of these categories of subpublics can be further divided. Employees, for example, would include part-time workers, blue-collar personnel, clerical staff, managers, and supervisors. Catering to the information needs of every group complicates the job of public relations agents in an organization.

At your college or university, for example, the PR staff working for the administration or development office likely divide the alumni subpublic into smaller categories. Alumni subpublics might include:

- Wealthy graduates of 50 years ago who might just come forth with a few million dollars if buildings were named for them
- Football fanatics whose loyalty depends largely on the win-loss record of this year's team
- Parents who are thinking of sending their children to the school from which they graduated
- English majors who now head corporations and think the school should offer a degree in business
- Engineers who work for industry but return to campus occasionally for refresher courses
- Scholars who earned Ph.D. degrees and are now college professors

Each subgroup is potentially helpful and influential, and thus the PR staff likely works hard to carefully target their messages and requests to each one. For example, a university may develop a dozen different publications catering to these subpublics, rather than relying on a single alumni magazine to satisfy everyone's needs and interests.

Setting Objectives. When implementing a program, PR professionals must also set clear goals and objectives. Press agent/publicity and public information specialists may be concerned with getting information to consumers, creating enthusiasm for an idea, motivating actions, or instilling confidence in a person or project. Thus their objectives are relatively simple and obvious: "Fill the stadium on Saturday" or "Let people know about the many uses of our products." In the two-way models, however, objectives are more complex: "Gain compliance with the new recycling laws" or "Help our employees find educational resources that will promote their career advancement."

Whatever the model, public relations people have to set specific objectives—the number of people reached or the number of consumers behaving in a certain manner—and specific time frames and deadlines so that the effects of the public relations program can be measured and demonstrated to management in numerical terms.

RACE formula
John E. Marston's construct for the implementation of a successful public relations program involving four steps: research, action, communication, and evaluation

Planning the Program. To ensure that they have followed all the steps in implementing a successful public relations program, many professionals follow a plan modeled after John E. Marston's **RACE formula.**[14] The letters stand for research, action, communication, and evaluation. Since evaluation at the end of a program is a kind of research that may lead to modifications or changes in the public relations program, the formula can be seen as a spiral that continually renews the process of analysis, program design, and communication.

Research includes measuring public opinion, analyzing all information currently available to publics, considering options, pretesting messages, assessing the impact of information channels, and making qualitative assessments of ideas that may prove effective. *Action* means laying out the program that will get the message across—planning events and organizing information that will persuade the consumer to accept the views (or product or candidate) put forth by the organization. *Communication* involves creating and conveying messages to audiences, and the *evaluation* of feedback as to whether and how the messages have been received and interpreted.

THE ROLES AND FUNCTIONS OF PUBLIC RELATIONS IN TODAY'S GLOBAL MARKETPLACE

In today's global marketplace, where communication is lightning fast, new technology is constantly developing, and many organizations aim to reach consumers all over the world, public relations continues to grow in prominence and importance. Moreover, the roles and functions of public relations continue to expand and evolve in response to these changes and challenges. Indeed, public relations today fulfills a variety of functions within a diverse set of contexts. While the following discussion is not exhaustive, it is a useful sampling of some of PR's most important roles.

damage control
the first phase of crisis communication in which PR practitioners identify how the crisis has negatively affected the public's perception of the organization and demonstrate that the organization is taking responsibility and has a plan for solving the crisis

Crisis Management

In the last few decades, one of the most important roles PR departments have played in many large organizations has been within the context of crisis management. Developing a crisis communication plan comprises one of the most important responsibilities of many PR bodies. Crisis communication consists of two important phases. The first is called **damage control.** It involves

Historical Case Study: The Tylenol Tragedy

In September of 1982, several deaths in the Chicago area were traced to arseniclaced Tylenol capsules. When it was revealed that the medicine was made by a subsidiary of Johnson & Johnson, the company's stock fell sharply in value.

The swift response of the J&J public relations department was to counsel management to remove the product from the shelves immediately. A team rushed to Chicago to work with the police in getting information to the public, and a national hotline was set up to answer questions from consumers. The chief executive officer of the company served as spokesperson throughout the crisis, and he assured the media and consumers that the company would put consumer safety before profits.

Rather than abandon the successful Tylenol brand, the company reintroduced it in tamper-resistant packaging after research showed that consumers trusted the company as a result of its handling of the Tylenol tragedy. Johnson & Johnson's management of the crisis became a model for industry to follow.

finding out what has happened and how it has negatively affected the public's perception of the organization. The immediate task is to demonstrate that the organization is taking responsibility and has the means of solving the crisis.

The second phase involves moving the organization from the crisis footing to one of **issues management.** While it may not be possible to undo the effects of the crisis or make it go away, it is possible to demonstrate to the public that the organization is working to solve or alleviate the problem through cooperation or negotiation with other organizations.

issues management the second phase of crisis communication in which PR practitioners aim to demonstrate to the public that the organization is working to solve or alleviate the problem through cooperation or negotiation with other organizations

An example is the exposure of a nonprofit charity organization whose executive director has been discovered misappropriating contributions and putting them to personal use. The damage control phase consists of showing that the wrongdoing has been stopped and the wrongdoer has been relieved of duty. The issues management phase consists of a program to reassure contributors that their money is being applied to the charitable programs for which it was intended, and that those programs continue to be worthy of public support.

High profile examples of poor crisis communication—the 1979 Three-Mile Island nuclear power plant accident, for instance, in which the federal government and plant operators took three days to effectively address the public—have set examples for today's corporations on how such crises *should not* be handled. As a result of these historical failures, many corporations nowadays specifically mandate how quickly media requests for information must be met in the event of a crisis, as well as which officer will serve as spokesperson for the company when a catastrophe occurs.

In 2007, after many of their toys were discovered to contain dangerous levels of lead paint, Mattel Inc. found itself mired in a serious crisis. In response, CEO Robert A. Eckert issued a direct apology on the company's Web site. The company then enacted a recall, followed by a revised safety plan that required more rigorous inspections for its products.[15] As Mattel demonstrated, effective public relations planning can mitigate a crisis, winning support for an organization by showing its

© Stefan Zaklin/epa/Corbis.

Robert Eckert testifies before the Senate about toys manufactured in China that needed to be recalled for safety issues.

willingness to talk openly about its mistakes. In following, a poor PR response to crisis can result in total loss of public trust and, potentially, loss of business for a company.

Corporate Rebranding

rebranding
the process through which a product, service, or organization is marketed and associated with new, different, and improved identity

corporate social responsibility (CSR)
the actions or programs adopted by organizations that reflect an interest in and concern for social and environmental issues

greenwashing
the practice of companies expressing environmental concerns and/or making their products appear to be environmentally sound

Another important role of public relations within a corporate context involves **rebranding**—that is, implementing initiatives that cause consumers to associate an organization with a new and improved identity. In some instances, rebranding may overlap with or follow crisis management, serving as a means to rehabilitate and change the image of a company marred by scandal or tragedy. In other cases, rebranding may represent an organization's attempt to increase their appeal to consumers, and in turn, their potential profits.

The demonstration of **corporate social responsibility,** or CSR, is at the heart of many PR rebranding efforts. The Turkcell case study that opened this chapter is just one among many examples of how companies today use PR to revamp their images, benefit society, and augment their bottom lines.

In recent years, the burgeoning Green Movement—an increased concern on sustainability and environmentally-friendly practices—has incited many organizations to emphasize their products or practices as environmentally altruistic. Critics refer to this PR tactic as **greenwashing,** and accuse organizations of exaggerating their environmental contributions or misrepresenting their practices for PR and monetary gain. In some instances—the development of a hybrid locomotive by GE as part of their Ecomagination initiative, for example—companies do seem to be making valid, and valuable, efforts to

Case Study: A "Green" Oil Company?

British Petroleum (BP), a major oil and chemicals company that operates across six continents to the tune of $277 billion in revenues in 2007, has tried, at least since the mid-1990s, to clean up its image and brand itself as the "environmentally responsible" oil company.[16] Its advertising and public relations campaign, which in the U.S. had adopted slogans such as "bp: beyond petroleum" and "bp: better petroleum," has been largely successful in changing the company's image.

BP's rebranding effort can be traced to the mid-1990s, years before the company's purchase of Amoco, a competing oil giant, and several years before its incorporation of ARCO, another major player. In 1996, BP resigned from and distanced itself from the Global Climate Coalition, a lobbying group that ridiculed the science behind global warming and tried to undermine the Kyoto treaty discussions. The move coincided with the promotion of John Browne as BP's CEO.

In 2000, BP hired Ogilvy & Mather Worldwide, one of the largest global advertising and PR firms, to design and launch the $200 million public relations and advertising campaign responsible for the "bp: beyond petroleum" slogan and the company's new yellow and green sun logo.[17] BP's public relations effort also includes publicizing the company's research into alternative energy sources, as well as its attempts to cut greenhouse gas emission levels in its refineries.

Despite some recent setbacks—in July 2006, BP had to shut off its gigantic Prudhoe Bay oilfield in Alaska, after a corroded and poorly maintained pipeline caused an oil spill in the area; in 2005, an explosion at a Texas BP refinery killed 15 workers—the BP rebranding effort has been mostly successful. In a field where consumers are hard pressed to find "good guys" among many perceived villains, BP has been able to elicit positive reactions from the general public.

improve the environment.[18] Other cases, such as the BP example outlined above, remain more ambiguous. Regardless, greenwashing will surely remain a key issue in public relations for years to come.

© Yaraz/Shutterstock.

In recent years, more companies have emphasized their environmentally-friendly products in PR campaigns.

Governments and Goodwill

The work of public relations is not limited to the business sector; public relations practitioners are key players in government agencies at the local, state, and federal level alike. Building strong ties with the community through programs and initiatives, keeping citizens informed about government issues, decisions, and services, and encouraging the public to participate in government-sponsored activities are a few of the varied functions of public relations within this realm.

Public relations officers at local and state health departments, for example, might foster goodwill within the community by promoting free health screenings or information sessions. In addition, public information specialists at a given government agency might explain the reasons for controversial policies or decisions to affected citizens. On a national level, PR programs have been implemented by governments in response to a variety of societal issues, from deterring alcohol and drug use, to preventing forest fires, to reducing violence through weapons buyback programs as mentioned in the case study from Central America.

Case Study: Reducing Violence in Central America

Since the late-1990s, public weapons buyback and exchange programs have been successfully implemented in Central and South America in an attempt to reduce societal violence. In countries such as Panama and El Salvador, which pioneered these programs, the campaigns' success can be largely credited to well-executed public relations campaigns set up by local and federal governments, in collaboration with social institutions and private companies.

In the mid-1990s, the United Nations warned that small weapons posed a very significant threat in developing (and developed) countries that had a history of civil unrest. Working with nonprofit organizations such as Rotary International and the Ford Foundation, the U.N. called for a "microdisarmament" that would reduce this threat.

Countries such as Panama and El Salvador were quick to respond to this call and set up comprehensive public relations and education campaigns that called on the general public to give up their guns in return for toys, food, or even cash. The public relations campaigns included public announcements in the mass media; press conferences with the organizers; paid advertisements in newspapers, radio and television; and flyers, among other tactics.

As a result, some areas that implemented the program in Panama registered a drop in violent crime from 5,124 cases to 1,588 cases in one year. In El Salvador, the United Nations observer mission collected more than 10,000 weapons, and the Guns for Goods exchange program collected 9,527 weapons, 3,157 magazines and 120,696 rounds of ammunition over four years.[19]

© U.S. Air Force photo by Staff Sgt. Paul Gonzales.

During the Presidential campaign, Barack Obama represented "change."

Politics and Entertainment

One need look no further than the 2008 U.S. Presidential election campaigns for evidence that public relations and politics go hand in hand. Interestingly, many of the principles applied to business apply to politics as well, albeit in slightly different ways. Politicians are often "branded" and "rebranded" in the hopes of capturing the public's attention and allegiance—John McCain and Sarah Palin, for example, were "mavericks, "while Barack Obama and Joe Biden represented "change." Developing a strong image for politicians is a key concern for PR people within this realm.

Moreover, crisis management also comes into play frequently in politics. When a scandal emerges surrounding a key political figure, PR people spring into action with plans to contain the damage and move forward as quickly as possible.

PR fulfills a similar role within the entertainment sector. When a major celebrity is involved in a scandal or breaks the law, a publicist usually scrambles to release a statement explaining or apologizing for the behavior. Many celebrities employ a team of public relations professionals who help shape the image of their clients by coordinating interviews and television appearances, orchestrating photo ops, and ensuring that their client's projects receive ample press attention and coverage.

spin
PR tactic in which a specific point of view of interpretation of an event is presented with the intention of influencing public opinion

In both politics and entertainment, **spin**—a PR tactic in which a specific point of view of interpretation of an event is presented with the intention of influencing public opinion—often comes into play. Successfully convincing the public to see ideas or actions that they may not understand or agree with in a positive light comprises a key preoccupation of many PR practitioners.

SKILLS AND TACTICS OF THE PR PROFESSIONAL

Because of the diversity of the field, today's PR professionals must possess a multitude of skills, employ a variety of tactics, and stay informed about key issues in the field.

Historical Case Study: Selling Kitchens . . . and Nixon

The American public's opinion of Vice-President Richard Nixon in the 1950s soared when he visited an American exhibition in Moscow. He was shown forcefully lecturing Soviet Premier Nikita Khrushchev about the benefits of the American way of life in front of a model American kitchen. One might suspect that Nixon's staff arranged the event. But it was the public relations man for the kitchenware firm who created the moment spontaneously. "Right this way, right this way!" he shouted at the two leaders as they moved through the exhibit. They moved toward the kitchen, and Nixon made an assertive gesture toward the American hardware. An Associated Press photographer tossed his camera to the public relations man inside the exhibit, who took the famous "Kitchen Debate" photos.[20] The public relations man, William Safire, became President Nixon's speechwriter a decade later, and now is a respected syndicated columnist.

Relations with the News Media

The most critical skills for public relations practitioners are those necessary for placing stories in the news media. Editors must be convinced that a story is interesting, factual, and relevant. While the advertising agency pays to insert its message in commercial space or time, the public relations counsel ethically cannot pay to control what goes in the news columns. The apparent newsworthiness of the item is what wins it credibility.

Not surprisingly, many of today's successful public relations professionals are former journalists who understand the workings of the newsroom. Fundamental skills for dealing with the press include:

- Writing an interesting news release following the journalistic format and style used by the news media.
- Explaining to a busy editor on the phone in just a few minutes why a story is interesting and important.
- Providing the contacts or resources the journalist needs to write a story; helping the journalist get through to the spokespeople for your organization.
- Arranging a press conference that is well-timed for the media and produces useful information.
- Understanding the special needs of the print and broadcast media, which often have different priorities.

Two-Way Benefits. When we discussed the creation of news in Chapter 11, we acknowledged the special relationship between the press and public relations professionals. Former Mobil vice-president for public affairs Herb Schmertz, to whom we referred early in this chapter, counsels public relations professionals to maintain good relations with reporters and editors because "information is currency. If you build a good relationship with a reporter, you may find you'll learn as much from him as he'll learn from you. . . when you talk with someone who's well-informed, not all of the information flows in the same direction."[21]

© Monkey Business Images/Shutterstock.

Press conferences ideally provide useful information for the media.

That special relationship between journalists and public relations people suggests they can be placed simultaneously as producers and consumers of information. For example, a public relations person may have information for a journalist about a company's efforts to comply with new pollution standards set by the state government. The reporter's questions in response to the briefing may reveal what the reporter has heard about another company's efforts to forestall enforcement of the new regulations. That information, in turn, may help the public relations person to advise management about the climate of opinion surrounding the issue.

Management by Objectives

MBO
management by objectives, a technique used by professional managers and borrowed by public relations professionals; it involves laying out specific, quantifiable goals for PR campaigns

In recent years, public relations has borrowed a business management technique known as MBO—management by objectives—in order to clearly demonstrate the worth and impact of their programs. In the past, when public relations departments made such promises as to "improve our organization's image" or "celebrate the organization's contribution to the community," they found it difficult to show their contribution to the bottom line of the organization. That is to say, they could not show that they enhanced the making of a profit or, in the case of nonprofit organizations, that they served the main goal of the organization.

However, by adopting MBO, public relations people developed the ability to demonstrate the worth of their programs in terms business people can understand. Today, PR professionals can use MBO to state the impact of PR program through quantitative measurement. Here is an example: "The information project reached 40,000 residents, and over half of them requested our information packet—three times as many as last year, when there was no information program."

Research Applications

public opinion poll
a research tool in which a large group of randomly selected consumers are surveyed on their opinions on a given topic

focus group interview
a research tool in which small groups of selected consumers are interviewed in a formal but open-ended way that allows them to make known to the researchers their interests, preferences, and concerns

The typical public relations professional of a generation ago was a former news reporter or editor hired to deal with former colleagues in the press. Today's public relations practitioner needs an important new skill: the ability to use research to understand how a public thinks and behaves in regard to issues that affect a client organization.

Just as the advertising industry became more sophisticated when it learned to measure the consumer's preferences and needs, so too has the public relations industry evolved as it has realized the importance of consumer research. Understanding the attitudes of consumers is critical to effectively reaching target publics with a message and persuading them to change their behaviors.

As with advertising, the survey or **public opinion poll** is a major research tool for public relations people. Another is the **focus group interview**, in which small groups of selected consumers are interviewed in a formal but open-ended way that allows them to make known to the researchers their interests, preferences, and concerns. Studying behaviors and quantifying them is another valid technique: How many people of what type attended an event, and how many of them subsequently requested information using the phone number provided?

© Monkey Business Images/Shutterstock.

A focus group interview gives researchers information on consumers' interests, preferences, and concerns.

The rise of research by public relations practitioners relates directly to the increase in MBO techniques. Research is needed to demonstrate exactly how and why an objective was set, and whether or not it was achieved.

Writing: The Essential Skill

Critics of public relations practitioners assume that the chief talent of the "PR person" is the ability to talk a good line, coupled with a propensity to "like other people." This limited view assumes that persuasion is accomplished by overwhelming another person with one's personality and depth of conviction.

In truth, persuasion is best accomplished by presenting factual data in a comprehensible, interesting, compelling, and believable manner. Consumers of the information should have the opportunity to think about the arguments, weigh the evidence, and persuade themselves that the idea or cause presented is the best one.

This is why writing is the basic skill of public relations. And this is also why, historically, so many public relations people have come from the ranks of reporters and editors. A premium is put on the individual who can gather information accurately, organize it coherently, and present it in a straightforward manner.

Journalistic writing, both feature articles and hard news reporting, provides the models that public relations people imitate when attempting to place a client's stories in the news media. The closer they come to the ideal, the greater the chances of placement. Because public relations also involves supporting the marketing of products and services, promotional writing modeled after advertising copy is a specialized writing skill that may prove helpful. Similarly, writing for the ear and following tight time formats are desirable specialized skills for public relations people who target the broadcast media.

Capitalizing on Emerging Technology

PR professionals need not only be skilled in media relations and writing, but also in the strategic use of the newest, cutting-edge technologies. Blogs and personal media such as Facebook provide forums for both research for and implementation of PR programs. Many corporate executives maintain blogs on their corporation's Web sites in order to appear accessible to consumers, for example, just as many actors, actresses, and music artists maintain personal pages or fan sites to promote their projects. In addition, podcasts, e-mails, and text messages can be keys to success in PR programs, keeping consumers informed and helping them to feel connected to a given cause or organization. In future years, the importance of emerging technology will likely only grow within the field of public relations.

CAREERS IN THE FIELD

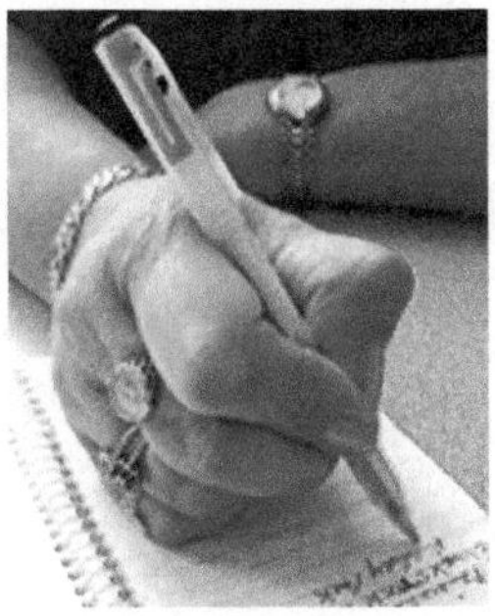

A compelling reason for studying public relations is that the field, far from being static in terms of growth as many other mass media fields are, provides increasing numbers of entry-level jobs for college graduates. Opportunities abound in a variety of areas, including government, education, nonprofit and social programs, business, politics, and entertainment.

Some organizations handle all public relations in-house, meaning they put together their own publications, do their own lobbying with legislative bodies, and prepare campaigns aimed at diverse external publics, from stockholders to customers to community groups. Most corporations, and many government bodies and trade associations, give several important segments of their public relations work to specialized agencies. These organizations often turn to agencies for campaigns aimed at promoting specific products, lobbying, community relations, and media relations.

Some agencies specialize by topic: politics and public affairs, health care, insurance, environmental concerns, or new product introductions. Other agencies specialize in types of service: video news releases, special events, publications, or crisis communication. Small agencies may consist of a principal and one or two assistants, while freelancers may handle only two or three accounts; the largest agencies, with dozens of account teams, serve dozens of clients in a variety of ways.

In public relations, the quest for credibility has raised questions about the need to accredit or even license practitioners, much as lawyers are admitted to the bar, doctors are licensed to practice, and accountants must pass exams in order to pursue their trade. The Public Relations Society of America (PRSA) and the International Association of Business Communicators (IABC) both offer accreditation exams. However, because accreditation is not necessary to practice public relations and because the majority of practitioners do not join either organization, professional accreditation is not yet as meaningful as it is in the fields of law, medicine, and accounting. Accredited or not, today's public relations practitioners find that the field is maturing, gaining acceptance, and taking an increasingly important role in the management of complex organizations that depend on the support of consumers in order to survive.

SUMMARY

- The concepts central to modern public relations can be traced to ancient texts, including Aristotle's *Rhetoric* and the Bible, as well as to the ideas of the founders of the United States.
- Amos Kendall and P.T. Barnum may be considered two of the earliest press agents; Barnum, in particular, was known for enacting elaborate publicity stunts. Ivy Lee pioneered the concept of public relations as a tool for businesses to gain support from consumers. Edward Bernays, with his emphasis on proactive public relations and astute analysis of target publics, shaped public relations as we know it today.
- The press agent/publicity model, public information model, two-way asymmetric model, and two-way symmetric model comprise the four theoretical constructs for approaching public relations. Although the two-way symmetric model tends to dominate in the contemporary landscape, all four models continue to coexist and may be used to achieve specific PR goals.
- The modern public relations industry is a media facilitator. Identifying subpublics, setting objectives, and implementing Marston's RACE formula are key components of effective PR programs.
- Public relations plays key roles in crisis management, corporate rebranding, government, politics, and entertainment.
- Cultivation of media relationships, management by objectives, research, writing, and the use of emerging technologies are integral skills for success in the public relations field.

DISCUSSION QUESTIONS

1. Discuss the ethical implications of the press agent/publicity model favored by P.T. Barnum. Is the predominance of hype over truth ethical? Why or why not? What contemporary examples illustrate this potential conflict?

2. Analyze the factors that have contributed to the predominance of the two-way symmetrical model in PR communications in recent years. What advantages does this model offer over other techniques? What potential problems can occur as a result of its use?

3. How would you characterize the "special relationship" that exists between public relations professionals and the media? How can it be helpful, and/or detrimental, to both parties? What about the public? Explain your response.

4. Consider how you would design a PR program to rehabilitate the image of an organization in crisis. If possible, choose a current example from the news to illustrate your ideas. What steps would you take? What objectives would you delineate? How, and why, would your program be effective?

5. What impact have technological, political, economic, and/or cultural developments of the past decade had on the PR industry as a whole, and, more specifically, on the skills necessary to succeed in the industry?

NOTES

1. Aydemir Okay and Aylar Okay, "Contemporary Girls of Contemporary Turkey: Case Study of a Public Relations Campaign." In *The evolution of public relations: Case studies from countries in transition*, Judy VanSlyke Turk and Linda H. Scanlan, eds. pp. 23–33. Gainesville, Florida: The Institute for Public Relations Research and Education, 2004. Available at http://www.instituteforpr.org/files/uploads/Int_CaseStudies.pdf.
2. Turkcell, Communication Activities. "IPRA Golden World Awards, 2007 Competition." Available at http://www.turkcell.com.tr/c/docs/ic/TURKCELL_SNOWDROPS.pdf.
3. Scott M. Cutlip and Allen H. Center. *Effective public relations.* Englewood Cliffs, New Jersey: 1952.
4. James E. Grunig and Todd Hunt, *Managing Public Relations* (New York: Holt, Rinehart & Winston, 1984), p. 15.
5. Scott Cutlip, "Public Relations and the American Revolution," *Public Relations Review*, Fall 1976, pp. 11–24.
6. Fred F. Endres, "Public Relations in the Jackson White House," *Public Relations Review*, Fall 1976, pp. 5–12.
7. Irving Wallace, "P.T. Barnum." *Encyclopedia Britannica* at http://search .eb.com/eb/article-9013431.
8. Edward L. Bernays, *Public Relations* (Norman: University of Oklahoma Press, 1952), p. 70.
9. Ray E. Hiebert, *Courtiers to the Crowd* (Ames: Iowa State University Press, 1966), p. 48.
10. Edward L. Bernays. *Propaganda.* New York: Horace Liveright, 1928.
11. Edward L. Bernays, *Crystallizing Public Opinion* (New York: Liveright, 1923).
12. James E. Grunig and Todd Hunt. *Managing Public Relations.* New York: Holt, Rinehart, Winston, 1984.
13. Herb Schmertz, *Goodbye to the Low Profile: The Art of Creative Confrontation.* New York: Little Brown, 1986.
14. John E. Marston. *Modern public relations.* New York: McGraw-Hill, 1979.
15. Nicholas Casey and Nicholas Zemiska, "Mattel Does Damage Control After New Recall" August 15, 2007, *Wall Street Journal* [Online Edition]. Available at http://online.wsj.com/article/SB118709567221897168.html?mod=googlenews_wsj.
16. Fortune Global 500 2007. *fortune* [Online edition at cnn.money.com] Available at http://money.cnn.com/magazines/fortune/global500/2007/snapshots/6327.html.
17. Sourcewatch, "BP". Available at http://www.sourcewatch.org/index.php?title=BP.
18. "GE Ecomagination: Hybrid Locomotive" GE Corporate Web Site. Available at http://ge.ecomagination.com/site/#hybr.
19. Mark Hucklebridge and William Godnick, "Public Relations Campaigns Reduce Violence in Panama and El Salvador." In *The evolution of public relations: Case studies from countries in transition*, Judy VanSlyke Turk and Linda H. Scanlan, eds. pp. 135–147. Gainesville, Florida: The Institute for Public Relations Research and Education, 2004. Available at http://www.instituteforpr.org/files/uploads/Int_CaseStudies.pdf.
20. Art Stevens, *The Persuasion Explosion* (Washington: Acropolis Books, 1985), pp. 70-71.
21. Herb Schmertz, *Good-bye to the Low Profile* (Boston: Little, Brown, 1986), p. 126.